Say I Love You.

by
Kanae
Hazuki

12

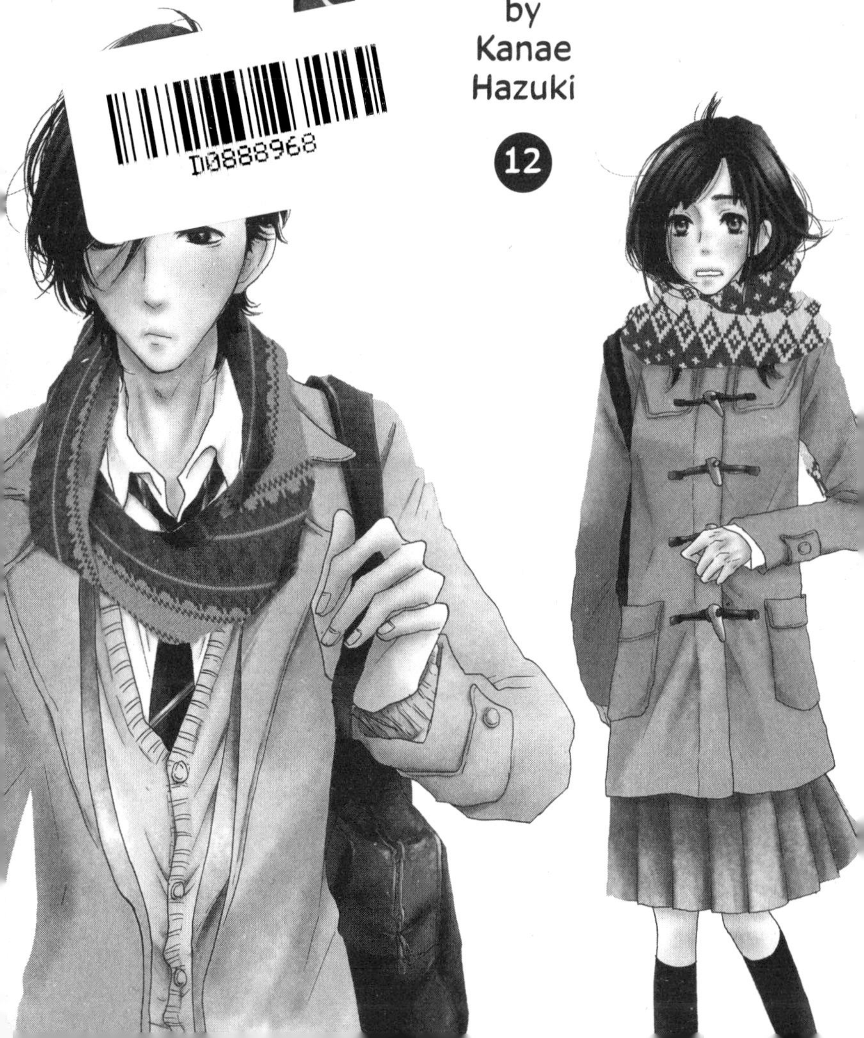

Kanae Hazuki
presents

Say I Love You.

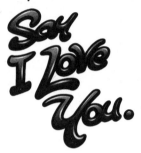

CHARACTER

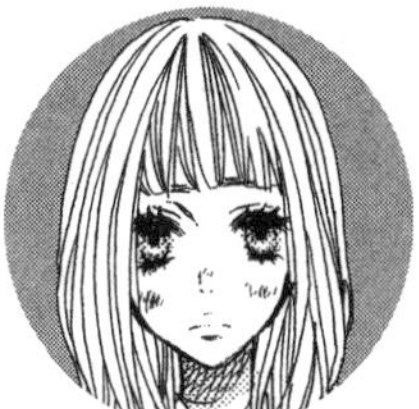

Mei Tachibana

A girl who hasn't had a single friend, let alone a boyfriend, in sixteen years and has lived her life trusting no one. She finds herself attracted to Yamato, who, for some reason, just won't leave her alone, and they start dating.

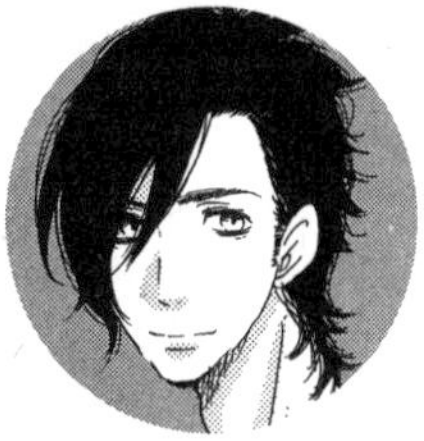

Yamato Kurosawa

The most popular boy at Mei's school. He has the love of many girls, yet for some reason, he is obsessed with Mei, the brooding weirdo girl from another class.

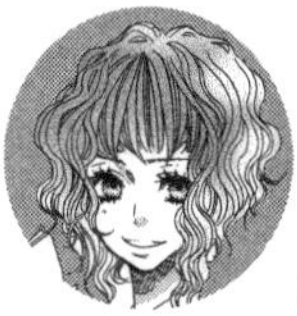

Megumi

An amateur model who had her sights set on Yamato. She transferred to his school and got him a modeling job, and the two gradually grew closer. In the end, Yamato rejected her, but now she has moved on and is going forward with a positive outlook.

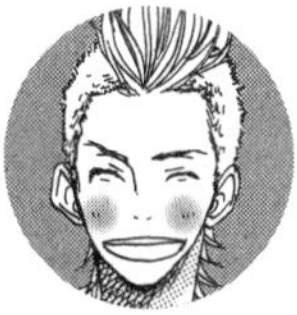

Kai

Yamato's classmate from middle school who had been the victim of bullying. For his own reasons, he started high school a year late. He likes Mei and told her so, but...?

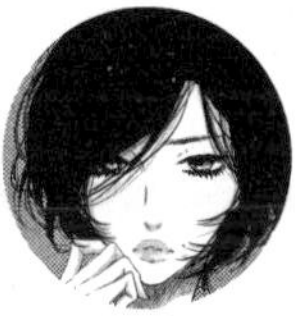

Rin Aoi

A new student at Mei's school, who is currently modeling under the name RIN. Kai caught her with one hand when she tripped on the stairs, and she fell in love at first sight?!

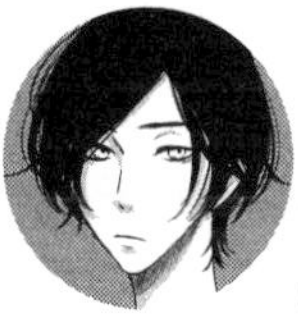

Len Aoi

A new student and Rin's twin brother. He helps Mei at the gym, which is run by his parents. The complete opposite of his sociable sister, he is rather unfriendly, but has a surprisingly kind side.

STORY

Mei Tachibana spent sixteen years without a single friend or boyfriend, but then, for some reason, Yamato Kurosawa, the most popular boy in school, took a liking to her. Mei was drawn in by Yamato's kindness and sincerity, and now it has been almost two years since they started dating. As they enter their third year of high school, all their classmates can talk about is what they're going to do after they graduate. Mei learns that Yamato is thinking of going to a vocational school to learn photography, and starts trying to find what she wants to do. Meanwhile, twins named Rin and Len start going to their school. These two are different in many ways, and as they become involved with Mei and her friends, their interpersonal relationships start to change...?!

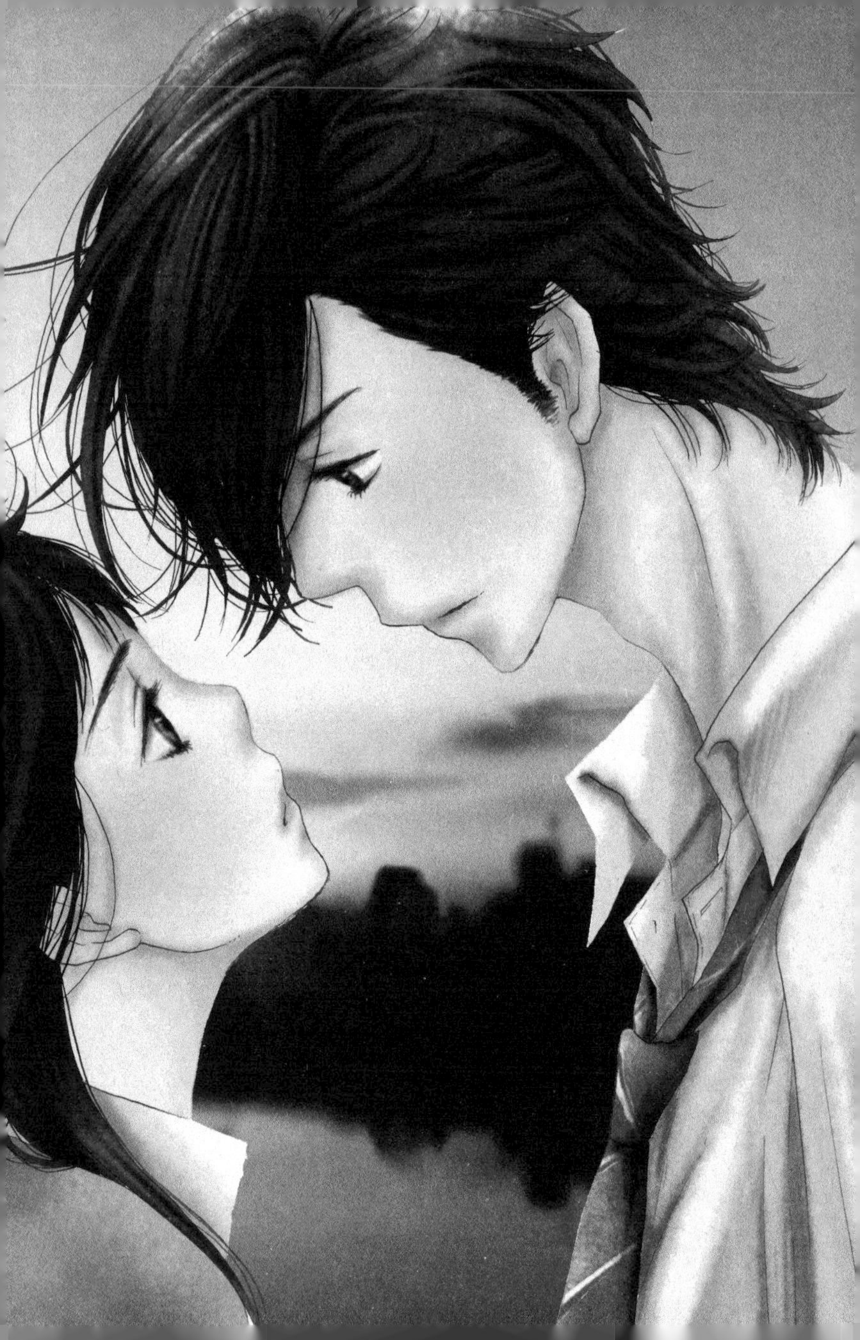

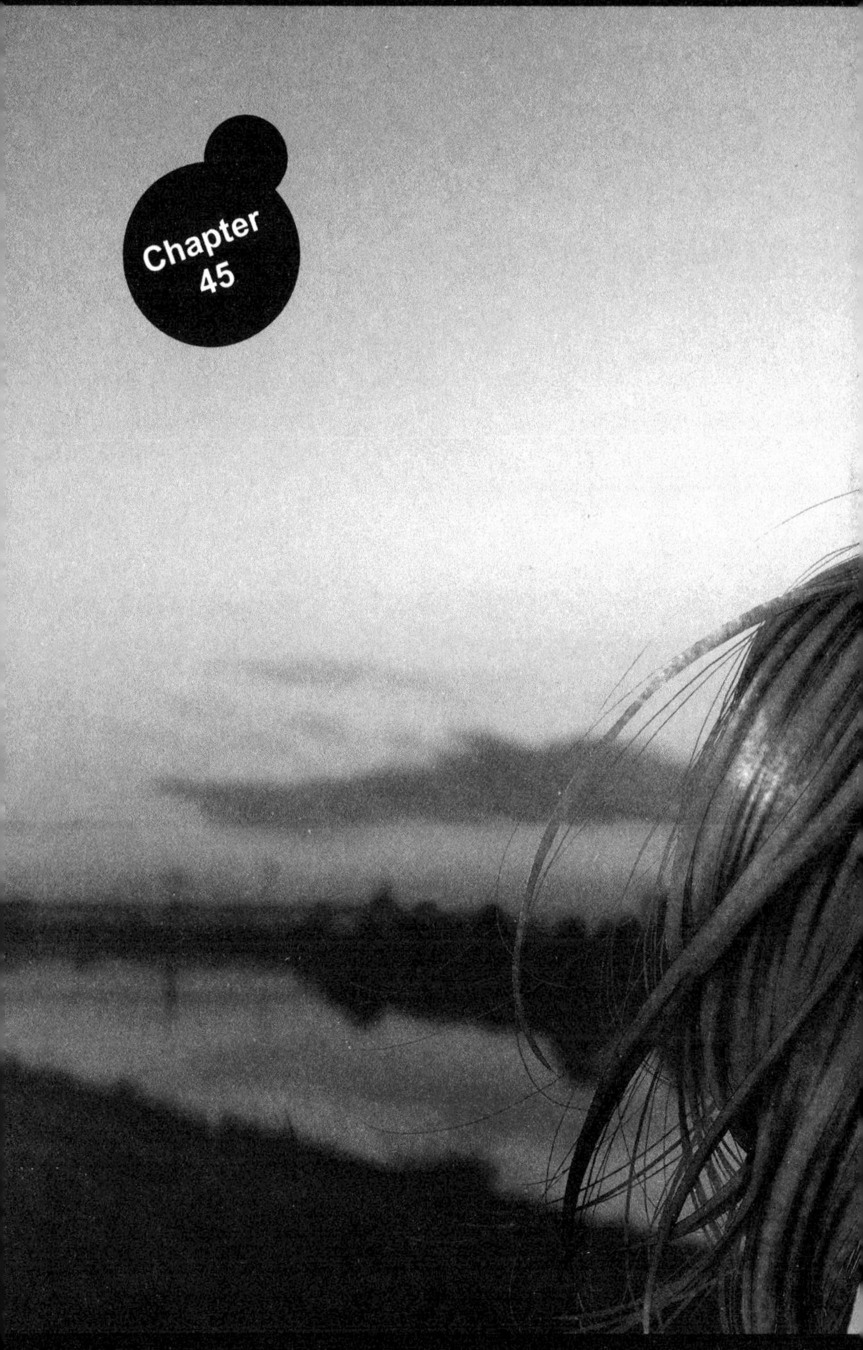
Chapter 45

Say "I love you".

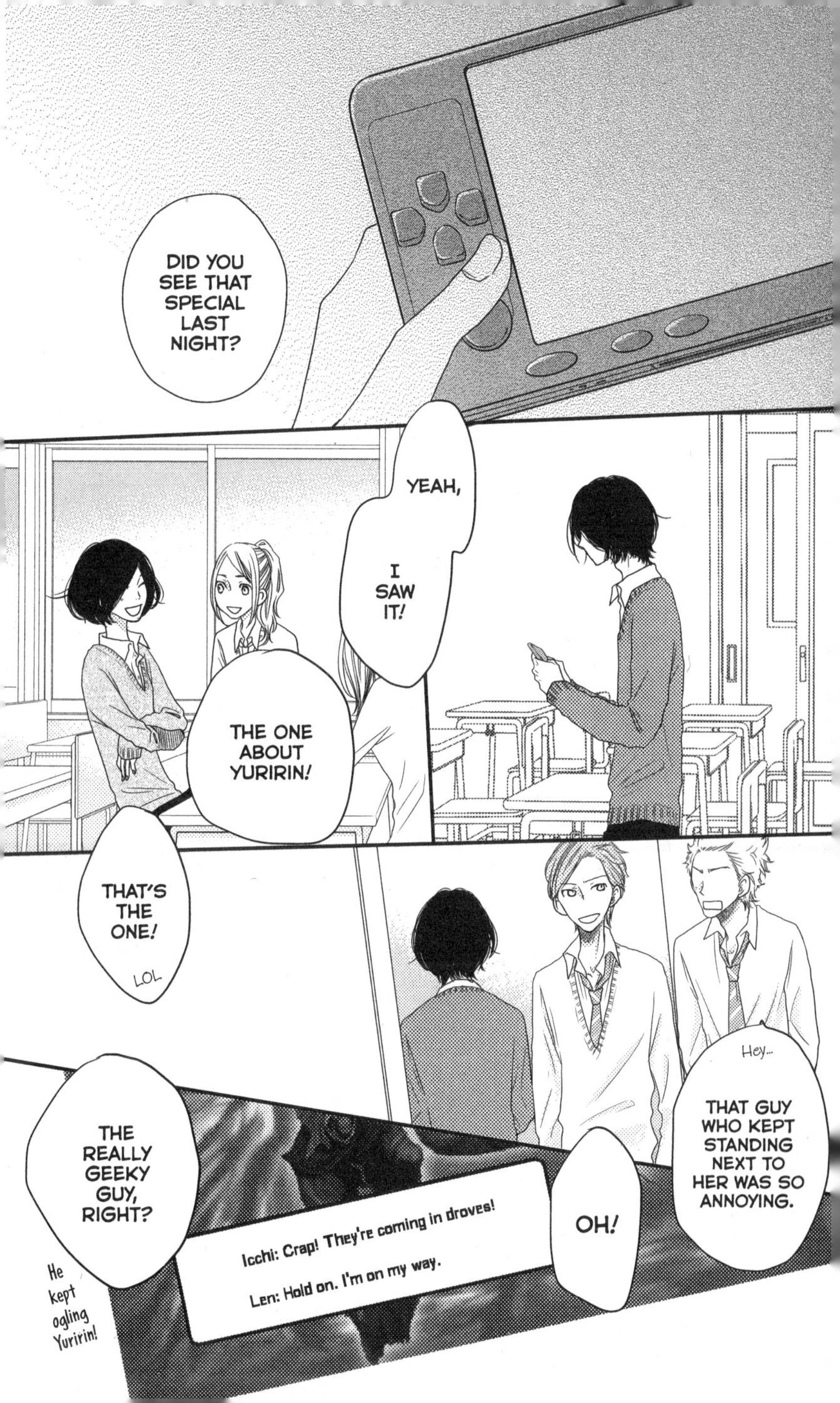
DID YOU SEE THAT SPECIAL LAST NIGHT?
YEAH, I SAW IT!
THE ONE ABOUT YURIRIN!
Hey...
THAT GUY WHO KEPT STANDING NEXT TO HER WAS SO ANNOYING.
THAT'S THE ONE!
LOL
THE REALLY GEEKY GUY, RIGHT?
He kept ogling Yuririn!
OH!
Icchi: Crap! They're coming in droves!
Len: Hold on. I'm on my way.

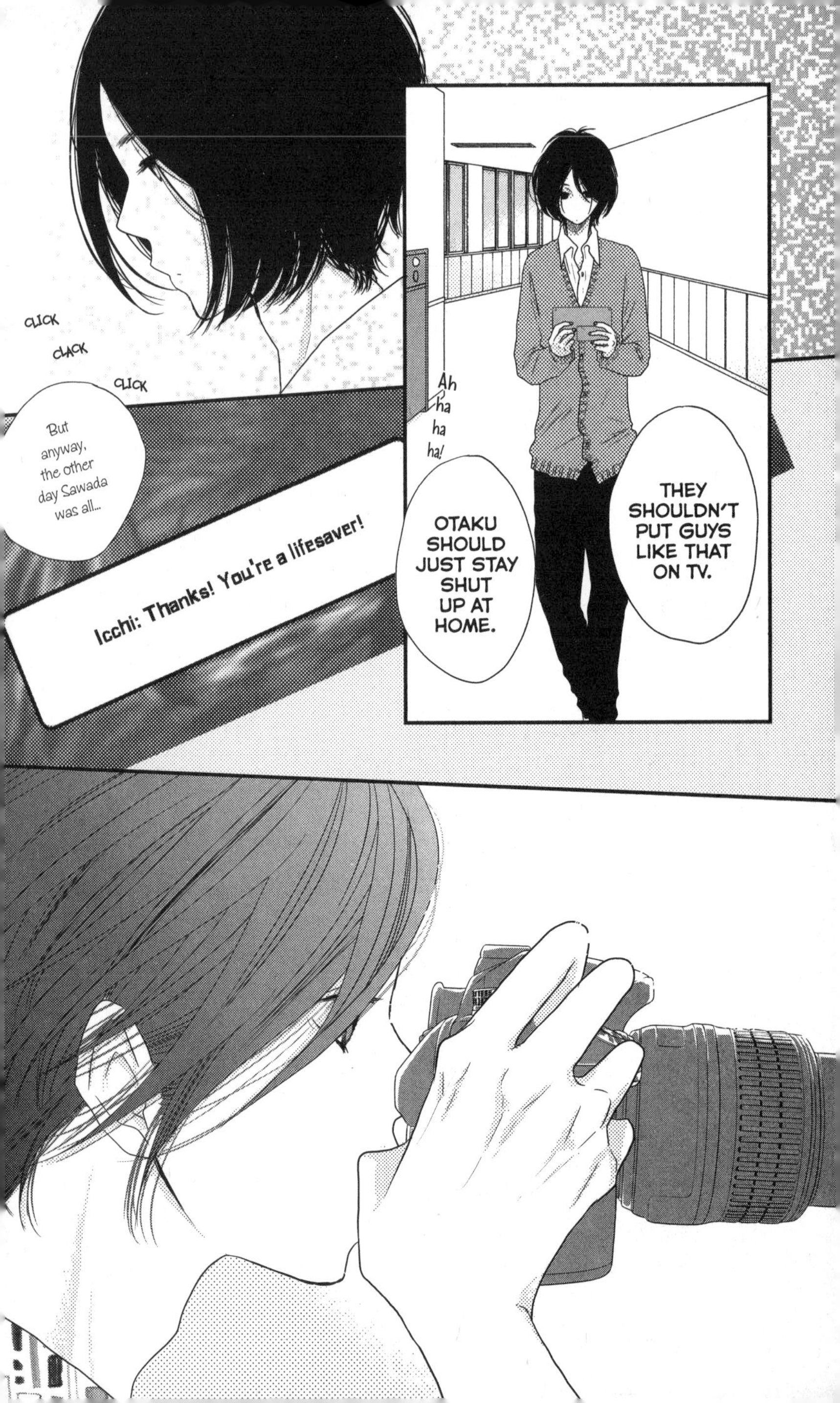
THEY SHOULDN'T PUT GUYS LIKE THAT ON TV.
OTAKU SHOULD JUST STAY SHUT UP AT HOME.
Ah ha ha ha!
CLICK
CLACK
CLICK
But anyway, the other day Sawada was all...
Icchi: Thanks! You're a lifesaver!

SNAP

SNAP

SNAP

Hmmm...

SOME-
THING'S
JUST NOT
RIGHT...

Nikon

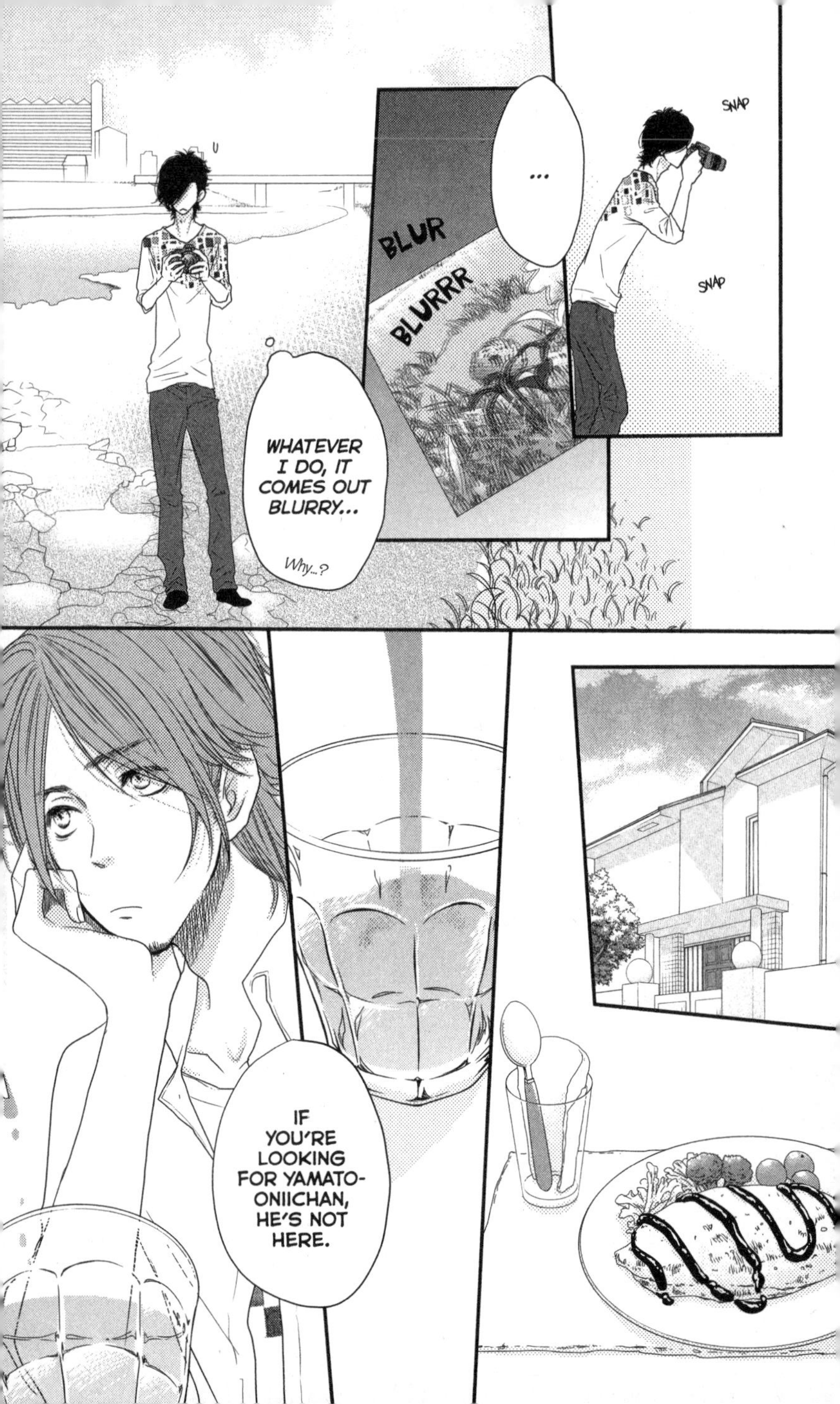
SNAP
SNAP
...
BLUR
BLURRR
WHATEVER I DO, IT COMES OUT BLURRY...
Why...?
IF YOU'RE LOOKING FOR YAMATO-ONIICHAN, HE'S NOT HERE.

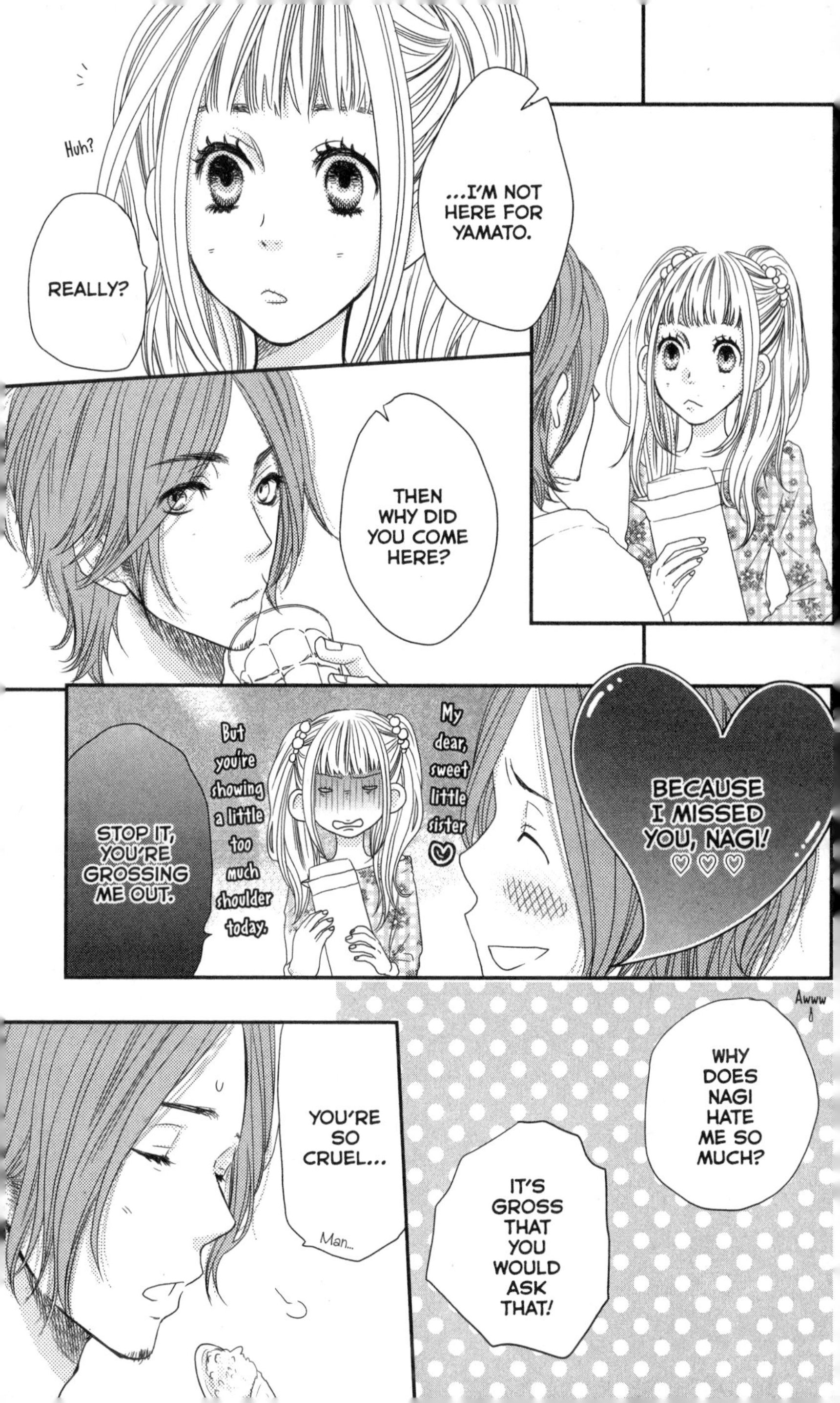
...I'M NOT HERE FOR YAMATO.
Huh?
REALLY?
THEN WHY DID YOU COME HERE?
BECAUSE I MISSED YOU, NAGI! ♡♡♡
My dear, sweet little sister ♡
But you're showing a little too much shoulder today.
STOP IT, YOU'RE GROSSING ME OUT.
Awww
WHY DOES NAGI HATE ME SO MUCH?
IT'S GROSS THAT YOU WOULD ASK THAT!
YOU'RE SO CRUEL...
Man...

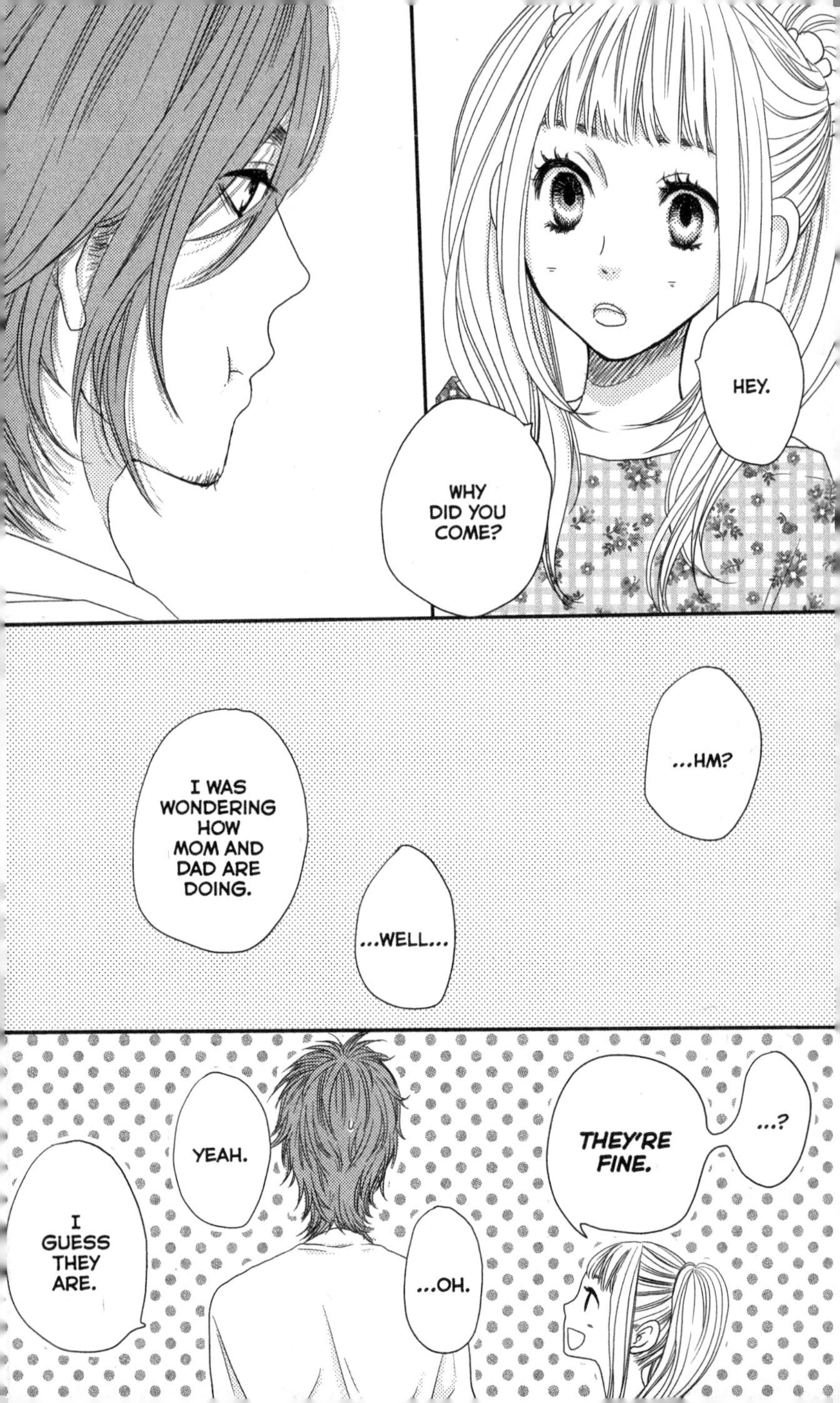
HEY.
WHY DID YOU COME?
...HM?
I WAS WONDERING HOW MOM AND DAD ARE DOING.
...WELL...
...?
THEY'RE FINE.
YEAH.
...OH.
I GUESS THEY ARE.

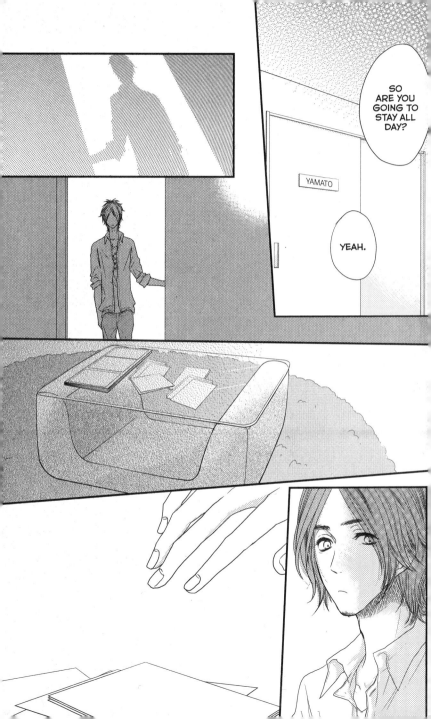

SO ARE YOU GOING TO STAY ALL DAY?

YAMATO

YEAH.

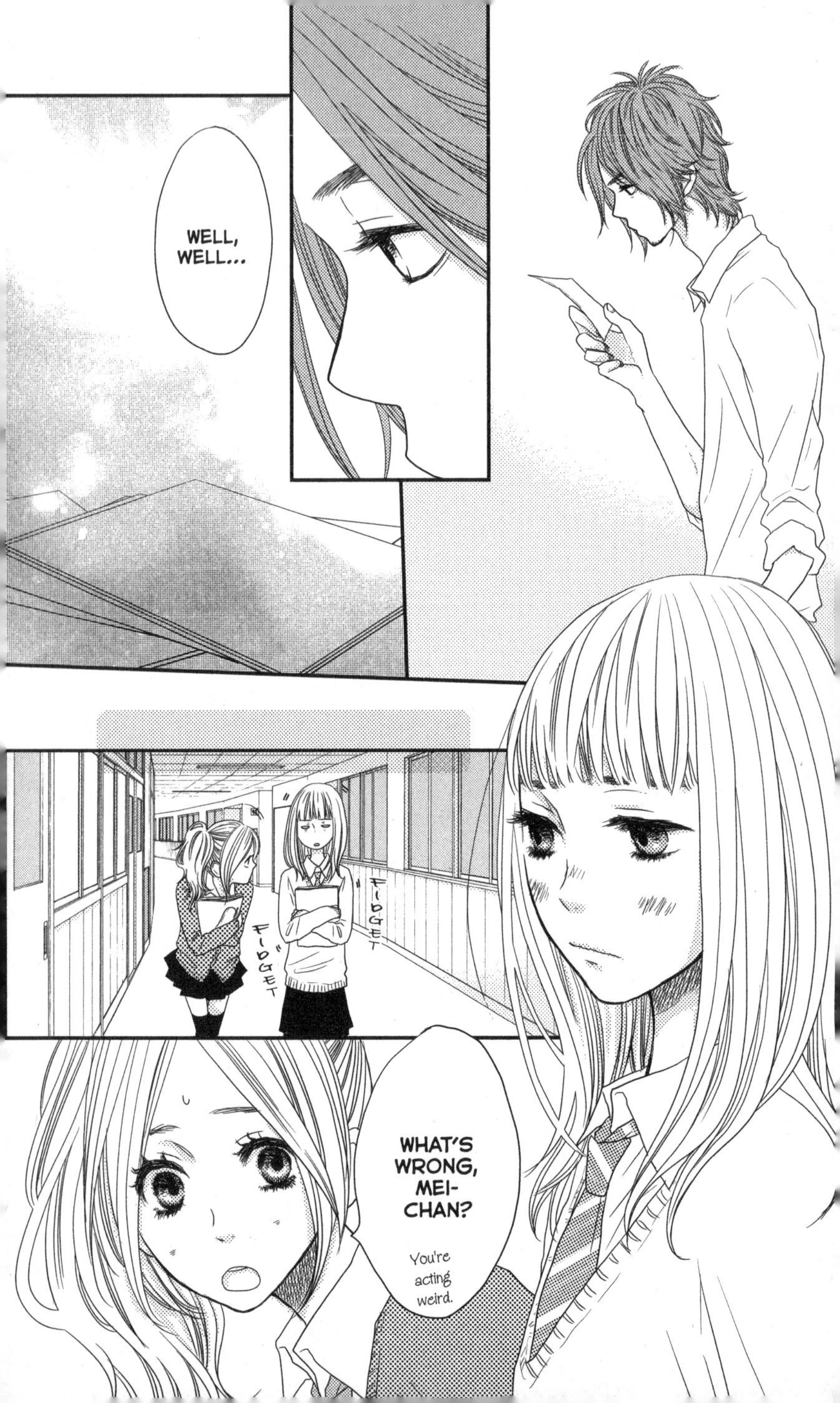
WELL, WELL...
FIDGET
FIDGET
WHAT'S WRONG, MEI-CHAN?
You're acting weird.

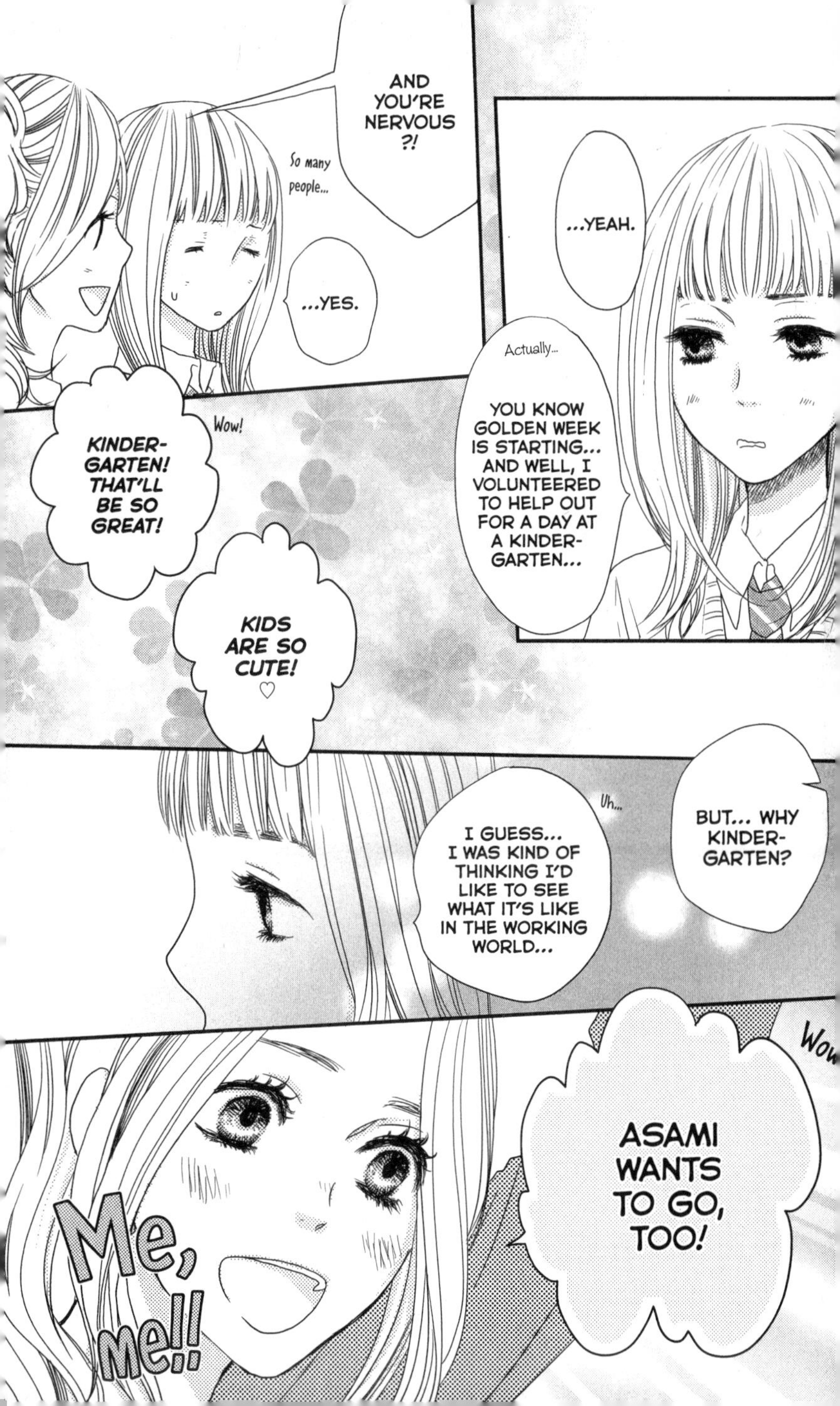
...YEAH.
Actually...
YOU KNOW GOLDEN WEEK IS STARTING... AND WELL, I VOLUNTEERED TO HELP OUT FOR A DAY AT A KINDER-GARTEN...
AND YOU'RE NERVOUS?!
So many people...
...YES.
Wow!
KINDER-GARTEN! THAT'LL BE SO GREAT!
KIDS ARE SO CUTE! ♡
BUT... WHY KINDER-GARTEN?
Uh...
I GUESS... I WAS KIND OF THINKING I'D LIKE TO SEE WHAT IT'S LIKE IN THE WORKING WORLD...
Wow
ASAMI WANTS TO GO, TOO!
Me, me!!

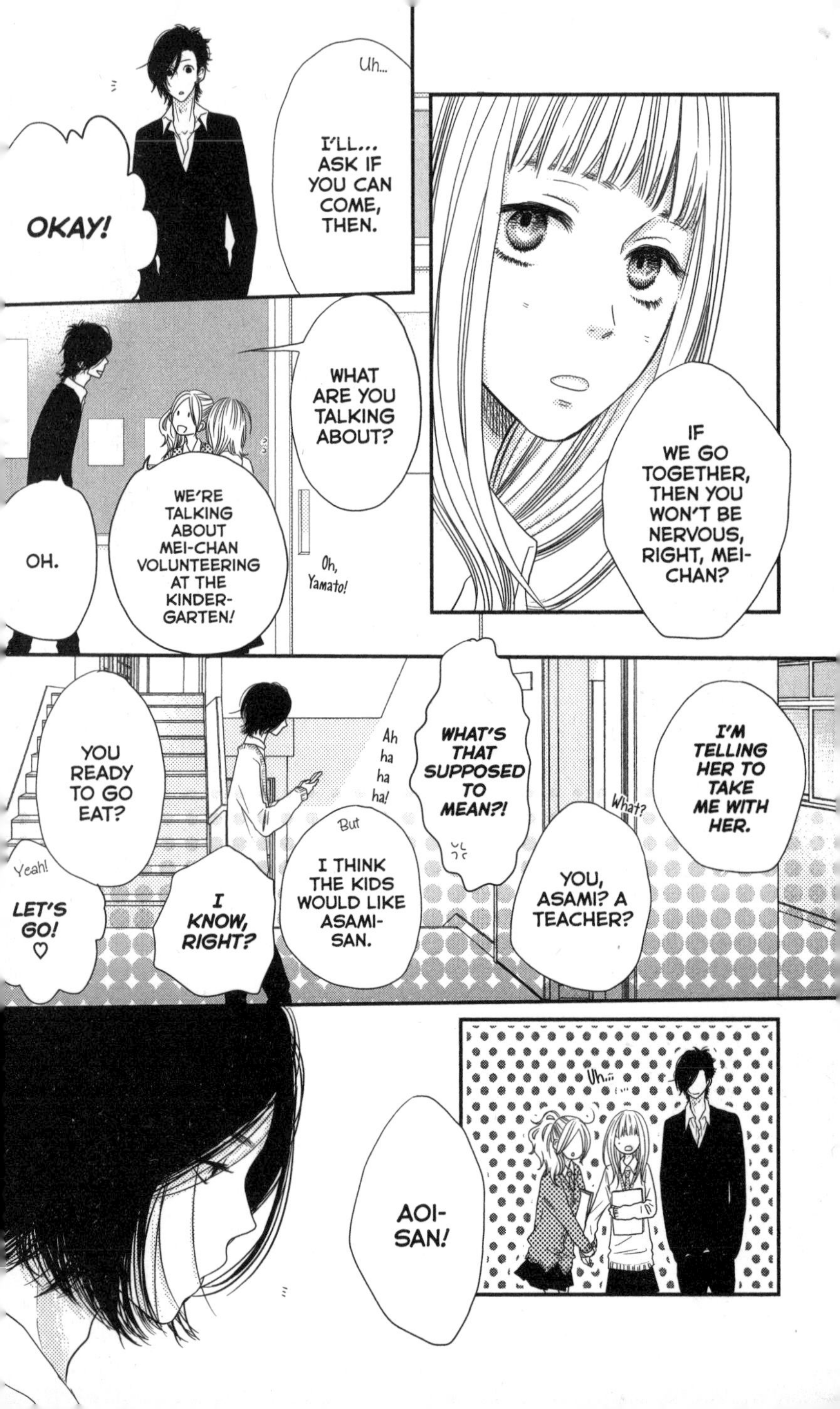
IF WE GO TOGETHER, THEN YOU WON'T BE NERVOUS, RIGHT, MEI-CHAN?
Uh...
I'LL... ASK IF YOU CAN COME, THEN.
OKAY!
Oh, Yamato!
WHAT ARE YOU TALKING ABOUT?
WE'RE TALKING ABOUT MEI-CHAN VOLUNTEERING AT THE KINDERGARTEN!
OH.
I'M TELLING HER TO TAKE ME WITH HER.
What?
YOU, ASAMI? A TEACHER?
WHAT'S THAT SUPPOSED TO MEAN?!
Ah ha ha ha!
But
I THINK THE KIDS WOULD LIKE ASAMI-SAN.
I KNOW, RIGHT?
YOU READY TO GO EAT?
Yeah!
LET'S GO! ♡
Uh...
AOI-SAN!

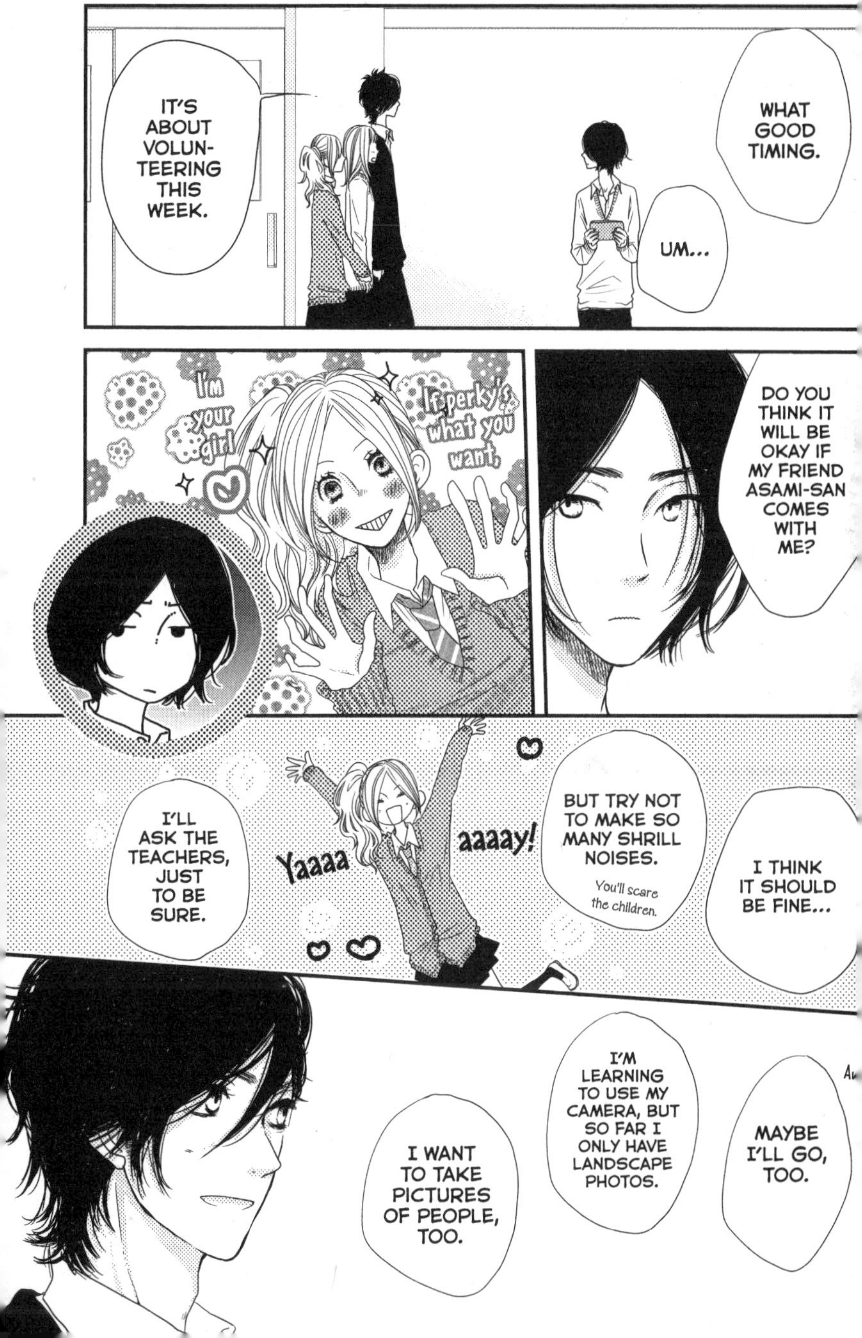
WHAT GOOD TIMING.
UM...
IT'S ABOUT VOLUNTEERING THIS WEEK.
DO YOU THINK IT WILL BE OKAY IF MY FRIEND ASAMI-SAN COMES WITH ME?
If perky's what you want,
I'm your girl
I THINK IT SHOULD BE FINE...
BUT TRY NOT TO MAKE SO MANY SHRILL NOISES.
You'll scare the children.
Yaaaa aaaay!
I'LL ASK THE TEACHERS, JUST TO BE SURE.
MAYBE I'LL GO, TOO.
I'M LEARNING TO USE MY CAMERA, BUT SO FAR I ONLY HAVE LANDSCAPE PHOTOS.
I WANT TO TAKE PICTURES OF PEOPLE, TOO.

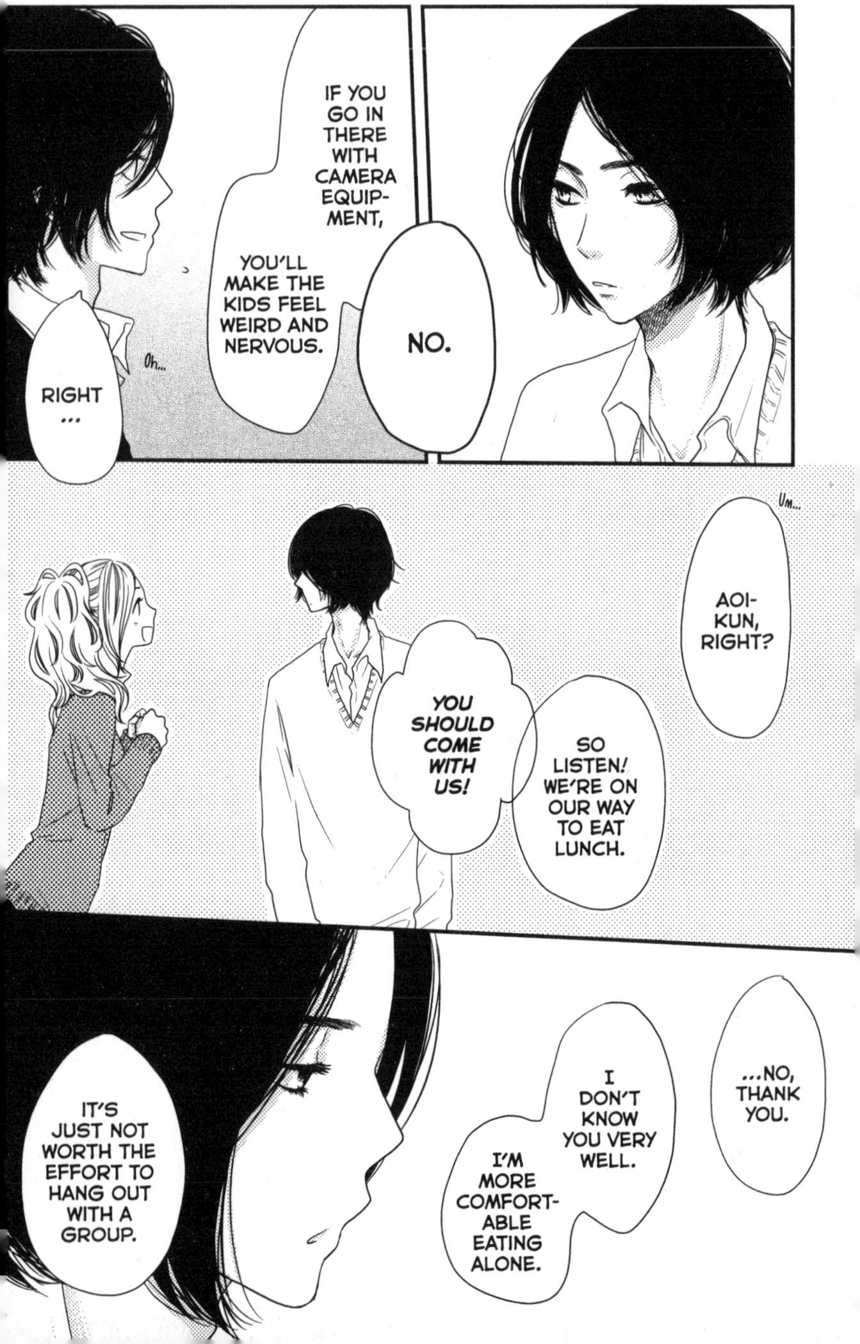
NO.
IF YOU GO IN THERE WITH CAMERA EQUIPMENT,
YOU'LL MAKE THE KIDS FEEL WEIRD AND NERVOUS.
Oh...
RIGHT...
Um...
AOI-KUN, RIGHT?
SO LISTEN! WE'RE ON OUR WAY TO EAT LUNCH.
YOU SHOULD COME WITH US!
...NO, THANK YOU.
I DON'T KNOW YOU VERY WELL.
I'M MORE COMFORTABLE EATING ALONE.
IT'S JUST NOT WORTH THE EFFORT TO HANG OUT WITH A GROUP.

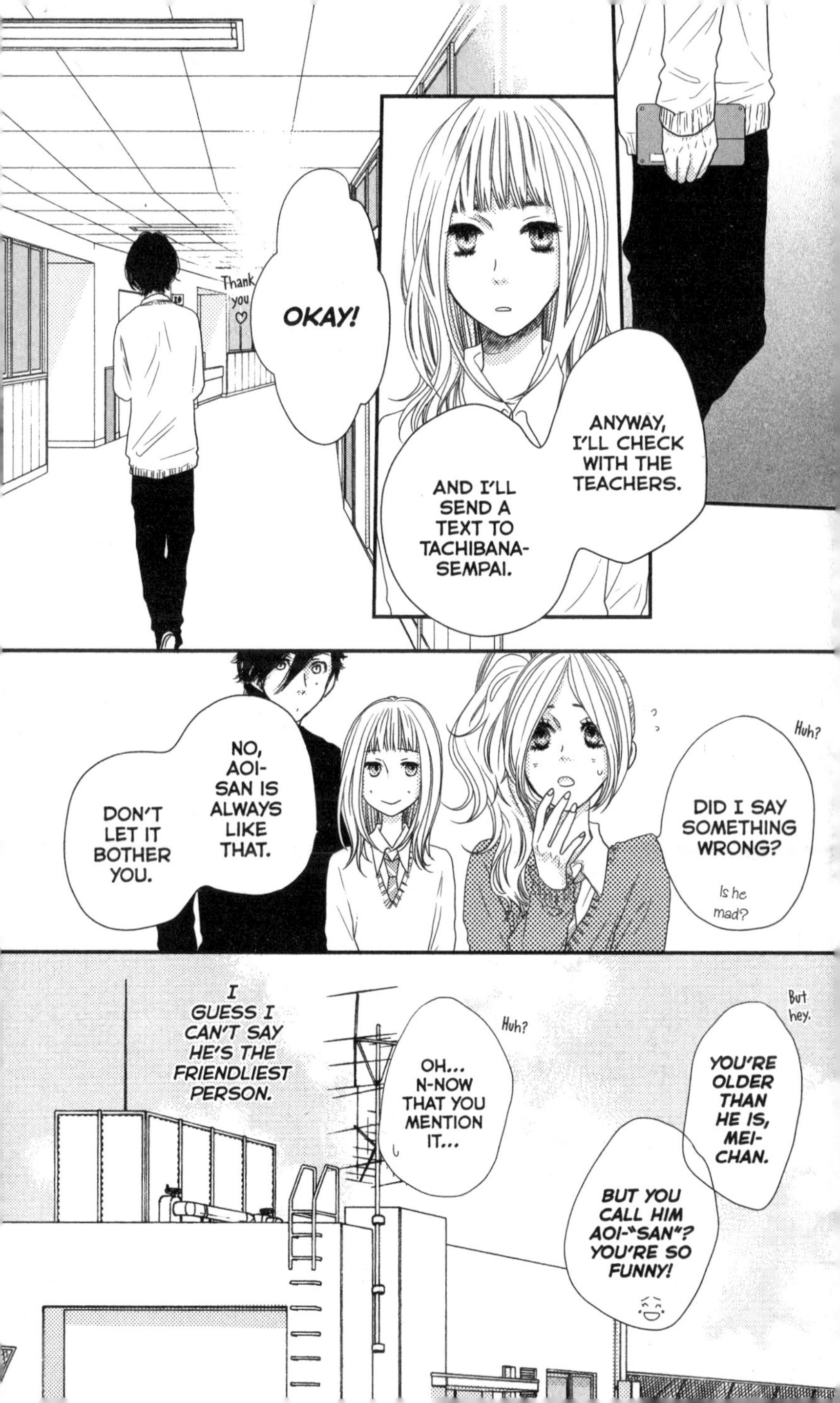
ANYWAY, I'LL CHECK WITH THE TEACHERS.
AND I'LL SEND A TEXT TO TACHIBANA-SEMPAI.
OKAY!
Thank you ♡
Huh?
DID I SAY SOMETHING WRONG?
Is he mad?
NO, AOI-SAN IS ALWAYS LIKE THAT.
DON'T LET IT BOTHER YOU.
But hey.
YOU'RE OLDER THAN HE IS, MEI-CHAN.
BUT YOU CALL HIM AOI-"SAN"? YOU'RE SO FUNNY!
Huh?
OH... N-NOW THAT YOU MENTION IT...
I GUESS I CAN'T SAY HE'S THE FRIENDLIEST PERSON.

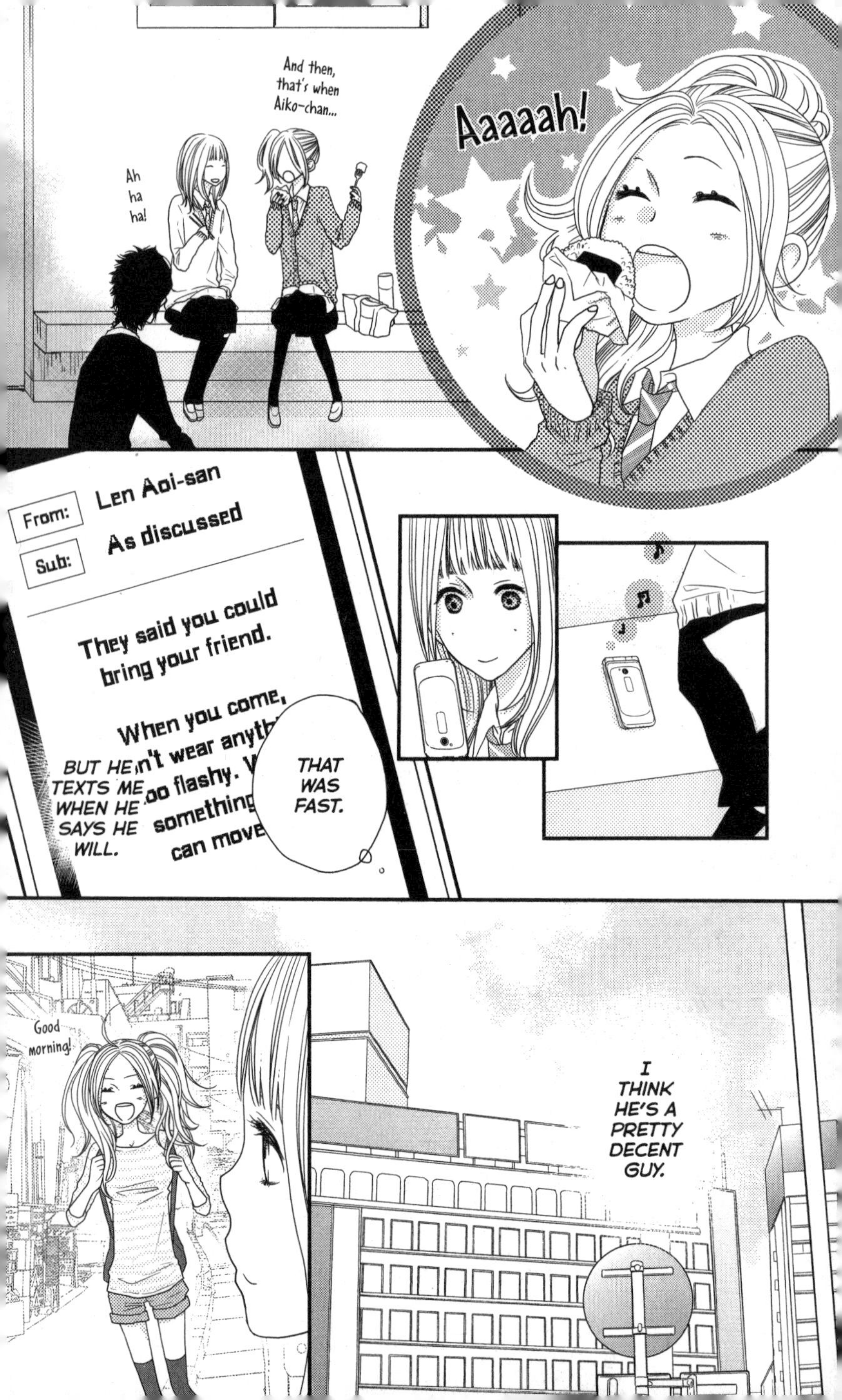

Aaaaah!
And then, that's when Aiko-chan...
Ah ha ha!
From:
Len Aoi-san
Sub:
As discussed
They said you could bring your friend.
When you come,
THAT WAS FAST.
BUT HE TEXTS ME WHEN HE SAYS HE WILL.
I THINK HE'S A PRETTY DECENT GUY.
Good morning!

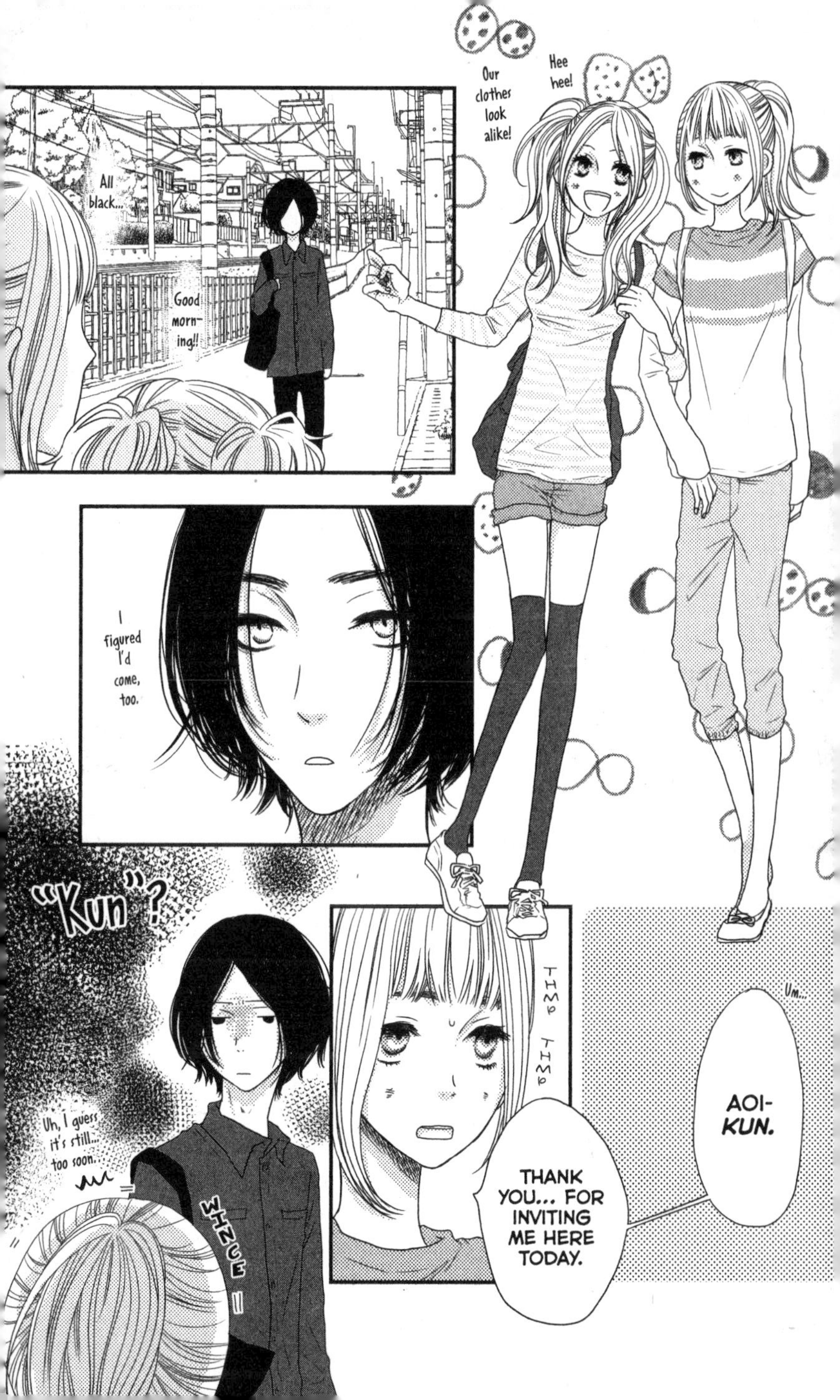
Hee hee!
Our clothes look alike!
All black...
Good morn-ing!!
I figured I'd come, too.
Um...
AOI-KUN.
THANK YOU... FOR INVITING ME HERE TODAY.
THMP THMP
"Kun"?
Uh, I guess it's still... too soon...
WINCE

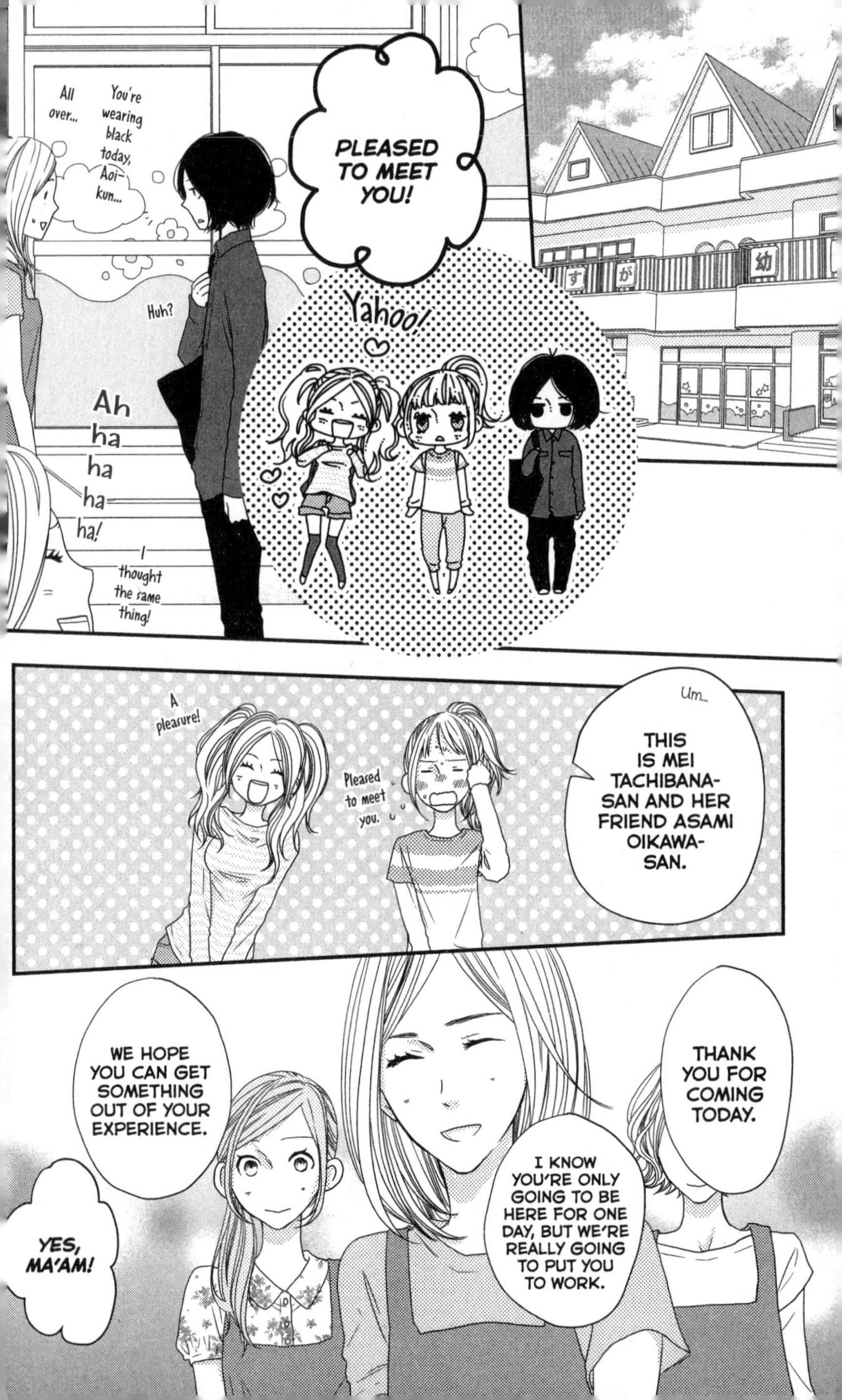
PLEASED TO MEET YOU!
Yahoo!
You're wearing black today, Aoi-kun...
All over...
Huh?
Ah ha ha ha ha!
I thought the same thing!
Um...
THIS IS MEI TACHIBANA-SAN AND HER FRIEND ASAMI OIKAWA-SAN.
Pleased to meet you.
A pleasure!
THANK YOU FOR COMING TODAY.
I KNOW YOU'RE ONLY GOING TO BE HERE FOR ONE DAY, BUT WE'RE REALLY GOING TO PUT YOU TO WORK.
WE HOPE YOU CAN GET SOMETHING OUT OF YOUR EXPERIENCE.
YES, MA'AM!

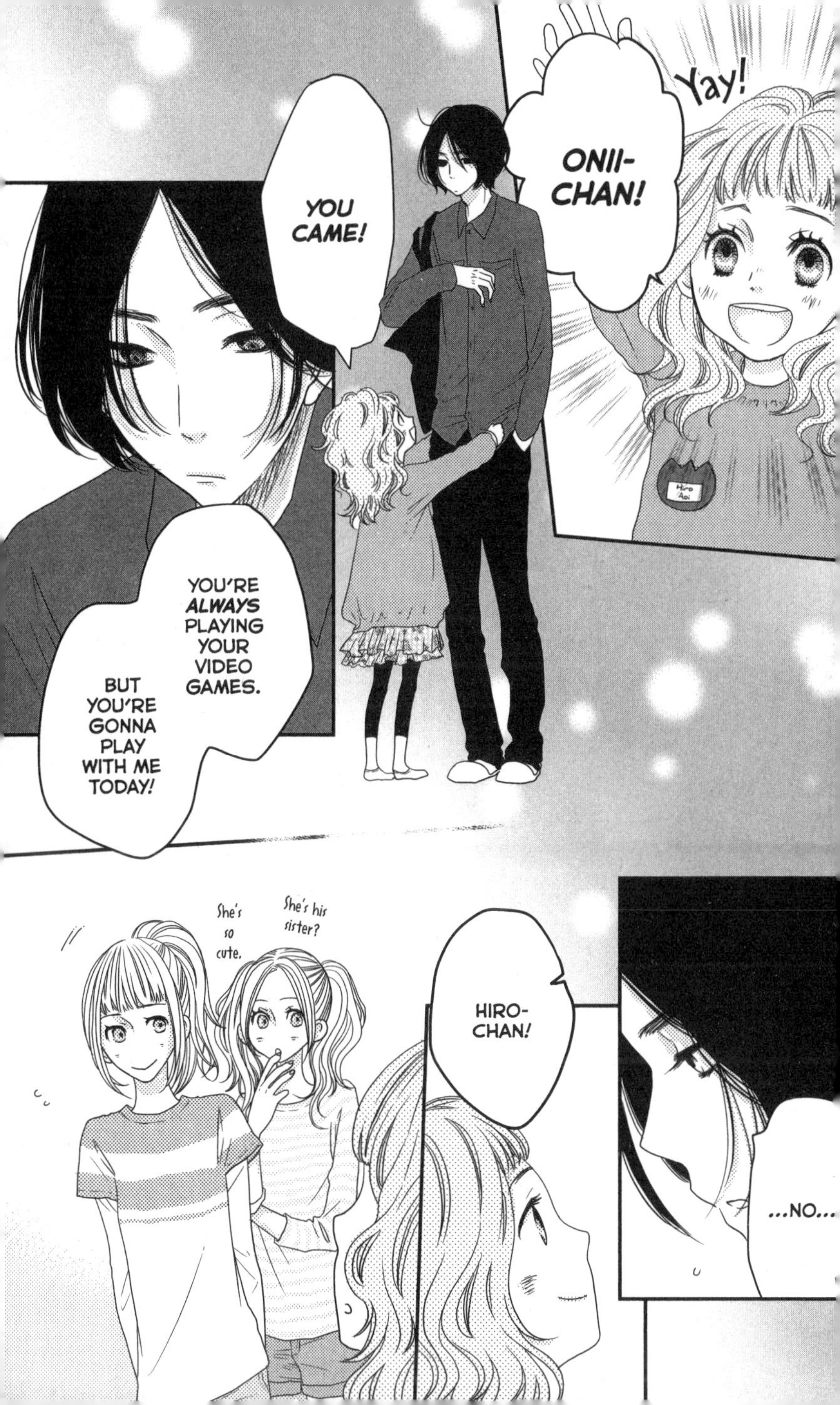
Yay!
ONII-CHAN!
Hiro Aoi
YOU CAME!
YOU'RE *ALWAYS* PLAYING YOUR VIDEO GAMES.
BUT YOU'RE GONNA PLAY WITH ME TODAY!
...NO...
HIRO-CHAN!
She's his sister?
She's so cute.

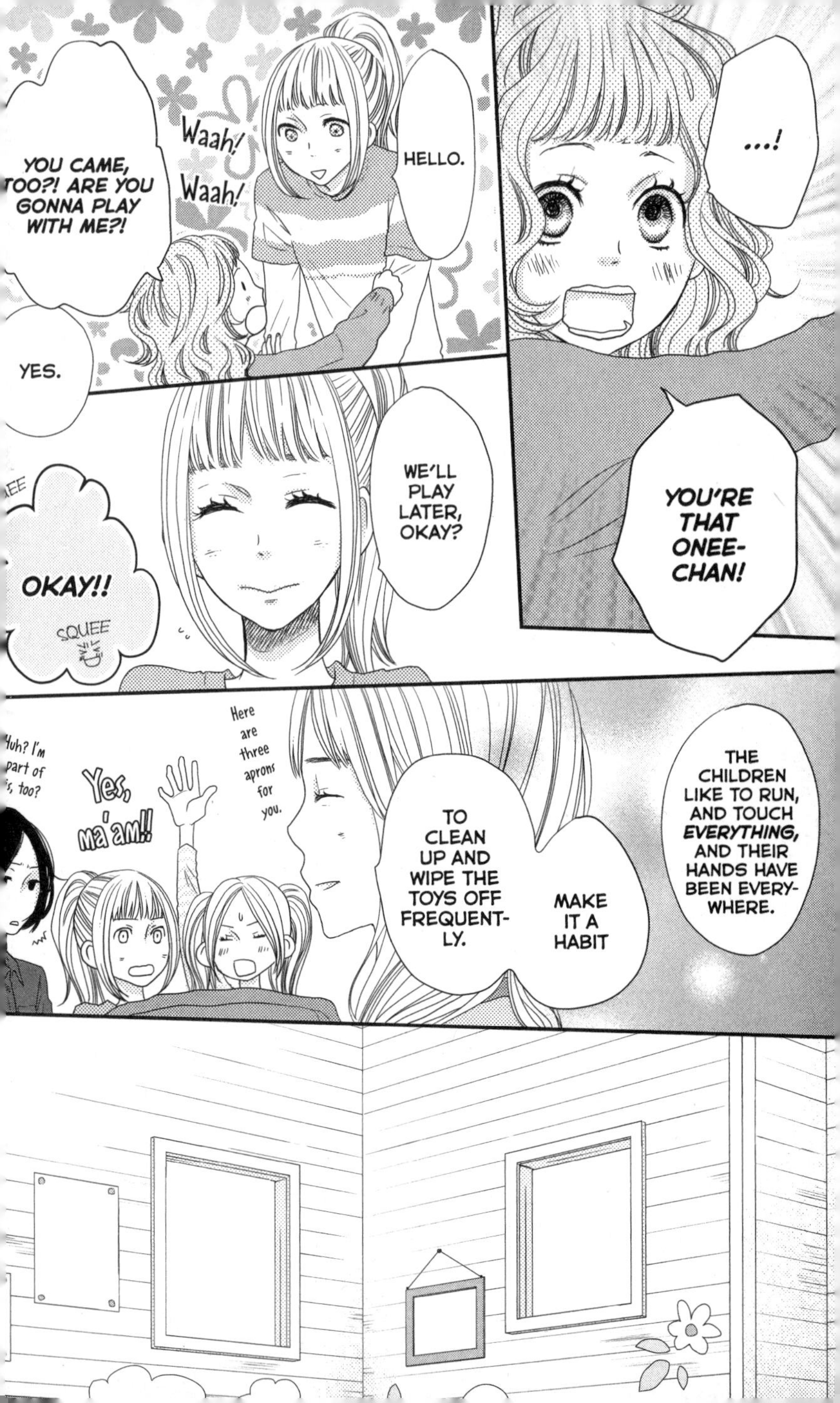
...!
YOU'RE THAT ONEE-CHAN!
HELLO.
Waah! Waah!
YOU CAME, TOO?! ARE YOU GONNA PLAY WITH ME?!
YES.
WE'LL PLAY LATER, OKAY?
OKAY!!
SQUEE
THE CHILDREN LIKE TO RUN, AND TOUCH *EVERYTHING*, AND THEIR HANDS HAVE BEEN EVERY-WHERE.
MAKE IT A HABIT
TO CLEAN UP AND WIPE THE TOYS OFF FREQUENT-LY.
Here are three aprons for you.
Yes, ma'am!!
Huh? I'm part of s, too?

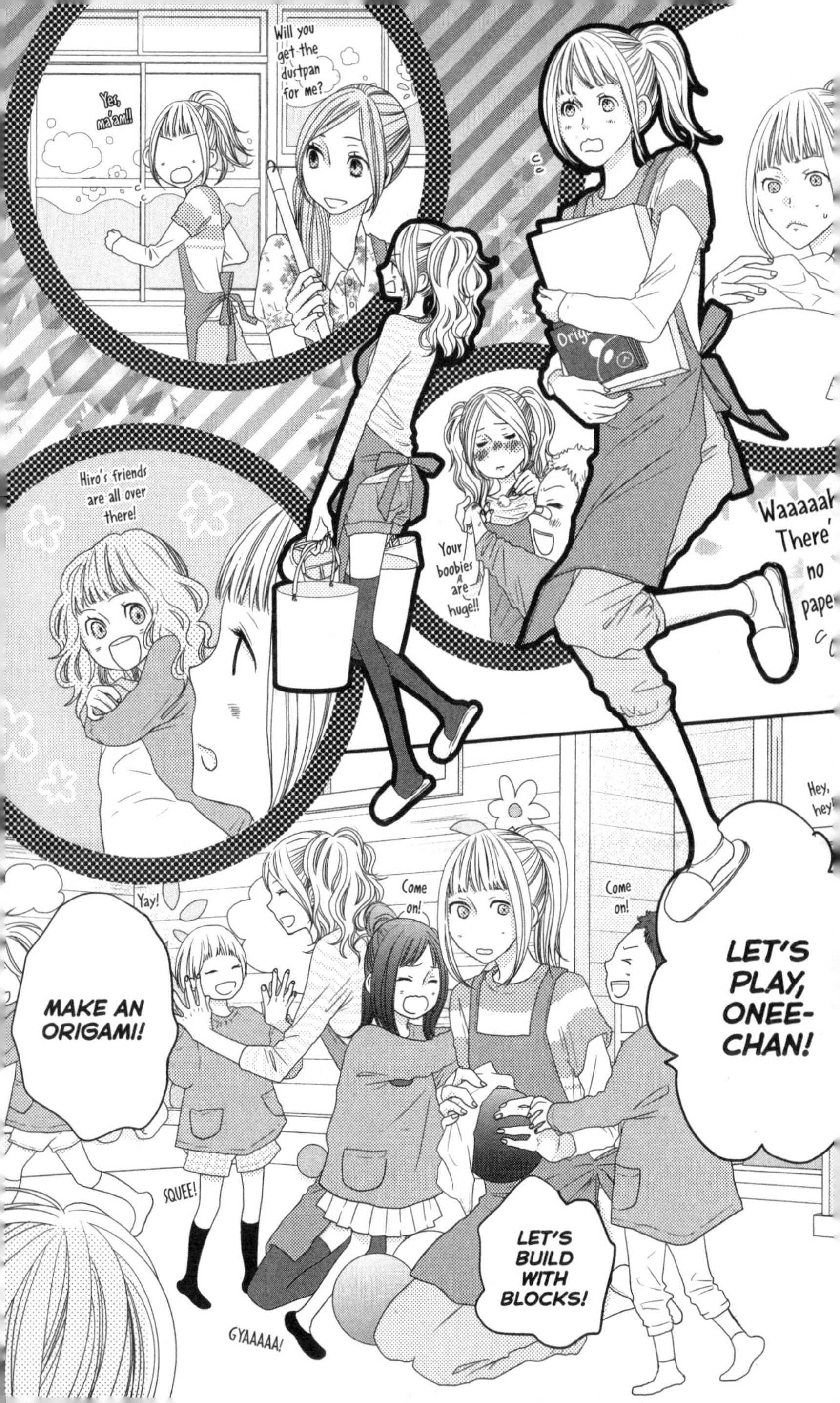
Will you get the dustpan for me?
Yes, ma'am!!
Waaaaa There' no pape
Your boobies are huge!!
Hiro's friends are all over there!
Hey, hey!
LET'S PLAY, ONEE-CHAN!
Come on!
Come on!
LET'S BUILD WITH BLOCKS!
Yay!
MAKE AN ORIGAMI!
SQUEE!
GYAAAAA!

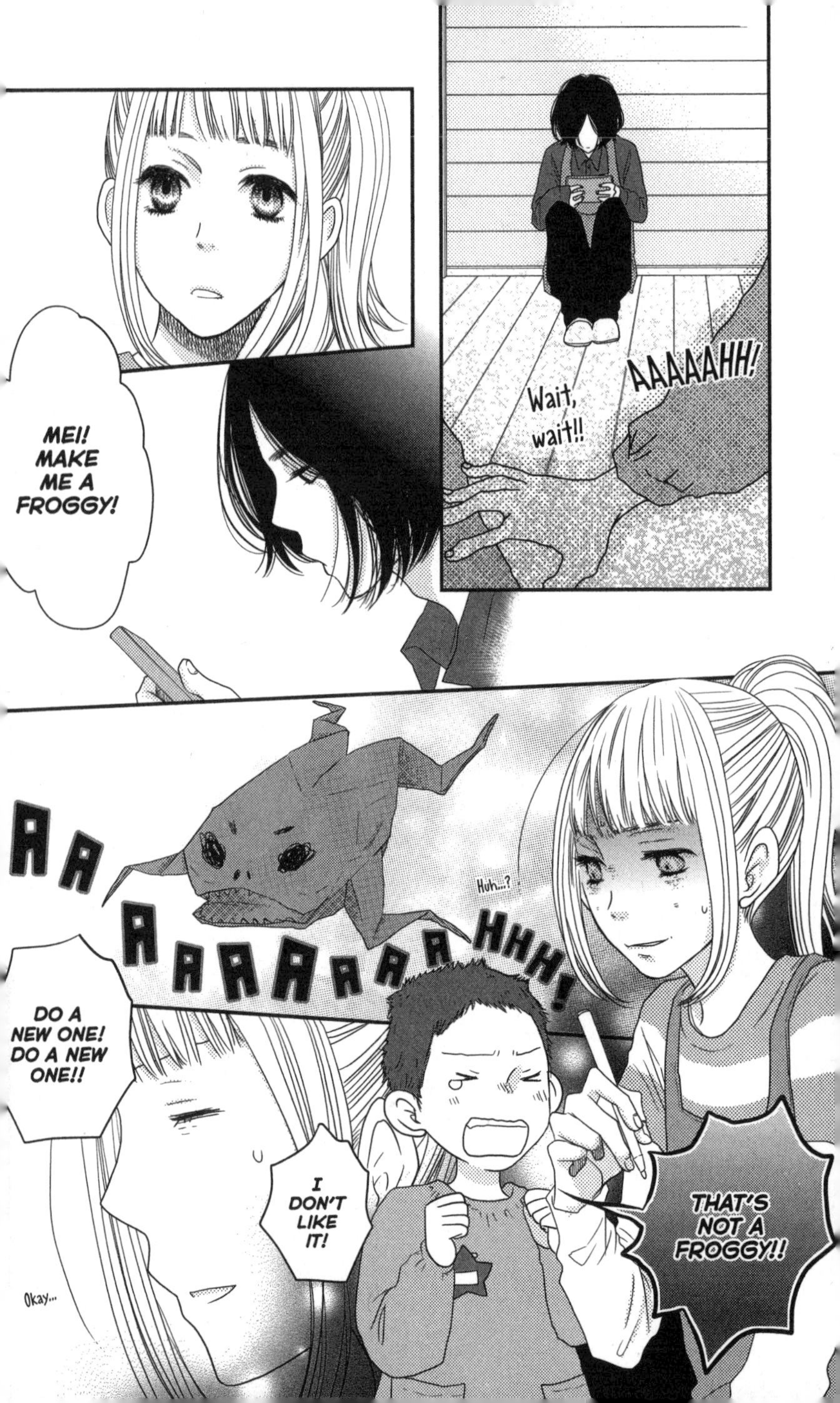
AAAAAHH!
Wait, wait!!
MEI! MAKE ME A FROGGY!
Huh...?
AAAAAAAAAHHH!
THAT'S NOT A FROGGY!!
DO A NEW ONE! DO A NEW ONE!!
I DON'T LIKE IT!
Okay...

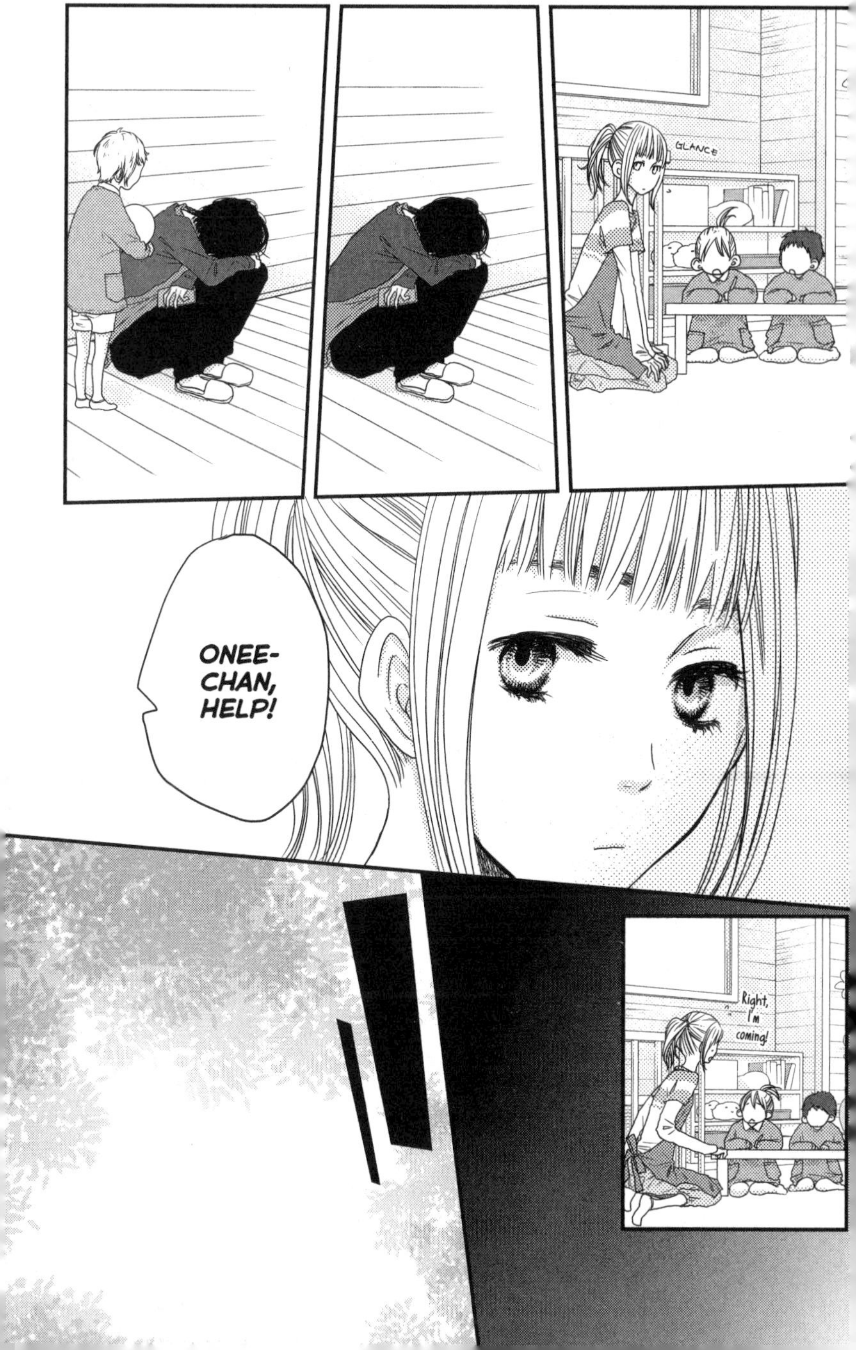
GLANCE
ONEE-CHAN, HELP!
Right, I'm coming!

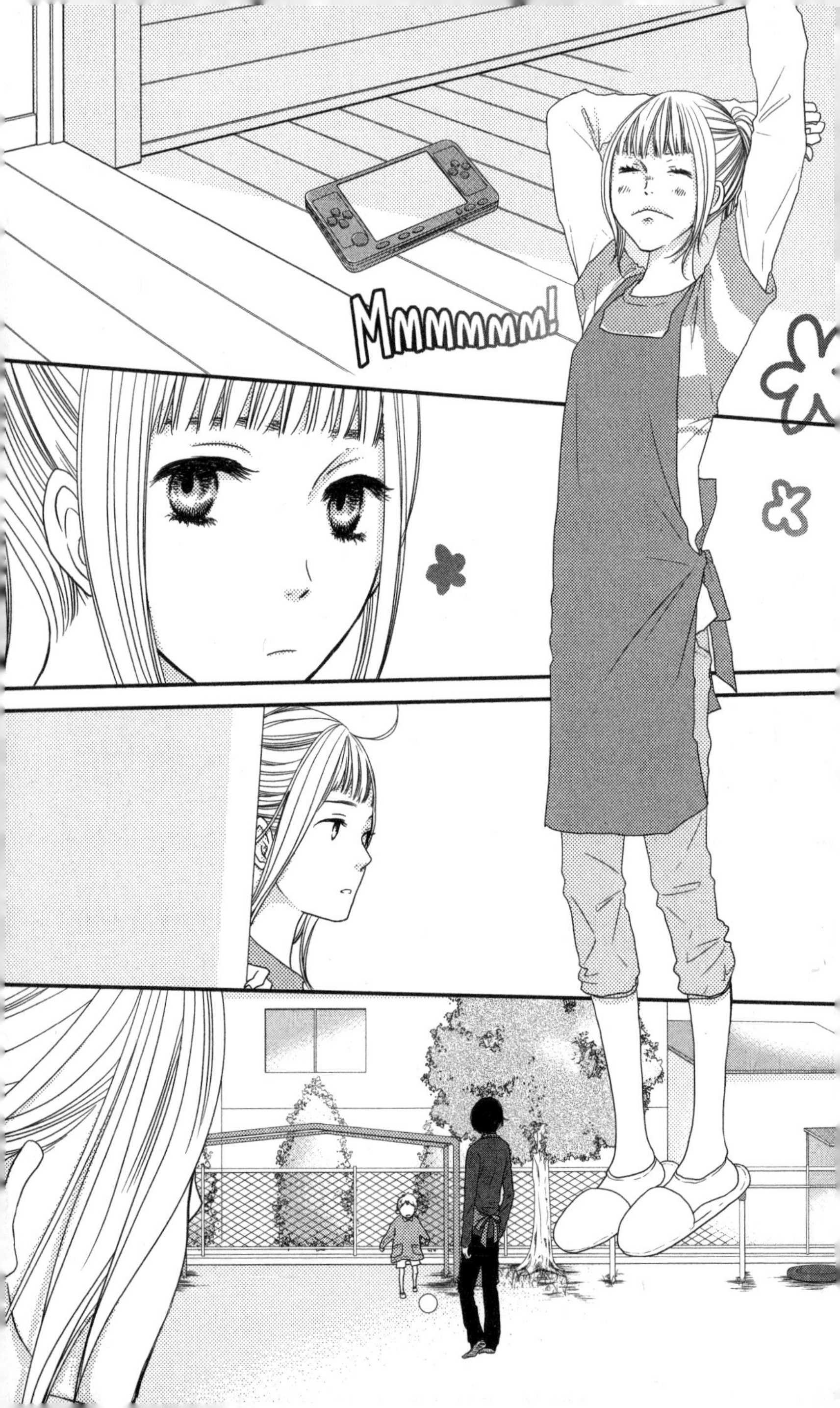
Mmmmmm!

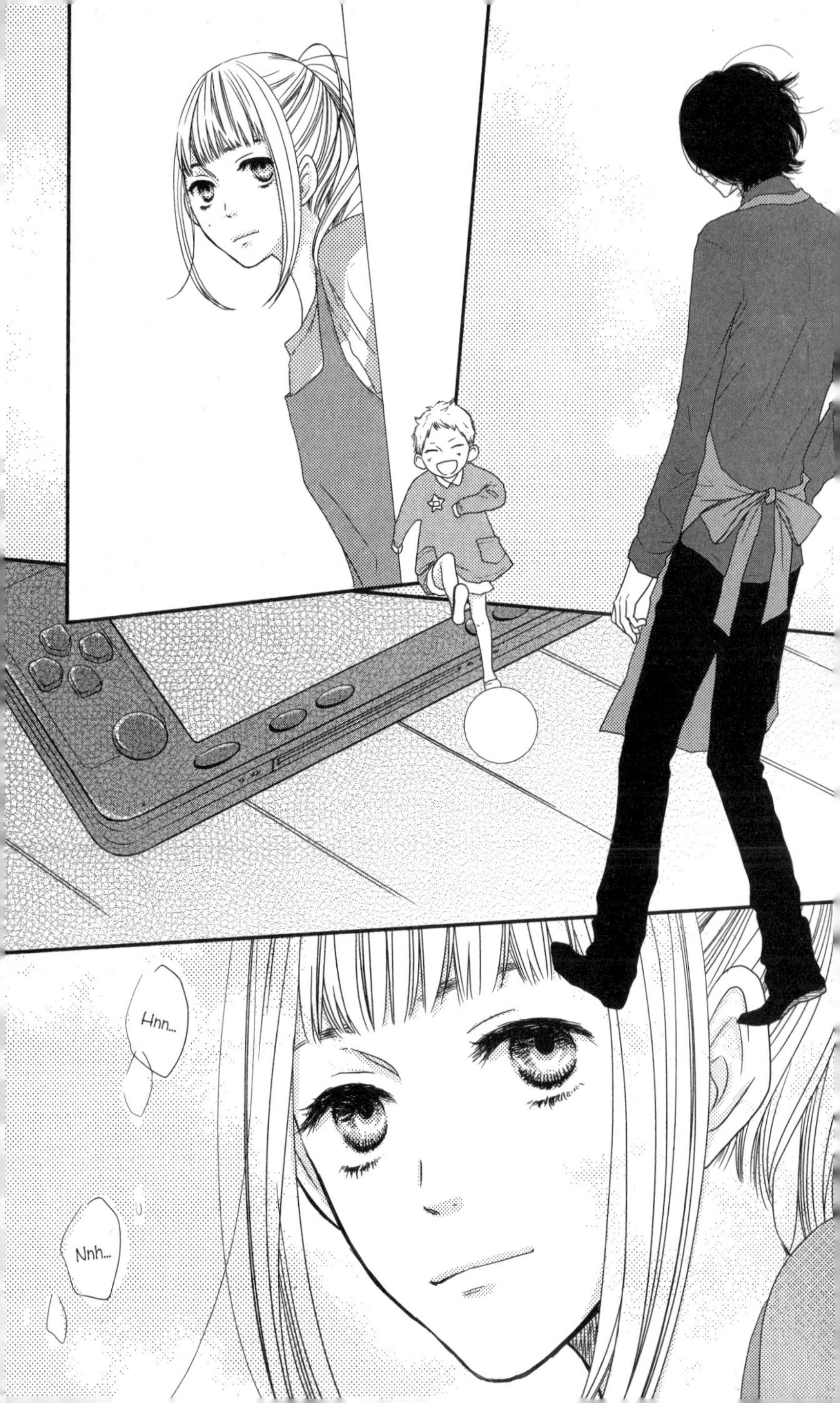
Hnn...
Nnh...

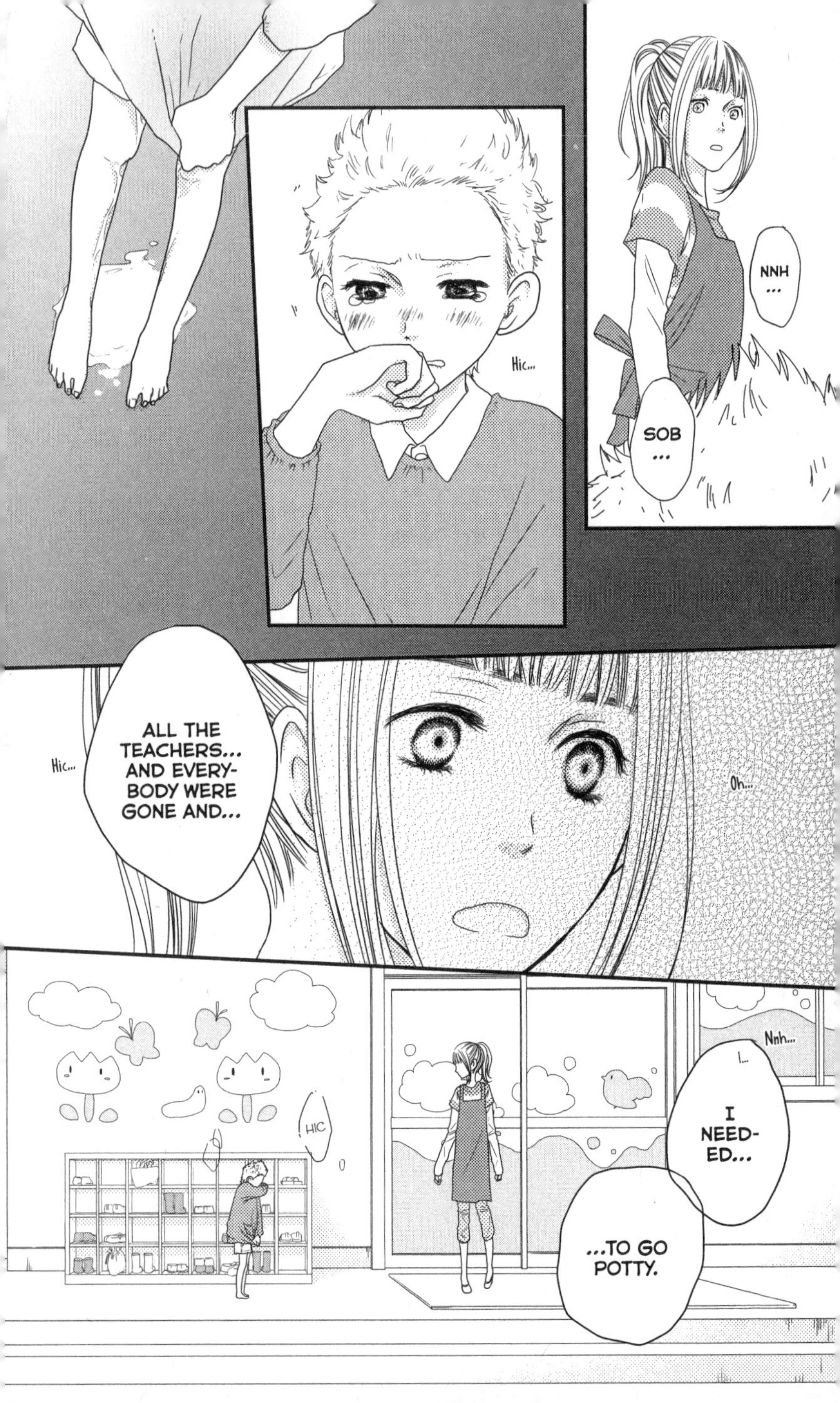
NNH...
SOB...
Hic...
Oh...
ALL THE TEACHERS... AND EVERY-BODY WERE GONE AND...
Hic...
Nnh...
I...
I NEED-ED...
...TO GO POTTY.
HIC

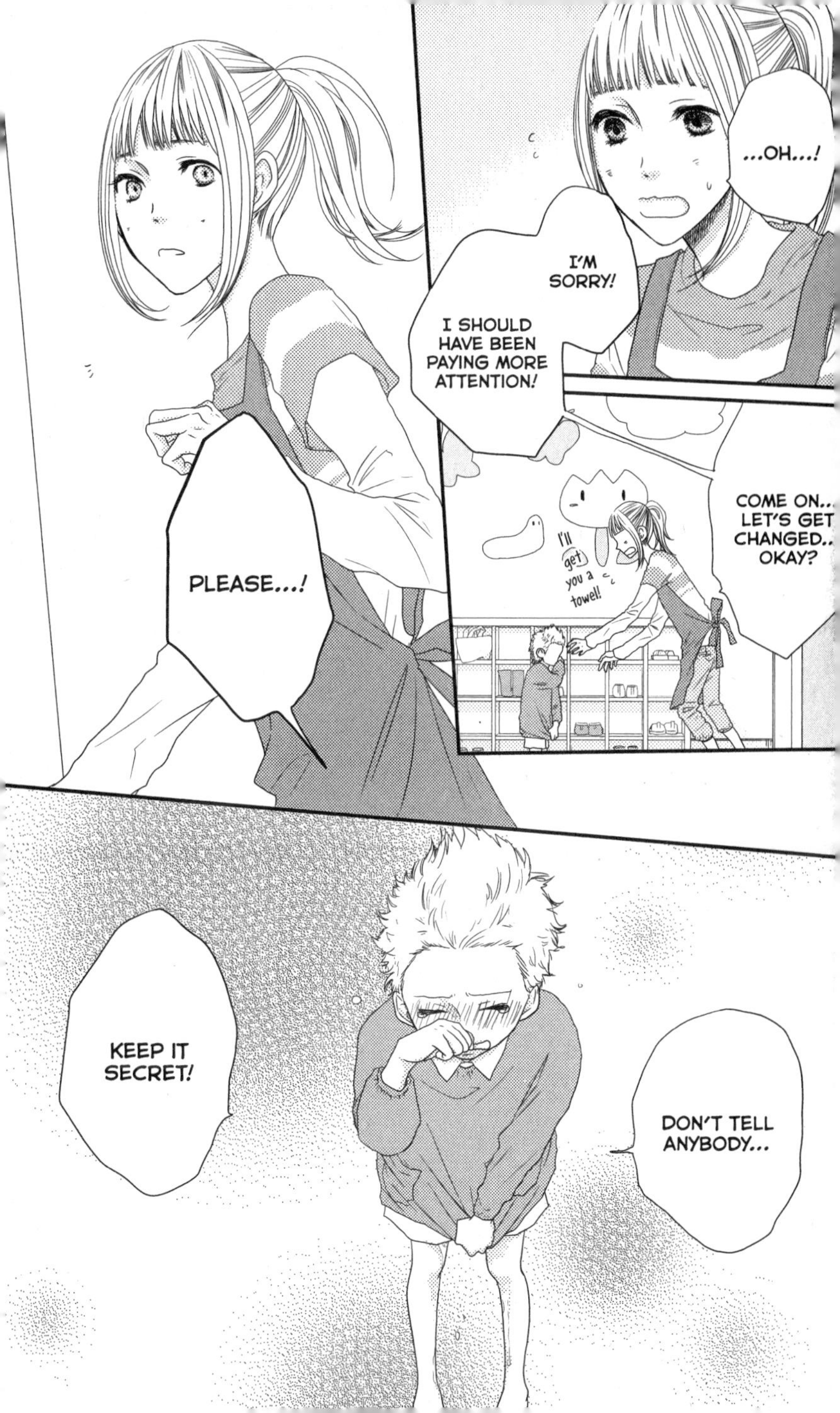
...OH...!
I'M SORRY!
I SHOULD HAVE BEEN PAYING MORE ATTENTION!
COME ON... LET'S GET CHANGED... OKAY?
I'll get you a towel!
PLEASE...!
DON'T TELL ANYBODY...
KEEP IT SECRET!

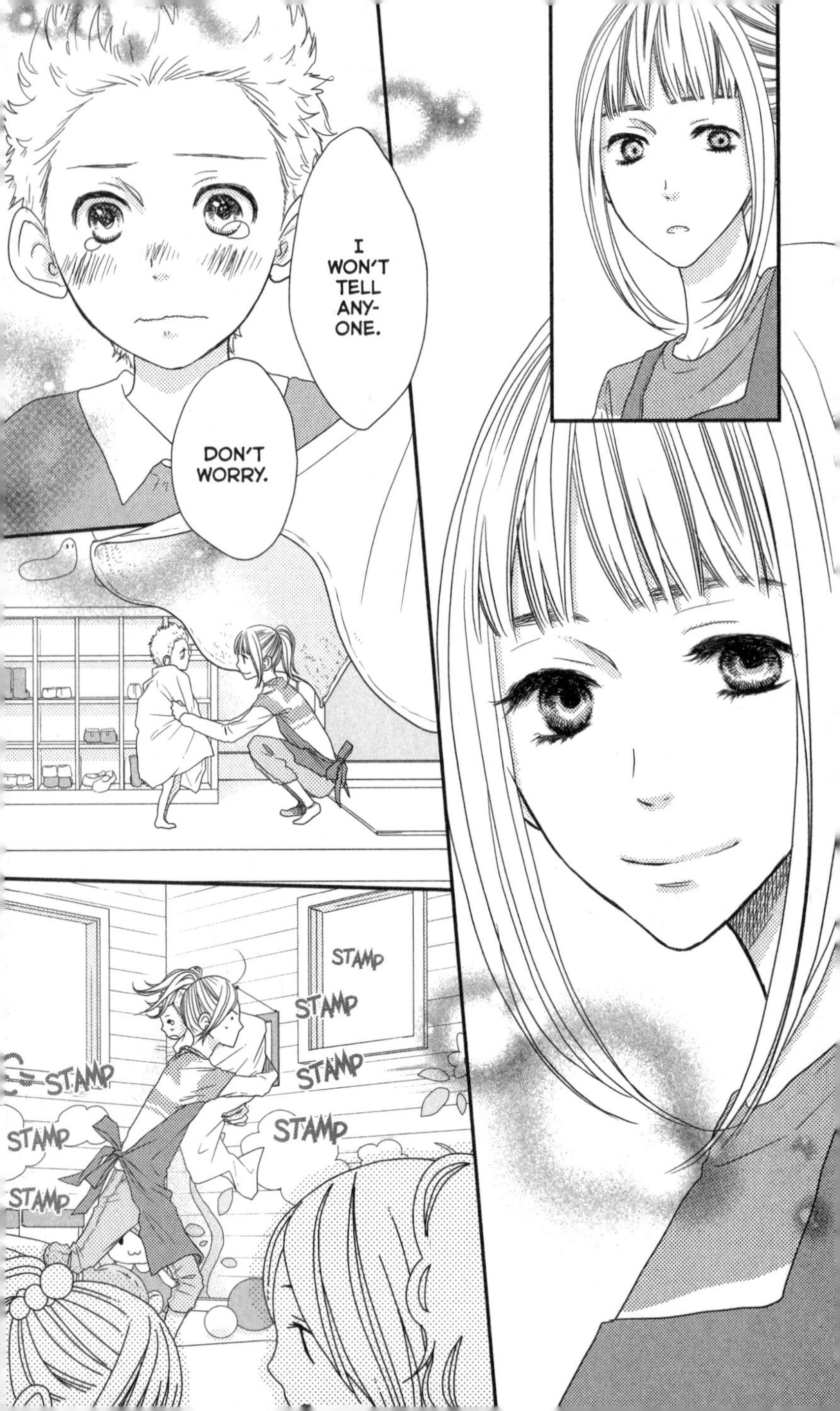
I WON'T TELL ANY-ONE.
DON'T WORRY.
STAMP
STAMP
STAMP
STAMP
STAMP
STAMP
STAMP

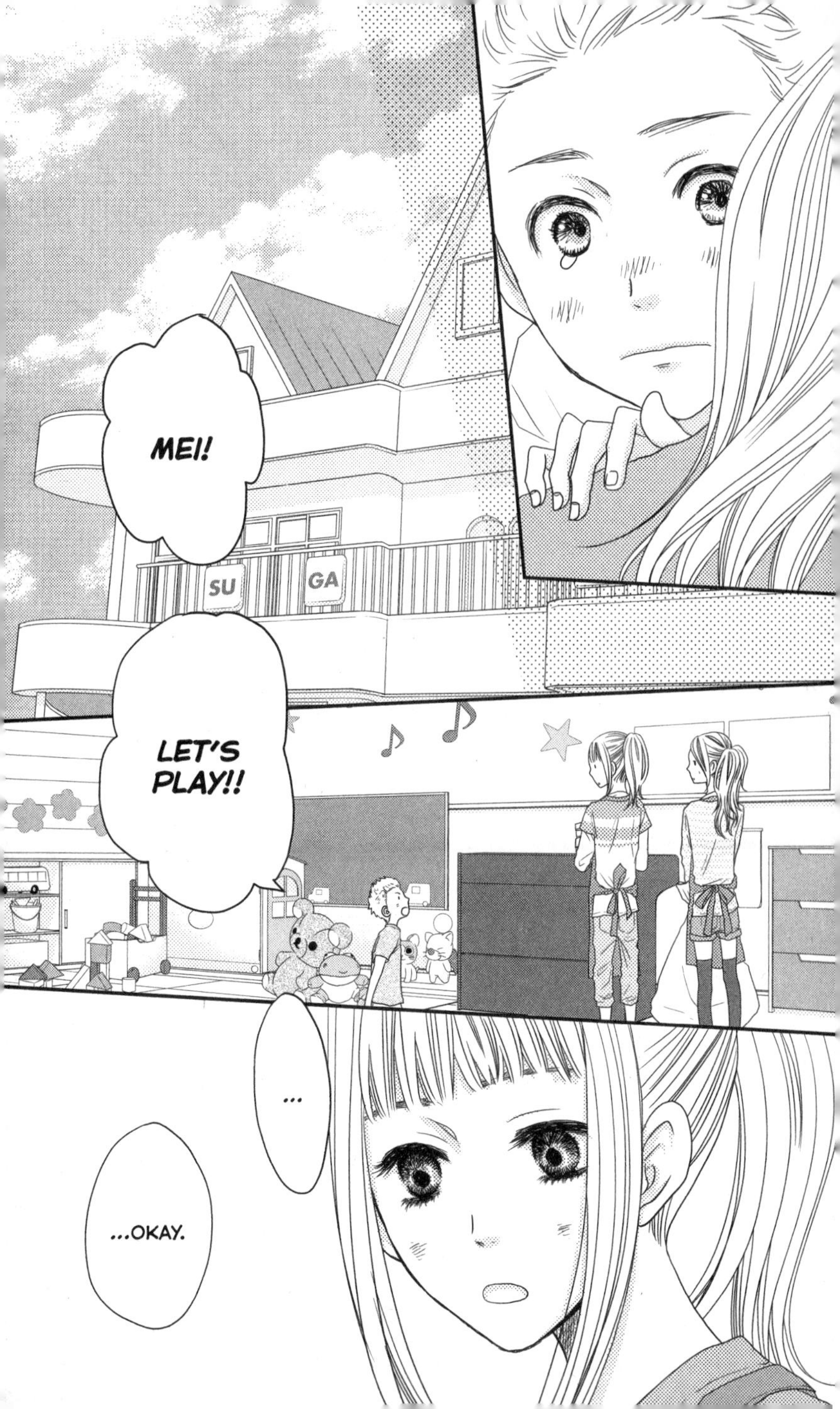
MEI!
SU
GA
LET'S PLAY!!
...
...OKAY.

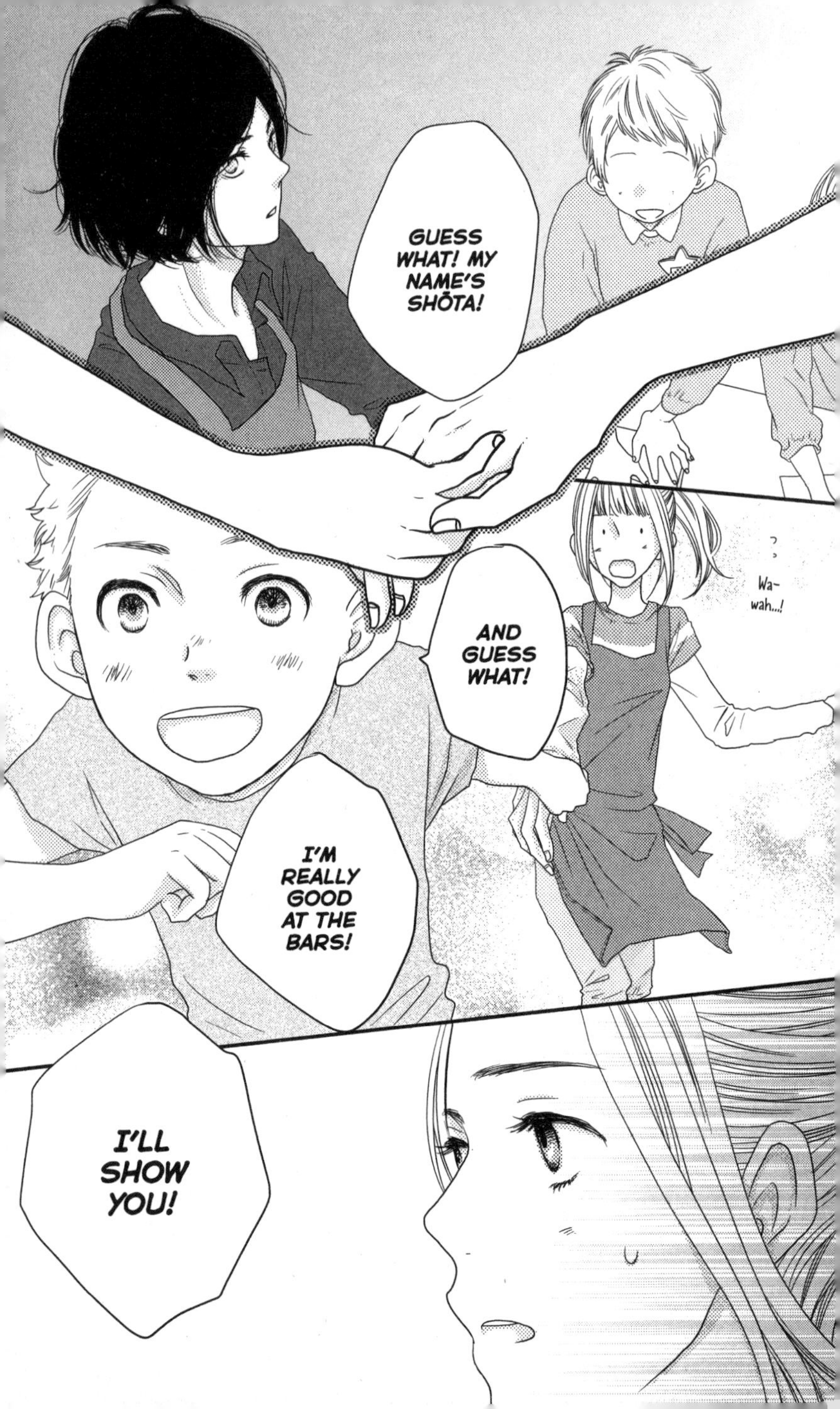
GUESS WHAT! MY NAME'S SHŌTA!
Wa-wah...!
AND GUESS WHAT!
I'M REALLY GOOD AT THE BARS!
I'LL SHOW YOU!

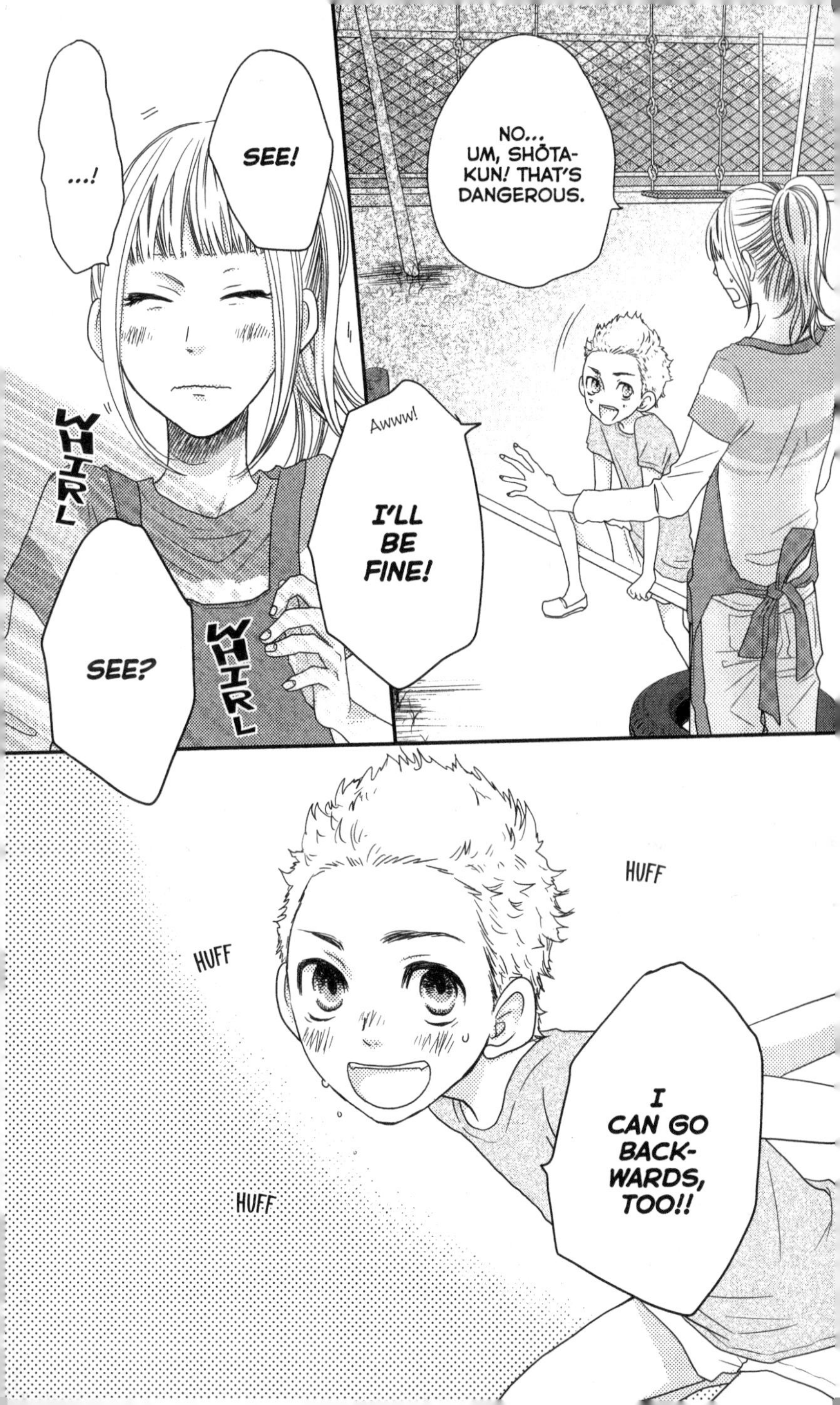
NO... UM, SHŌTA-KUN! THAT'S DANGEROUS.
Awww!
I'LL BE FINE!
SEE!
...!
WHIRL
WHIRL
SEE?
HUFF
I CAN GO BACKWARDS, TOO!!
HUFF
HUFF

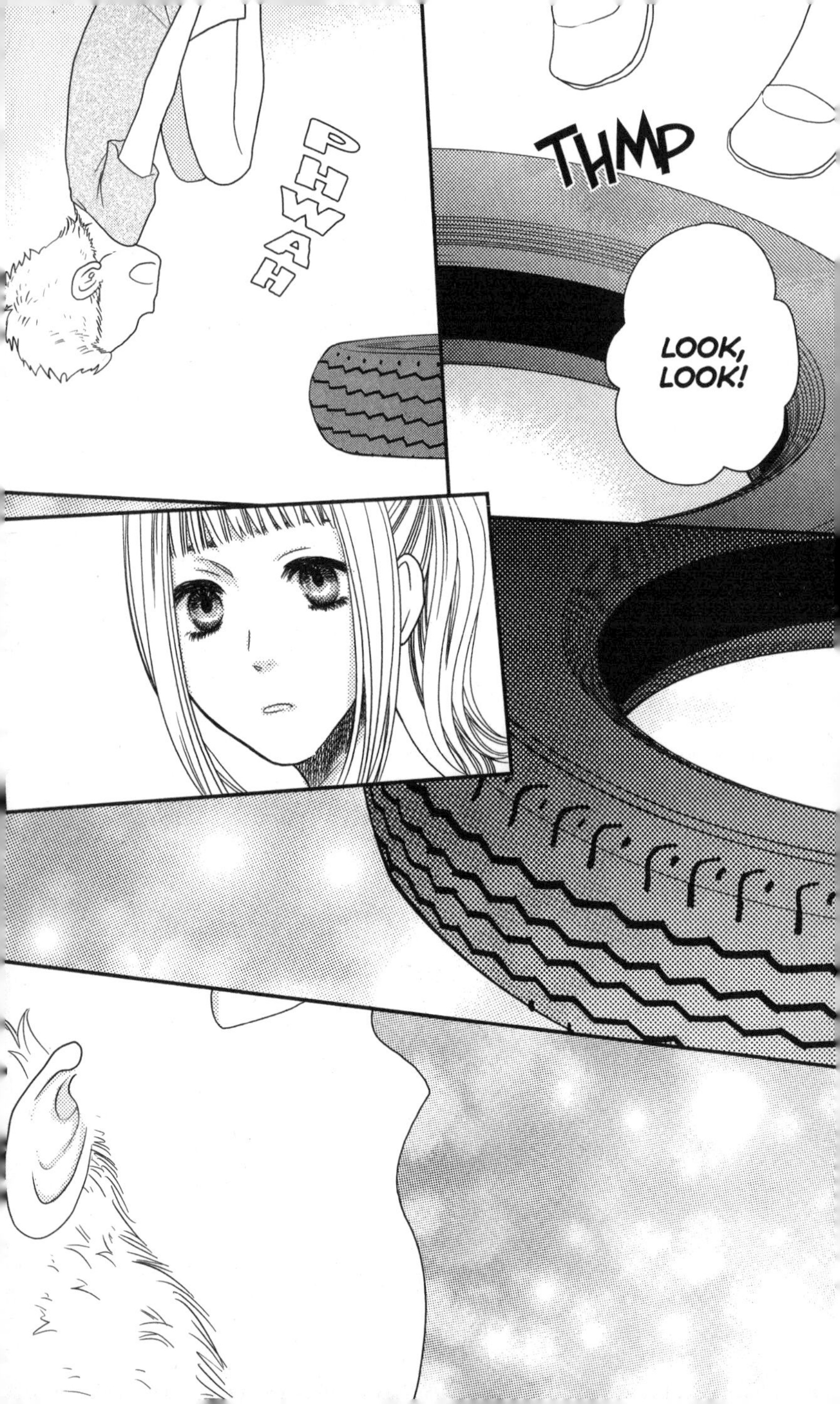
THMP
LOOK, LOOK!
PHWAH

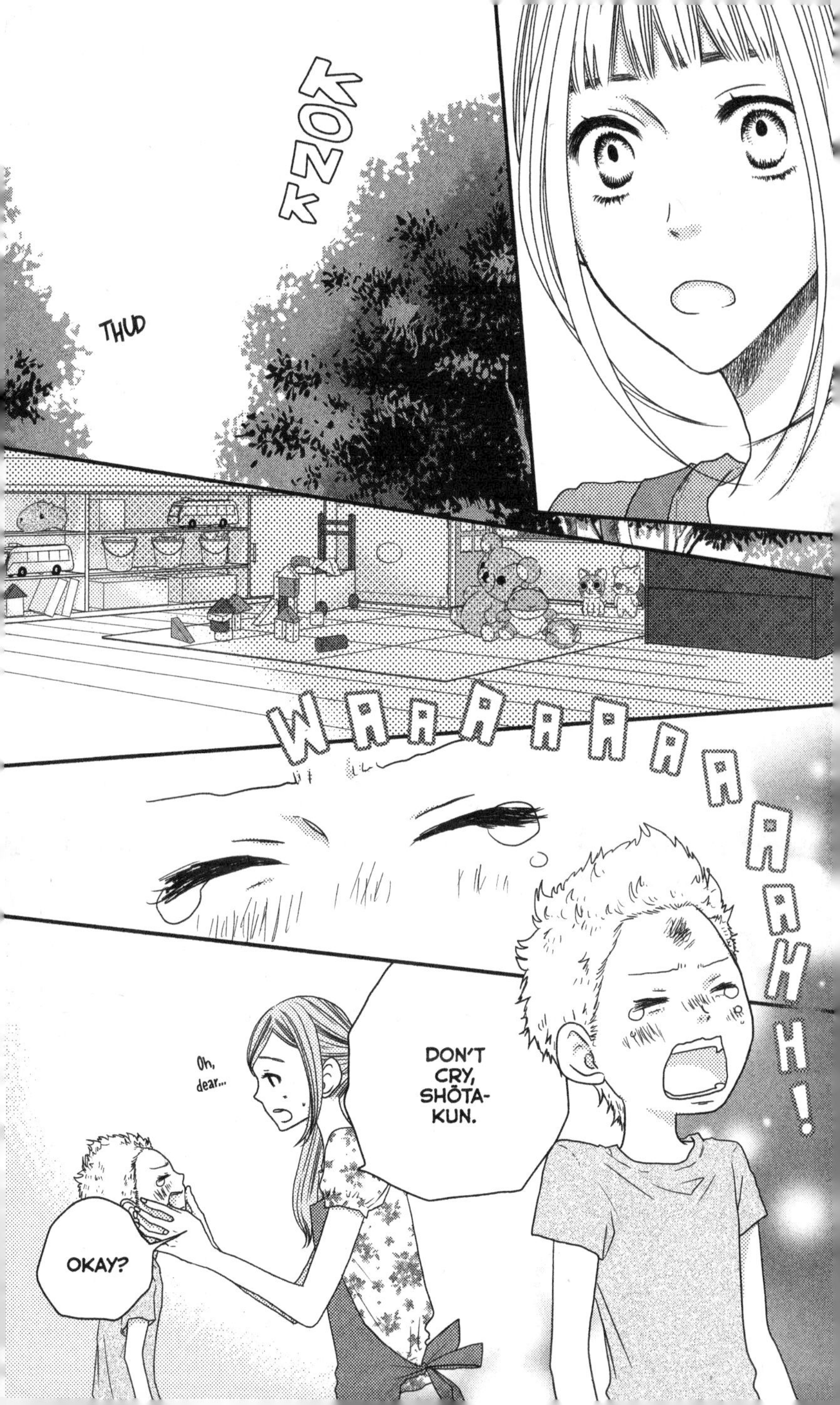
KONK
THUD
WAAAAAAAAAAAHHH!
DON'T CRY, SHŌTA-KUN.
Oh, dear...
OKAY?

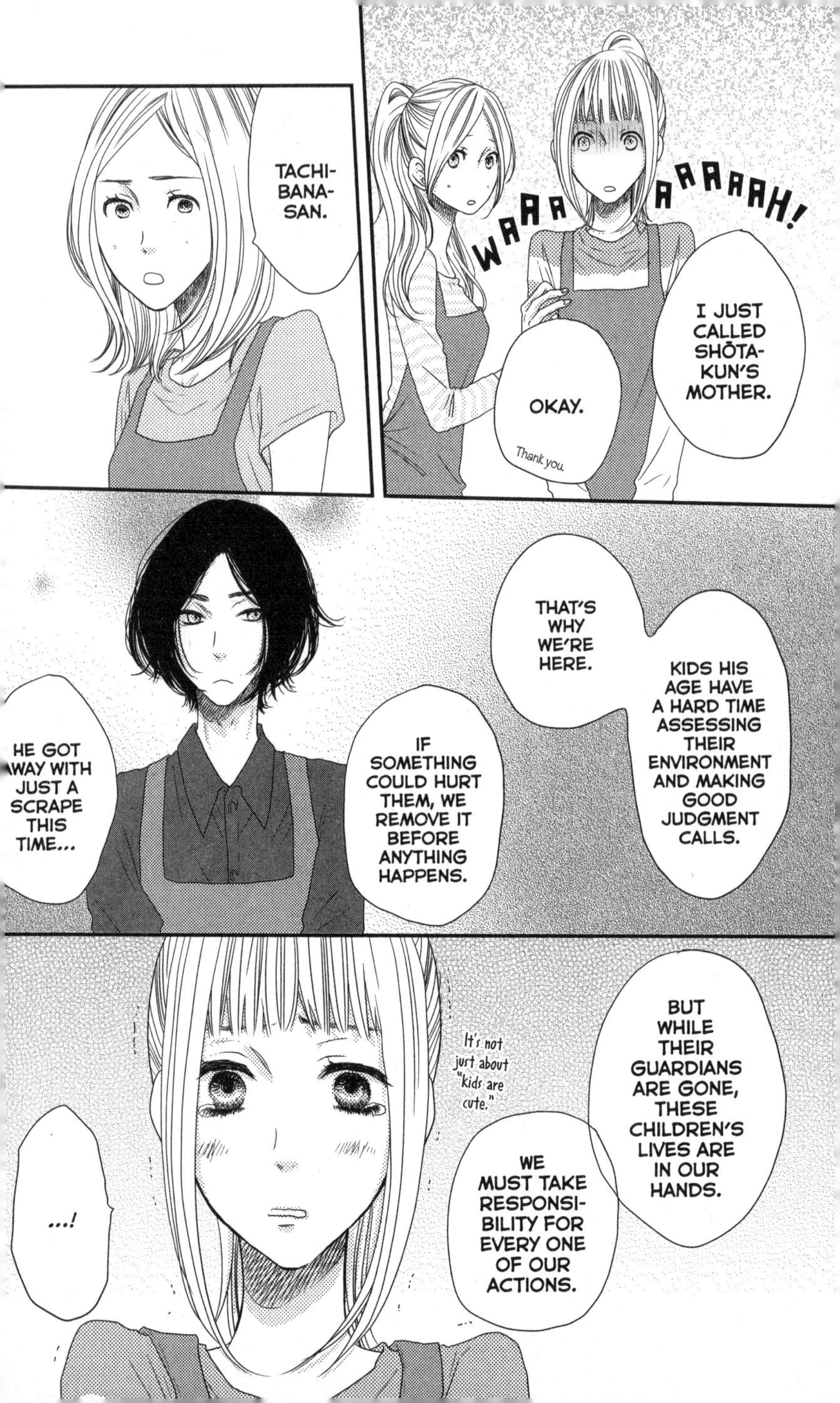
WAAAA AAAAAH!
I JUST CALLED SHŌTA-KUN'S MOTHER.
OKAY.
Thank you.
TACHI-BANA-SAN.
KIDS HIS AGE HAVE A HARD TIME ASSESSING THEIR ENVIRONMENT AND MAKING GOOD JUDGMENT CALLS.
THAT'S WHY WE'RE HERE.
IF SOMETHING COULD HURT THEM, WE REMOVE IT BEFORE ANYTHING HAPPENS.
HE GOT AWAY WITH JUST A SCRAPE THIS TIME...
BUT WHILE THEIR GUARDIANS ARE GONE, THESE CHILDREN'S LIVES ARE IN OUR HANDS.
WE MUST TAKE RESPONSIBILITY FOR EVERY ONE OF OUR ACTIONS.
It's not just about "kids are cute."
...!

NO...

NO!

MEI DIDN'T DO ANYTHING WRONG!

I'M SORRY.

...!

SHE SAID IT WAS DANGEROUS.

THAT'S WHY...!

BUT I MADE HER WATCH ME ANYWAY!

I TOLD HER...

...TO WATCH ME ON THE BARS!

IT DOESN'T HURT ANY-MORE!

HE'S...

...SO SMALL.

BUT HIS FRANK...

...CANDID...

.WORDS...

...STRUCK ME...

...TO THE HEART.

DON'T YELL AT MEI!!

I'M SORRY, SHŌTA-KUN.

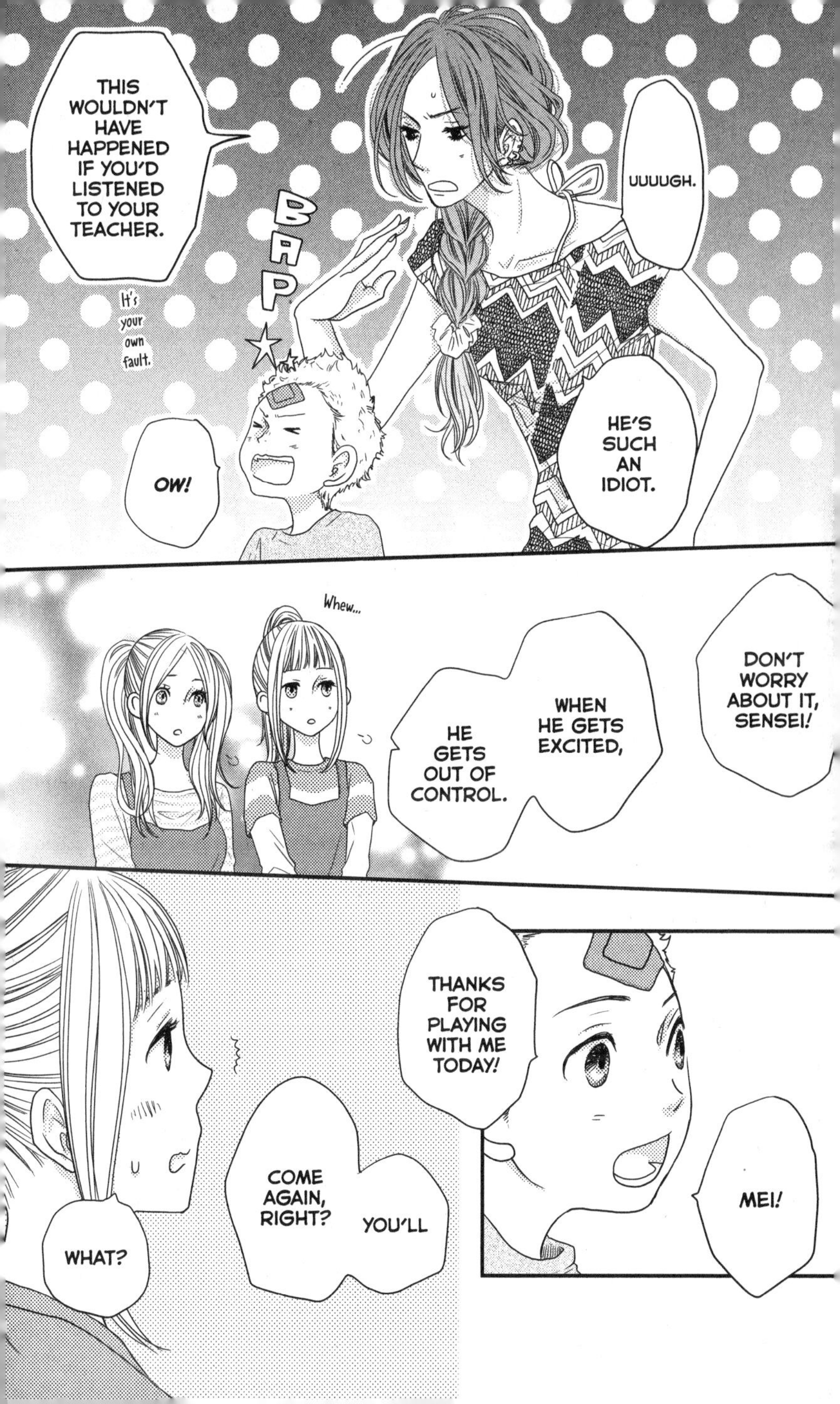
UUUUGH.
THIS WOULDN'T HAVE HAPPENED IF YOU'D LISTENED TO YOUR TEACHER.
BAP
It's your own fault.
HE'S SUCH AN IDIOT.
OW!
DON'T WORRY ABOUT IT, SENSEI!
WHEN HE GETS EXCITED,
HE GETS OUT OF CONTROL.
Whew...
THANKS FOR PLAYING WITH ME TODAY!
MEI!
YOU'LL
COME AGAIN, RIGHT?
WHAT?

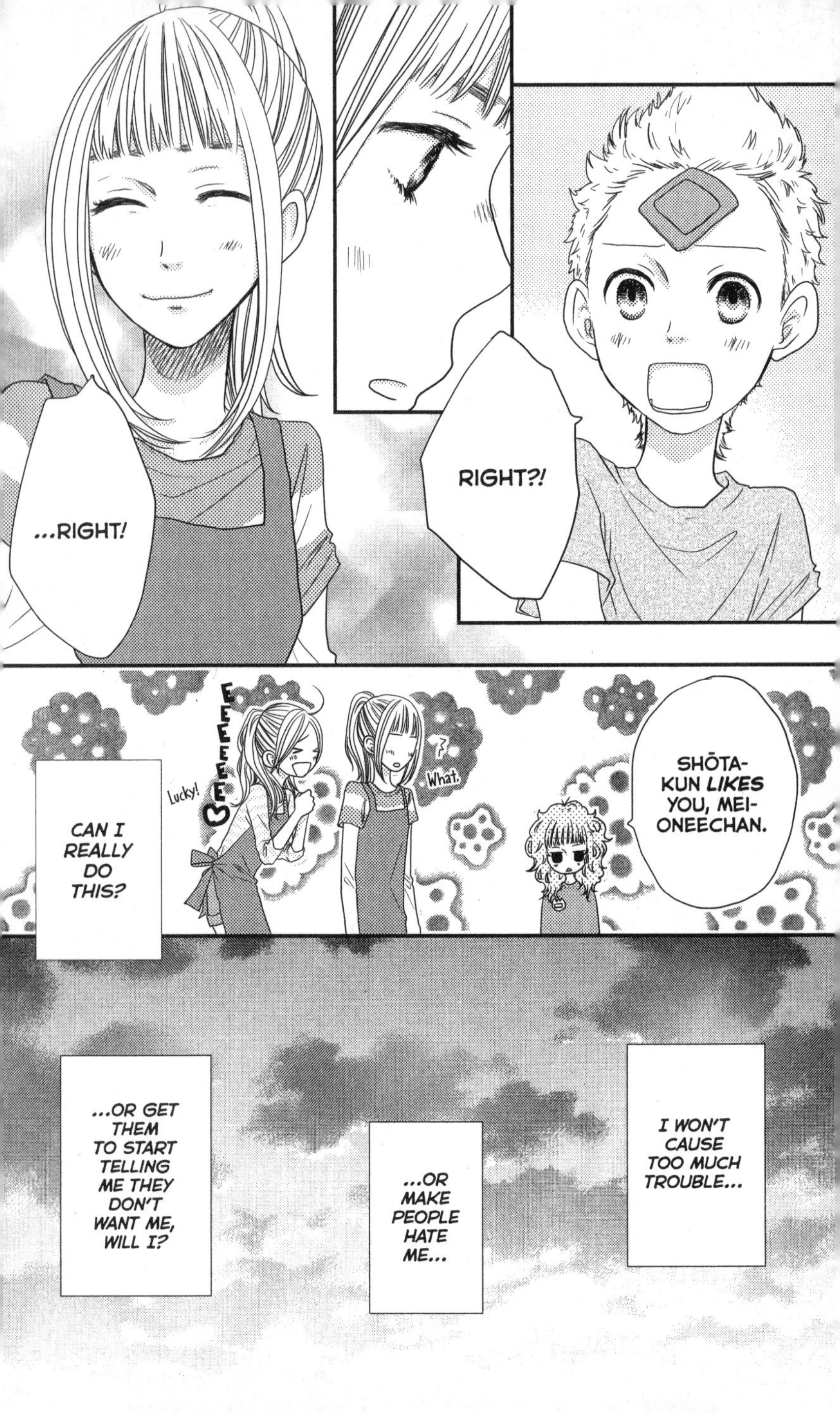
RIGHT?!
...RIGHT!
SHŌTA-KUN **LIKES** YOU, MEI-ONEECHAN.
?
What.
EEEEEE
Lucky!
CAN I REALLY DO THIS?
I WON'T CAUSE TOO MUCH TROUBLE...
...OR MAKE PEOPLE HATE ME...
...OR GET THEM TO START TELLING ME THEY DON'T WANT ME, WILL I?

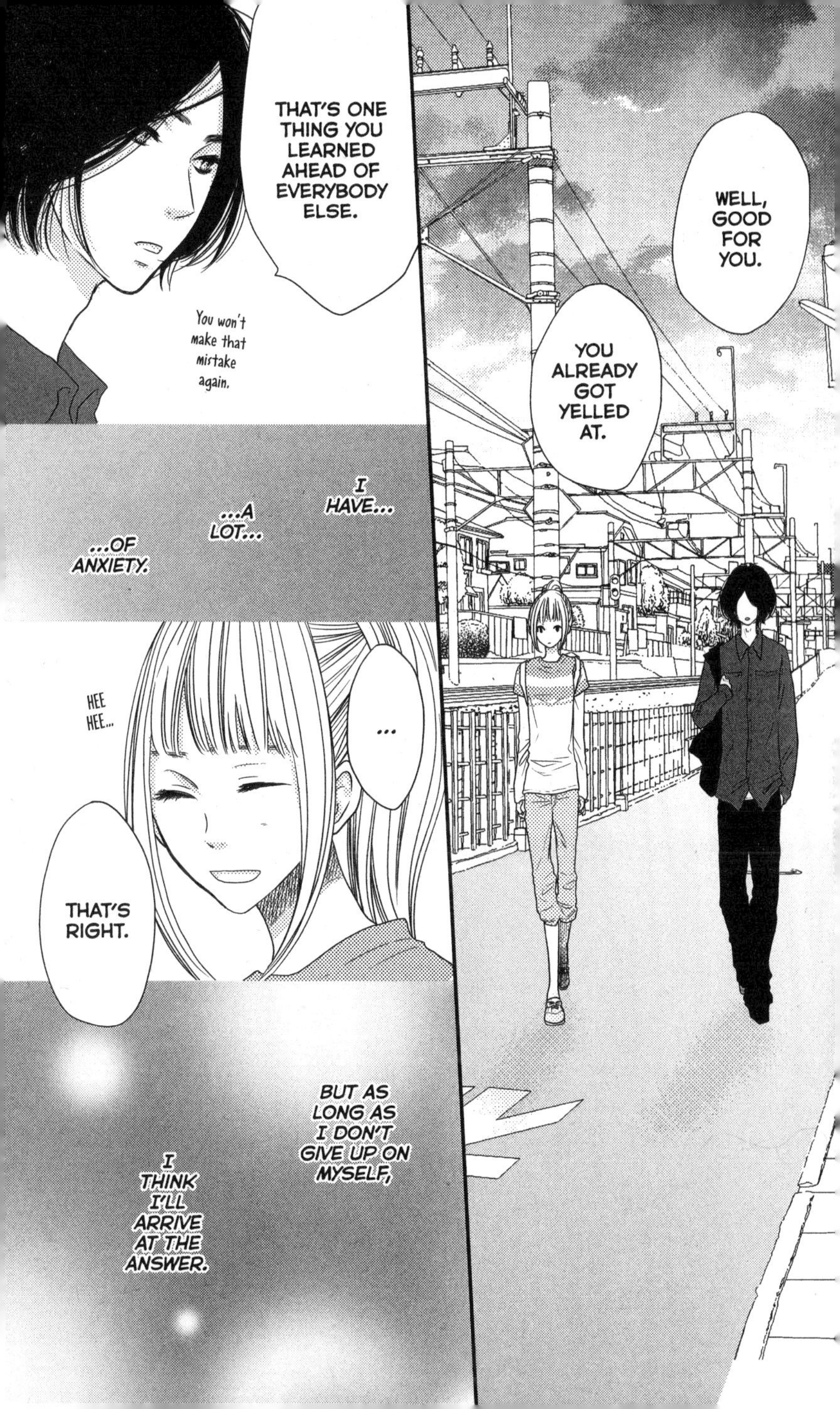
WELL, GOOD FOR YOU.
YOU ALREADY GOT YELLED AT.
THAT'S ONE THING YOU LEARNED AHEAD OF EVERYBODY ELSE.
You won't make that mistake again.
I HAVE...
...A LOT...
...OF ANXIETY.
...
HEE HEE...
THAT'S RIGHT.
BUT AS LONG AS I DON'T GIVE UP ON MYSELF,
I THINK I'LL ARRIVE AT THE ANSWER.

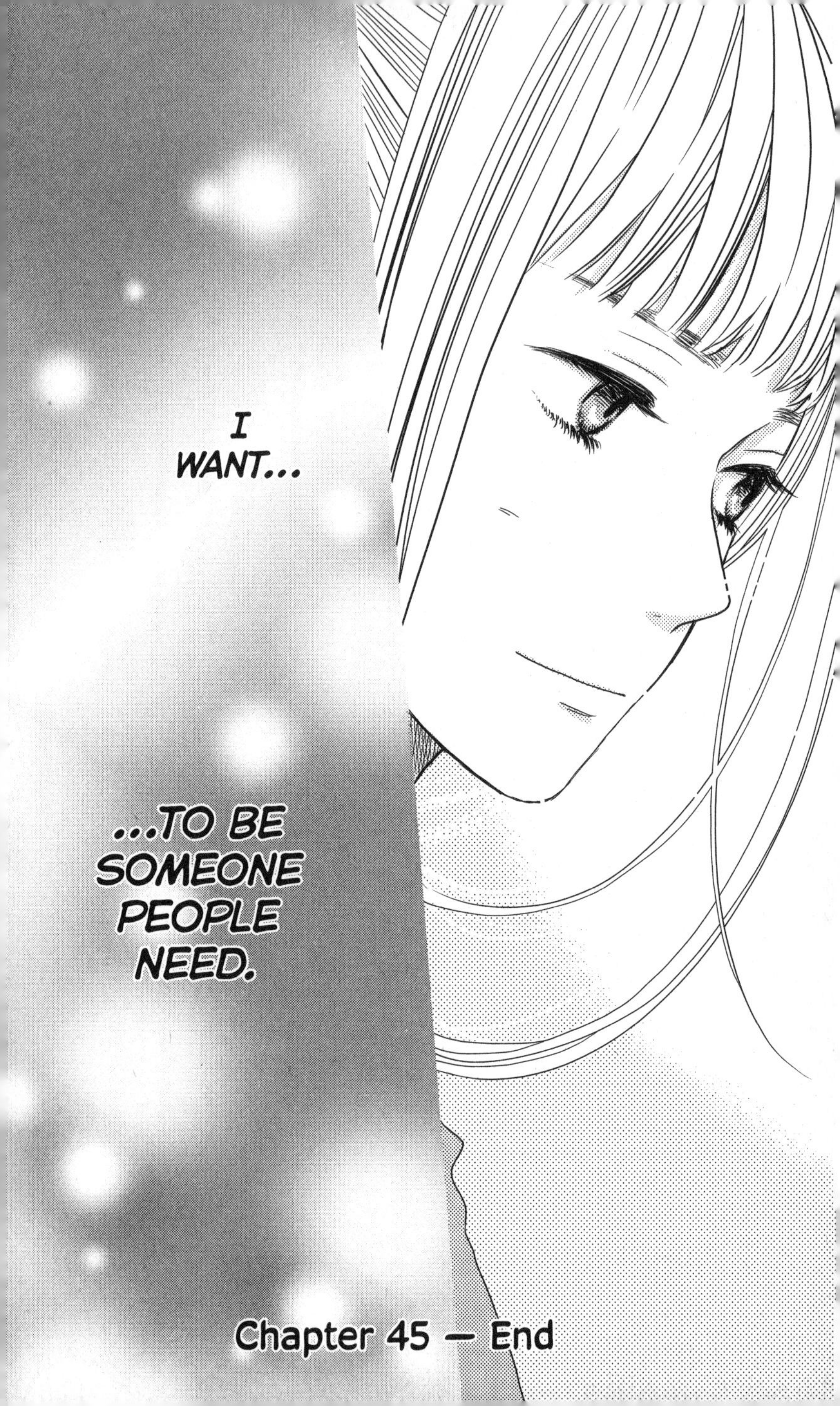
I WANT...
...TO BE SOMEONE PEOPLE NEED.
Chapter 45 — End

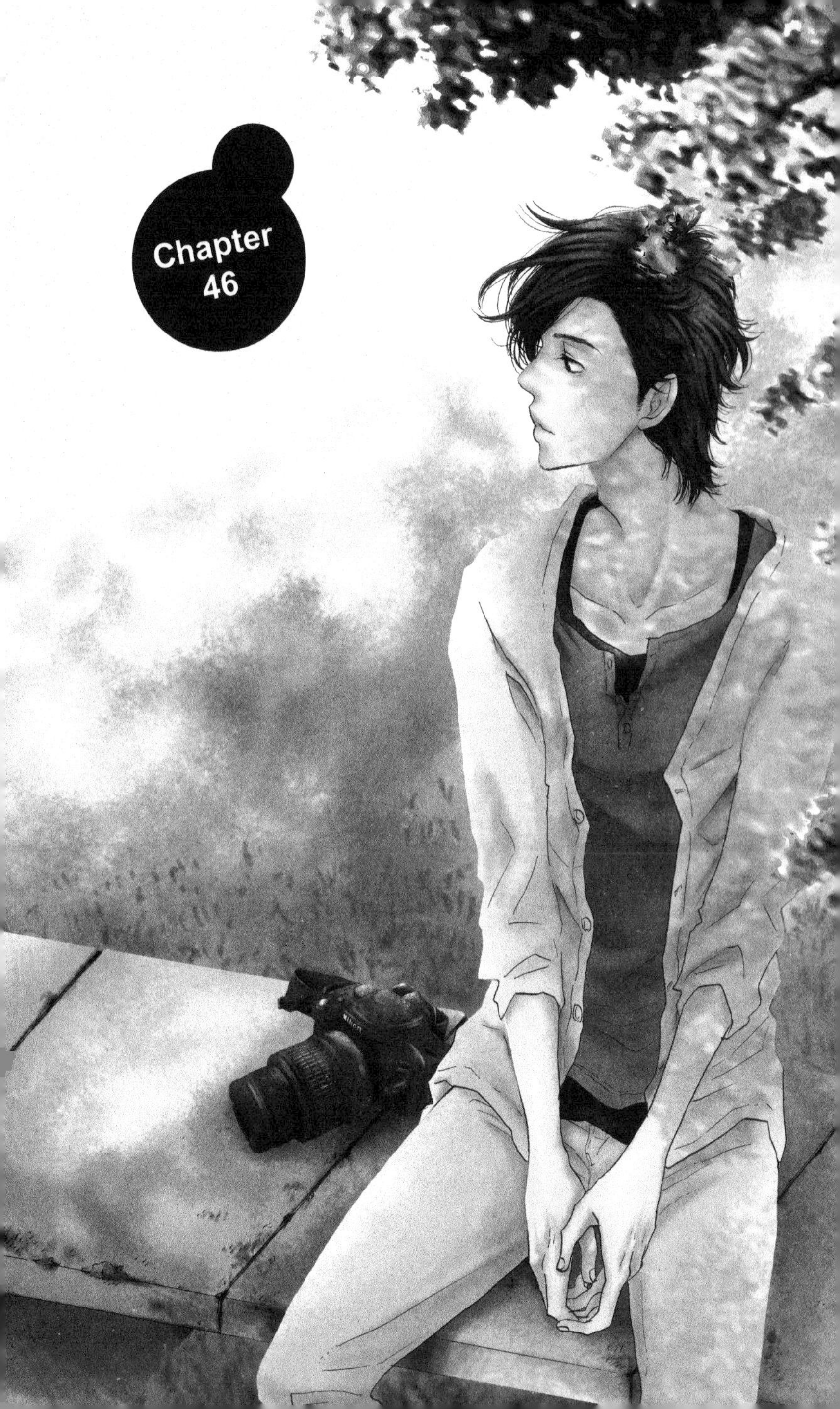
Chapter
46

Say "I love you".

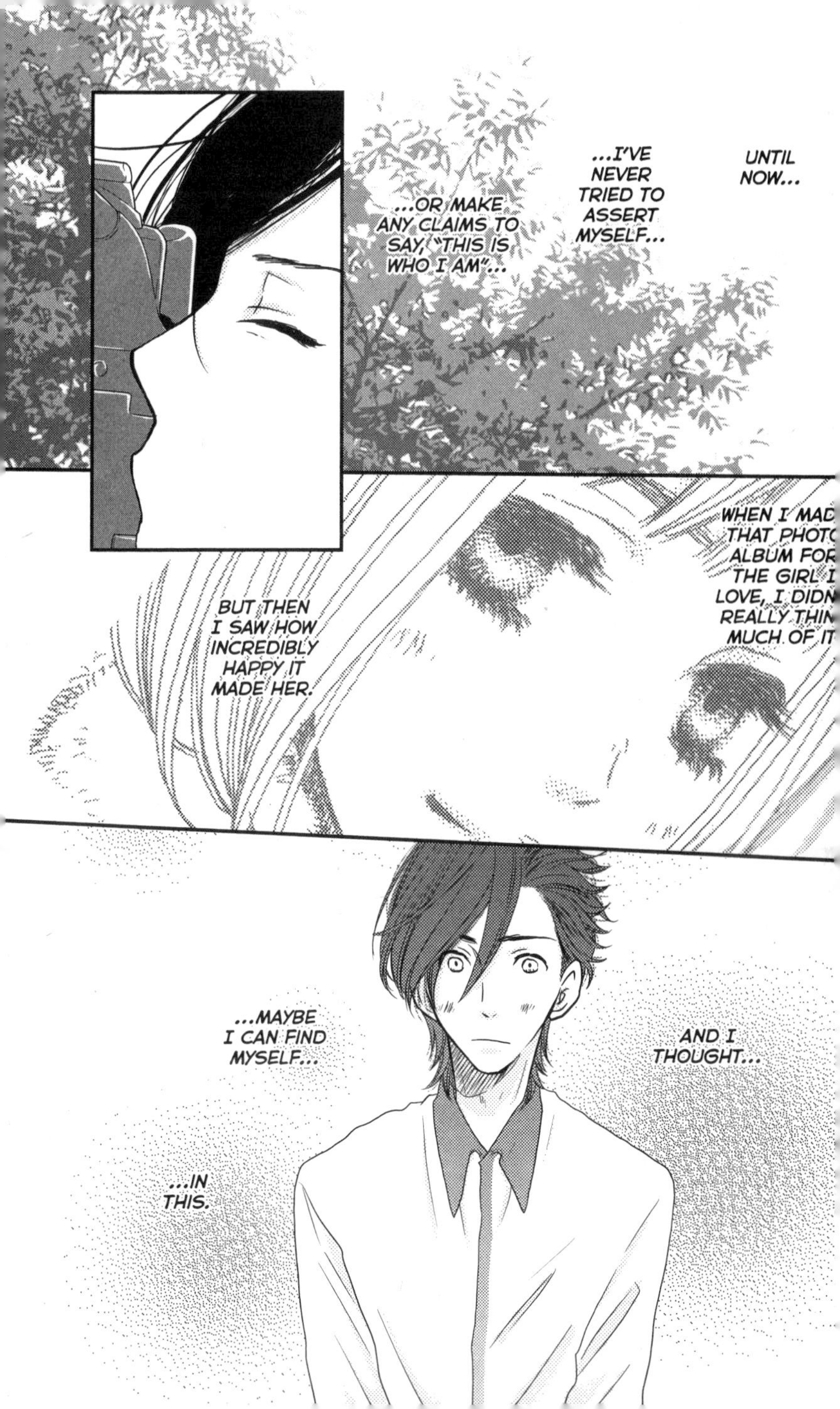
UNTIL NOW...
...I'VE NEVER TRIED TO ASSERT MYSELF...
...OR MAKE ANY CLAIMS TO SAY, "THIS IS WHO I AM"...
WHEN I MAD THAT PHOT ALBUM FOR THE GIRL I LOVE, I DIDN REALLY THIN MUCH OF IT
BUT THEN I SAW HOW INCREDIBLY HAPPY IT MADE HER.
AND I THOUGHT...
...MAYBE I CAN FIND MYSELF...
...IN THIS.

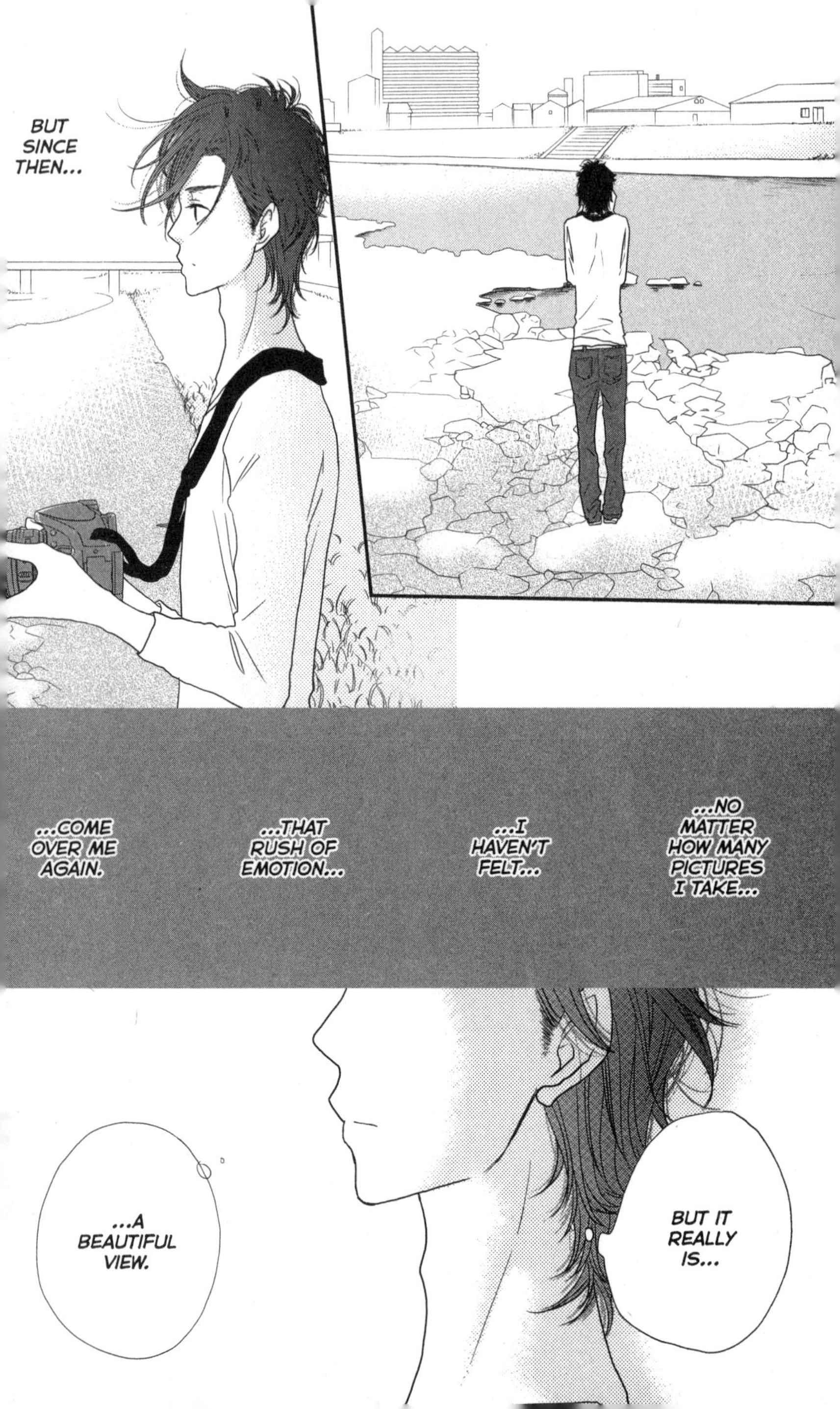
BUT SINCE THEN...
...NO MATTER HOW MANY PICTURES I TAKE...
...I HAVEN'T FELT...
...THAT RUSH OF EMOTION...
...COME OVER ME AGAIN.
BUT IT REALLY IS...
...A BEAUTIFUL VIEW.

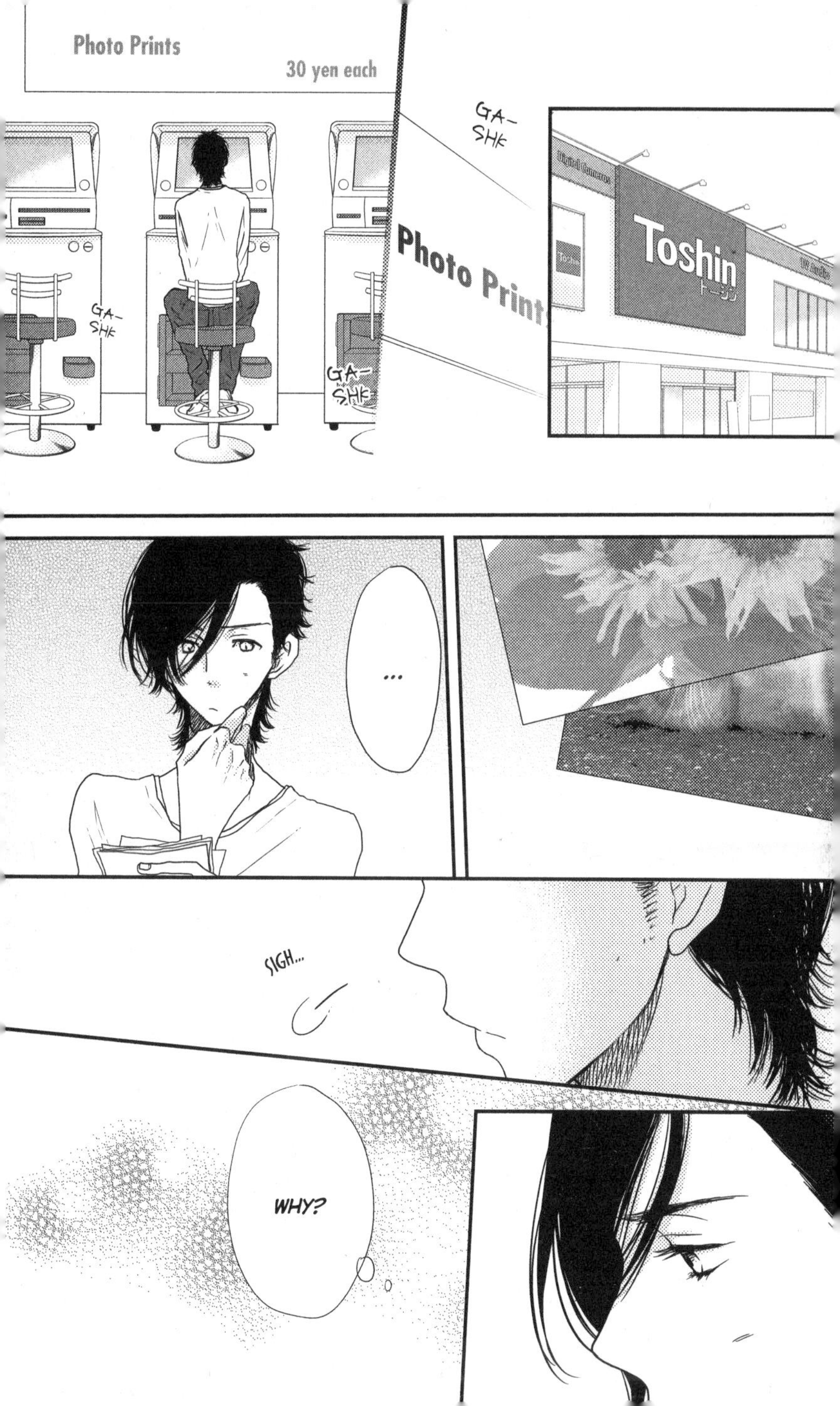
Toshin
トーシン
Digital Cameras
TV Audio
Toshin
GA-
SHK
Photo Prints
Photo Prints
30 yen each
GA-
SHK
GA-
SHK
...
SIGH...
WHY?

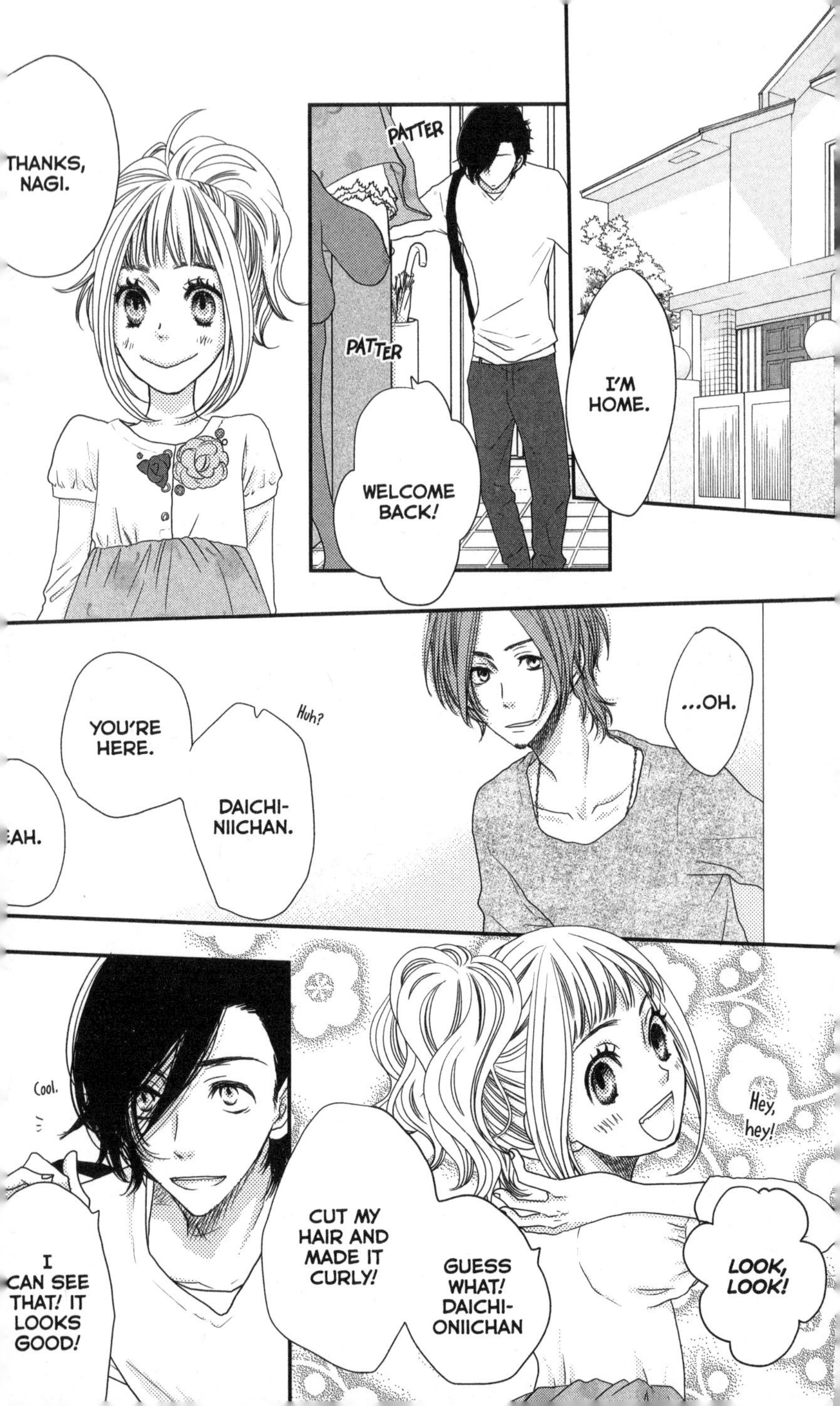

I'M HOME.
PATTER
PATTER
WELCOME BACK!
THANKS, NAGI.
...OH.
Huh?
DAICHI-NIICHAN.
YOU'RE HERE.
EAH.
Hey, hey!
LOOK, LOOK!
GUESS WHAT! DAICHI-ONIICHAN
CUT MY HAIR AND MADE IT CURLY!
Cool.
I CAN SEE THAT! IT LOOKS GOOD!

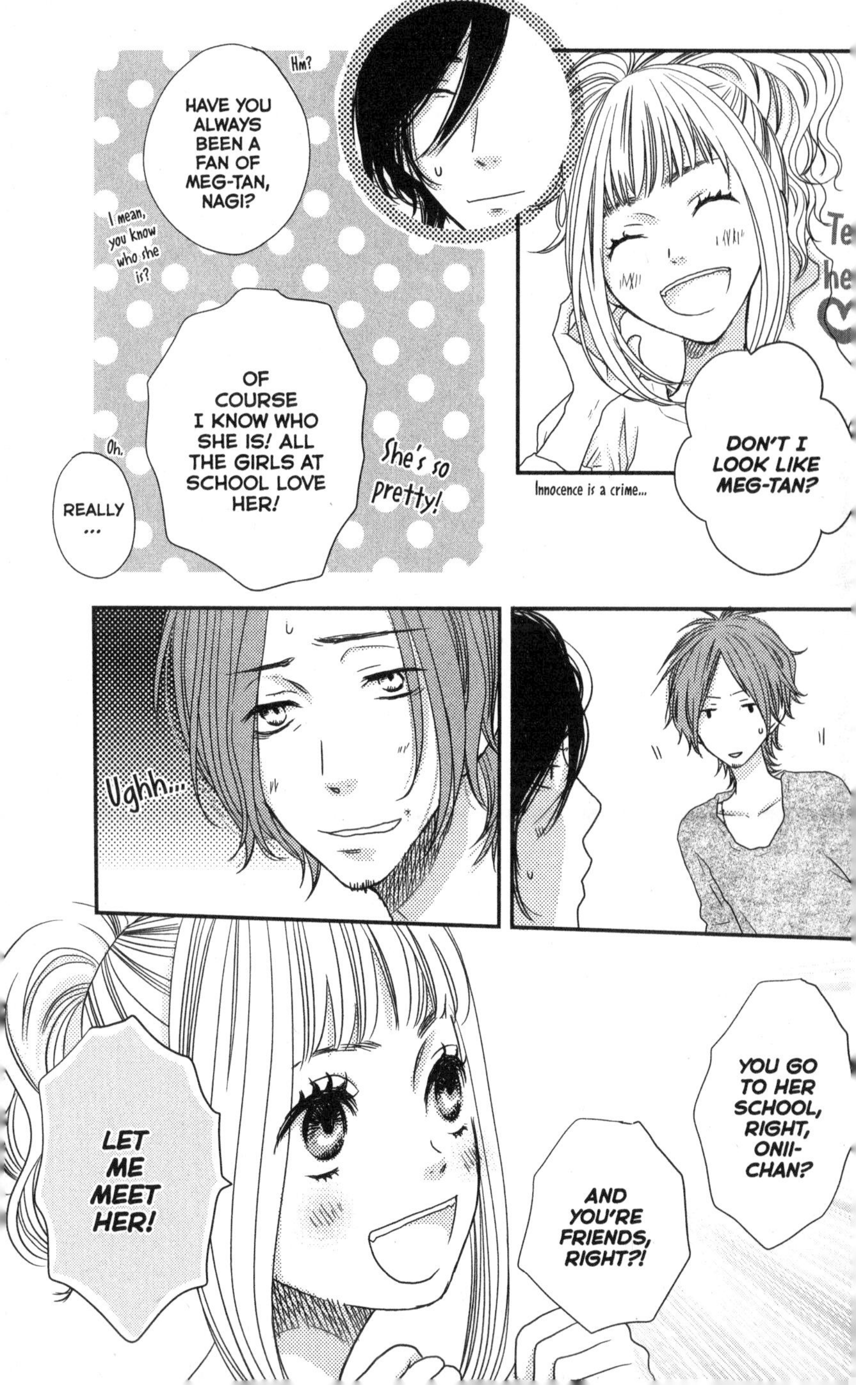
Tehe
DON'T I LOOK LIKE MEG-TAN?
Innocence is a crime...
Hm?
HAVE YOU ALWAYS BEEN A FAN OF MEG-TAN, NAGI?
I mean, you know who she is?
OF COURSE I KNOW WHO SHE IS! ALL THE GIRLS AT SCHOOL LOVE HER!
She's so pretty!
Oh.
REALLY...
Ughh...
YOU GO TO HER SCHOOL, RIGHT, ONII-CHAN?
AND YOU'RE FRIENDS, RIGHT?!
LET ME MEET HER!

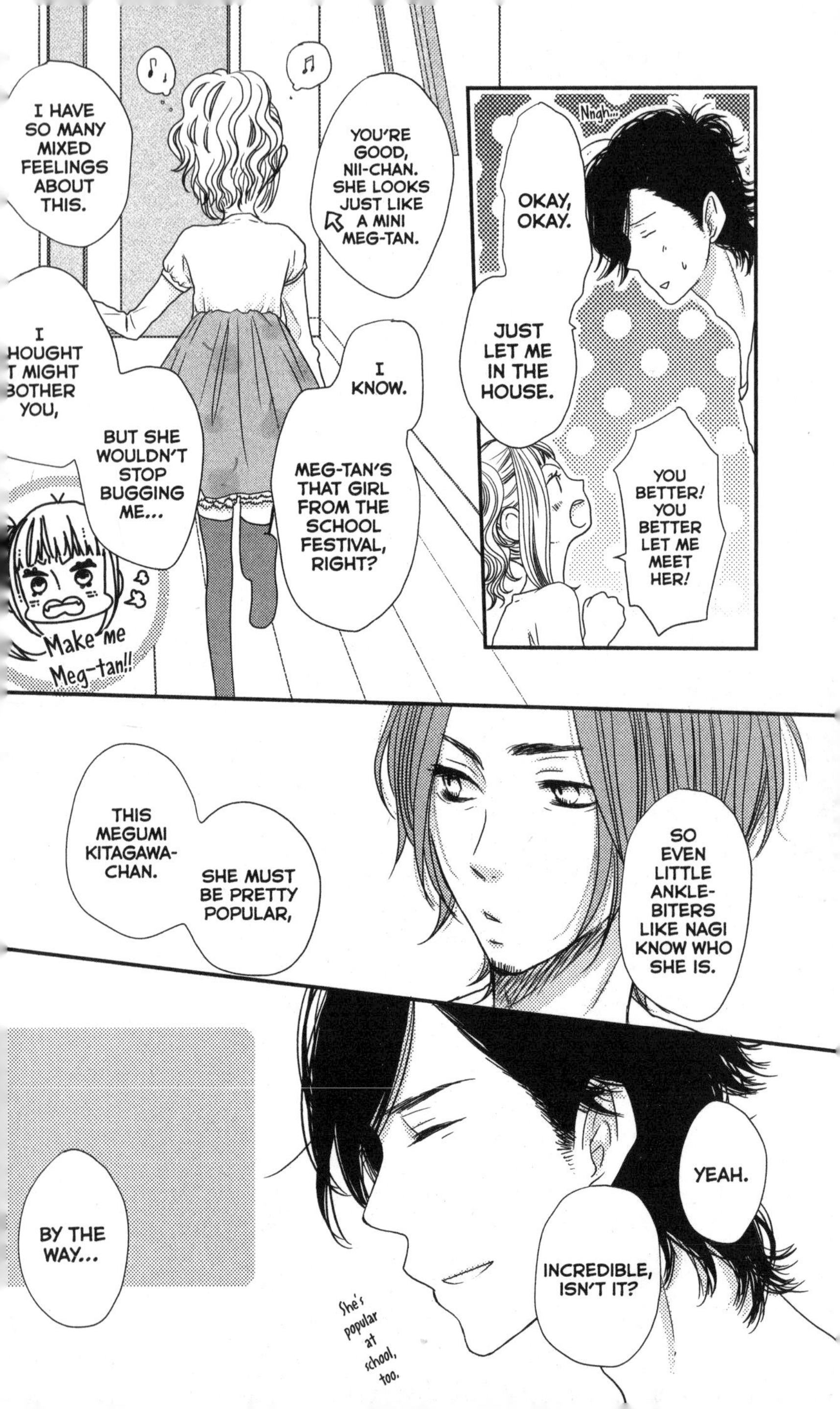
Nngh...
OKAY, OKAY.
JUST LET ME IN THE HOUSE.
YOU BETTER! YOU BETTER LET ME MEET HER!
YOU'RE GOOD, NII-CHAN. SHE LOOKS JUST LIKE A MINI MEG-TAN.
I HAVE SO MANY MIXED FEELINGS ABOUT THIS.
I KNOW.
MEG-TAN'S THAT GIRL FROM THE SCHOOL FESTIVAL, RIGHT?
I HOUGHT T MIGHT BOTHER YOU,
BUT SHE WOULDN'T STOP BUGGING ME...
Make me Meg-tan!!
SO EVEN LITTLE ANKLE-BITERS LIKE NAGI KNOW WHO SHE IS.
THIS MEGUMI KITAGAWA-CHAN.
SHE MUST BE PRETTY POPULAR,
YEAH.
INCREDIBLE, ISN'T IT?
She's popular at school, too.
BY THE WAY...

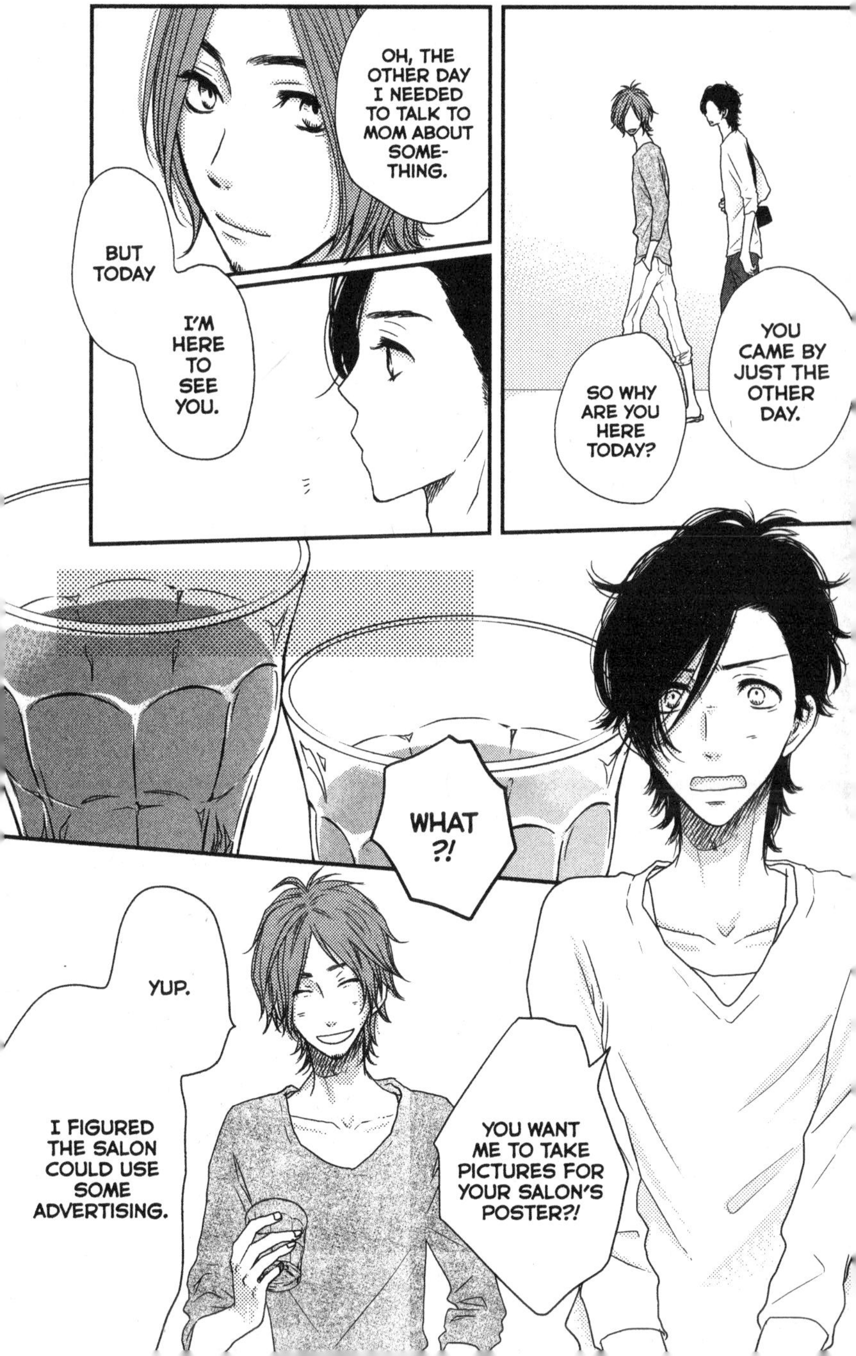
YOU CAME BY JUST THE OTHER DAY.
SO WHY ARE YOU HERE TODAY?
OH, THE OTHER DAY I NEEDED TO TALK TO MOM ABOUT SOME-THING.
BUT TODAY
I'M HERE TO SEE YOU.
WHAT ?!
YOU WANT ME TO TAKE PICTURES FOR YOUR SALON'S POSTER?!
YUP.
I FIGURED THE SALON COULD USE SOME ADVERTISING.

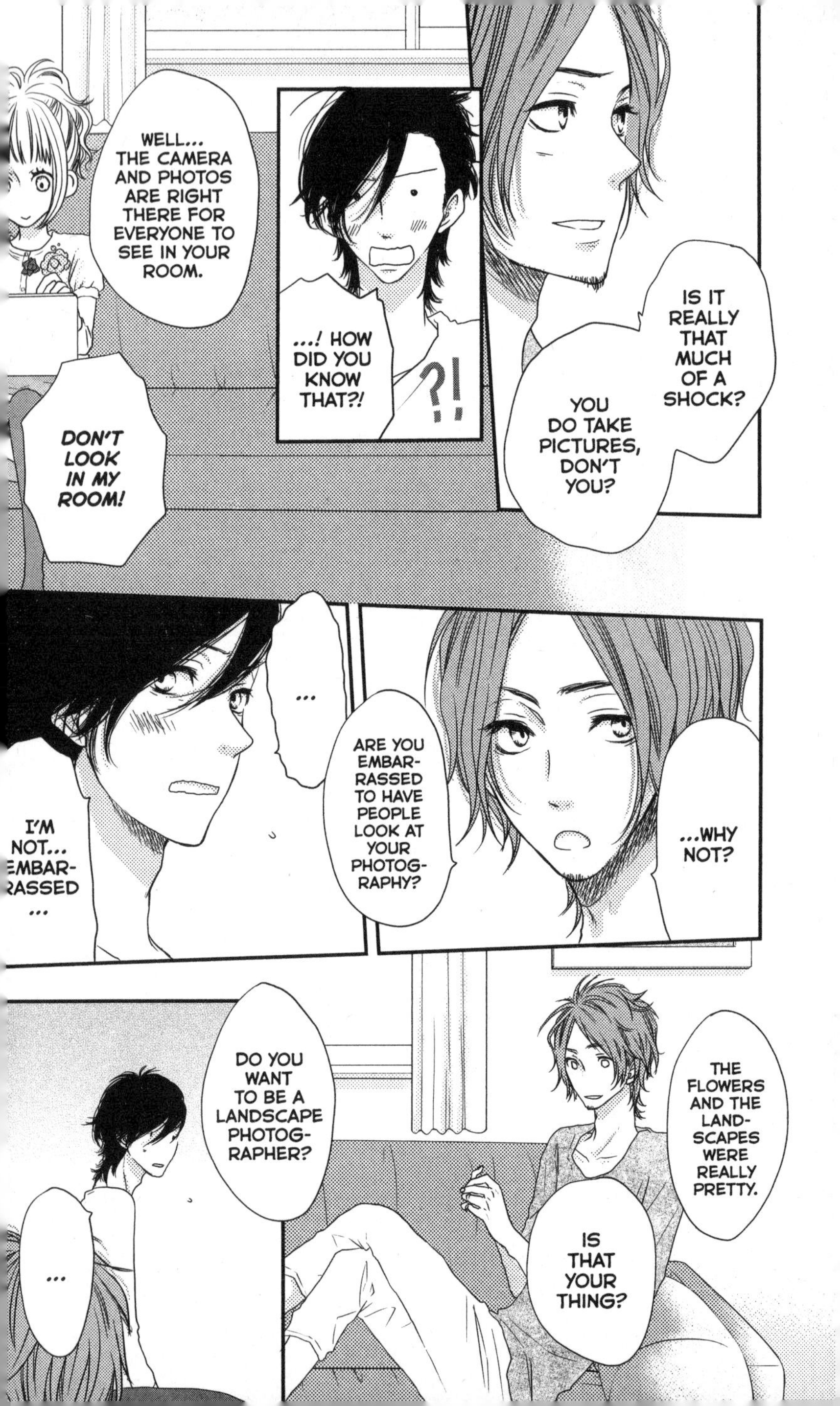
IS IT REALLY THAT MUCH OF A SHOCK?
YOU DO TAKE PICTURES, DON'T YOU?
...! HOW DID YOU KNOW THAT?!
?!
WELL... THE CAMERA AND PHOTOS ARE RIGHT THERE FOR EVERYONE TO SEE IN YOUR ROOM.
DON'T LOOK IN MY ROOM!
...WHY NOT?
ARE YOU EMBARRASSED TO HAVE PEOPLE LOOK AT YOUR PHOTOGRAPHY?
...
I'M NOT... EMBARRASSED...
THE FLOWERS AND THE LANDSCAPES WERE REALLY PRETTY.
IS THAT YOUR THING?
DO YOU WANT TO BE A LANDSCAPE PHOTOGRAPHER?
...

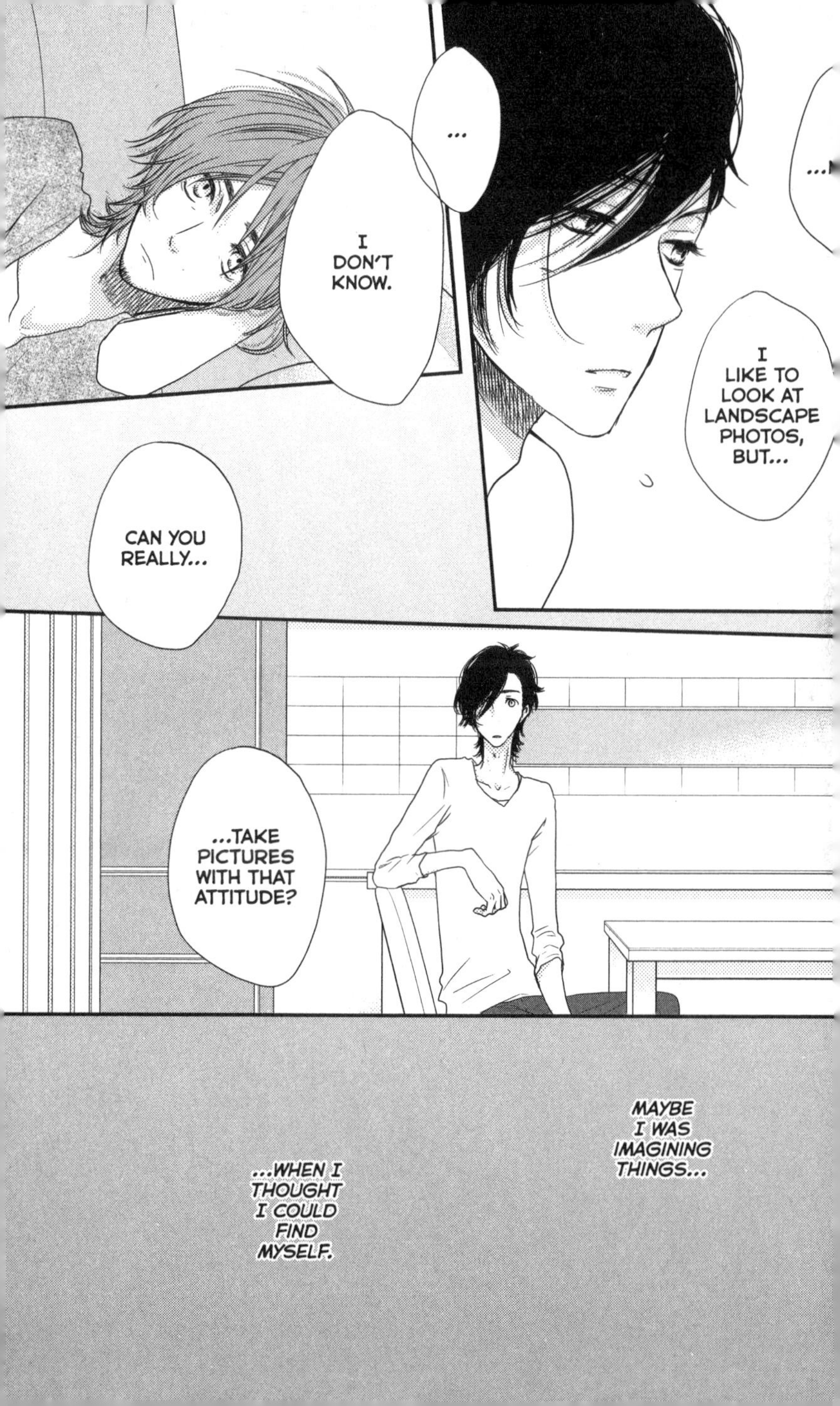
...
I LIKE TO LOOK AT LANDSCAPE PHOTOS, BUT...
I DON'T KNOW.
CAN YOU REALLY...
...TAKE PICTURES WITH THAT ATTITUDE?
MAYBE I WAS IMAGINING THINGS...
...WHEN I THOUGHT I COULD FIND MYSELF.

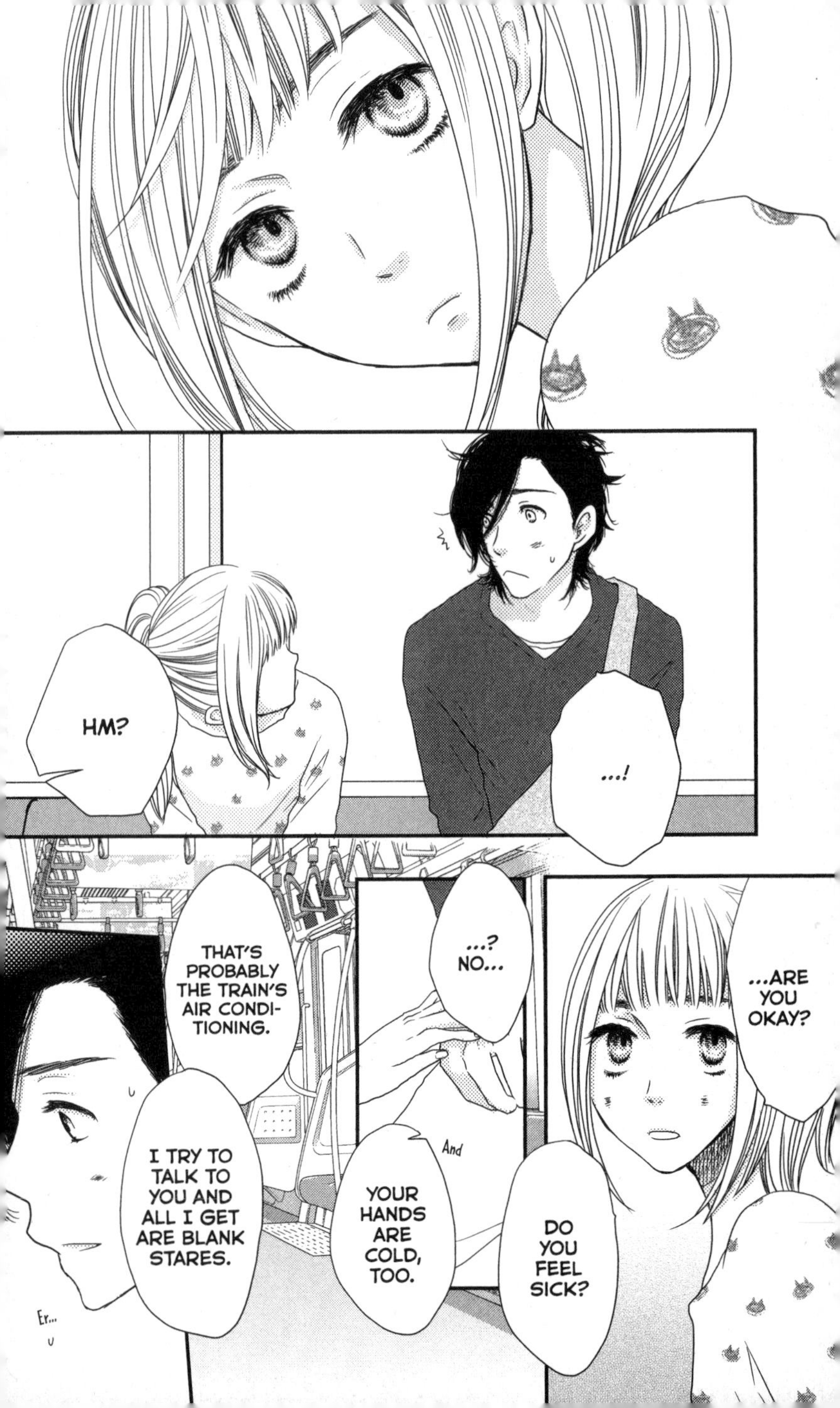
...!
HM?
...ARE YOU OKAY?
DO YOU FEEL SICK?
...? NO...
And
YOUR HANDS ARE COLD, TOO.
THAT'S PROBABLY THE TRAIN'S AIR CONDITIONING.
I TRY TO TALK TO YOU AND ALL I GET ARE BLANK STARES.
Er...

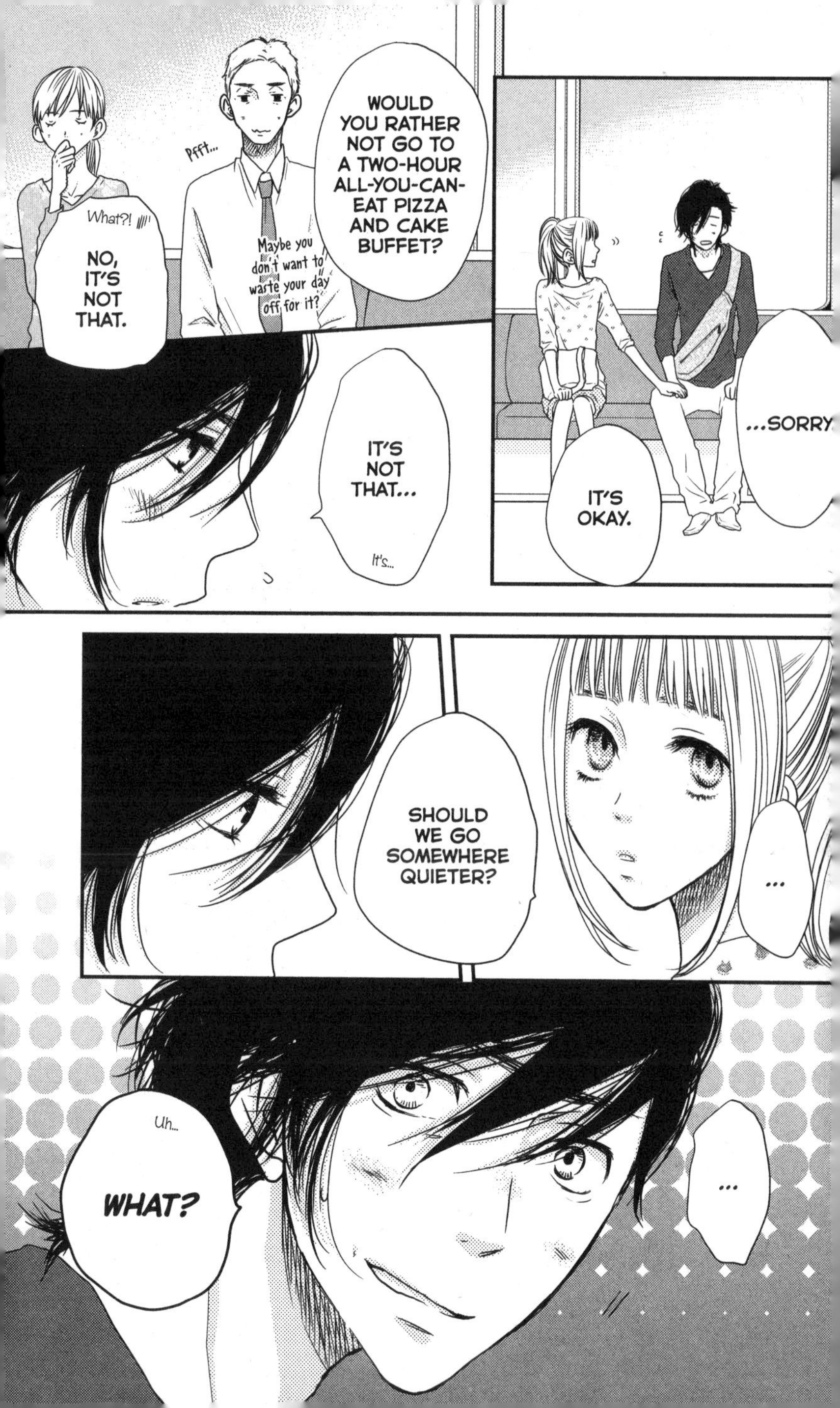
WOULD YOU RATHER NOT GO TO A TWO-HOUR ALL-YOU-CAN-EAT PIZZA AND CAKE BUFFET?
Pfft...
Maybe you don't want to waste your day off for it?
What?!
NO, IT'S NOT THAT.
...SORRY.
IT'S OKAY.
IT'S NOT THAT...
It's...
...
SHOULD WE GO SOMEWHERE QUIETER?
...
Uh...
WHAT?

Cat Café
A Cat Life.

↑2F

We have feeding time at noon!

Come see Kuromame, born last February!

OPEN 11:00～20:00

I'm sorry I pictured something else, Mei.

WE COULD HAVE GONE TO THE PARK, TOO.

SO, I THINK

BUT IT'S ALMOST JULY, SO I THOUGHT IT MIGHT BE TOO HOT.

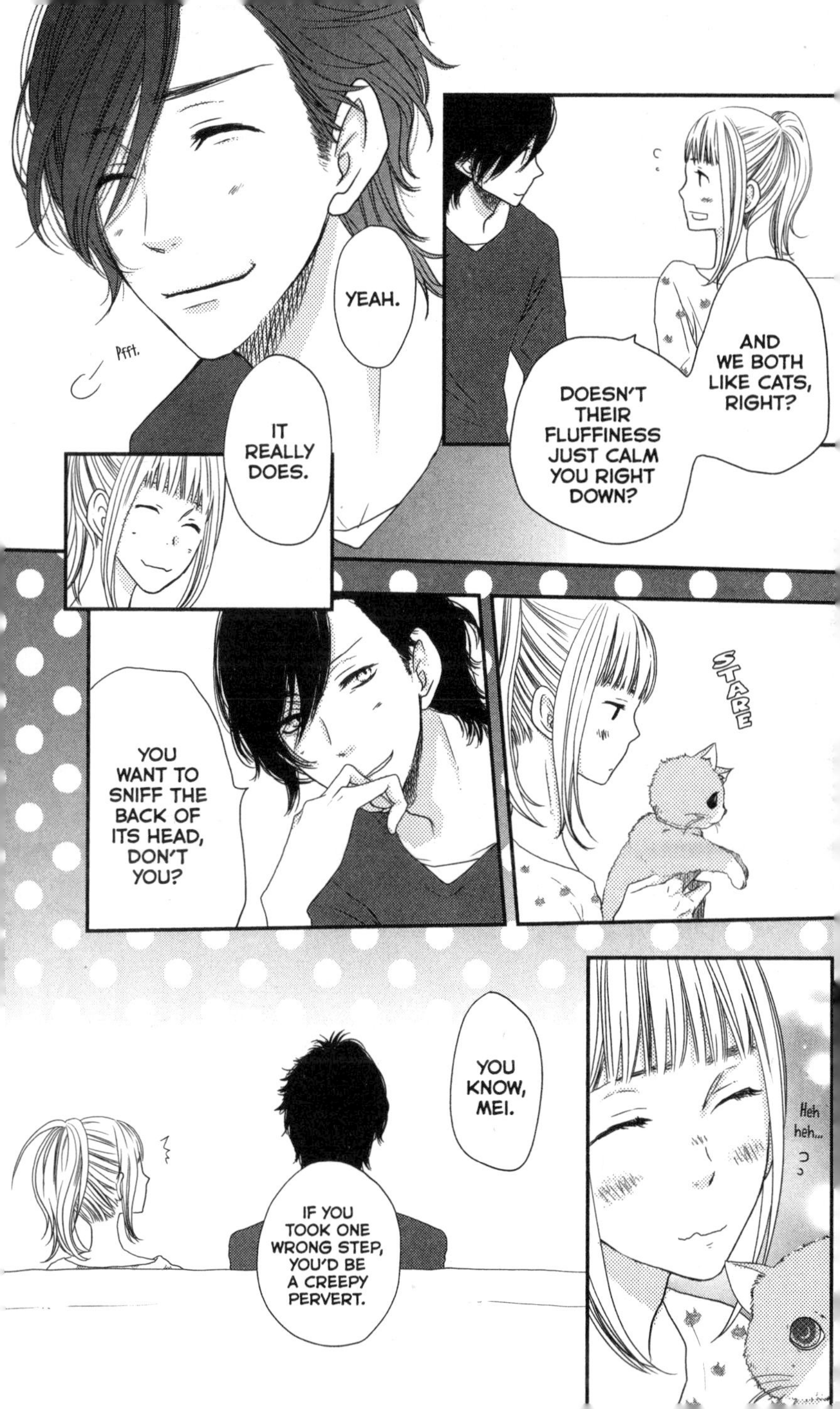
AND WE BOTH LIKE CATS, RIGHT?
DOESN'T THEIR FLUFFINESS JUST CALM YOU RIGHT DOWN?
YEAH.
IT REALLY DOES.
Pfft.
STARE
YOU WANT TO SNIFF THE BACK OF ITS HEAD, DON'T YOU?
Heh heh...
YOU KNOW, MEI.
IF YOU TOOK ONE WRONG STEP, YOU'D BE A CREEPY PERVERT.

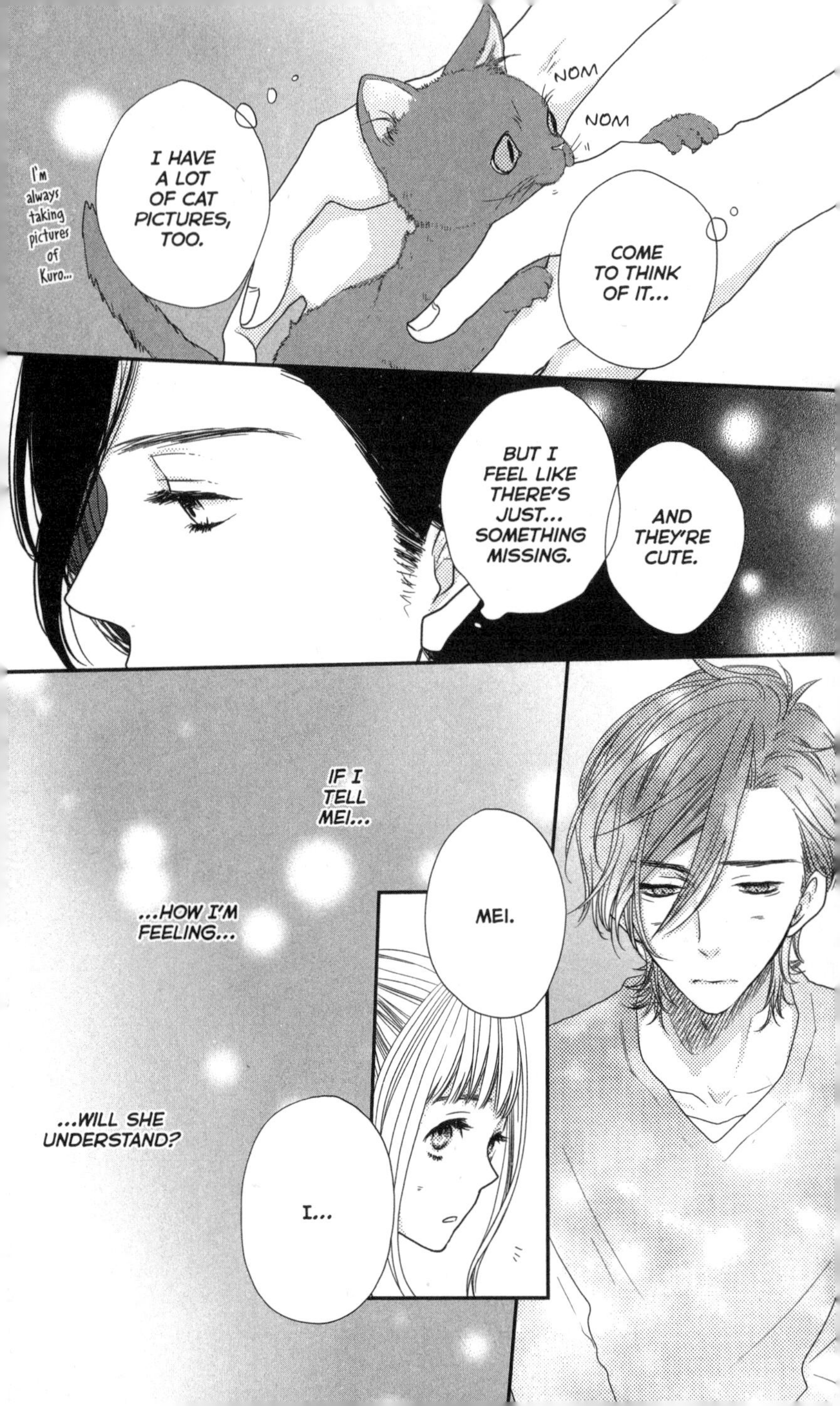
NOM
NOM
COME TO THINK OF IT...
I HAVE A LOT OF CAT PICTURES, TOO.
I'm always taking pictures of Kuro...
AND THEY'RE CUTE.
BUT I FEEL LIKE THERE'S JUST... SOMETHING MISSING.
MEI.
I...
IF I TELL MEI...
...HOW I'M FEELING...
...WILL SHE UNDERSTAND?

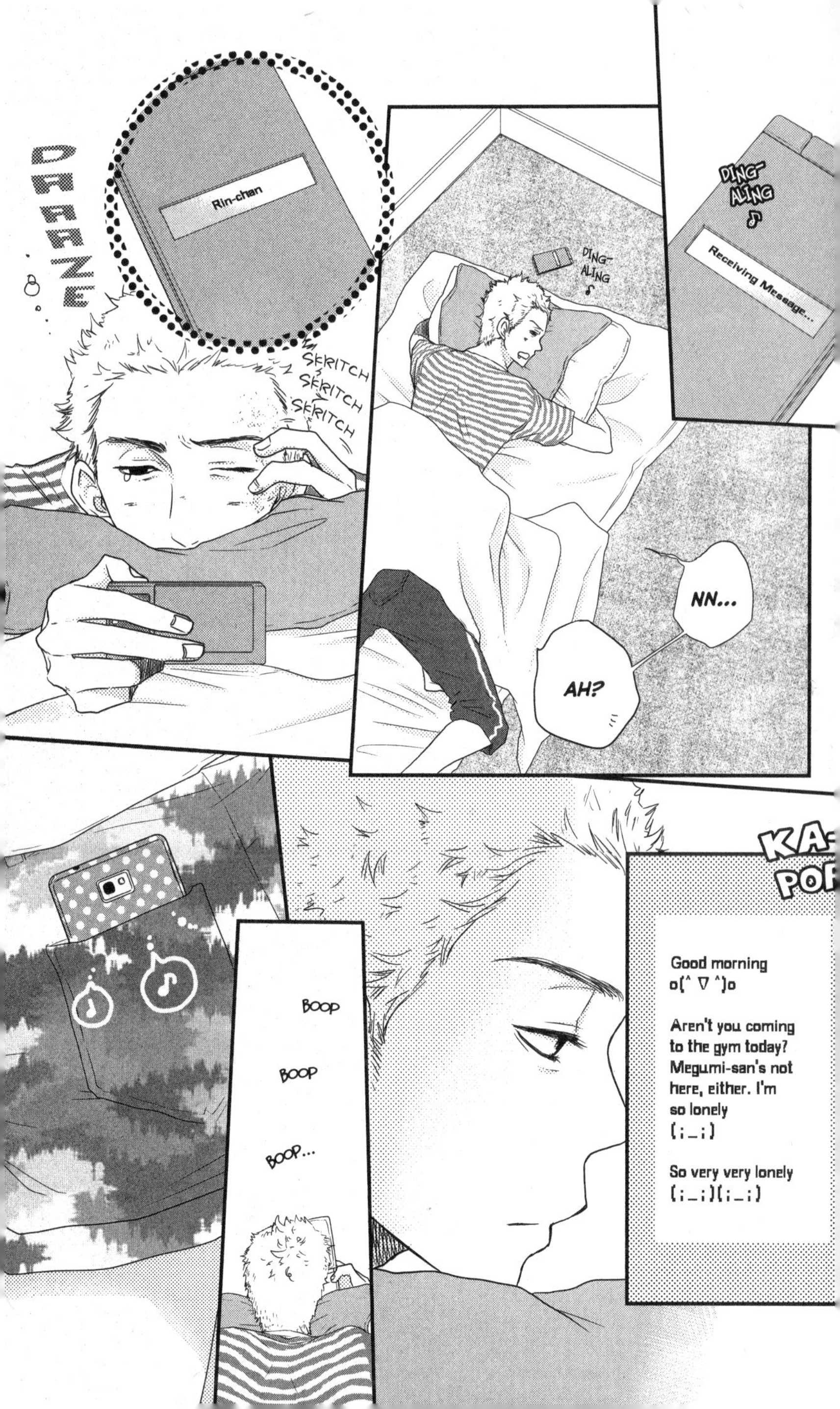
DING-ALING ♪
Receiving Message...
DING-ALING ♪
NN...
AH?
Rin-chan
DRAAZE
SKRITCH SKRITCH SKRITCH
KA-POP
Good morning
o(^ ∇ ^)o
Aren't you coming to the gym today? Megumi-san's not here, either. I'm so lonely
(;_;)
So very very lonely
(;_;)(;_;)
BOOP
BOOP
BOOP...

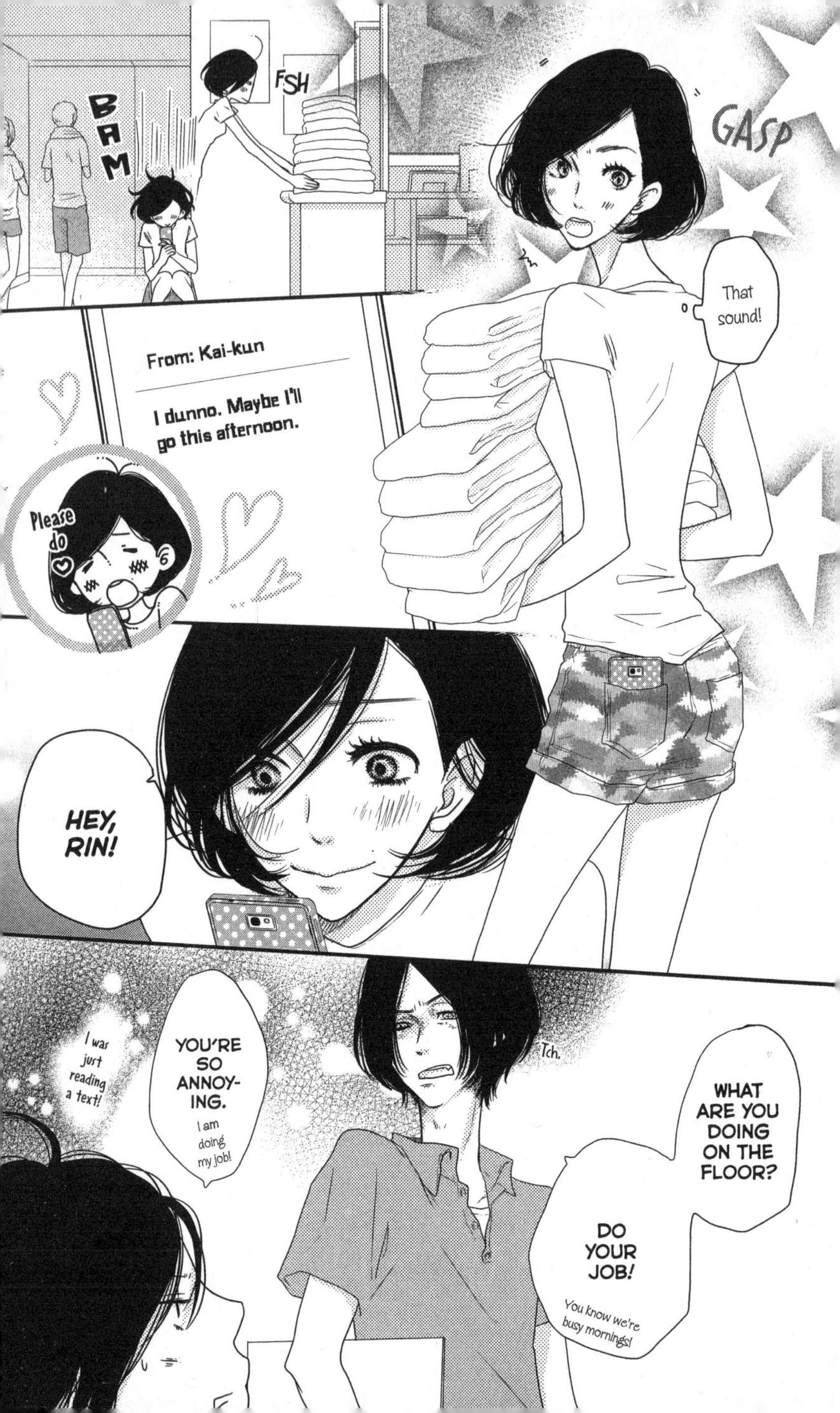
GASP
That sound!
FSH
BAM
From: Kai-kun
I dunno. Maybe I'll go this afternoon.
Please do
HEY, RIN!
WHAT ARE YOU DOING ON THE FLOOR?
DO YOUR JOB!
You know we're busy mornings!
Tch.
YOU'RE SO ANNOY-ING.
I am doing my job!
I was just reading a text!

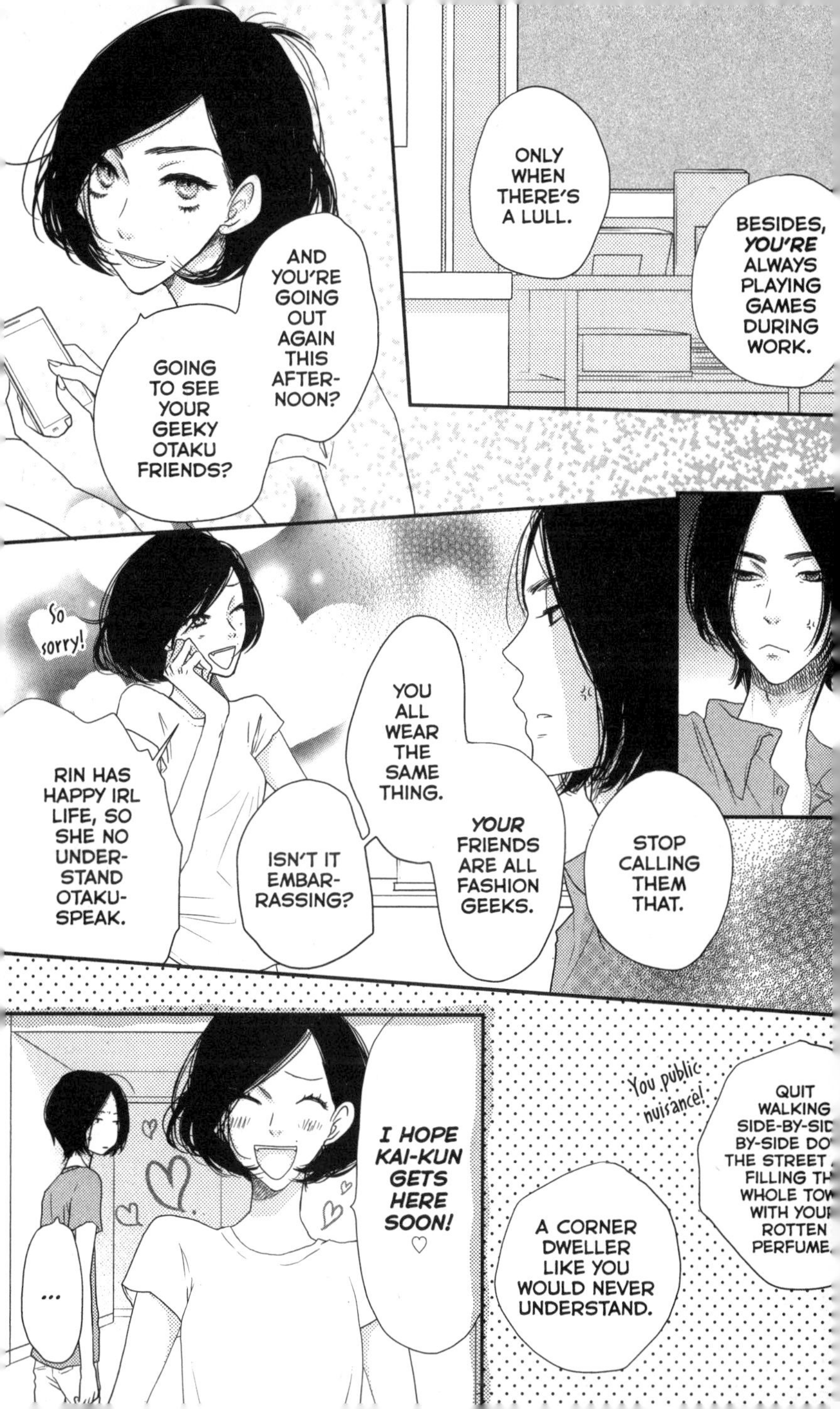
BESIDES, *YOU'RE* ALWAYS PLAYING GAMES DURING WORK.
ONLY WHEN THERE'S A LULL.
AND YOU'RE GOING OUT AGAIN THIS AFTER-NOON?
GOING TO SEE YOUR GEEKY OTAKU FRIENDS?
STOP CALLING THEM THAT.
YOUR FRIENDS ARE ALL FASHION GEEKS.
YOU ALL WEAR THE SAME THING.
ISN'T IT EMBAR-RASSING?
So sorry!
RIN HAS HAPPY IRL LIFE, SO SHE NO UNDER-STAND OTAKU-SPEAK.
QUIT WALKING SIDE-BY-SID BY-SIDE DO THE STREET FILLING TH WHOLE TOW WITH YOU ROTTEN PERFUME.
You public nuisance!
A CORNER DWELLER LIKE YOU WOULD NEVER UNDERSTAND.
I HOPE KAI-KUN GETS HERE SOON! ♡
...

THAT REMINDS ME, RIN. THEY PUT YOU IN CHARGE OF SOME COLUMN FOR YOUR MAGAZINE, RIGHT?

DOES THAT MEAN...

...THERE'S GONNA BE MORE DAYS YOU CAN'T HELP OUT HERE?

Hmmm.

NO?

I DON'T THINK IT'LL CHANGE THAT MUCH.

Today's Releases

LuLu vol. 9

Want to be RIN?

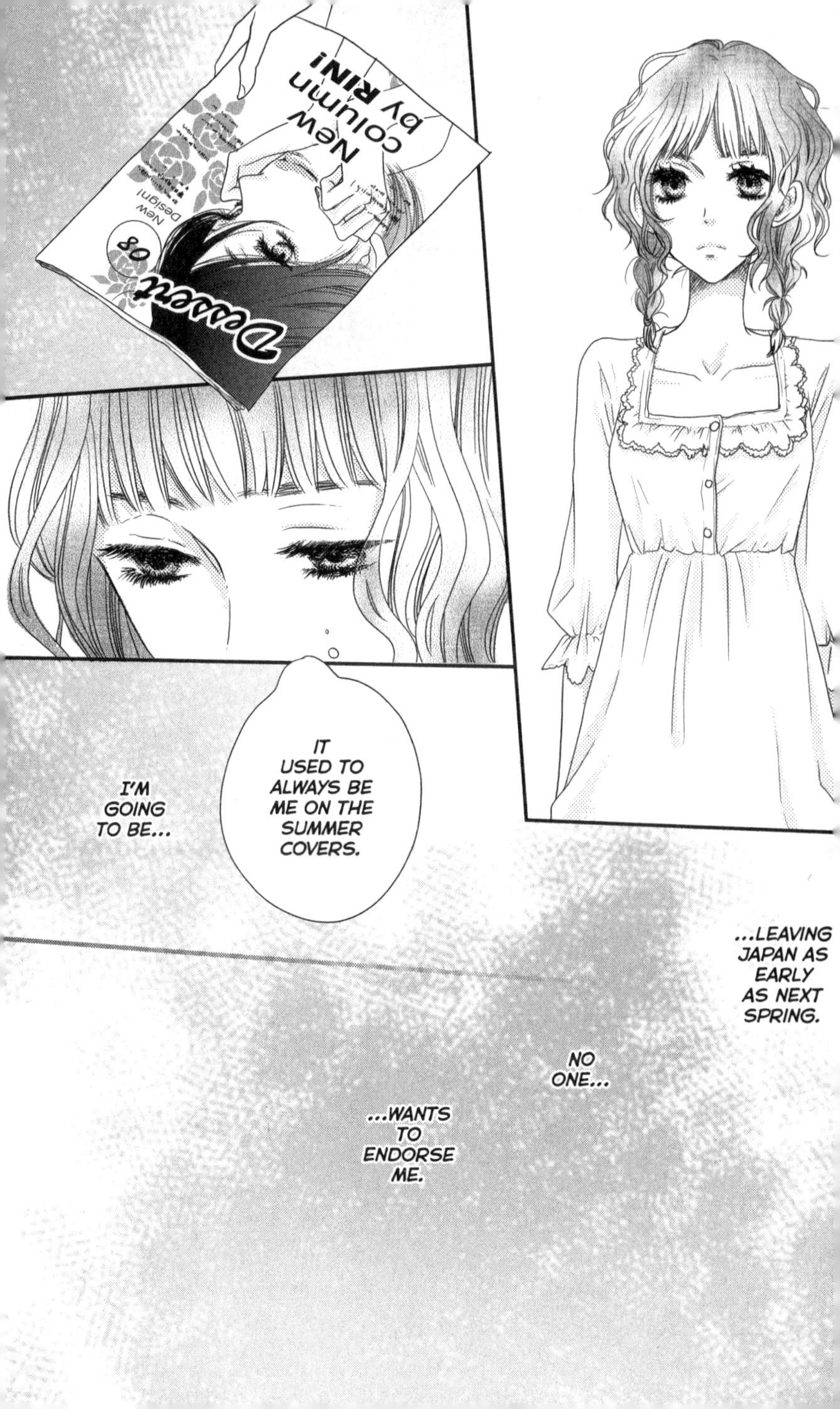
Dessert
08
New Design!
New column by RIN!
IT USED TO ALWAYS BE ME ON THE SUMMER COVERS.
I'M GOING TO BE...
...LEAVING JAPAN AS EARLY AS NEXT SPRING.
NO ONE...
...WANTS TO ENDORSE ME.

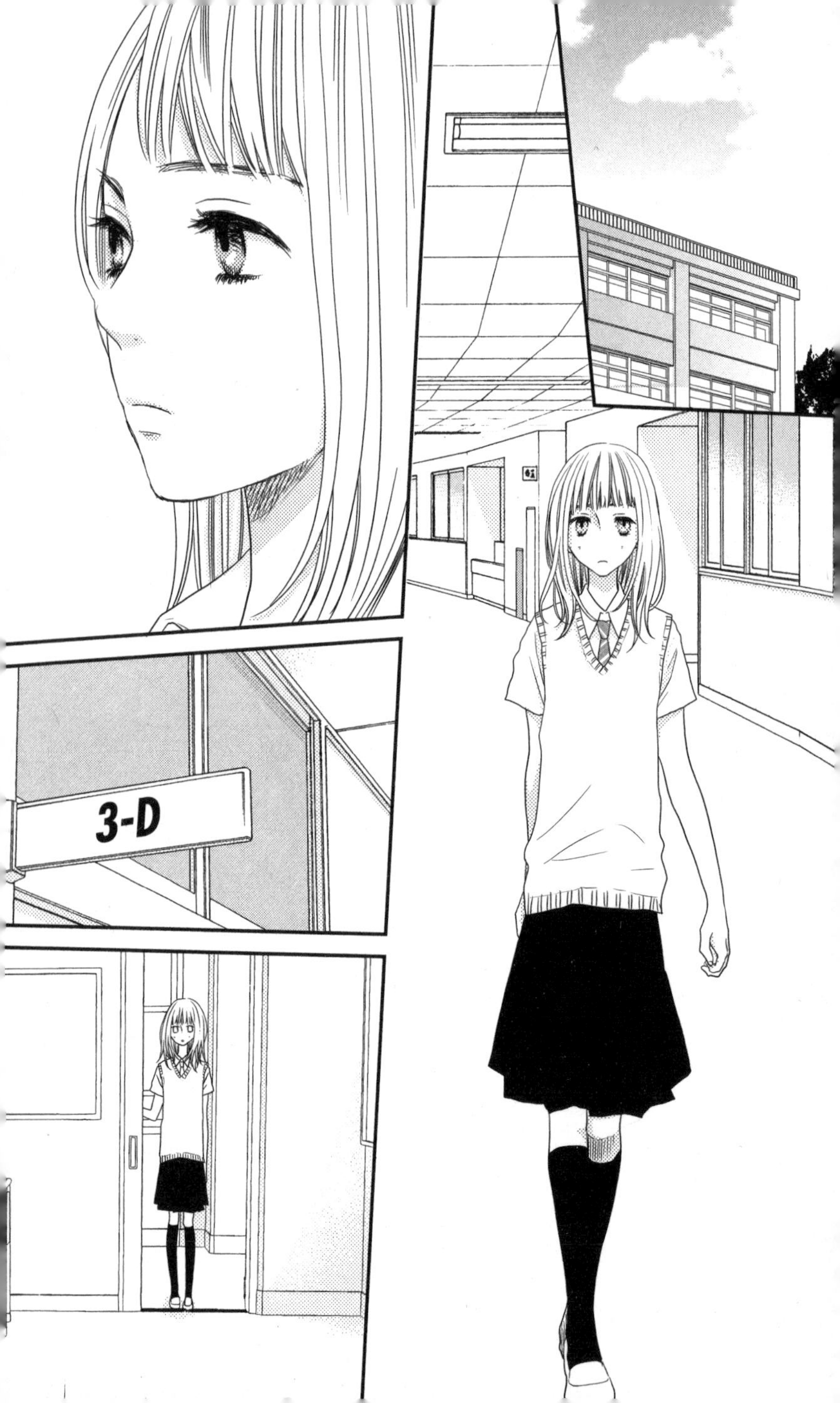
3-D

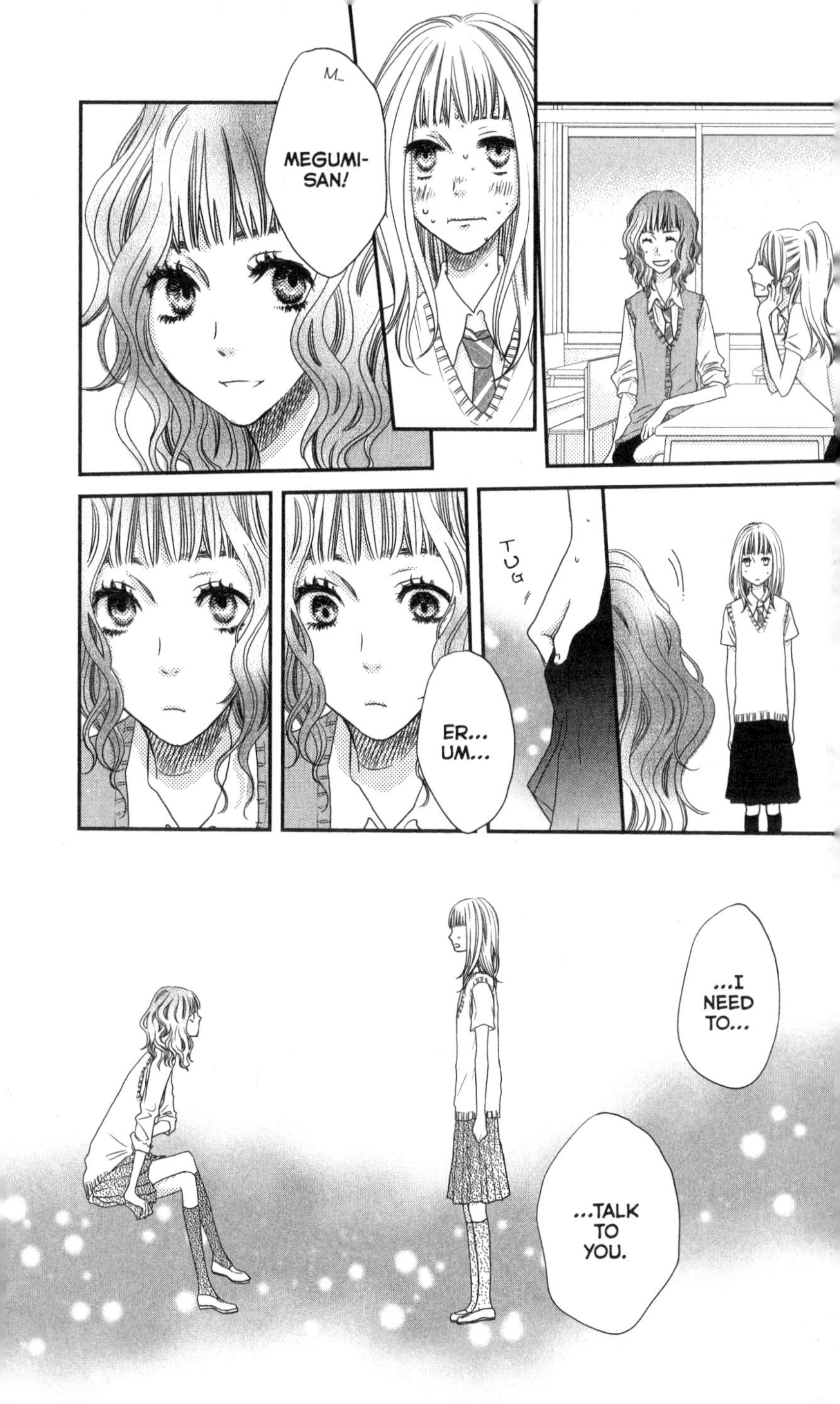
M... MEGUMI-SAN!
TUG
ER... UM...
...I NEED TO...
...TALK TO YOU.

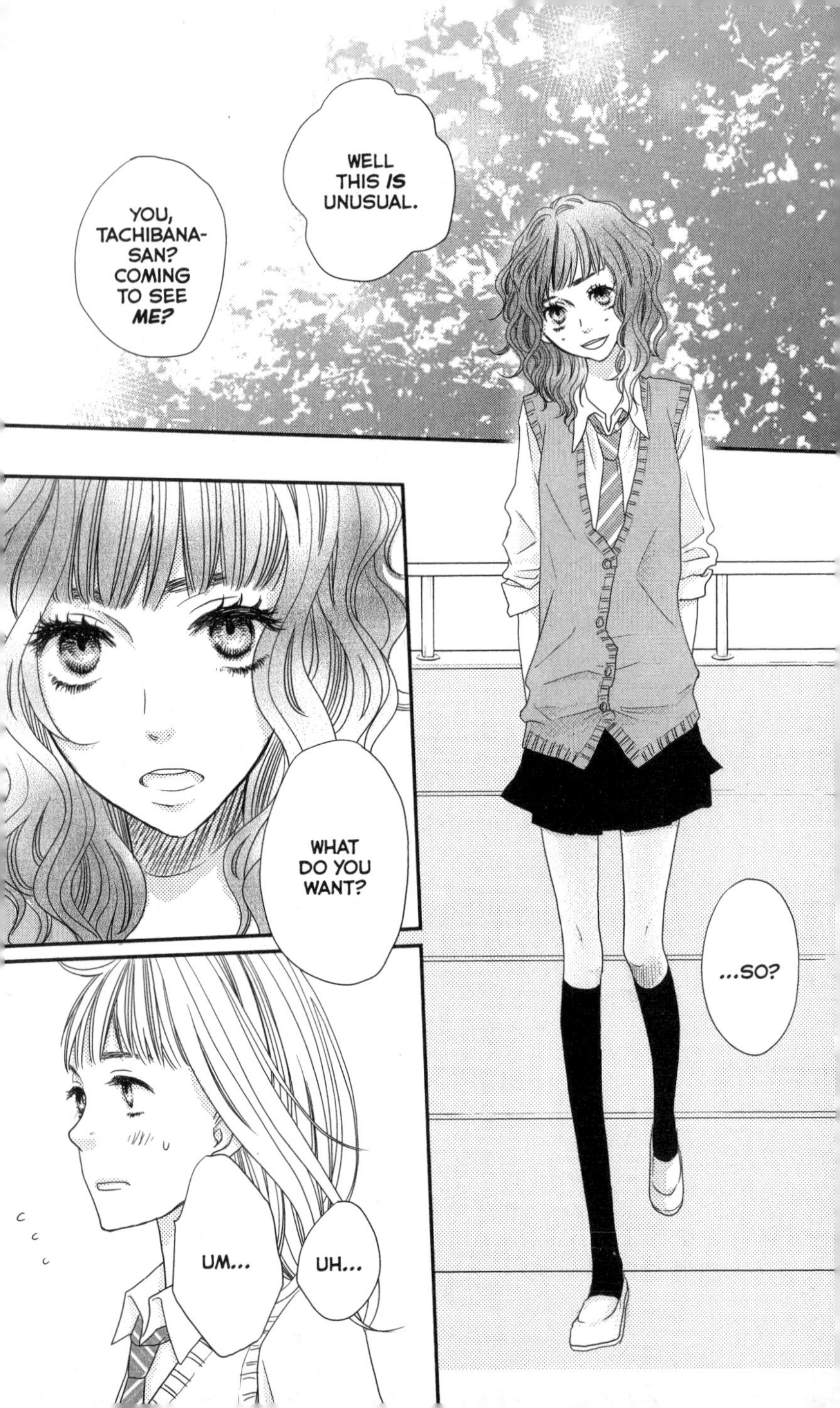
WELL THIS *IS* UNUSUAL.
YOU, TACHIBANA-SAN? COMING TO SEE *ME?*
...SO?
WHAT DO YOU WANT?
UH...
UM...

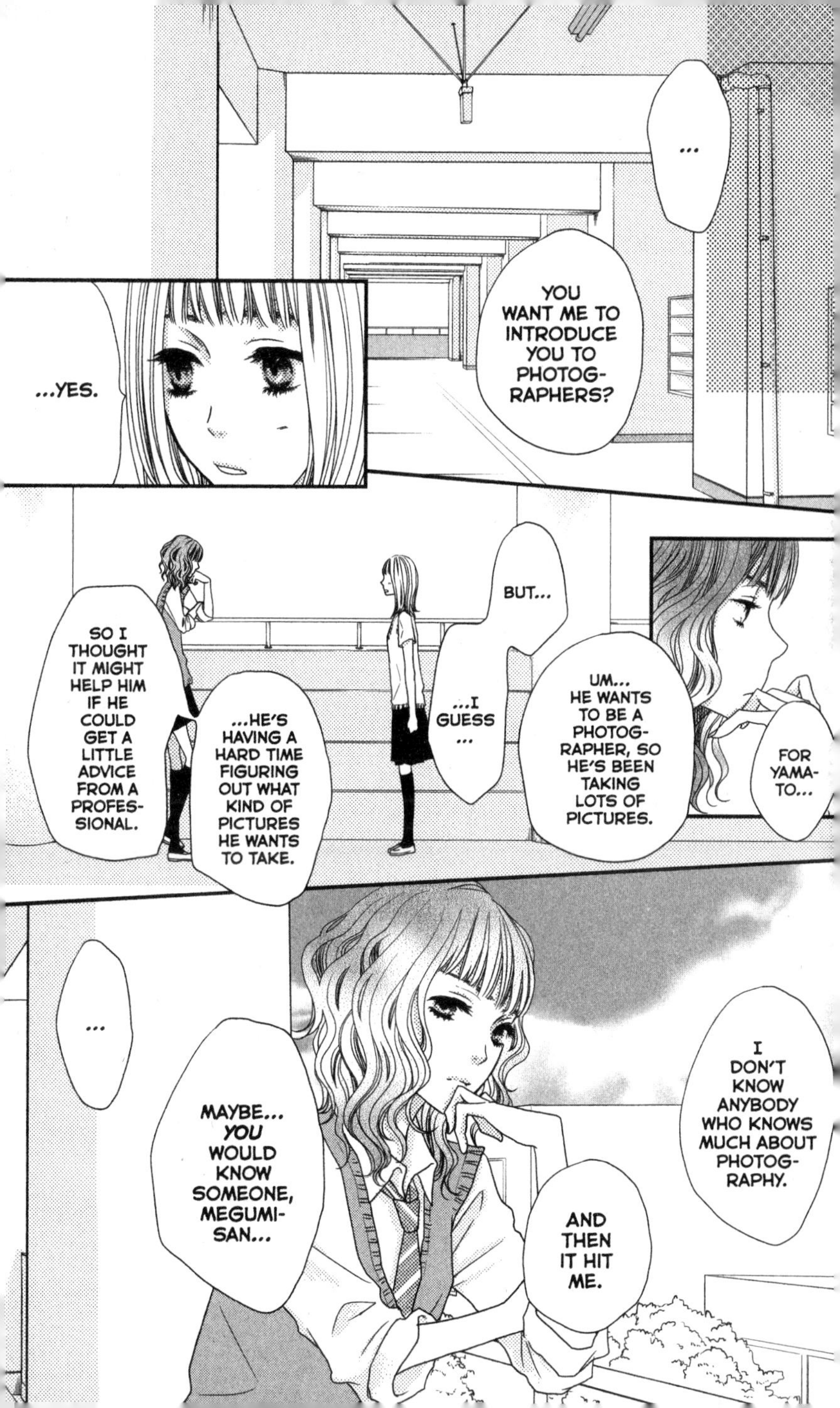
...
YOU WANT ME TO INTRODUCE YOU TO PHOTOGRAPHERS?
...YES.
FOR YAMATO...
UM... HE WANTS TO BE A PHOTOGRAPHER, SO HE'S BEEN TAKING LOTS OF PICTURES.
BUT...
...I GUESS...
...HE'S HAVING A HARD TIME FIGURING OUT WHAT KIND OF PICTURES HE WANTS TO TAKE.
SO I THOUGHT IT MIGHT HELP HIM IF HE COULD GET A LITTLE ADVICE FROM A PROFESSIONAL.
I DON'T KNOW ANYBODY WHO KNOWS MUCH ABOUT PHOTOGRAPHY.
AND THEN IT HIT ME.
MAYBE... *YOU* WOULD KNOW SOMEONE, MEGUMI-SAN...
...

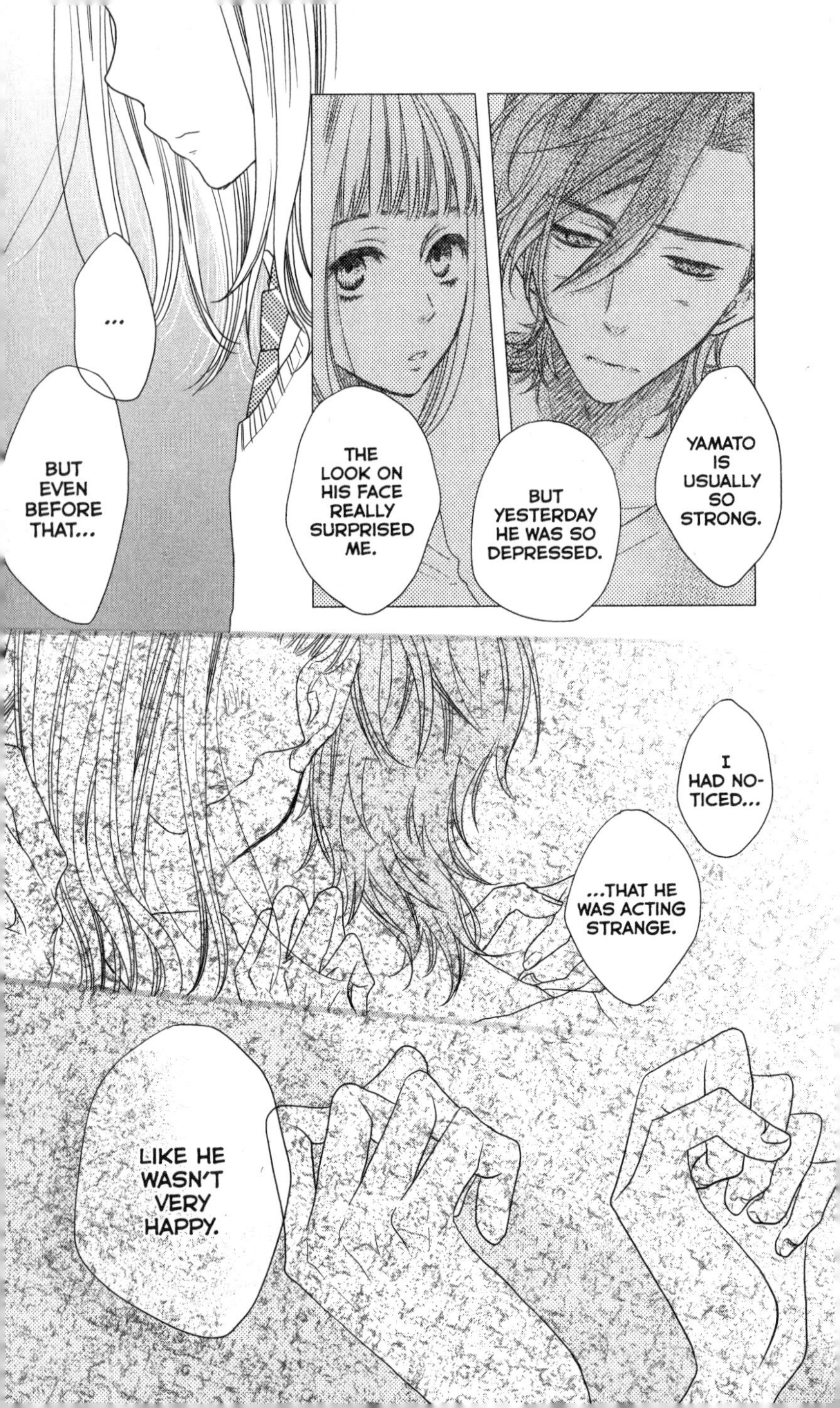
YAMATO IS USUALLY SO STRONG.
BUT YESTERDAY HE WAS SO DEPRESSED.
THE LOOK ON HIS FACE REALLY SURPRISED ME.
...
BUT EVEN BEFORE THAT...
I HAD NO-TICED...
...THAT HE WAS ACTING STRANGE.
LIKE HE WASN'T VERY HAPPY.

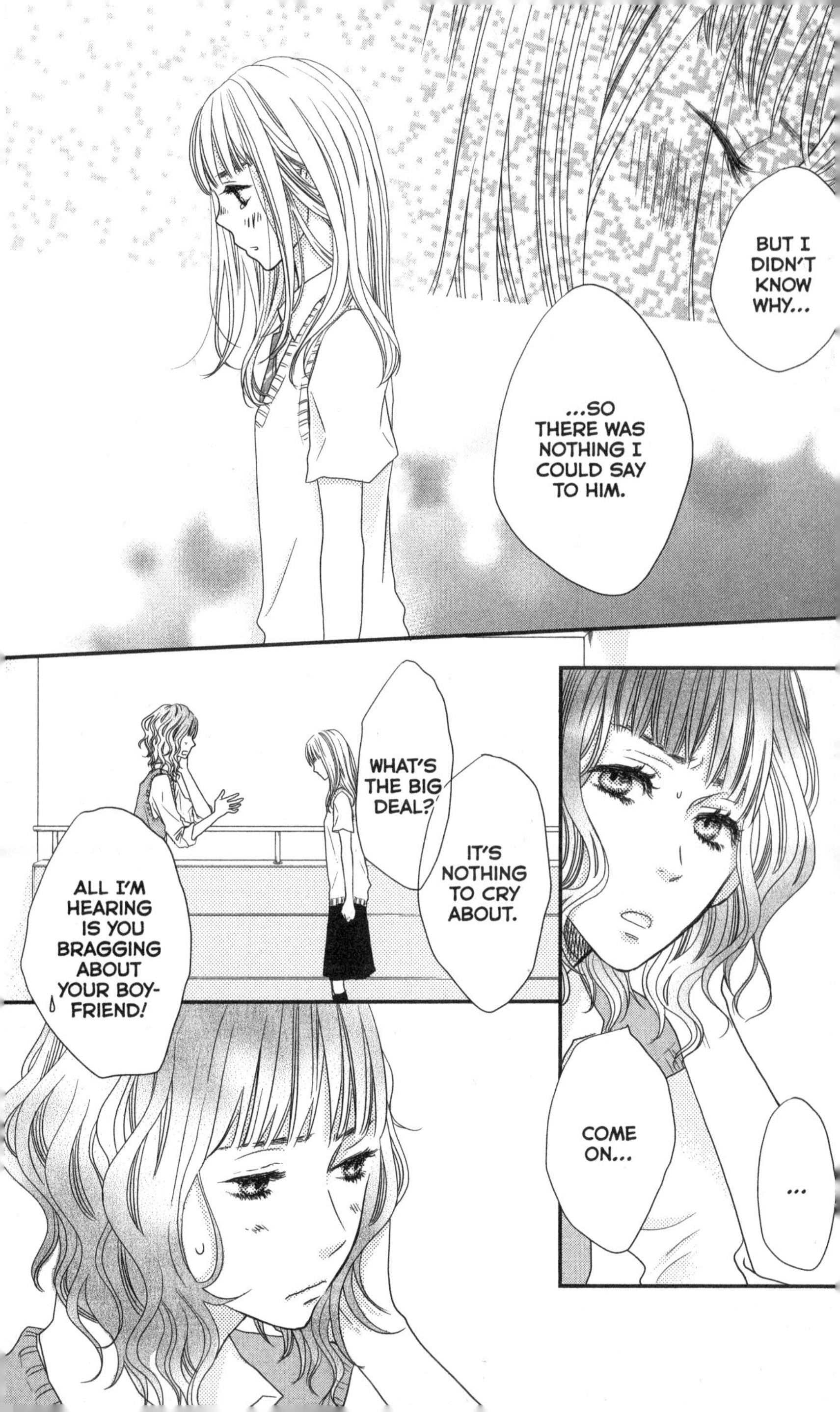
BUT I DIDN'T KNOW WHY...
...SO THERE WAS NOTHING I COULD SAY TO HIM.
COME ON...
...
WHAT'S THE BIG DEAL?
IT'S NOTHING TO CRY ABOUT.
ALL I'M HEARING IS YOU BRAGGING ABOUT YOUR BOY-FRIEND!

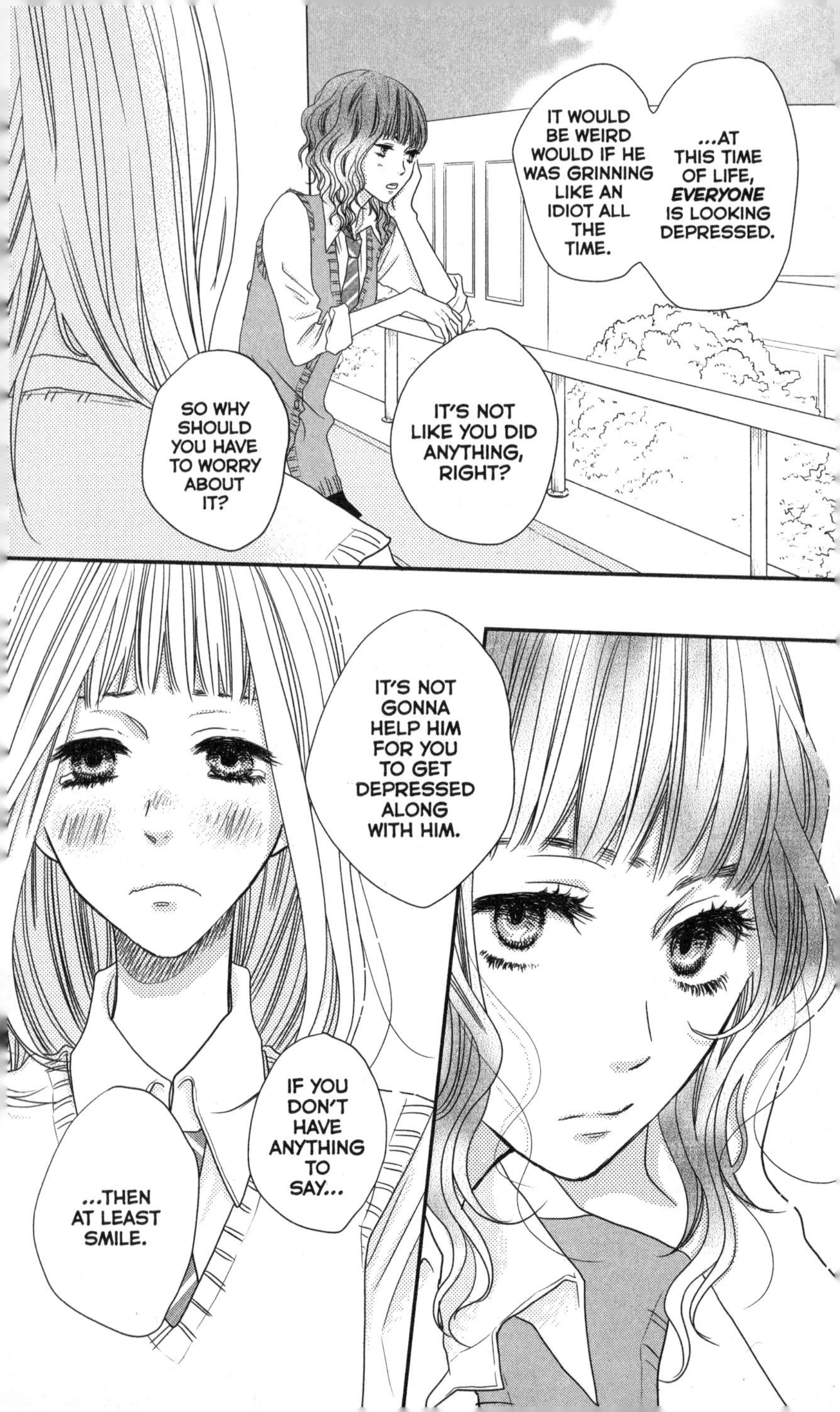
...AT THIS TIME OF LIFE, *EVERYONE* IS LOOKING DEPRESSED.
IT WOULD BE WEIRD WOULD IF HE WAS GRINNING LIKE AN IDIOT ALL THE TIME.
IT'S NOT LIKE YOU DID ANYTHING, RIGHT?
SO WHY SHOULD YOU HAVE TO WORRY ABOUT IT?
IT'S NOT GONNA HELP HIM FOR YOU TO GET DEPRESSED ALONG WITH HIM.
IF YOU DON'T HAVE ANYTHING TO SAY...
...THEN AT LEAST SMILE.

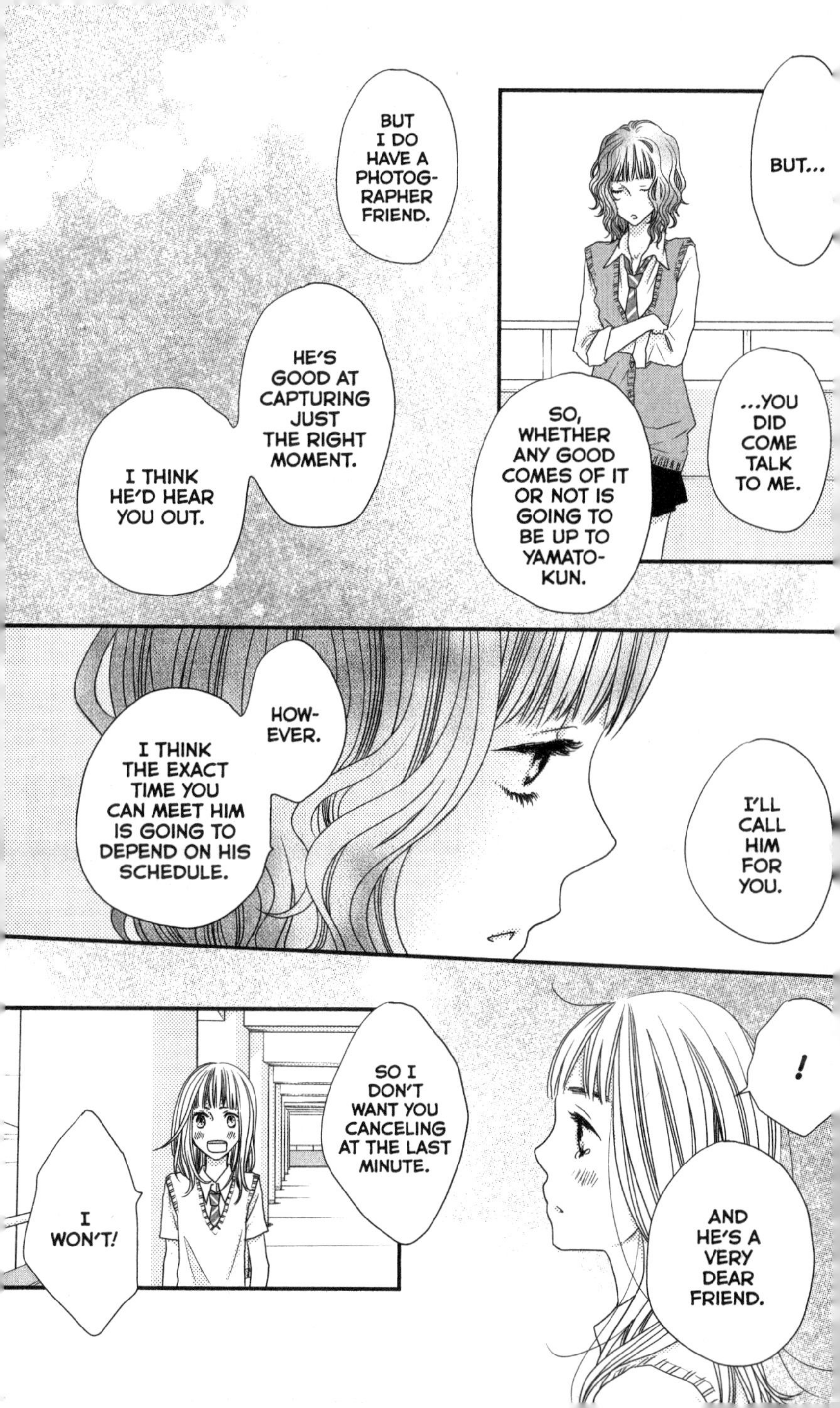

BUT...
...YOU DID COME TALK TO ME.
SO, WHETHER ANY GOOD COMES OF IT OR NOT IS GOING TO BE UP TO YAMATO-KUN.
BUT I DO HAVE A PHOTOG-RAPHER FRIEND.
HE'S GOOD AT CAPTURING JUST THE RIGHT MOMENT.
I THINK HE'D HEAR YOU OUT.
I'LL CALL HIM FOR YOU.
HOW-EVER.
I THINK THE EXACT TIME YOU CAN MEET HIM IS GOING TO DEPEND ON HIS SCHEDULE.
!
AND HE'S A VERY DEAR FRIEND.
SO I DON'T WANT YOU CANCELING AT THE LAST MINUTE.
I WON'T!

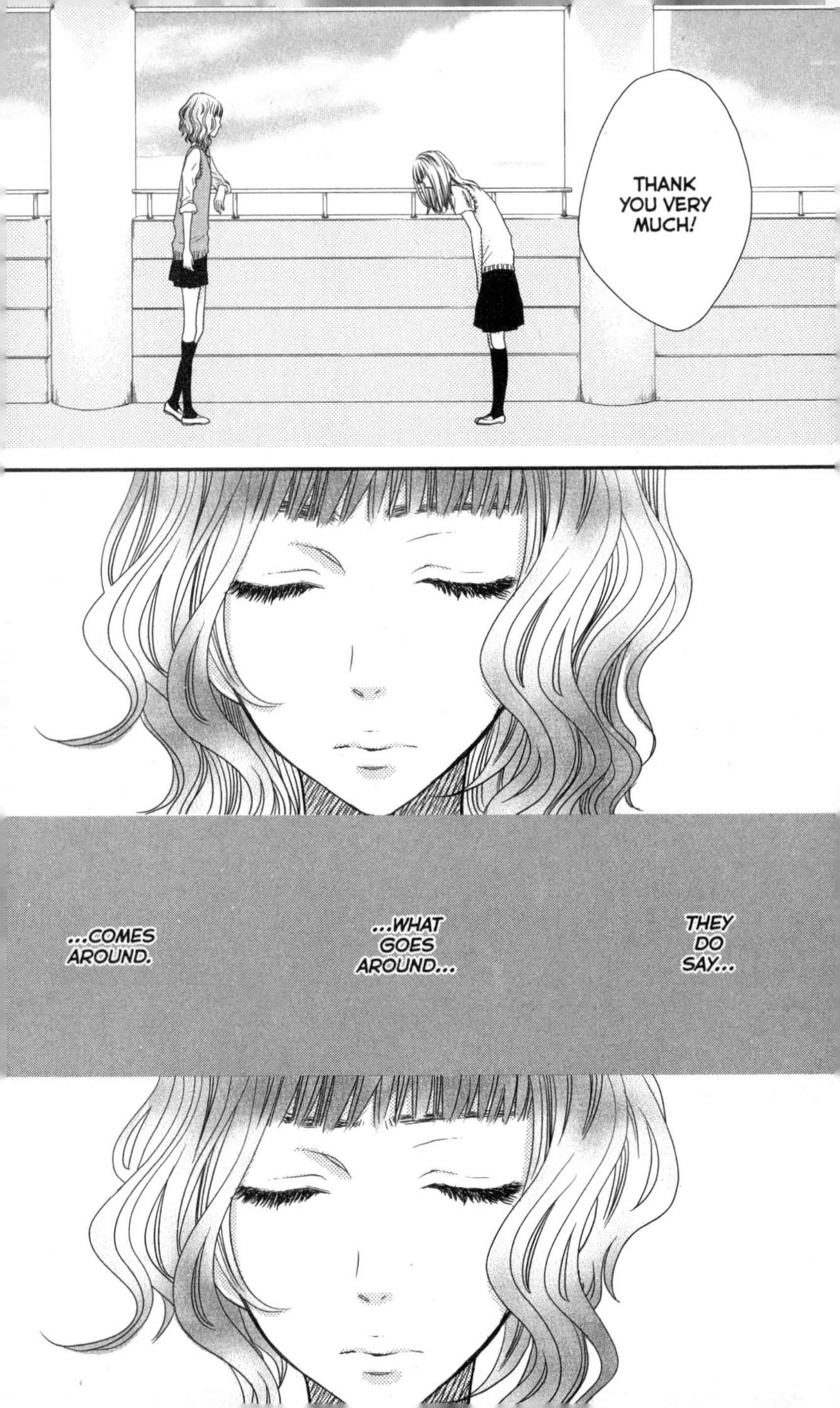
THANK YOU VERY MUCH!
THEY DO SAY...
...WHAT GOES AROUND...
...COMES AROUND.

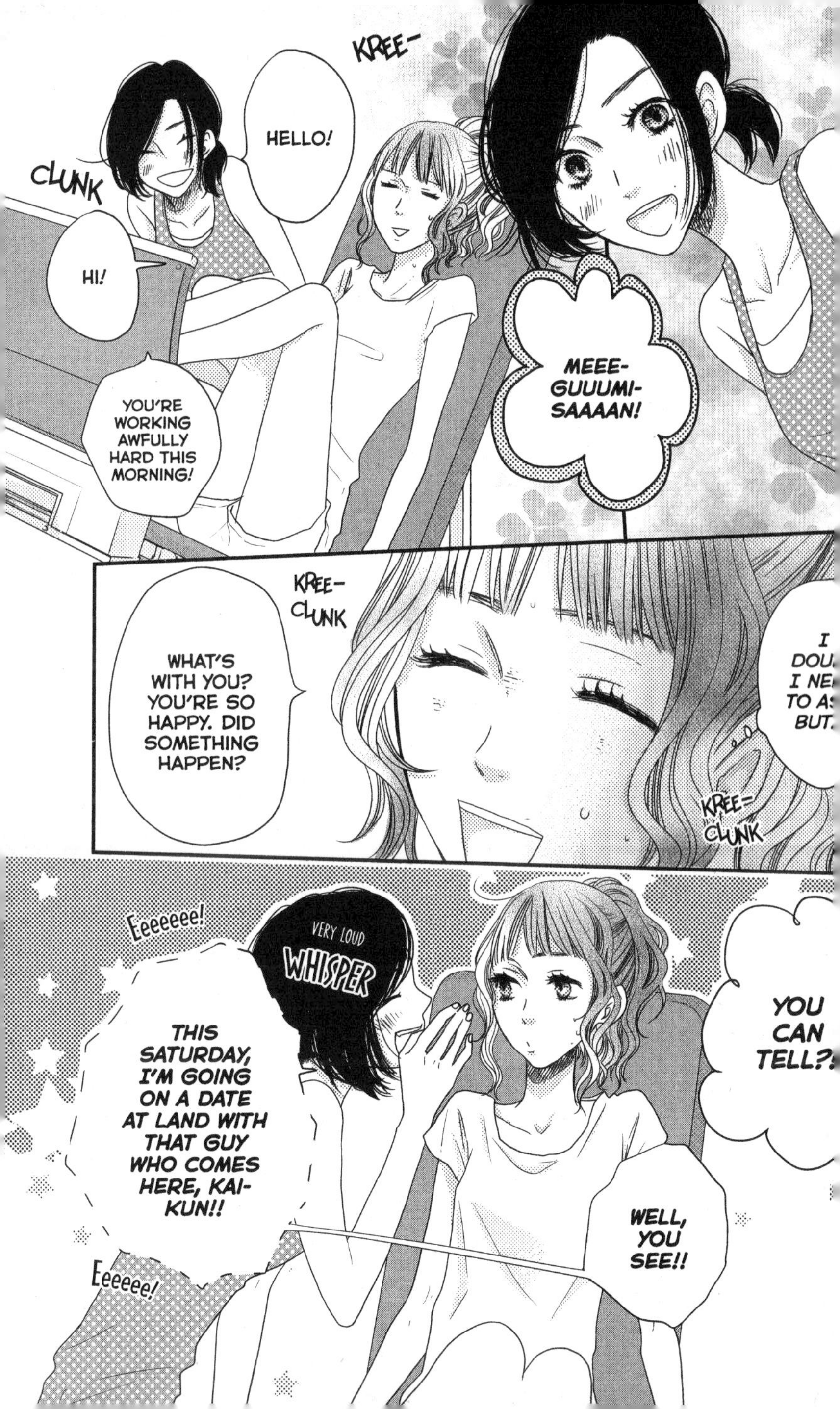
MEEE-GUUUMI-SAAAAN!
KREE-
HELLO!
CLUNK
HI!
YOU'RE WORKING AWFULLY HARD THIS MORNING!
I DOU I NE TO AS BUT
KREE-CLUNK
KREE-CLUNK
WHAT'S WITH YOU? YOU'RE SO HAPPY. DID SOMETHING HAPPEN?
YOU CAN TELL?!
WELL, YOU SEE!!
VERY LOUD WHISPER
THIS SATURDAY, I'M GOING ON A DATE AT LAND WITH THAT GUY WHO COMES HERE, KAI-KUN!!
Eeeeeee!
Eeeeee!

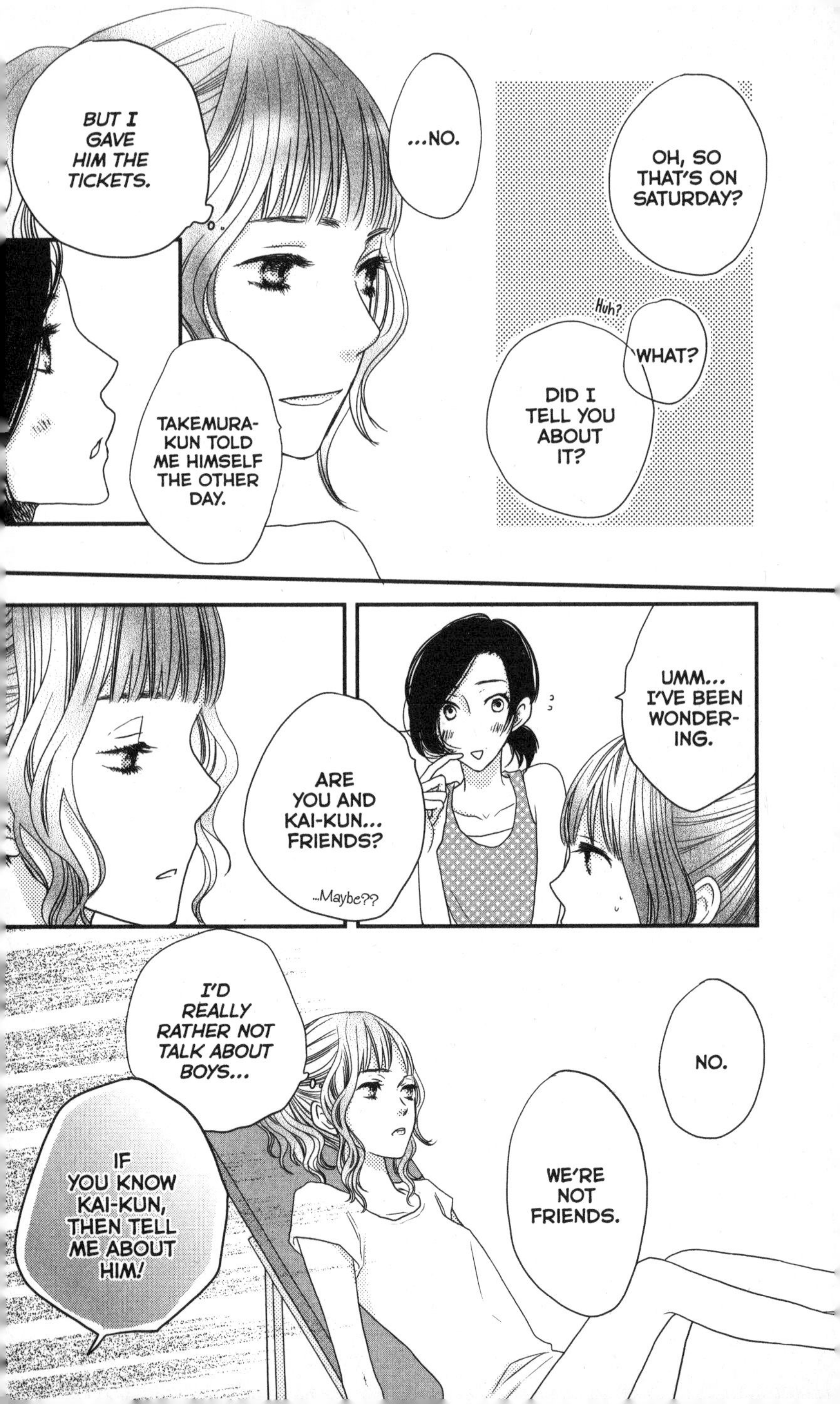
OH, SO THAT'S ON SATURDAY?
Huh?
WHAT?
DID I TELL YOU ABOUT IT?
...NO.
BUT I GAVE HIM THE TICKETS.
TAKEMURA-KUN TOLD ME HIMSELF THE OTHER DAY.
UMM... I'VE BEEN WONDERING.
ARE YOU AND KAI-KUN... FRIENDS?
...Maybe??
NO.
WE'RE NOT FRIENDS.
I'D REALLY RATHER NOT TALK ABOUT BOYS...
IF YOU KNOW KAI-KUN, THEN TELL ME ABOUT HIM!

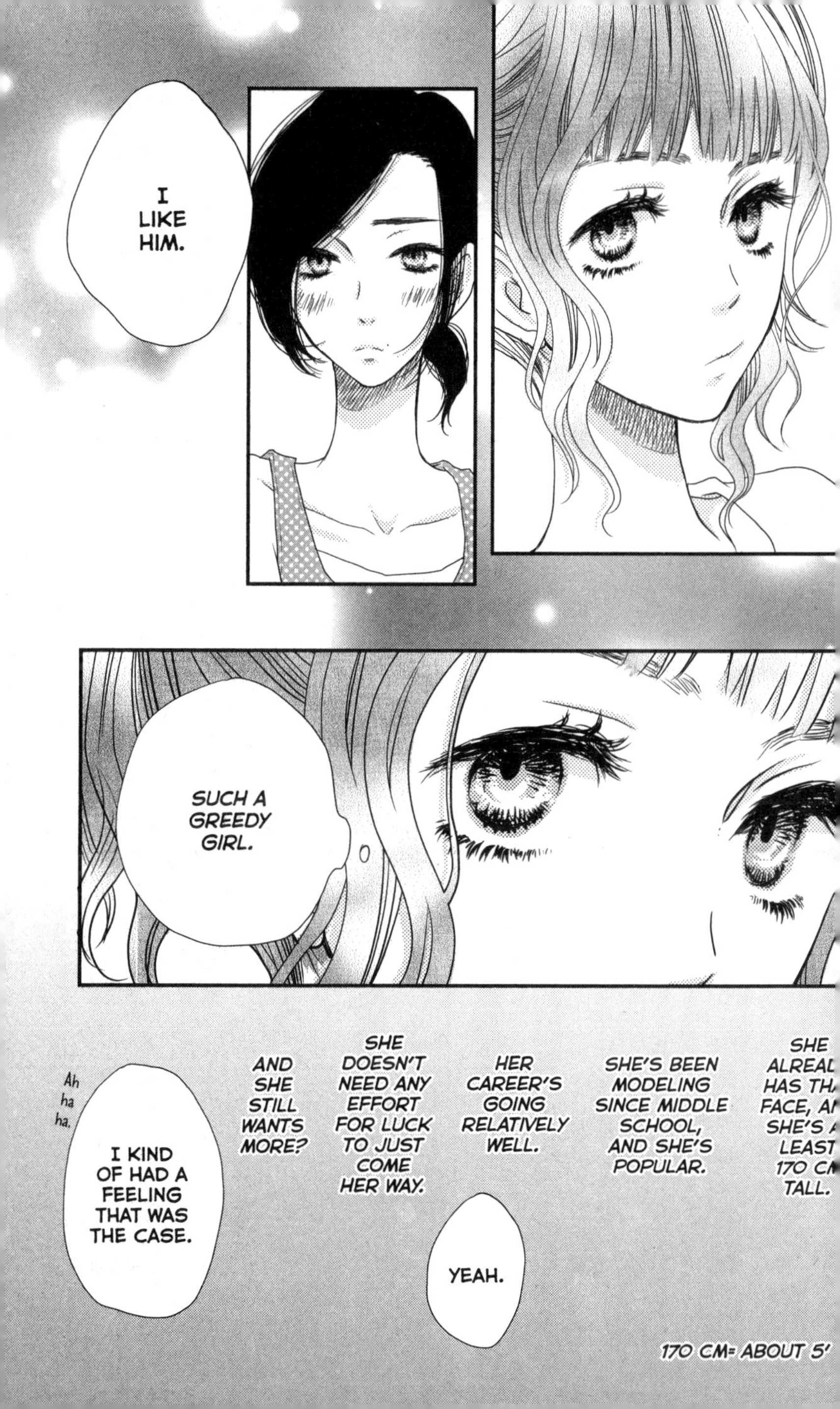
I LIKE HIM.
SUCH A GREEDY GIRL.
SHE ALREAD HAS TH FACE, A SHE'S A LEAST 170 C TALL.
SHE'S BEEN MODELING SINCE MIDDLE SCHOOL, AND SHE'S POPULAR.
HER CAREER'S GOING RELATIVELY WELL.
SHE DOESN'T NEED ANY EFFORT FOR LUCK TO JUST COME HER WAY.
AND SHE STILL WANTS MORE?
Ah ha ha.
I KIND OF HAD A FEELING THAT WAS THE CASE.
YEAH.

170 CM= ABOUT 5'

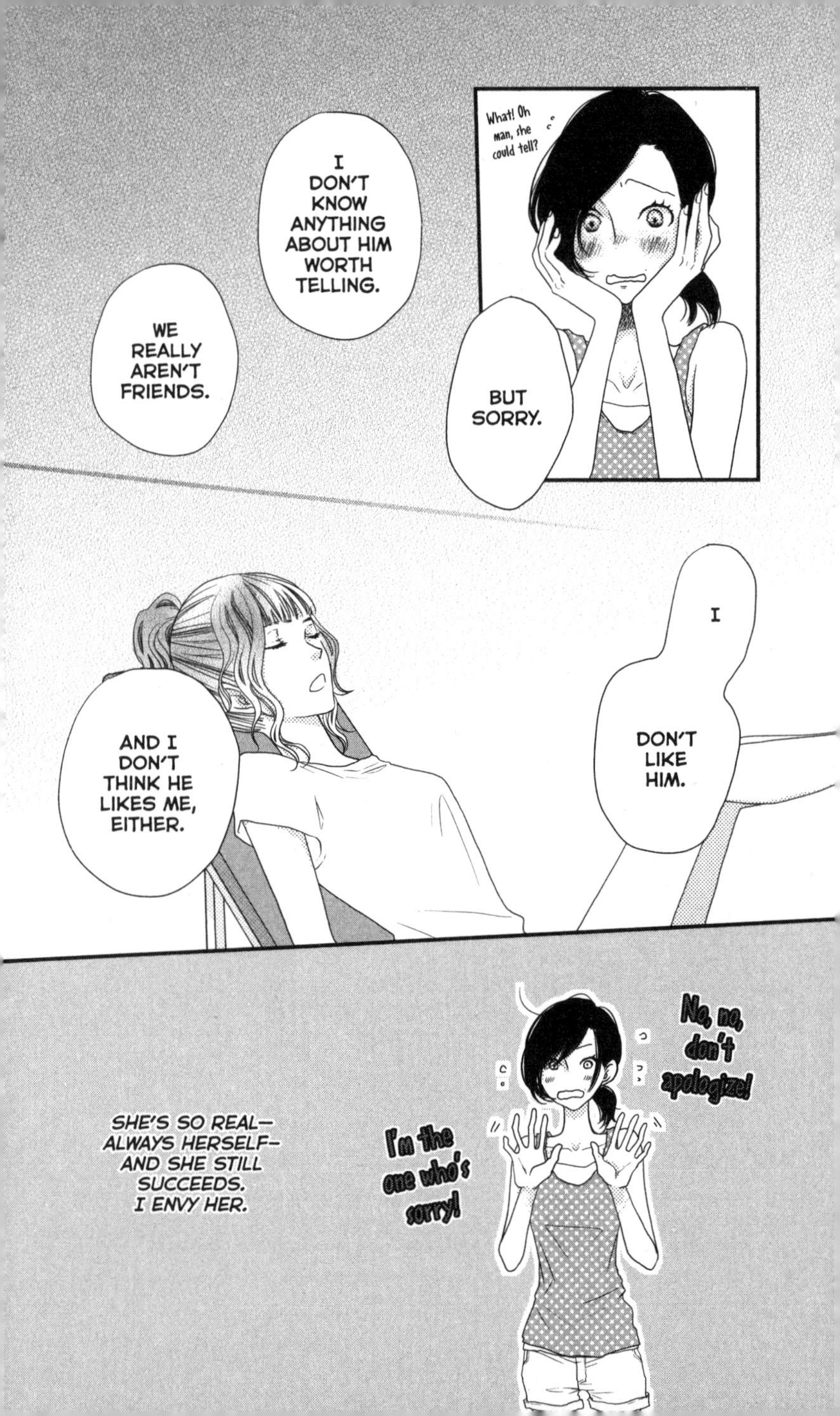
What! Oh man, she could tell?
I DON'T KNOW ANYTHING ABOUT HIM WORTH TELLING.
WE REALLY AREN'T FRIENDS.
BUT SORRY.
I DON'T LIKE HIM.
AND I DON'T THINK HE LIKES ME, EITHER.
No, no, don't apologize!
I'm the one who's sorry!
SHE'S SO REAL—ALWAYS HERSELF—AND SHE STILL SUCCEEDS. I ENVY HER.

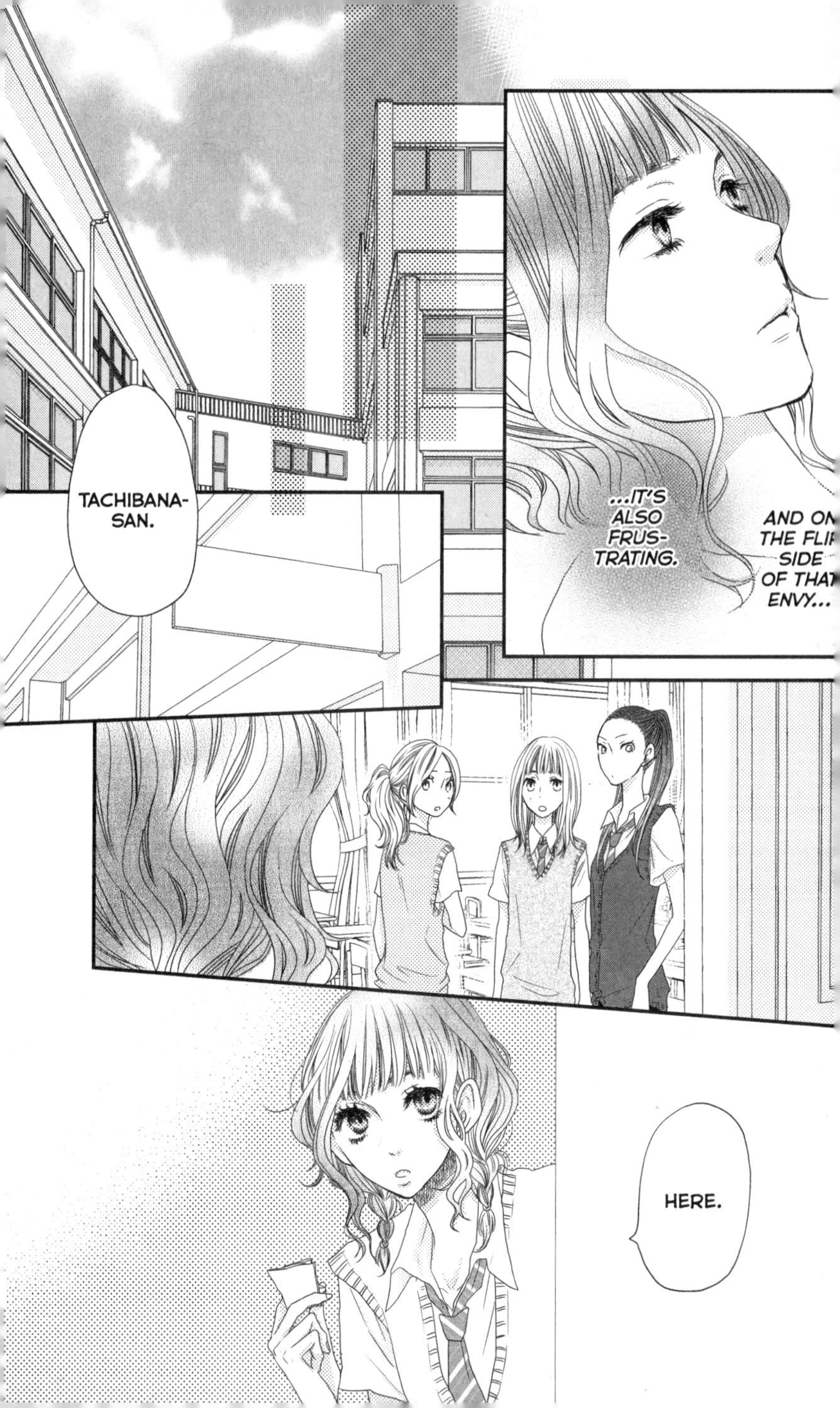
AND ON THE FLIP SIDE OF THAT ENVY...
...IT'S ALSO FRUS-TRATING.
TACHIBANA-SAN.
HERE.

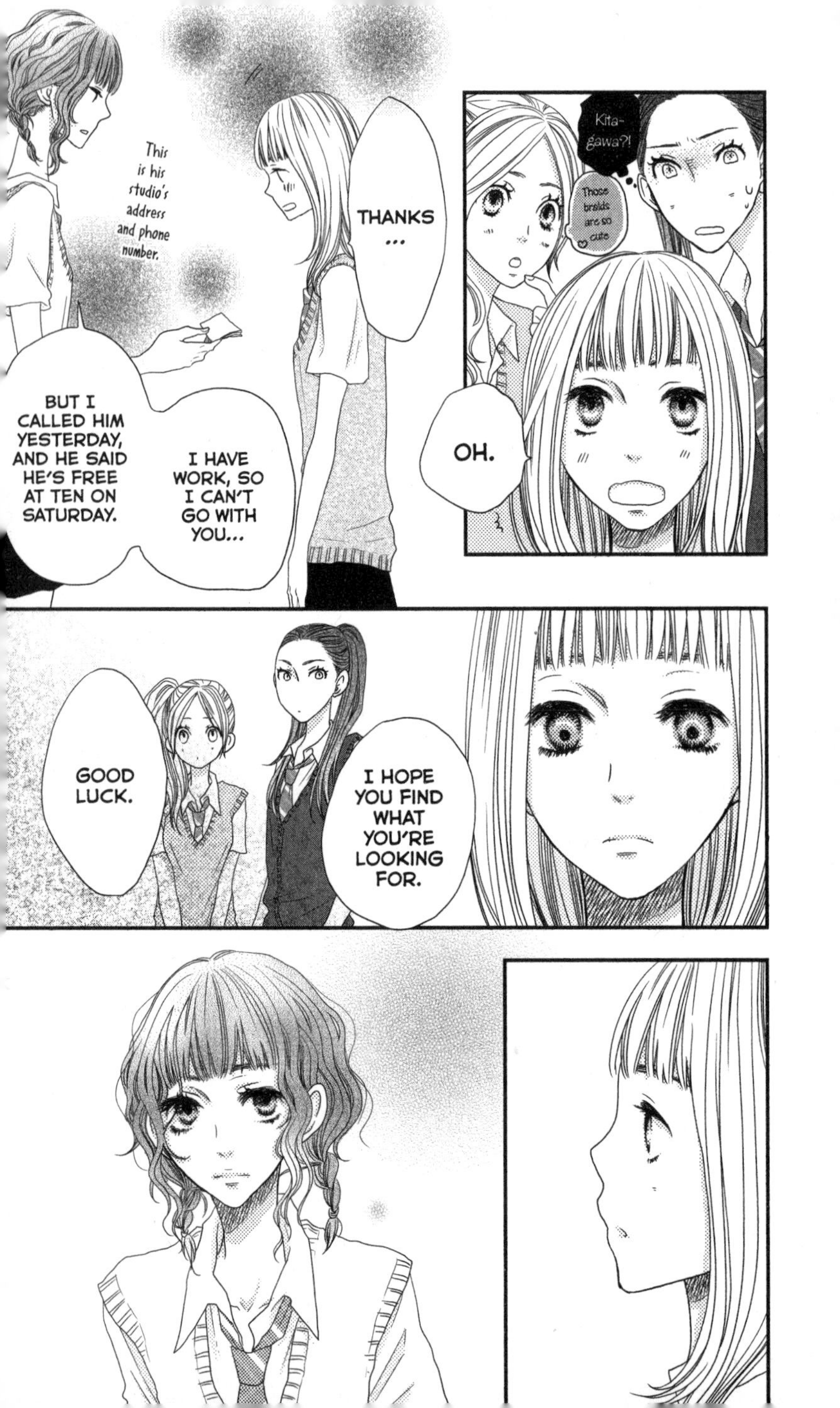
Kita-gawa?!
Those braids are so cute
OH.
THANKS...
This is his studio's address and phone number.
I HAVE WORK, SO I CAN'T GO WITH YOU...
BUT I CALLED HIM YESTERDAY, AND HE SAID HE'S FREE AT TEN ON SATURDAY.
I HOPE YOU FIND WHAT YOU'RE LOOKING FOR.
GOOD LUCK.

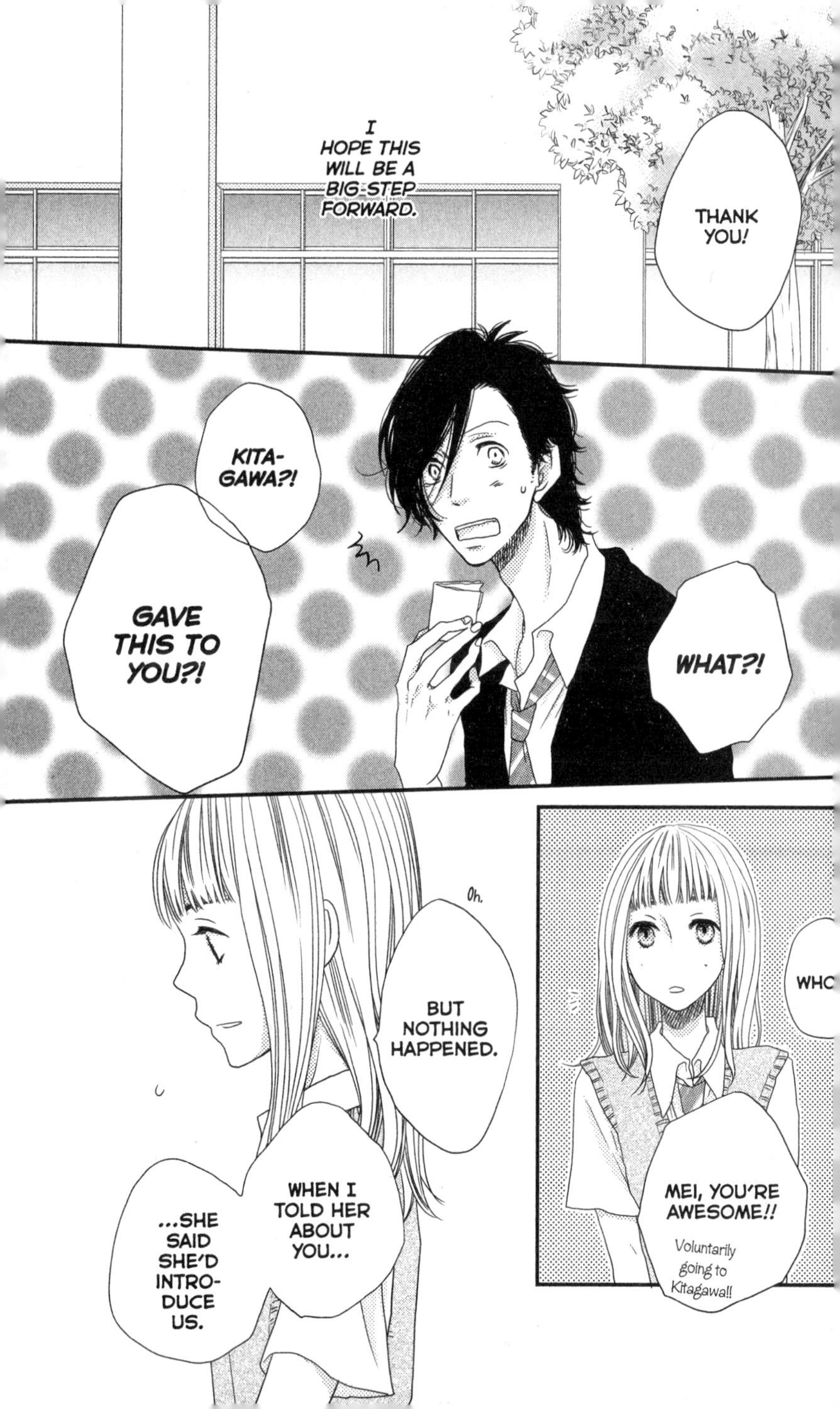
THANK YOU!
I HOPE THIS WILL BE A BIG STEP FORWARD.
WHAT?!
KITA-GAWA?!
GAVE THIS TO YOU?!
WHO
MEI, YOU'RE AWESOME!!
Voluntarily going to Kitagawa!!
Oh.
BUT NOTHING HAPPENED.
WHEN I TOLD HER ABOUT YOU...
...SHE SAID SHE'D INTRO-DUCE US.

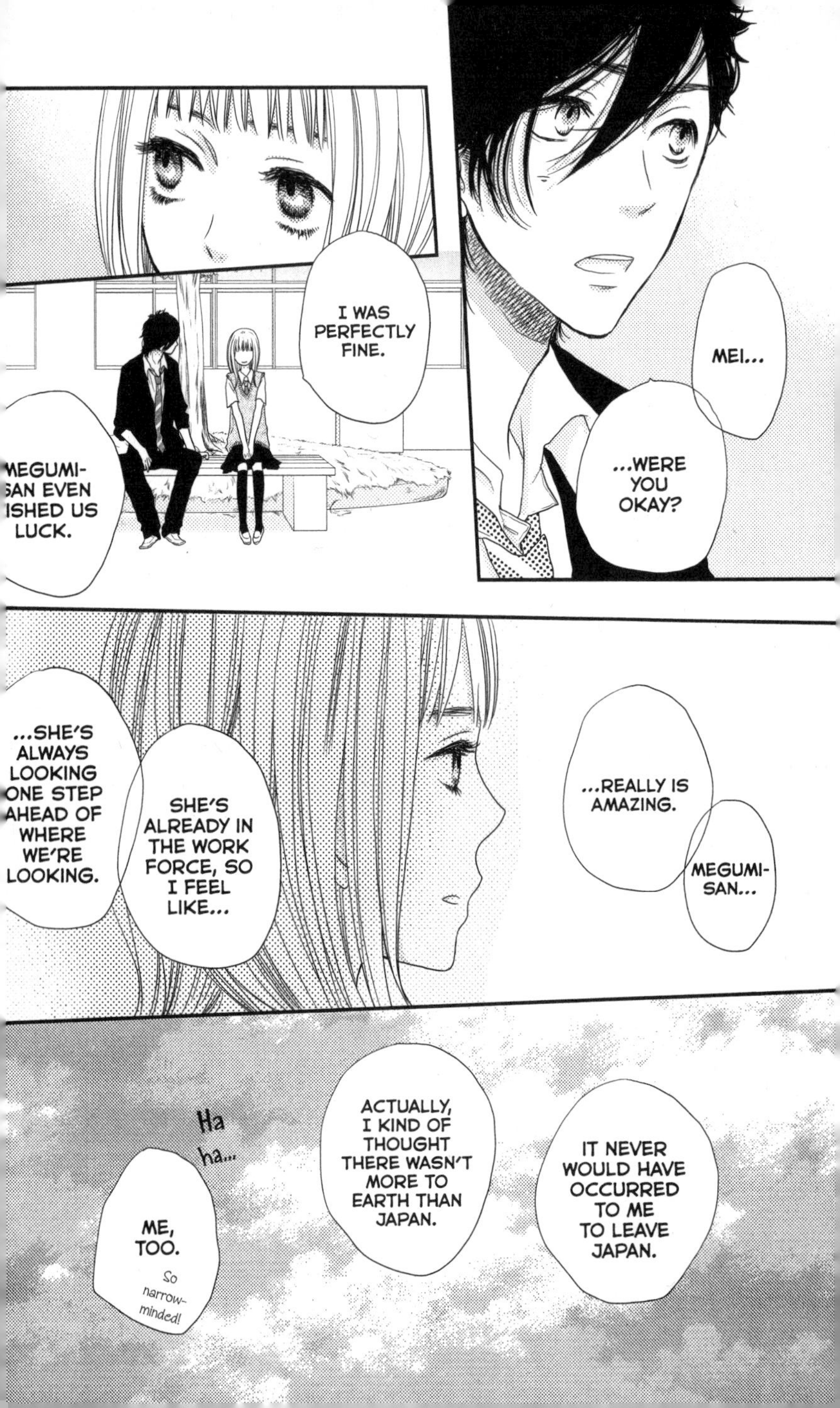
MEI...
...WERE YOU OKAY?
I WAS PERFECTLY FINE.
MEGUMI-SAN EVEN ISHED US LUCK.
MEGUMI-SAN...
...REALLY IS AMAZING.
SHE'S ALREADY IN THE WORK FORCE, SO I FEEL LIKE...
...SHE'S ALWAYS LOOKING ONE STEP AHEAD OF WHERE WE'RE LOOKING.
IT NEVER WOULD HAVE OCCURRED TO ME TO LEAVE JAPAN.
ACTUALLY, I KIND OF THOUGHT THERE WASN'T MORE TO EARTH THAN JAPAN.
Ha ha...
ME, TOO.
So narrow-minded!

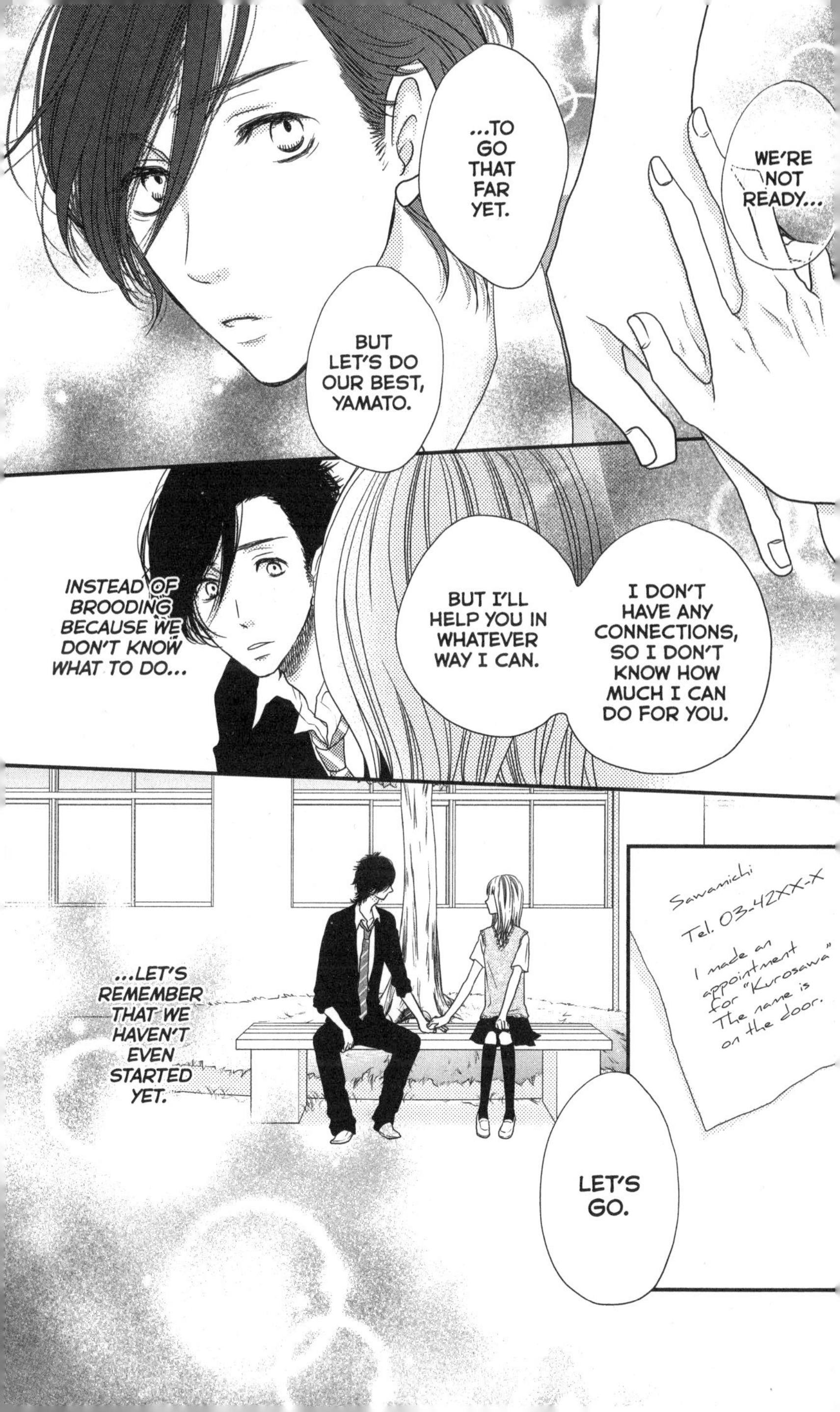
WE'RE NOT READY...
...TO GO THAT FAR YET.
BUT LET'S DO OUR BEST, YAMATO.
I DON'T HAVE ANY CONNECTIONS, SO I DON'T KNOW HOW MUCH I CAN DO FOR YOU.
BUT I'LL HELP YOU IN WHATEVER WAY I CAN.
INSTEAD OF BROODING BECAUSE WE DON'T KNOW WHAT TO DO...
Sawamichi
Tel. 03-42XX-X
I made an appointment for "Kurosawa" The name is on the door.
LET'S GO.
...LET'S REMEMBER THAT WE HAVEN'T EVEN STARTED YET.

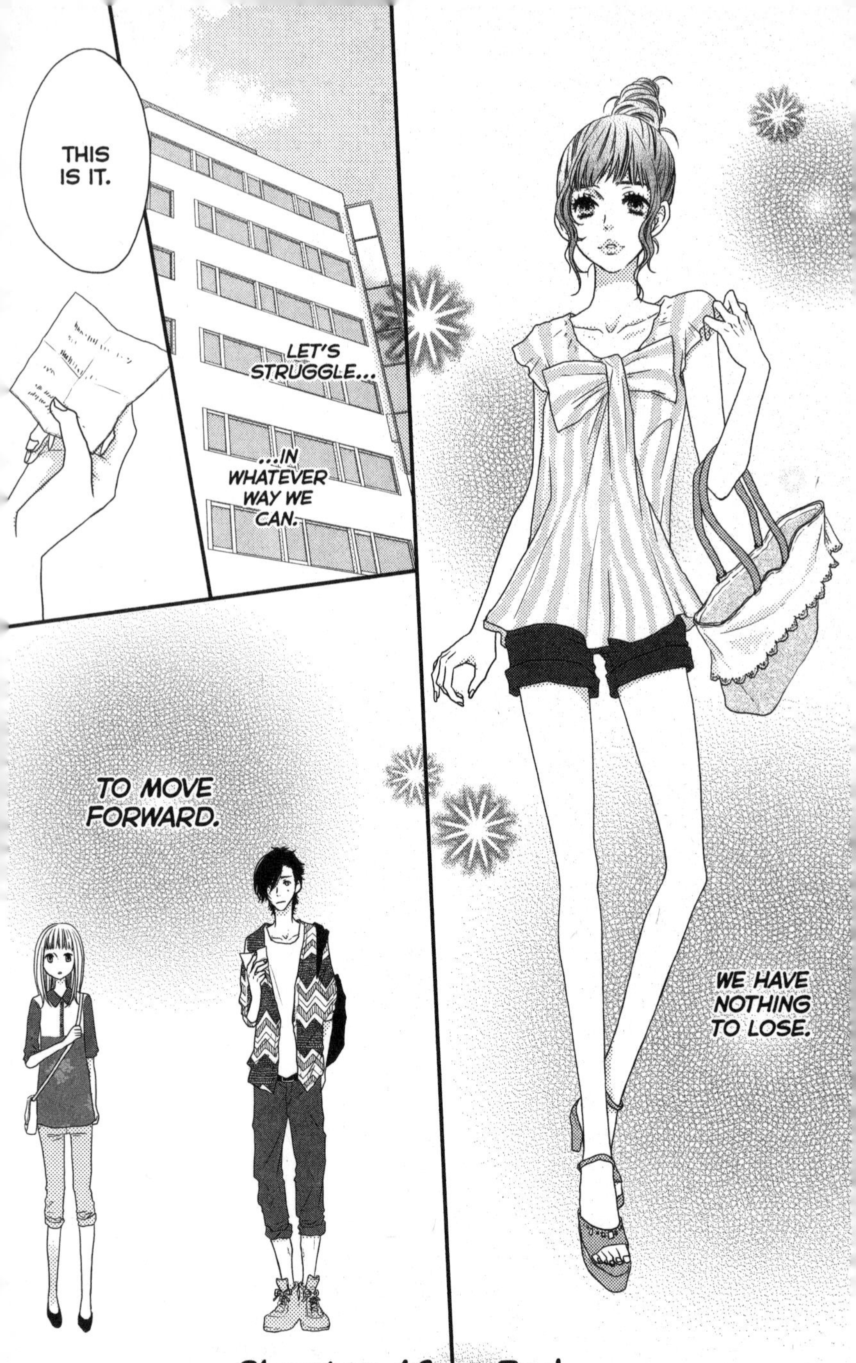
WE HAVE NOTHING TO LOSE.
LET'S STRUGGLE...
...IN WHATEVER WAY WE CAN.
THIS IS IT.
TO MOVE FORWARD.

Chapter 46 — End

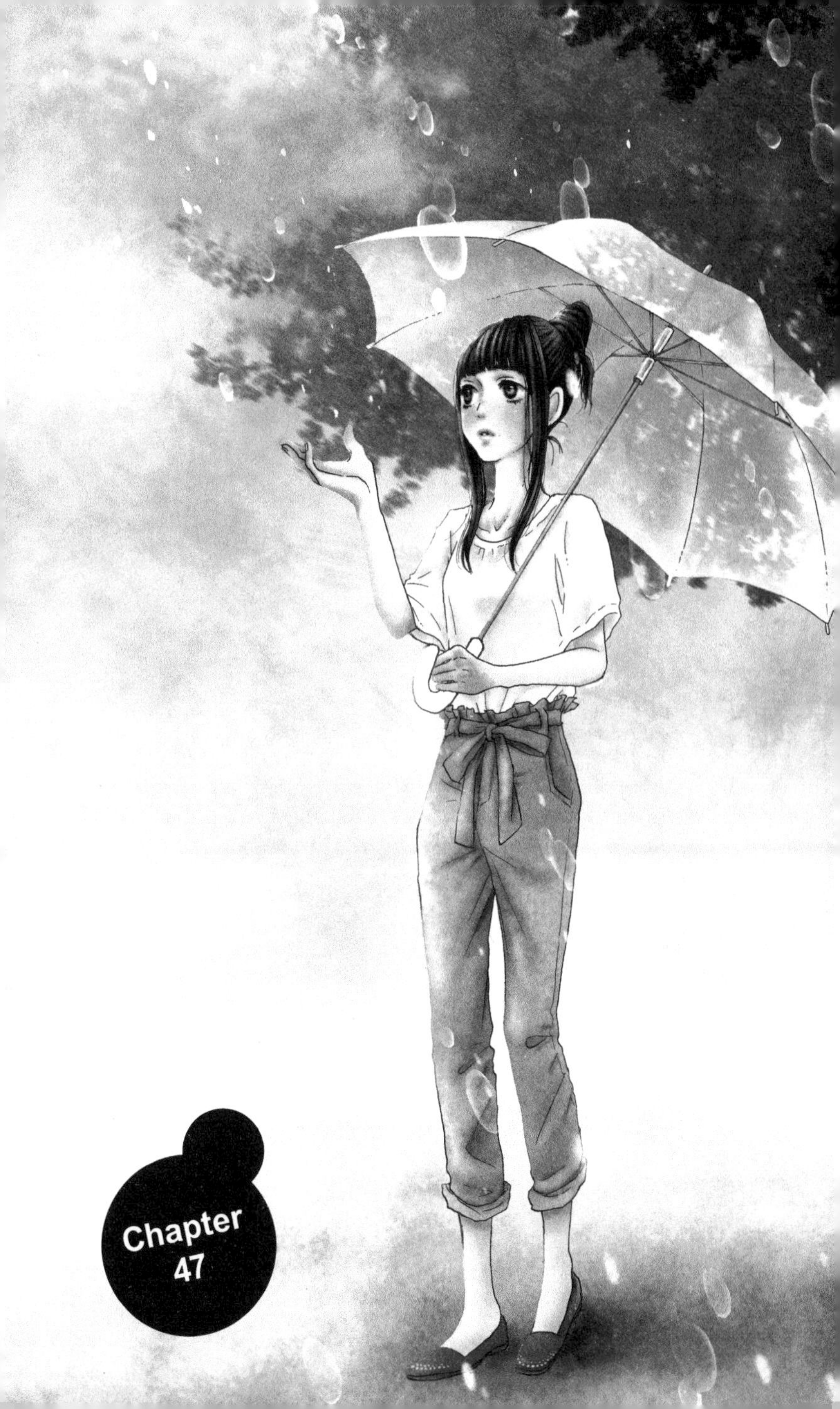
Chapter
47

Say "I love you".

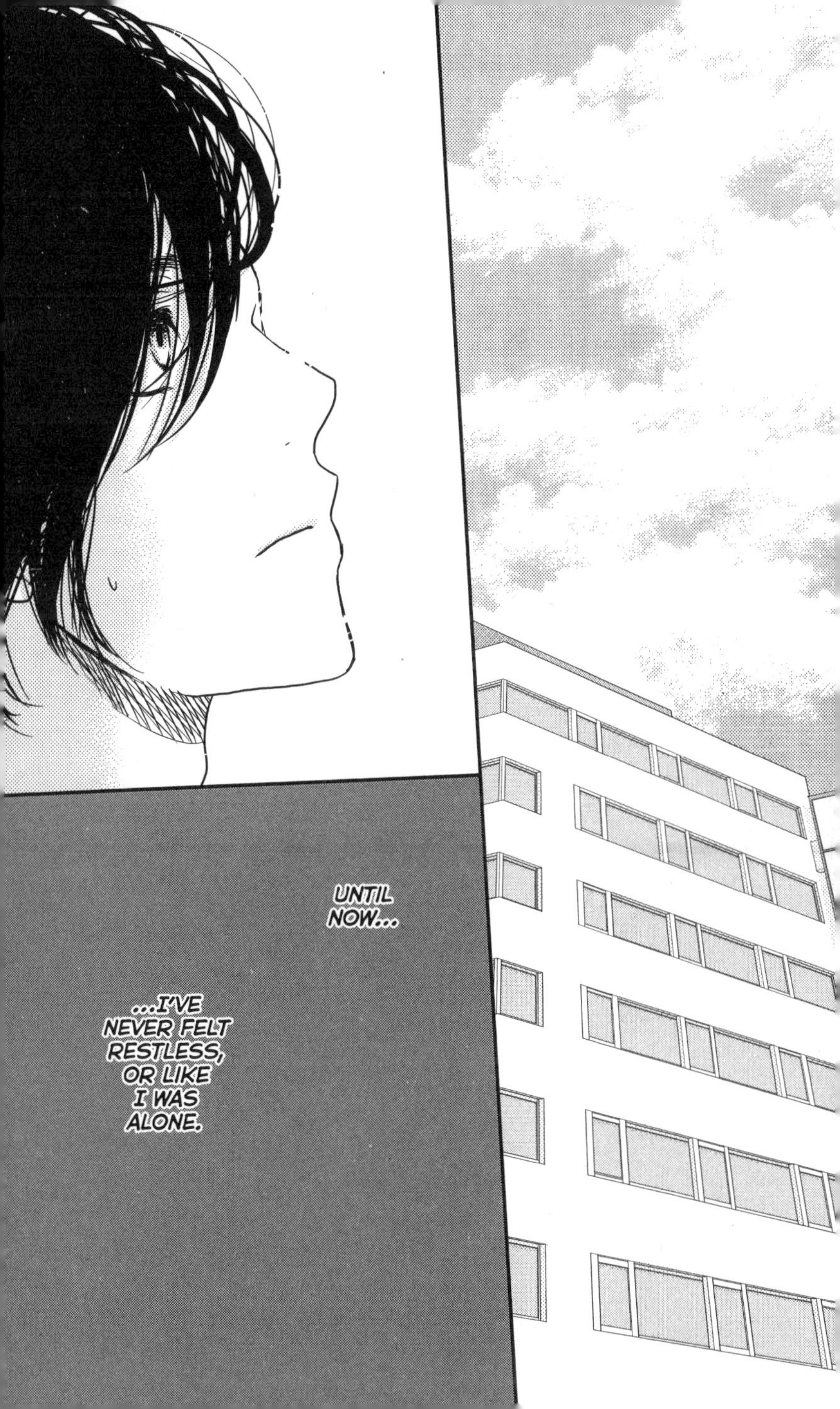
UNTIL NOW...
...I'VE NEVER FELT RESTLESS, OR LIKE I WAS ALONE.

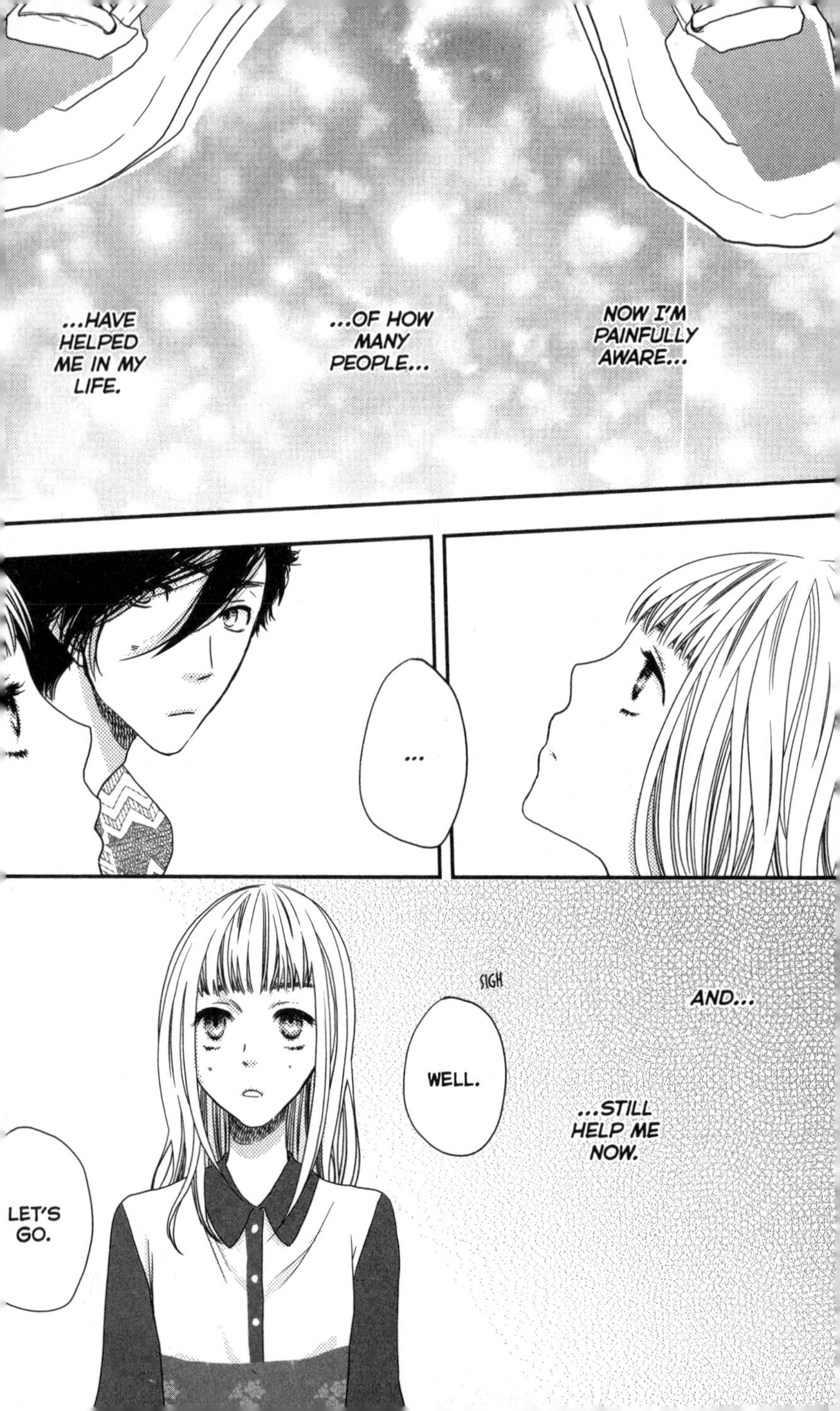
NOW I'M PAINFULLY AWARE...
...OF HOW MANY PEOPLE...
...HAVE HELPED ME IN MY LIFE.
...
AND...
...STILL HELP ME NOW.
SIGH
WELL.
LET'S GO.

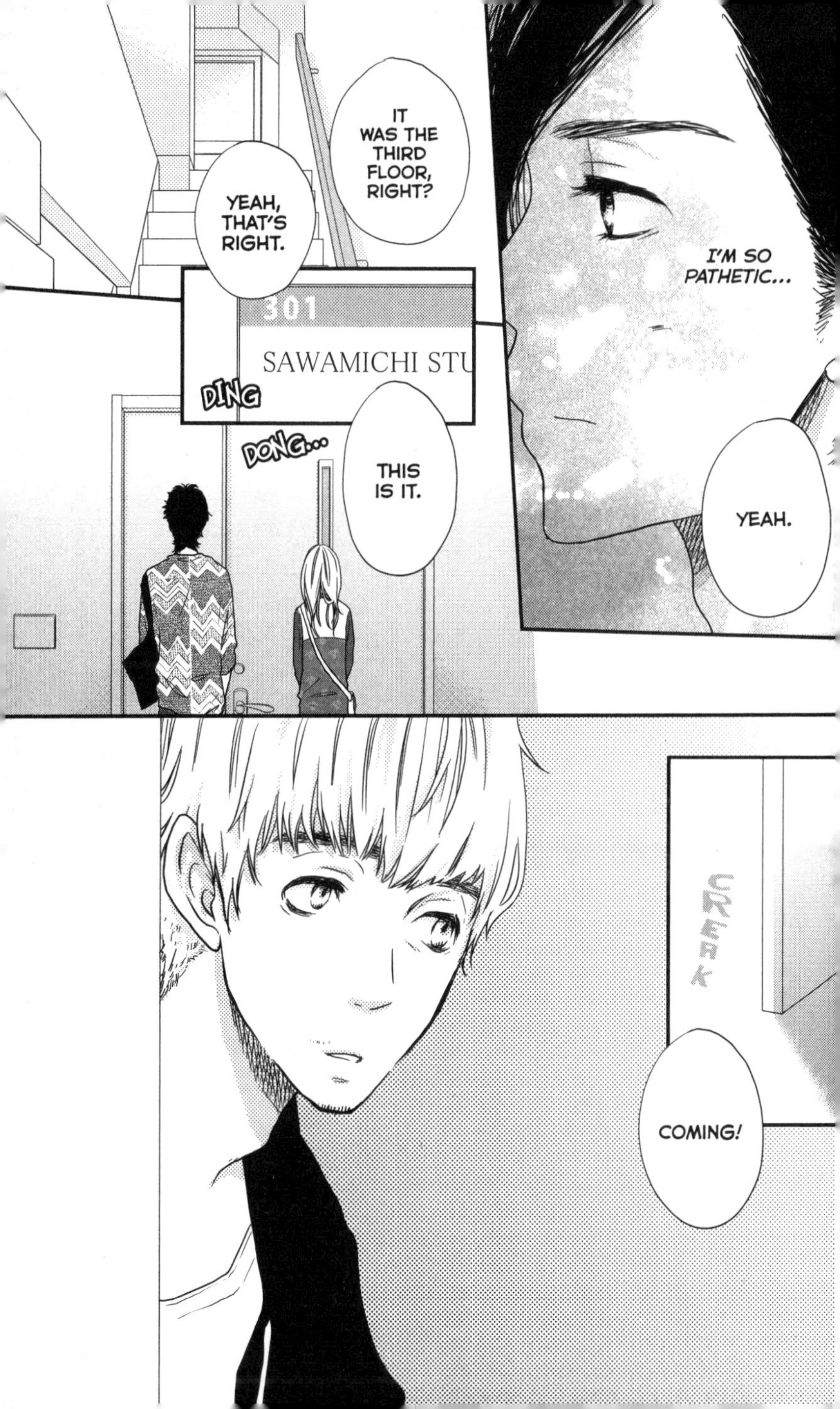
I'M SO PATHETIC...
YEAH.
IT WAS THE THIRD FLOOR, RIGHT?
YEAH, THAT'S RIGHT.
301
SAWAMICHI STU
DING
DONG...
THIS IS IT.
CREAK
COMING!

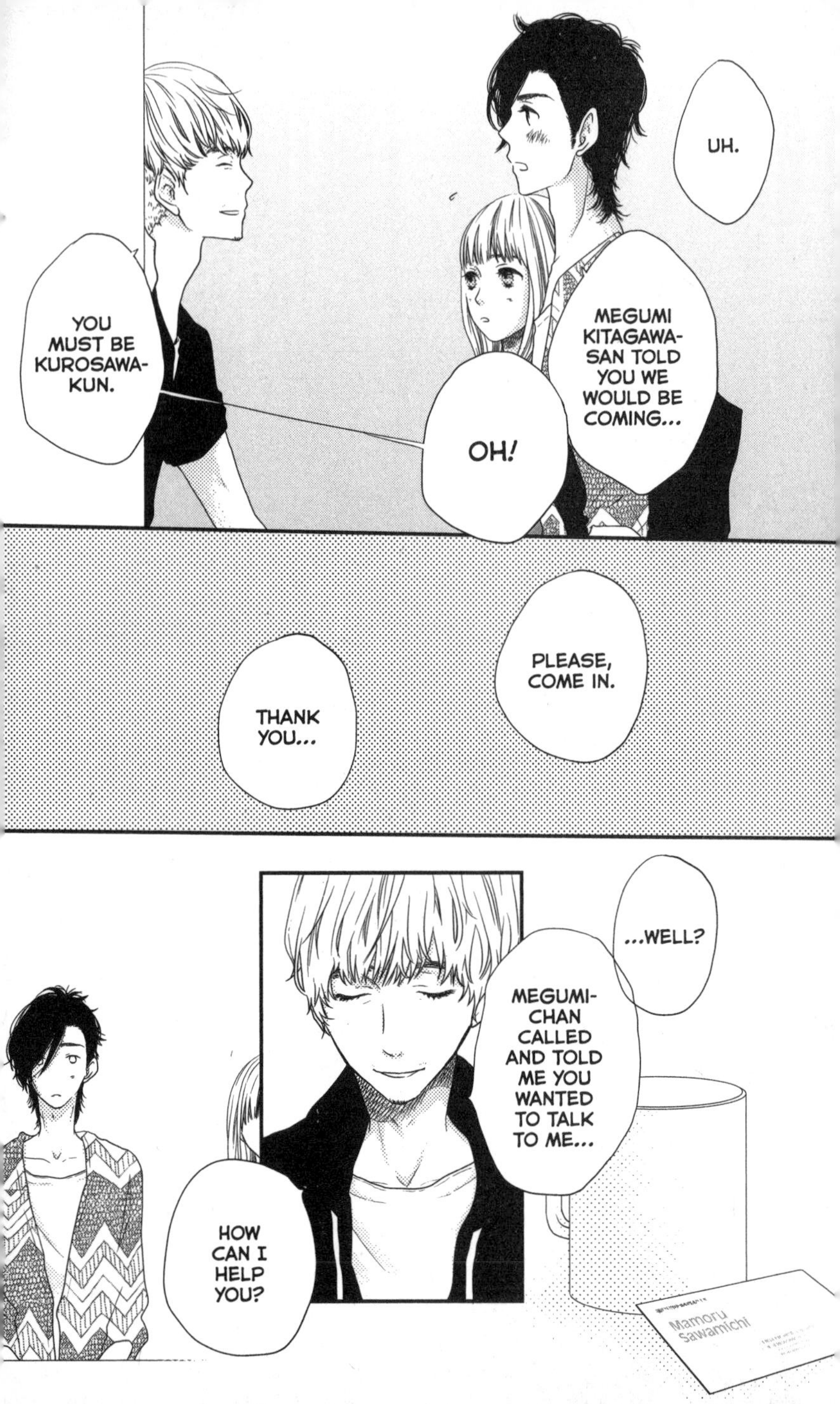
UH.
MEGUMI KITAGAWA-SAN TOLD YOU WE WOULD BE COMING...
YOU MUST BE KUROSAWA-KUN.
OH!
PLEASE, COME IN.
THANK YOU...
...WELL?
MEGUMI-CHAN CALLED AND TOLD ME YOU WANTED TO TALK TO ME...
HOW CAN I HELP YOU?
Mamoru Sawamichi

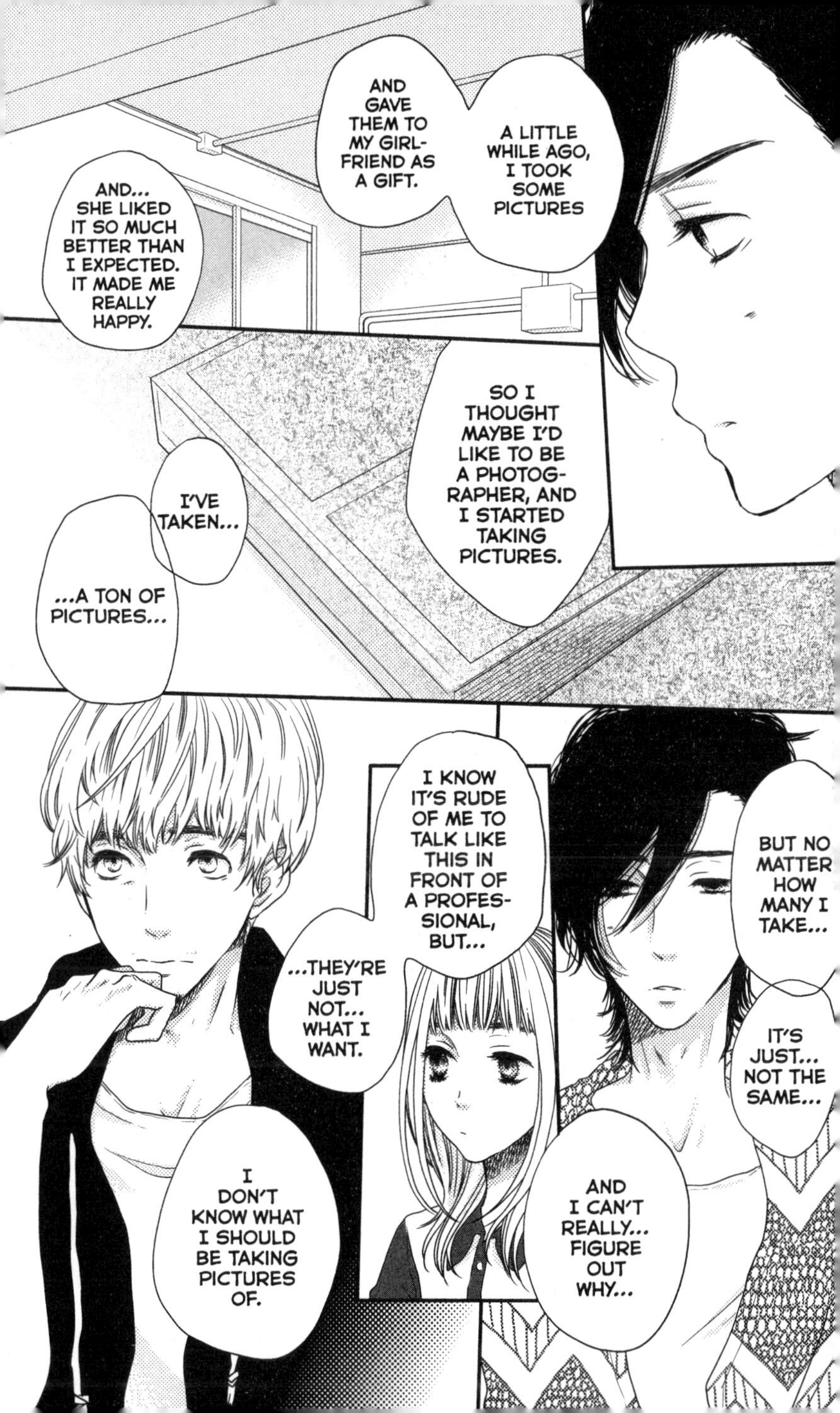
A LITTLE WHILE AGO, I TOOK SOME PICTURES
AND GAVE THEM TO MY GIRL-FRIEND AS A GIFT.
AND... SHE LIKED IT SO MUCH BETTER THAN I EXPECTED. IT MADE ME REALLY HAPPY.
SO I THOUGHT MAYBE I'D LIKE TO BE A PHOTOG-RAPHER, AND I STARTED TAKING PICTURES.
I'VE TAKEN...
...A TON OF PICTURES...
BUT NO MATTER HOW MANY I TAKE...
IT'S JUST... NOT THE SAME...
I KNOW IT'S RUDE OF ME TO TALK LIKE THIS IN FRONT OF A PROFES-SIONAL, BUT...
...THEY'RE JUST NOT... WHAT I WANT.
AND I CAN'T REALLY... FIGURE OUT WHY...
I DON'T KNOW WHAT I SHOULD BE TAKING PICTURES OF.

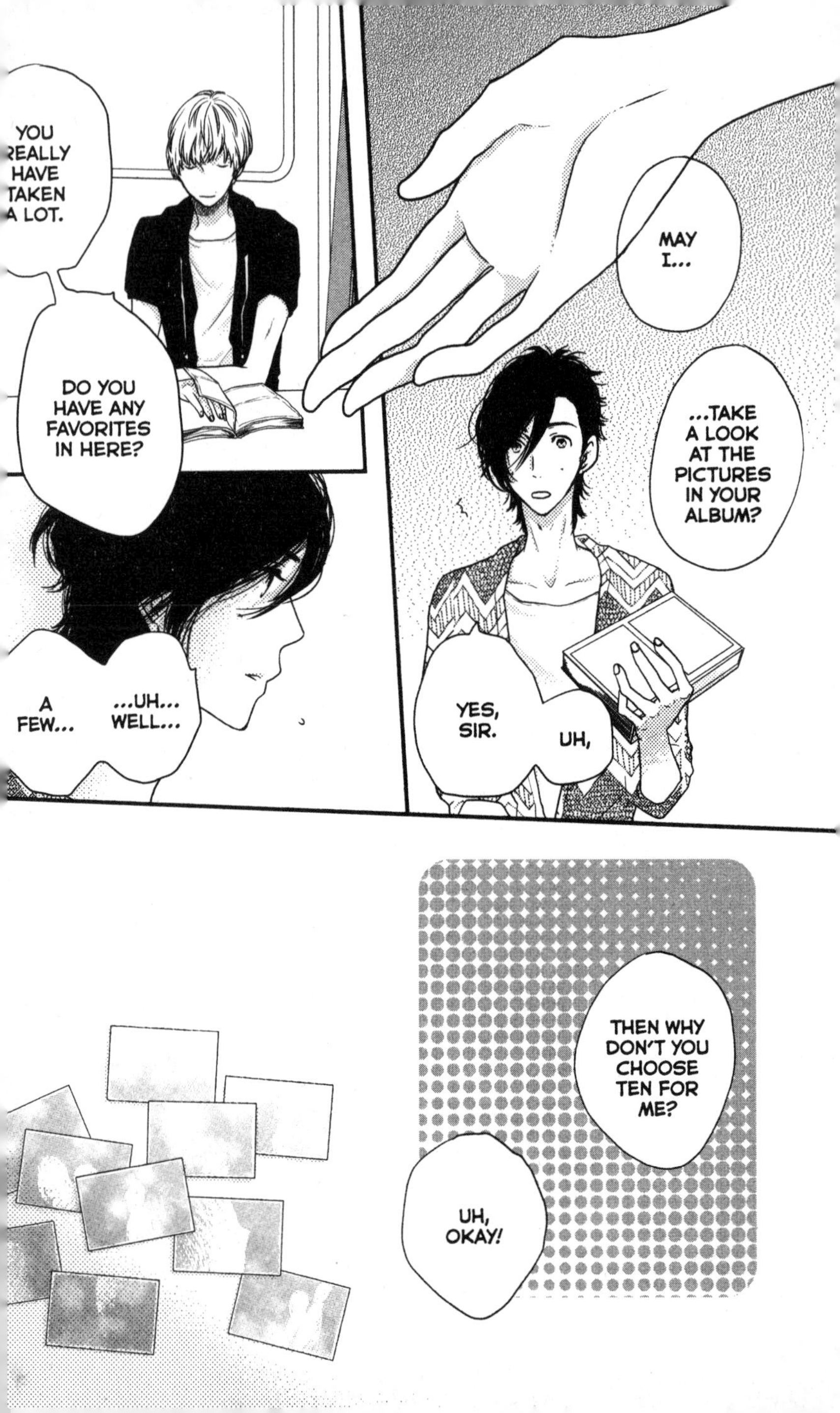
MAY I...
...TAKE A LOOK AT THE PICTURES IN YOUR ALBUM?
UH,
YES, SIR.
YOU REALLY HAVE TAKEN A LOT.
DO YOU HAVE ANY FAVORITES IN HERE?
...UH... WELL...
A FEW...
THEN WHY DON'T YOU CHOOSE TEN FOR ME?
UH, OKAY!

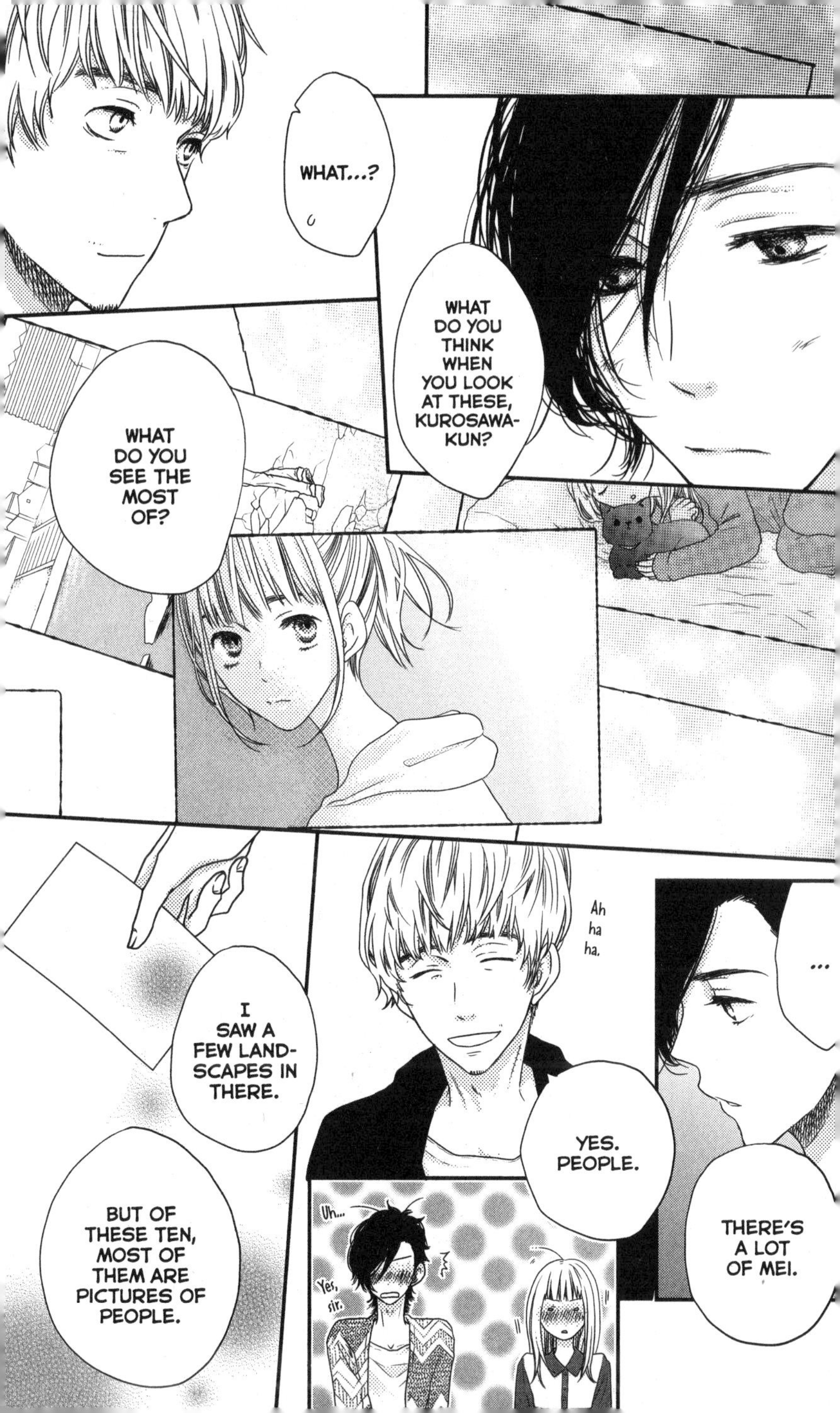
WHAT DO YOU THINK WHEN YOU LOOK AT THESE, KUROSAWA-KUN?
WHAT...?
WHAT DO YOU SEE THE MOST OF?
...
THERE'S A LOT OF MEI.
Ah ha ha.
YES. PEOPLE.
Uh...
Yes, sir.
I SAW A FEW LAND-SCAPES IN THERE.
BUT OF THESE TEN, MOST OF THEM ARE PICTURES OF PEOPLE.

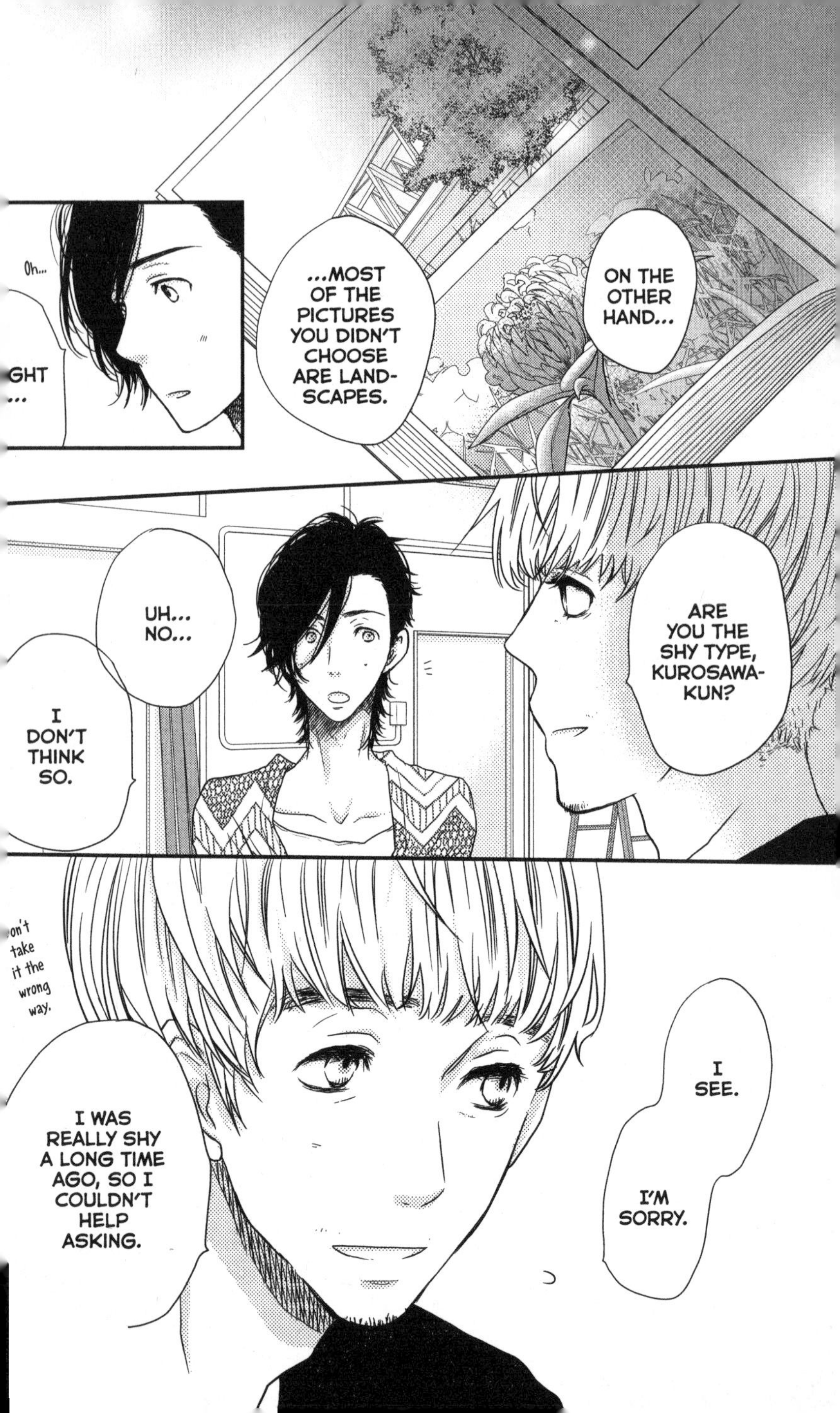
ON THE OTHER HAND...
...MOST OF THE PICTURES YOU DIDN'T CHOOSE ARE LAND-SCAPES.
Oh...
GHT ...
ARE YOU THE SHY TYPE, KUROSAWA-KUN?
UH... NO...
I DON'T THINK SO.
I SEE.
I'M SORRY.
I WAS REALLY SHY A LONG TIME AGO, SO I COULDN'T HELP ASKING.
on't take it the wrong way.

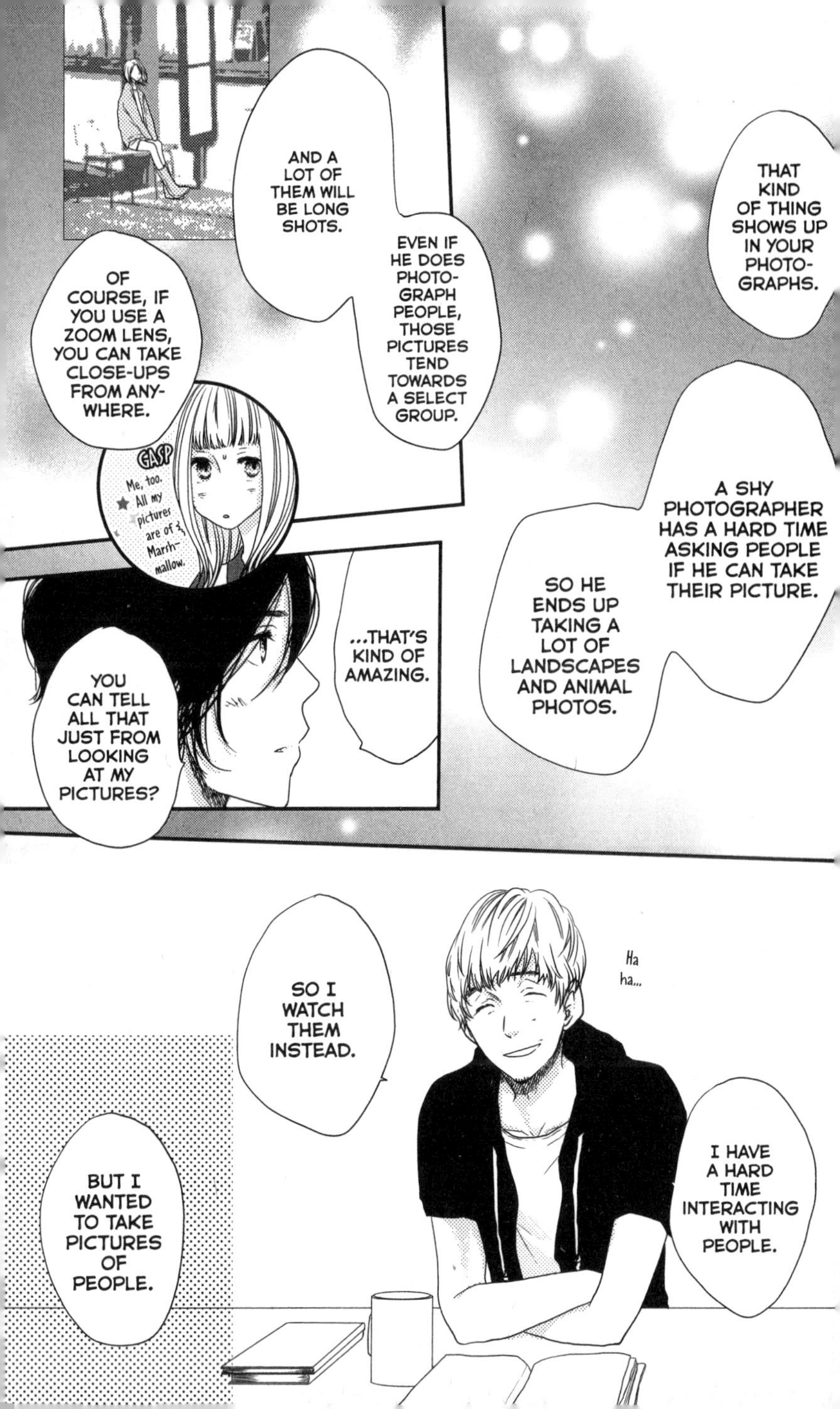
THAT KIND OF THING SHOWS UP IN YOUR PHOTOGRAPHS.
A SHY PHOTOGRAPHER HAS A HARD TIME ASKING PEOPLE IF HE CAN TAKE THEIR PICTURE.
SO HE ENDS UP TAKING A LOT OF LANDSCAPES AND ANIMAL PHOTOS.
AND A LOT OF THEM WILL BE LONG SHOTS.
EVEN IF HE DOES PHOTOGRAPH PEOPLE, THOSE PICTURES TEND TOWARDS A SELECT GROUP.
OF COURSE, IF YOU USE A ZOOM LENS, YOU CAN TAKE CLOSE-UPS FROM ANYWHERE.
GASP
Me, too. All my pictures are of Marshmallow.
...THAT'S KIND OF AMAZING.
YOU CAN TELL ALL THAT JUST FROM LOOKING AT MY PICTURES?
Ha ha...
I HAVE A HARD TIME INTERACTING WITH PEOPLE.
SO I WATCH THEM INSTEAD.
BUT I WANTED TO TAKE PICTURES OF PEOPLE.

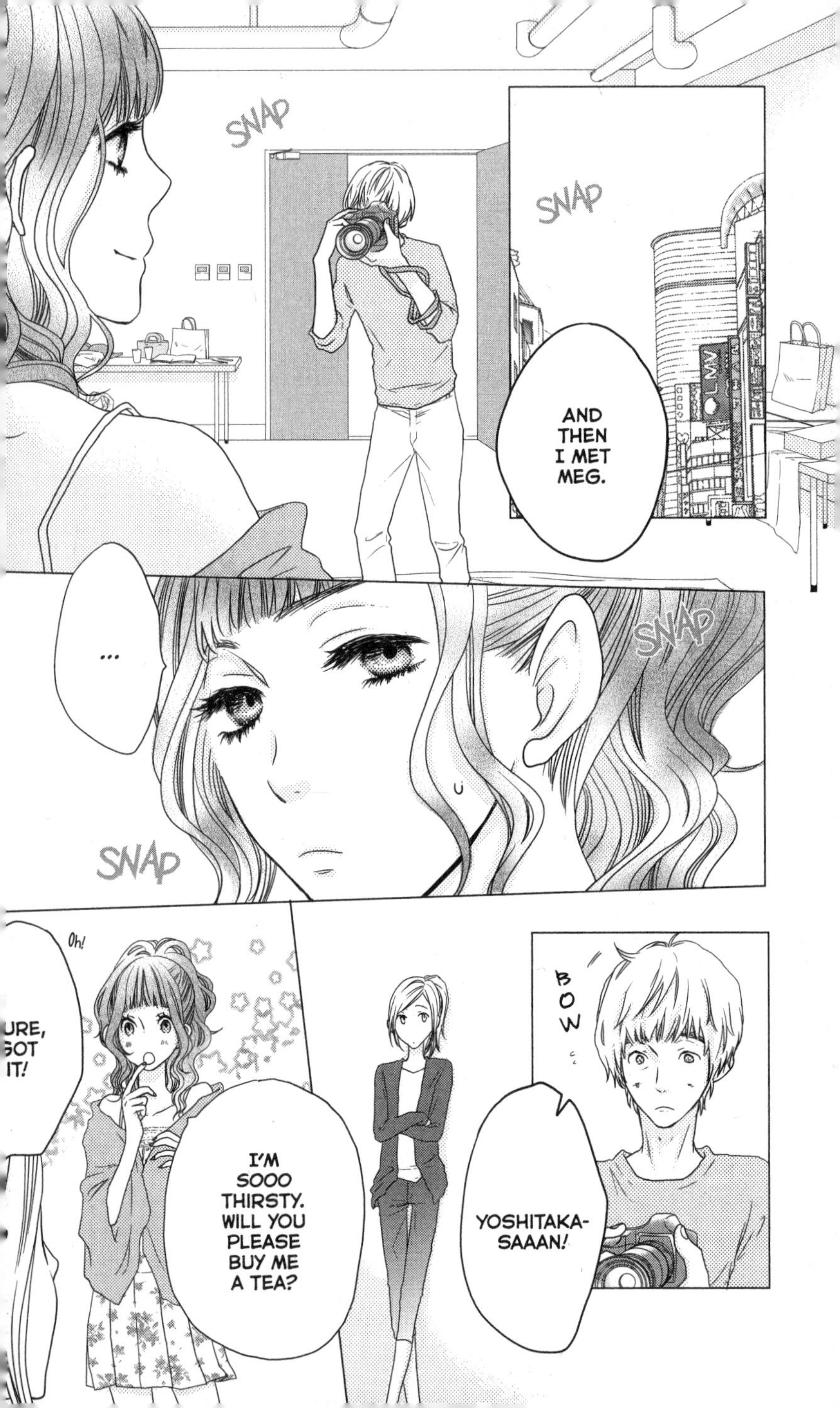

SNAP
AND THEN I MET MEG.
SNAP
SNAP
...
SNAP
BOW
YOSHITAKA-SAAAN!
I'M SOOO THIRSTY. WILL YOU PLEASE BUY ME A TEA?
Oh!
URE, GOT IT!

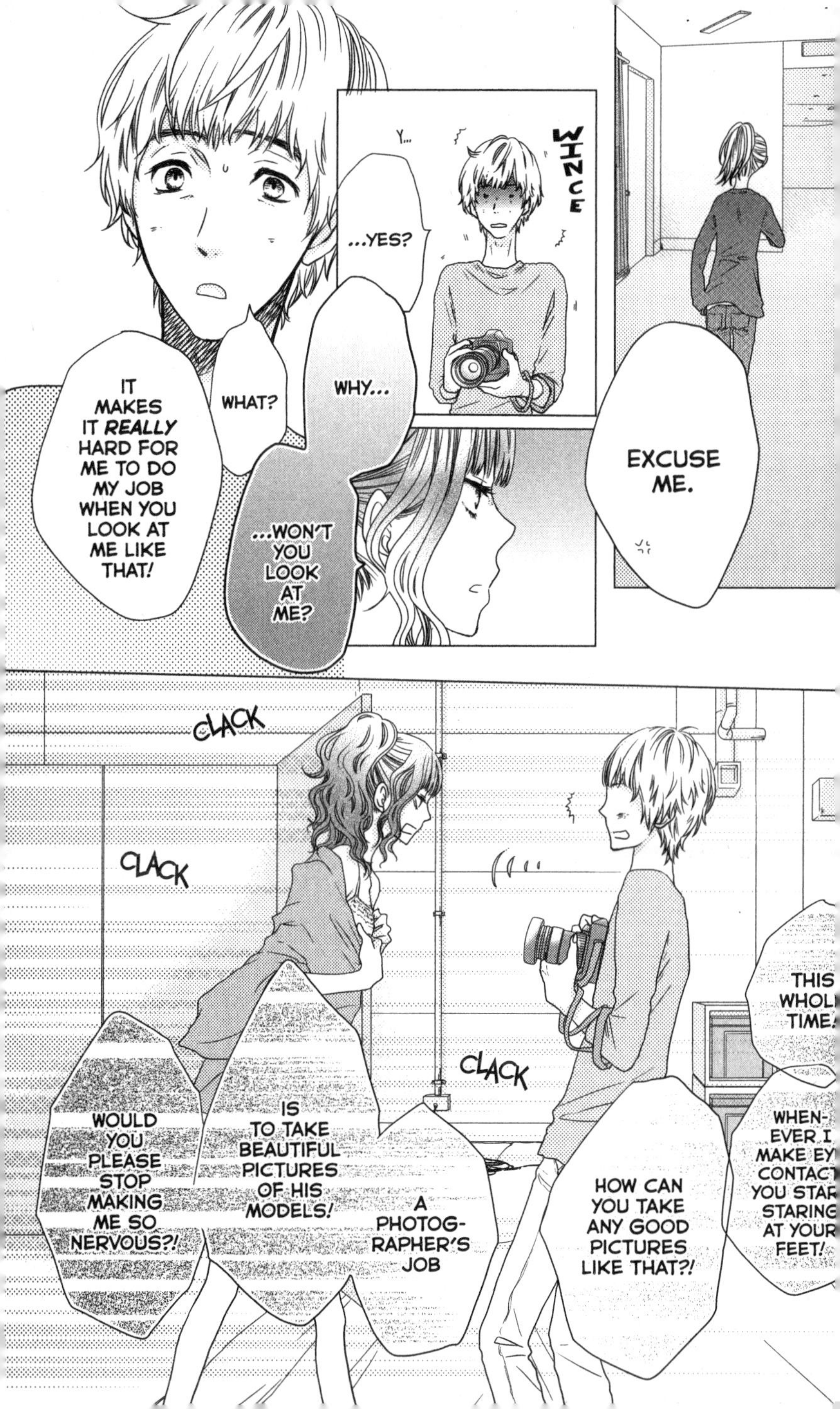

EXCUSE ME.
Y...
WINCE
...YES?
WHY...
...WON'T YOU LOOK AT ME?
WHAT?
IT MAKES IT *REALLY* HARD FOR ME TO DO MY JOB WHEN YOU LOOK AT ME LIKE THAT!
CLACK
CLACK
CLACK
THIS WHOL TIME.
WHEN-EVER I MAKE EY CONTAC YOU STAR STARING AT YOUR FEET!
HOW CAN YOU TAKE ANY GOOD PICTURES LIKE THAT?!
A PHOTOG-RAPHER'S JOB
IS TO TAKE BEAUTIFUL PICTURES OF HIS MODELS!
WOULD YOU PLEASE STOP MAKING ME SO NERVOUS?!

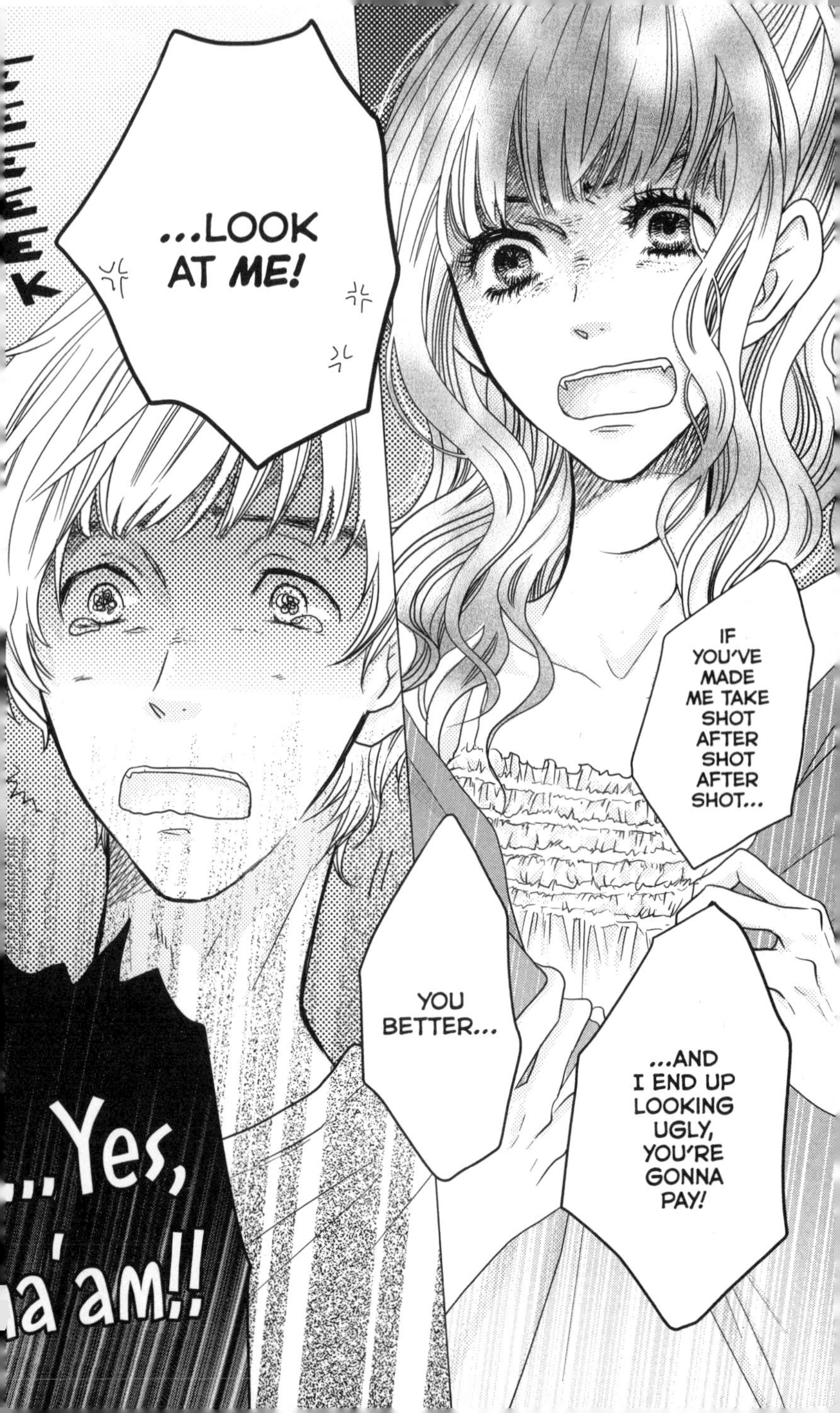
IF YOU'VE MADE ME TAKE SHOT AFTER SHOT AFTER SHOT...
...AND I END UP LOOKING UGLY, YOU'RE GONNA PAY!
YOU BETTER...
...LOOK AT *ME!*
...Yes,
a'am!!

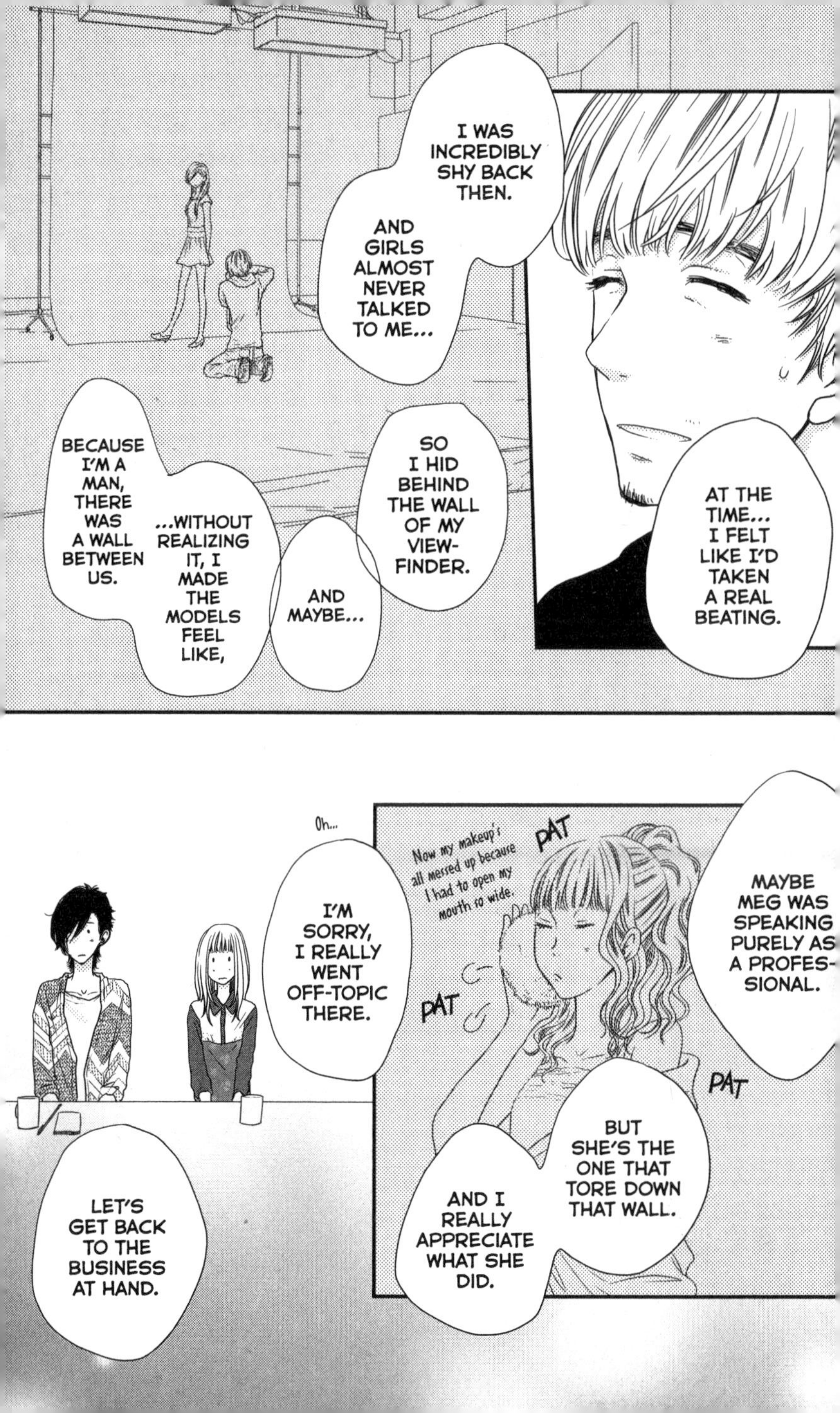
I WAS INCREDIBLY SHY BACK THEN.
AND GIRLS ALMOST NEVER TALKED TO ME...
SO I HID BEHIND THE WALL OF MY VIEW-FINDER.
AND MAYBE...
...WITHOUT REALIZING IT, I MADE THE MODELS FEEL LIKE,
BECAUSE I'M A MAN, THERE WAS A WALL BETWEEN US.
AT THE TIME... I FELT LIKE I'D TAKEN A REAL BEATING.
MAYBE MEG WAS SPEAKING PURELY AS A PROFES-SIONAL.
PAT
Now my makeup's all messed up because I had to open my mouth so wide.
PAT
PAT
BUT SHE'S THE ONE THAT TORE DOWN THAT WALL.
AND I REALLY APPRECIATE WHAT SHE DID.
Oh...
I'M SORRY, I REALLY WENT OFF-TOPIC THERE.
LET'S GET BACK TO THE BUSINESS AT HAND.

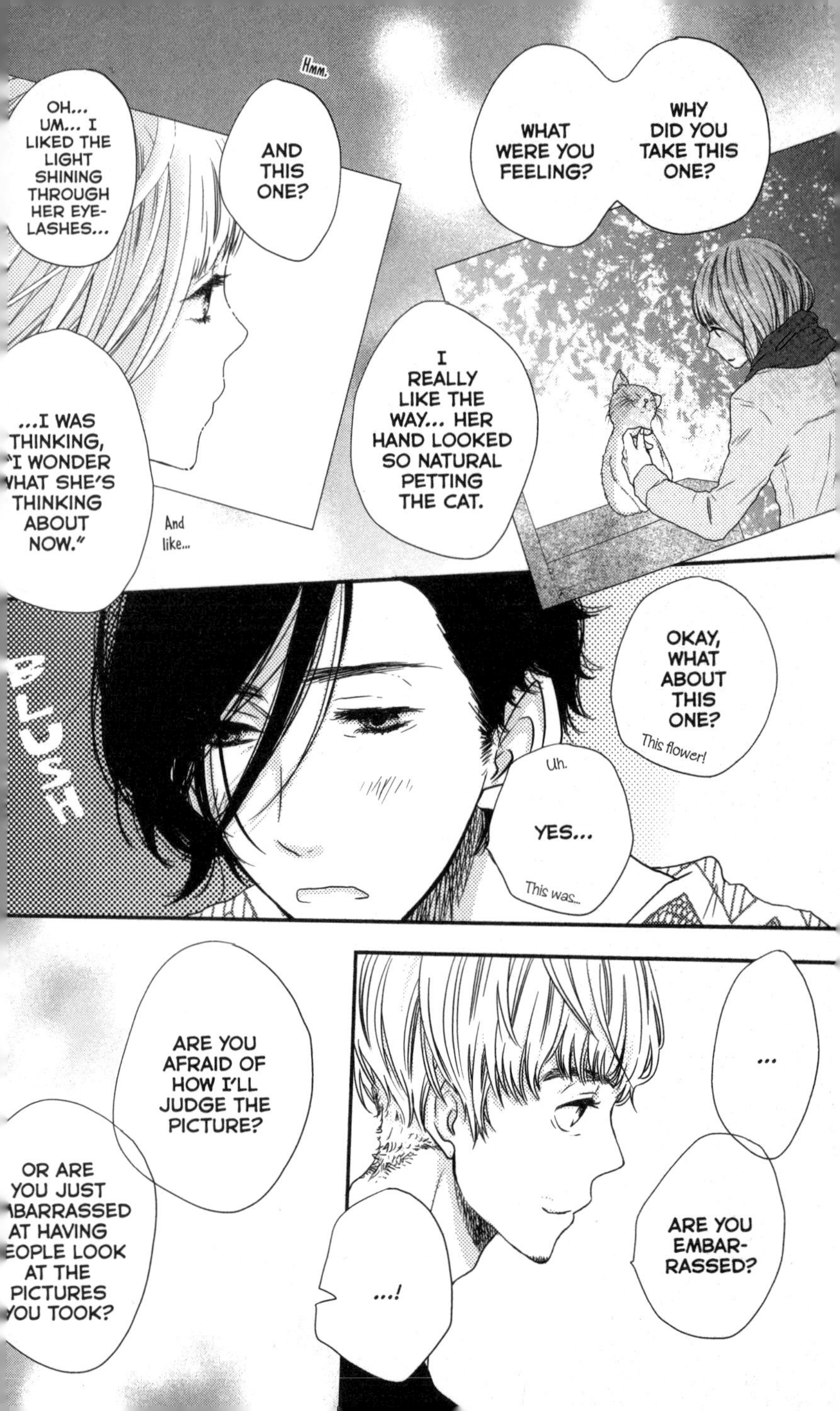
WHY DID YOU TAKE THIS ONE?
WHAT WERE YOU FEELING?
Hmm.
AND THIS ONE?
OH... UM... I LIKED THE LIGHT SHINING THROUGH HER EYE-LASHES...
I REALLY LIKE THE WAY... HER HAND LOOKED SO NATURAL PETTING THE CAT.
And like...
...I WAS THINKING, "I WONDER WHAT SHE'S THINKING ABOUT NOW."
OKAY, WHAT ABOUT THIS ONE?
This flower!
Uh.
YES...
This was...
BLUSH
...
ARE YOU EMBAR-RASSED?
...!
ARE YOU AFRAID OF HOW I'LL JUDGE THE PICTURE?
OR ARE YOU JUST BARRASSED AT HAVING EOPLE LOOK AT THE PICTURES YOU TOOK?

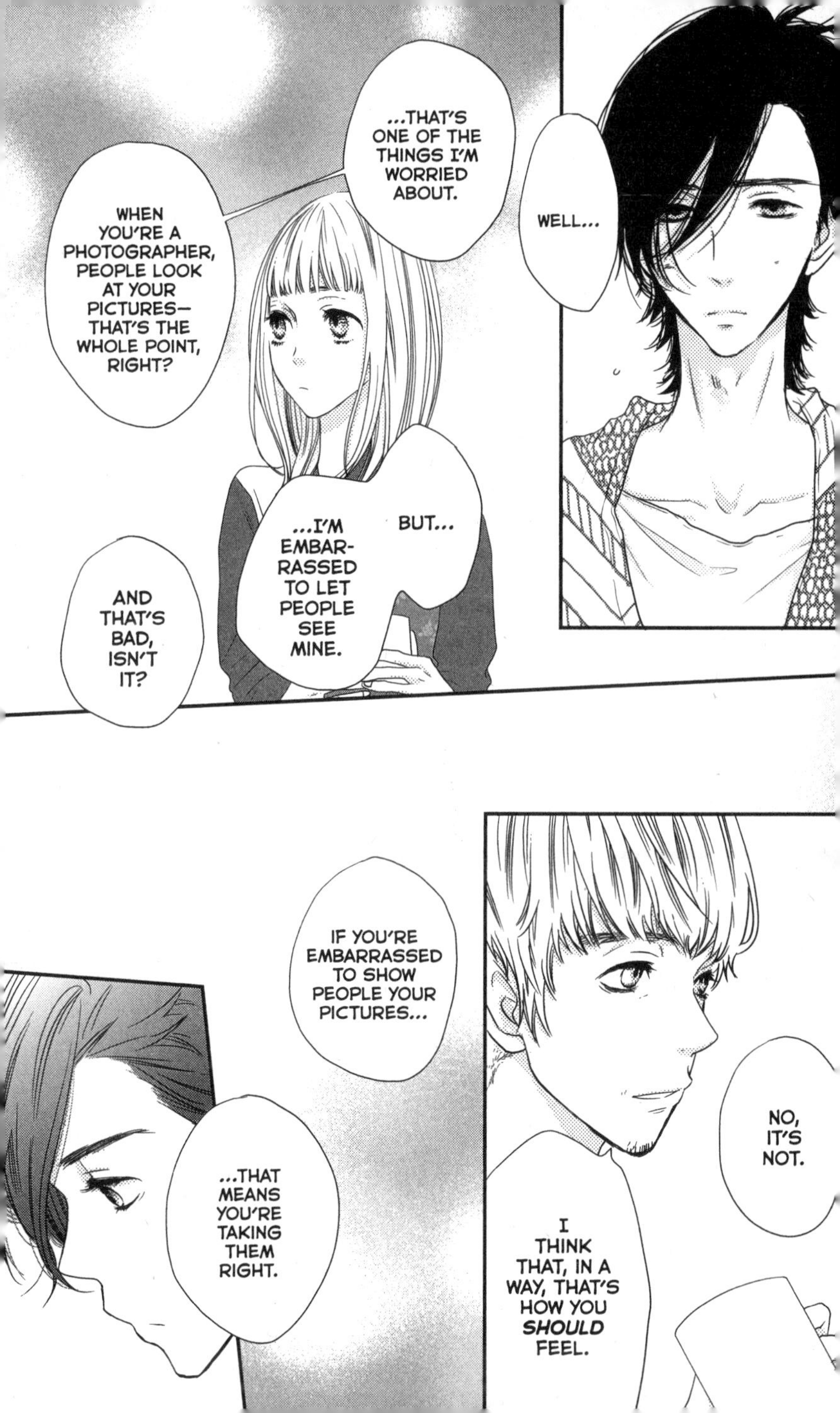
WELL...
...THAT'S ONE OF THE THINGS I'M WORRIED ABOUT.
WHEN YOU'RE A PHOTOGRAPHER, PEOPLE LOOK AT YOUR PICTURES—THAT'S THE WHOLE POINT, RIGHT?
BUT... ...I'M EMBARRASSED TO LET PEOPLE SEE MINE.
AND THAT'S BAD, ISN'T IT?
NO, IT'S NOT.
I THINK THAT, IN A WAY, THAT'S HOW YOU *SHOULD* FEEL.
IF YOU'RE EMBARRASSED TO SHOW PEOPLE YOUR PICTURES...
...THAT MEANS YOU'RE TAKING THEM RIGHT.

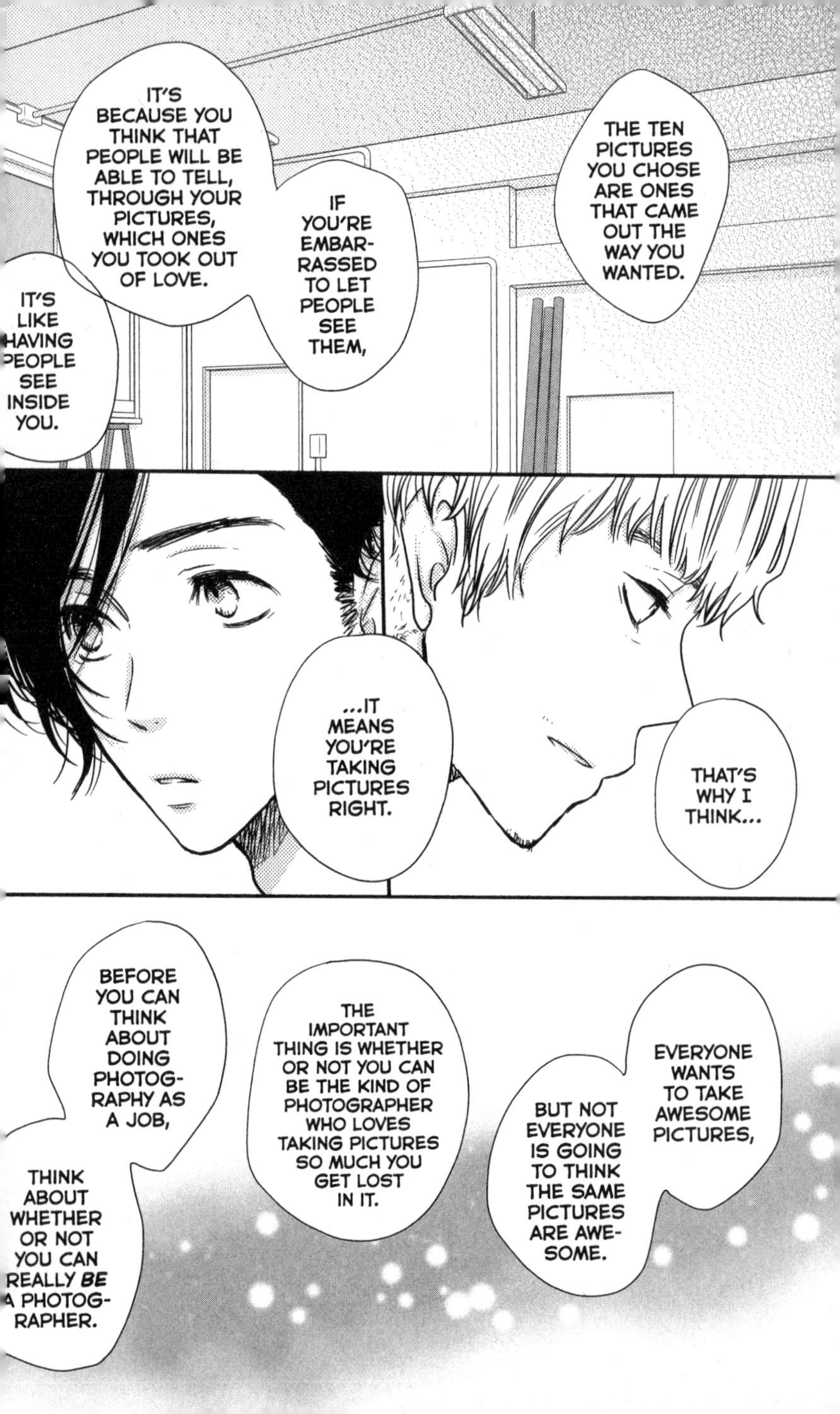
THE TEN PICTURES YOU CHOSE ARE ONES THAT CAME OUT THE WAY YOU WANTED.
IF YOU'RE EMBARRASSED TO LET PEOPLE SEE THEM,
IT'S BECAUSE YOU THINK THAT PEOPLE WILL BE ABLE TO TELL, THROUGH YOUR PICTURES, WHICH ONES YOU TOOK OUT OF LOVE.
IT'S LIKE HAVING PEOPLE SEE INSIDE YOU.
THAT'S WHY I THINK...
...IT MEANS YOU'RE TAKING PICTURES RIGHT.
EVERYONE WANTS TO TAKE AWESOME PICTURES,
BUT NOT EVERYONE IS GOING TO THINK THE SAME PICTURES ARE AWESOME.
THE IMPORTANT THING IS WHETHER OR NOT YOU CAN BE THE KIND OF PHOTOGRAPHER WHO LOVES TAKING PICTURES SO MUCH YOU GET LOST IN IT.
BEFORE YOU CAN THINK ABOUT DOING PHOTOGRAPHY AS A JOB,
THINK ABOUT WHETHER OR NOT YOU CAN REALLY *BE* A PHOTOGRAPHER.

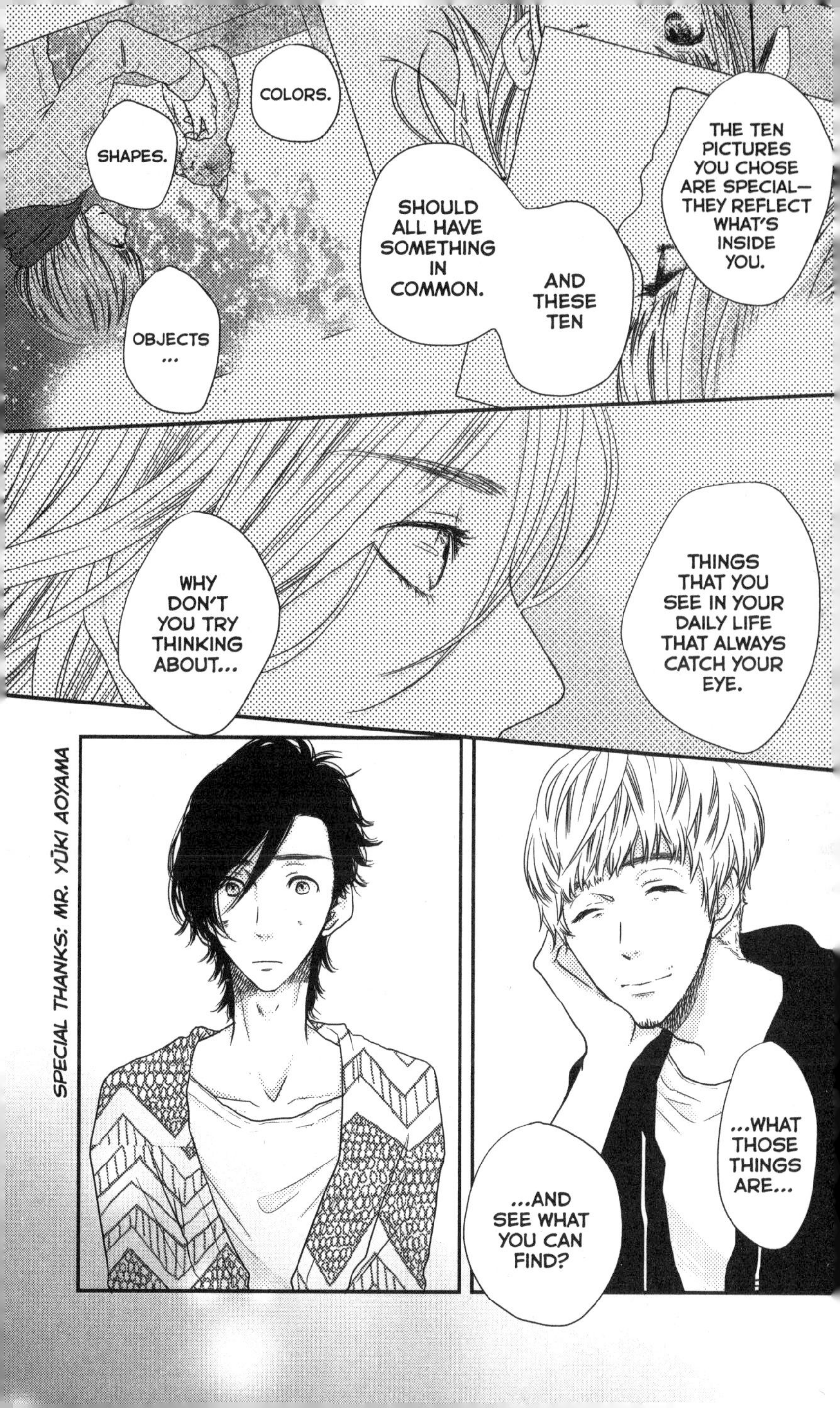
THE TEN PICTURES YOU CHOSE ARE SPECIAL—THEY REFLECT WHAT'S INSIDE YOU.
AND THESE TEN
SHOULD ALL HAVE SOMETHING IN COMMON.
COLORS.
SHAPES.
OBJECTS ...
WHY DON'T YOU TRY THINKING ABOUT...
THINGS THAT YOU SEE IN YOUR DAILY LIFE THAT ALWAYS CATCH YOUR EYE.
...WHAT THOSE THINGS ARE...
...AND SEE WHAT YOU CAN FIND?
SPECIAL THANKS: MR. YŪKI AOYAMA

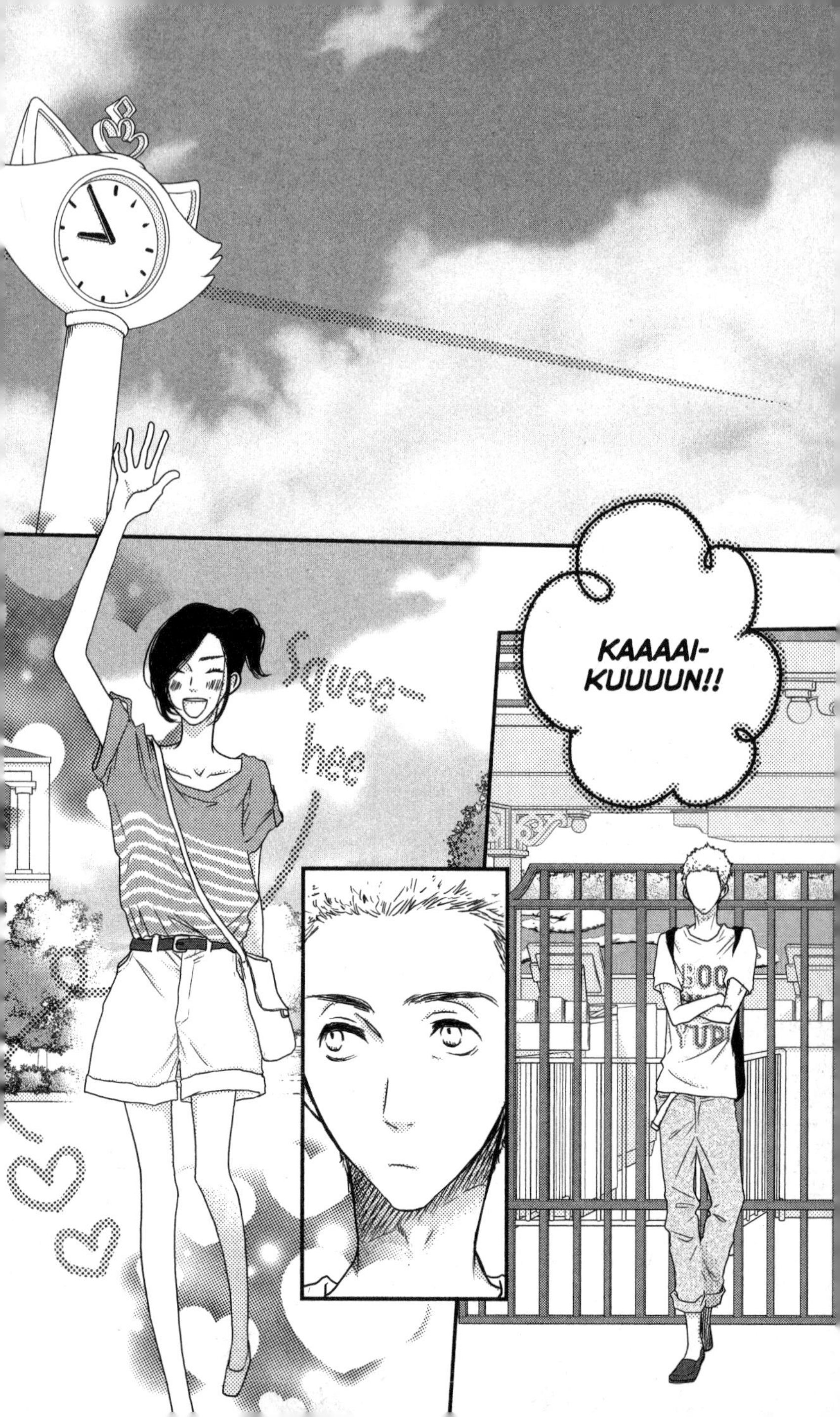
KAAAAI-
KUUUUN!!
Squee-hee

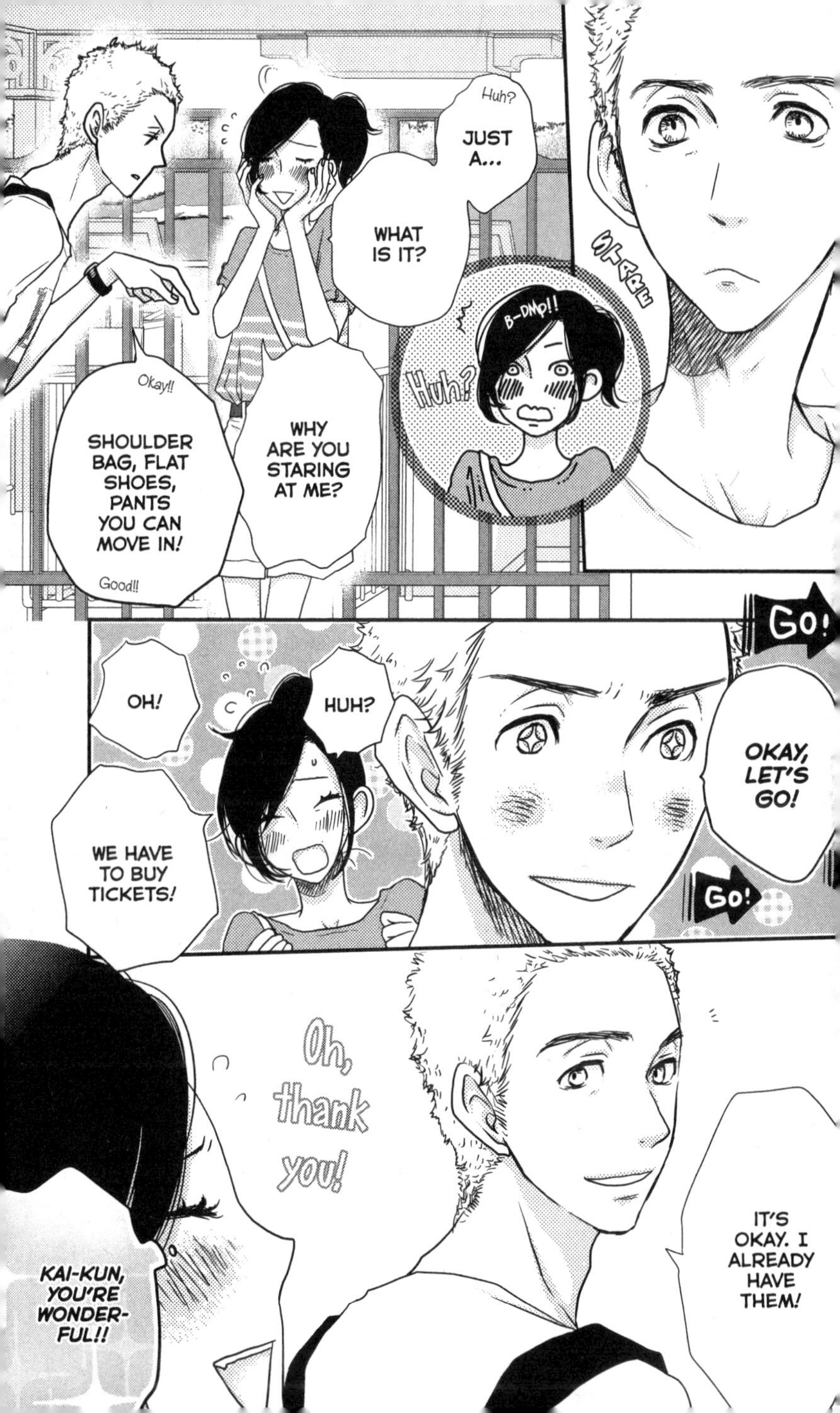
STARE
Huh?
JUST A...
WHAT IS IT?
B-DMP!!
Huh?
WHY ARE YOU STARING AT ME?
Okay!!
SHOULDER BAG, FLAT SHOES, PANTS YOU CAN MOVE IN!
Good!!
GO!
OKAY, LET'S GO!
GO!
HUH?
OH!
WE HAVE TO BUY TICKETS!
IT'S OKAY. I ALREADY HAVE THEM!
Oh, thank you!
KAI-KUN, YOU'RE WONDER-FUL!!

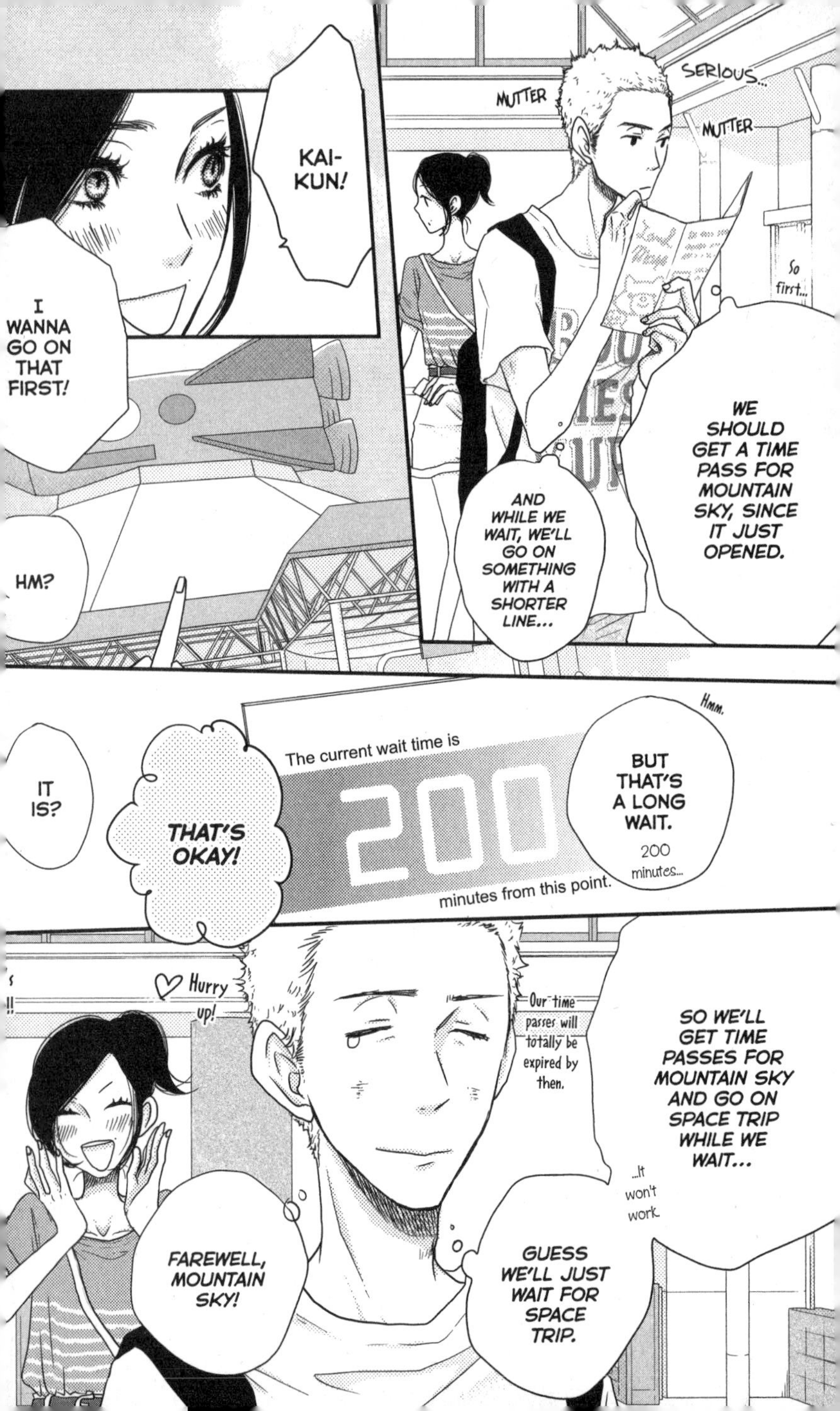
SERIOUS...
MUTTER
MUTTER
So first...
WE SHOULD GET A TIME PASS FOR MOUNTAIN SKY, SINCE IT JUST OPENED.
AND WHILE WE WAIT, WE'LL GO ON SOMETHING WITH A SHORTER LINE...
KAI-KUN!
I WANNA GO ON THAT FIRST!
HM?
Hmm.
BUT THAT'S A LONG WAIT.
200 minutes...
The current wait time is
200
minutes from this point.
THAT'S OKAY!
IT IS?
SO WE'LL GET TIME PASSES FOR MOUNTAIN SKY AND GO ON SPACE TRIP WHILE WE WAIT...
...It won't work.
Our time passes will totally be expired by then.
GUESS WE'LL JUST WAIT FOR SPACE TRIP.
Hurry up!
FAREWELL, MOUNTAIN SKY!

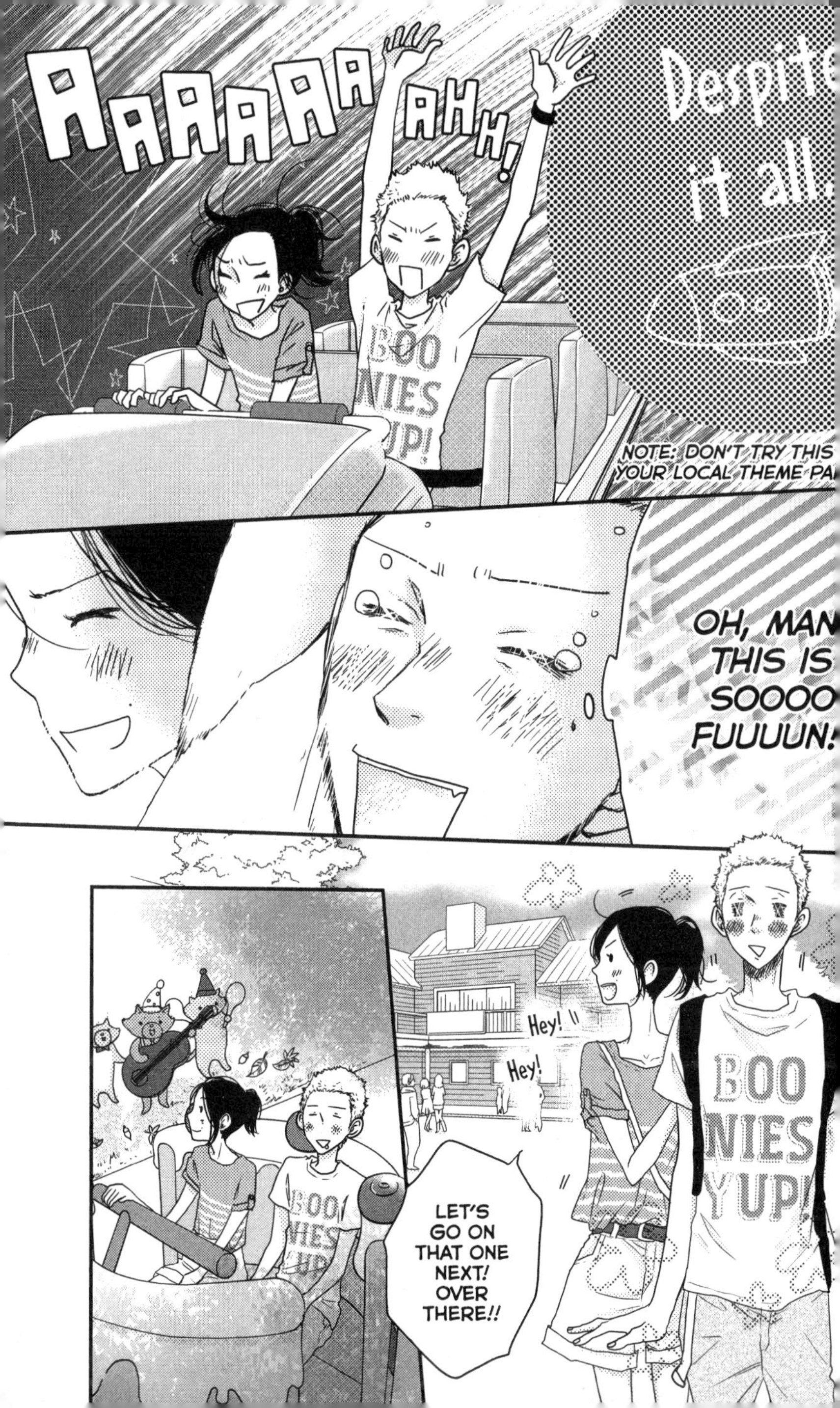
Despite it all.
AAAAAAAAHH!
NOTE: DON'T TRY THIS
YOUR LOCAL THEME PA
OH, MAN THIS IS SOOOO FUUUUN!
Hey!
Hey!
LET'S GO ON THAT ONE NEXT! OVER THERE!!

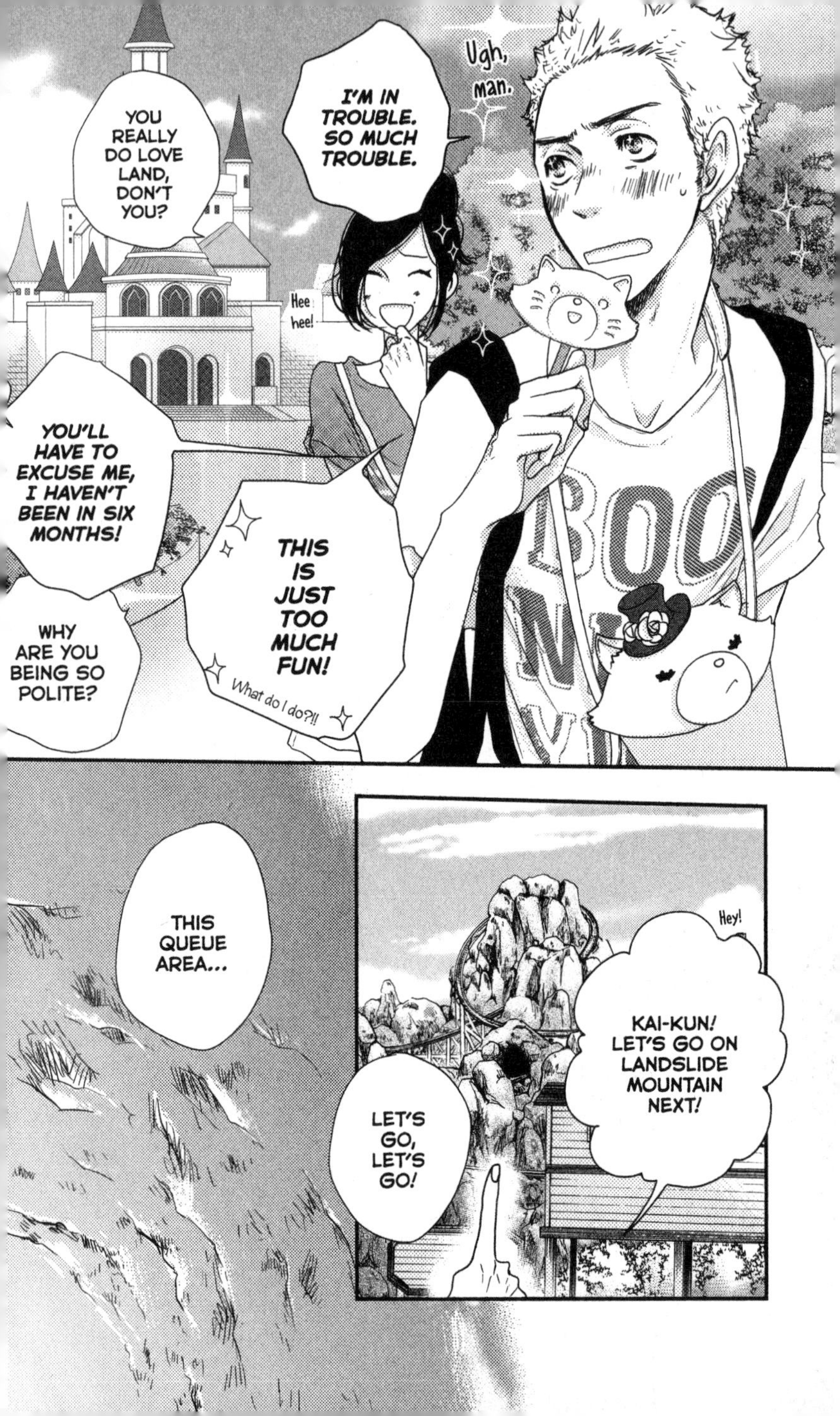
Ugh, man.
I'M IN TROUBLE. SO MUCH TROUBLE.
YOU REALLY DO LOVE LAND, DON'T YOU?
Hee hee!
THIS IS JUST TOO MUCH FUN!
What do I do?!!
YOU'LL HAVE TO EXCUSE ME, I HAVEN'T BEEN IN SIX MONTHS!
WHY ARE YOU BEING SO POLITE?
Hey!
KAI-KUN! LET'S GO ON LANDSLIDE MOUNTAIN NEXT!
LET'S GO, LET'S GO!
THIS QUEUE AREA...

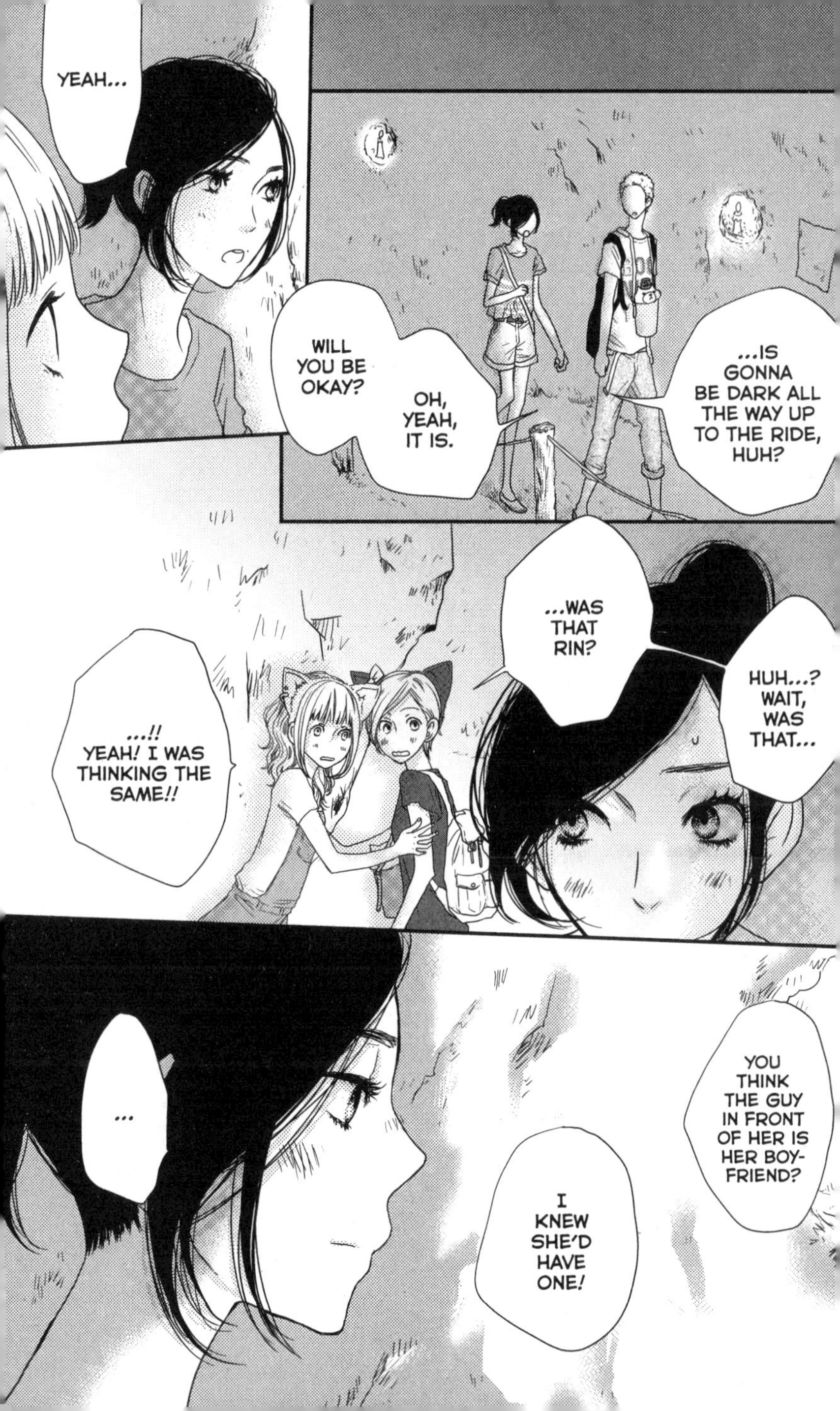
...IS GONNA BE DARK ALL THE WAY UP TO THE RIDE, HUH?
OH, YEAH, IT IS.
WILL YOU BE OKAY?
YEAH...
HUH...? WAIT, WAS THAT...
...WAS THAT RIN?
...!! YEAH! I WAS THINKING THE SAME!!
YOU THINK THE GUY IN FRONT OF HER IS HER BOY-FRIEND?
I KNEW SHE'D HAVE ONE!
...

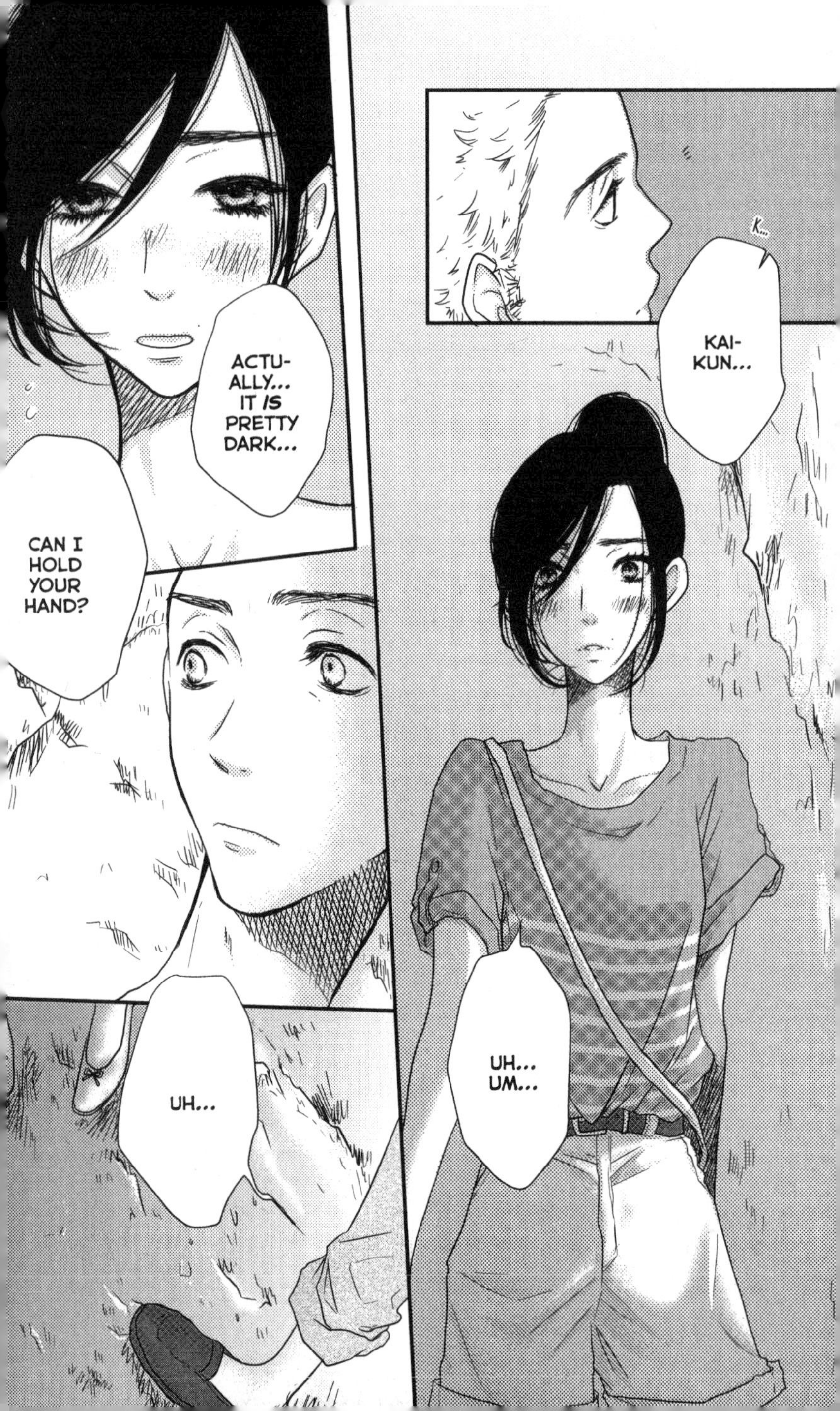

K...
KAI-KUN...
UH... UM...
ACTU-ALLY... IT *IS* PRETTY DARK...
CAN I HOLD YOUR HAND?
UH...

No...

IT'S OKAY!

SORRY FOR JUST BARGING ON AHEAD.

YEAH. IT *IS* DARK.

THANKS ...

WHOOOOOOSH

CRASH

POW P

THAT'S ALL I CAN THINK ABOUT.

THE WARMTH FROM HER SLENDER HAND...

LIKE SHE'S ENJOYING LETTING ME BE THE ONE TO HOLD HER HAND.

SHE'S HOLDING ON JUST TIGHT ENOUGH THAT IF I LET GO, OUR HANDS WILL COME APART.

RUMBLE

RUMBLE

RUMBLE

AAAAHH!

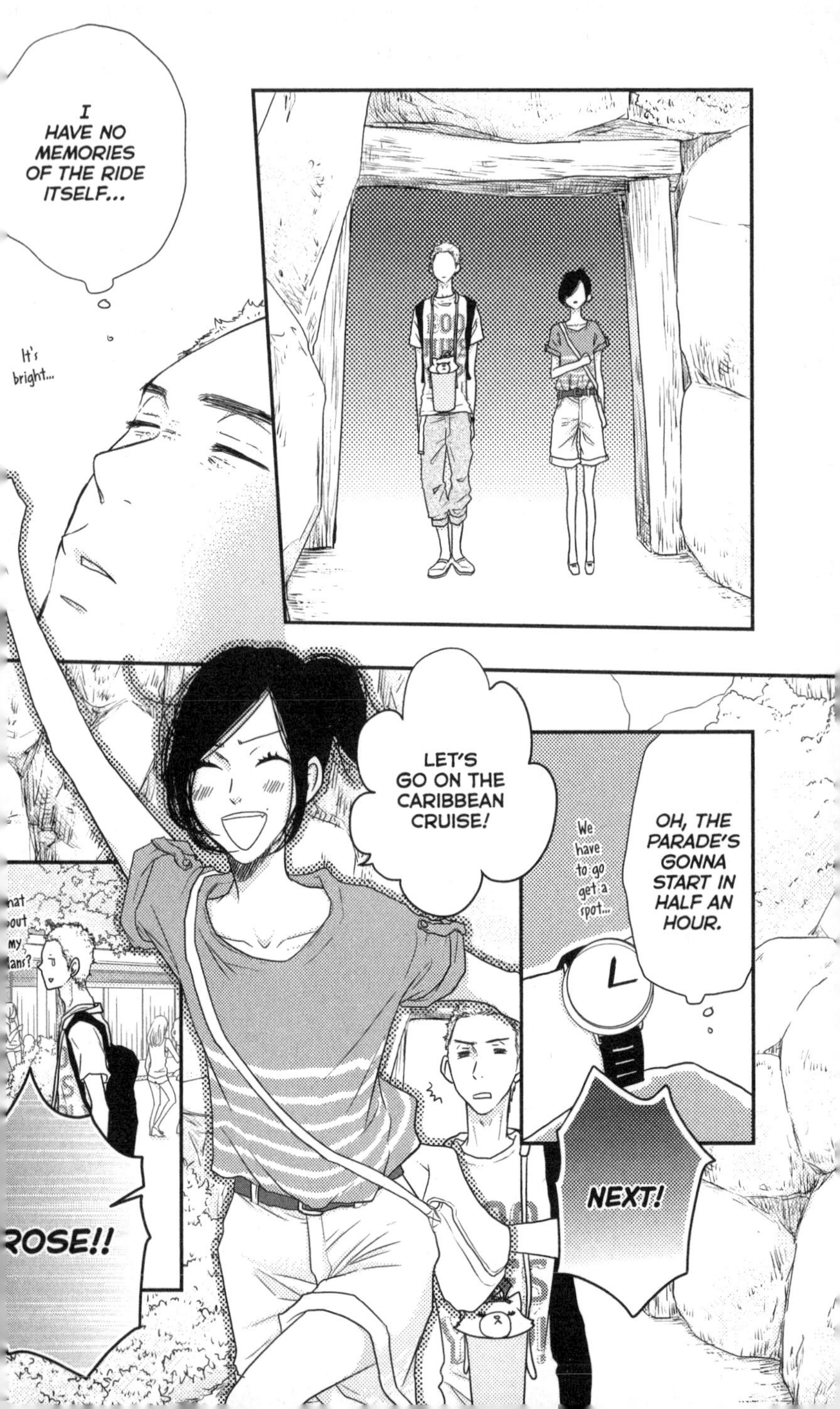

I HAVE NO MEMORIES OF THE RIDE ITSELF...
It's bright...
OH, THE PARADE'S GONNA START IN HALF AN HOUR.
We have to go get a spot...
NEXT!
LET'S GO ON THE CARIBBEAN CRUISE!
ROSE!!

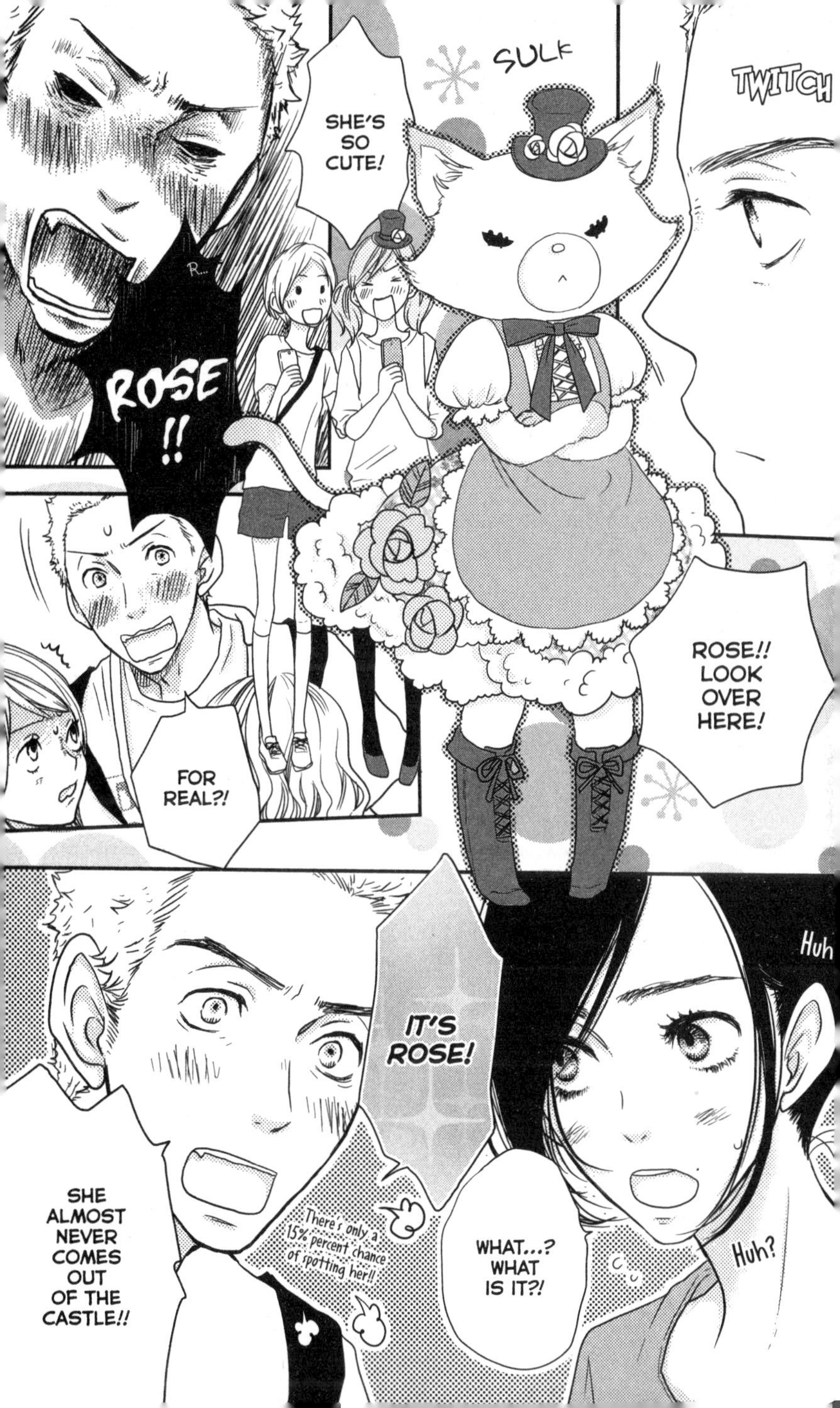
TWITCH
SULK
SHE'S SO CUTE!
ROSE!! LOOK OVER HERE!
R...
ROSE!!
FOR REAL?!
Huh
Huh?
WHAT...? WHAT IS IT?!
IT'S ROSE!
There's only a 15% percent chance of spotting her!!
SHE ALMOST NEVER COMES OUT OF THE CASTLE!!

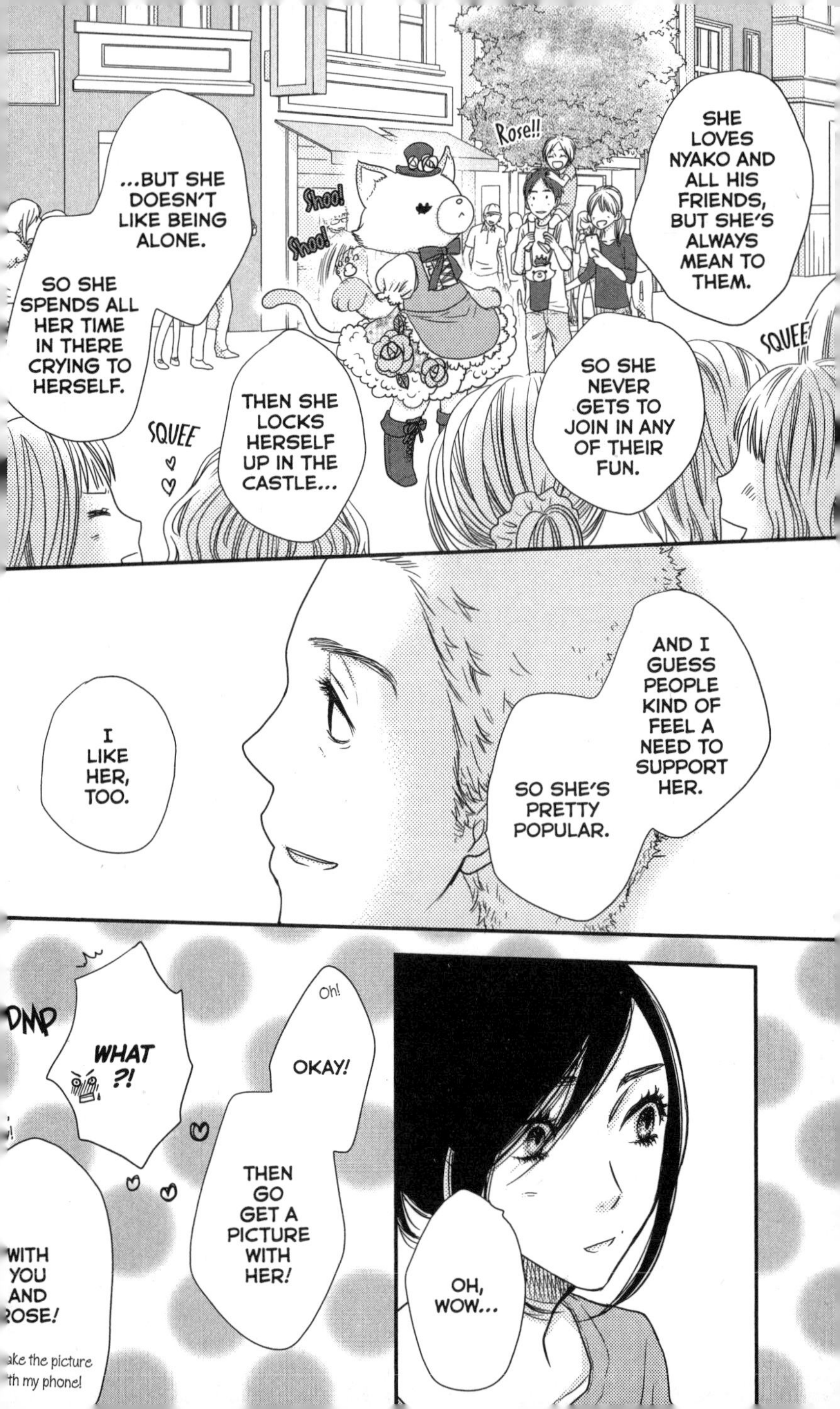
SHE LOVES NYAKO AND ALL HIS FRIENDS, BUT SHE'S ALWAYS MEAN TO THEM.
Rose!!
SQUEE
SO SHE NEVER GETS TO JOIN IN ANY OF THEIR FUN.
Shoo!
Shoo!
THEN SHE LOCKS HERSELF UP IN THE CASTLE...
...BUT SHE DOESN'T LIKE BEING ALONE.
SO SHE SPENDS ALL HER TIME IN THERE CRYING TO HERSELF.
SQUEE
AND I GUESS PEOPLE KIND OF FEEL A NEED TO SUPPORT HER.
SO SHE'S PRETTY POPULAR.
I LIKE HER, TOO.
OH, WOW...
Oh!
OKAY!
THEN GO GET A PICTURE WITH HER!
WHAT ?!
DMP
WITH YOU AND ROSE!

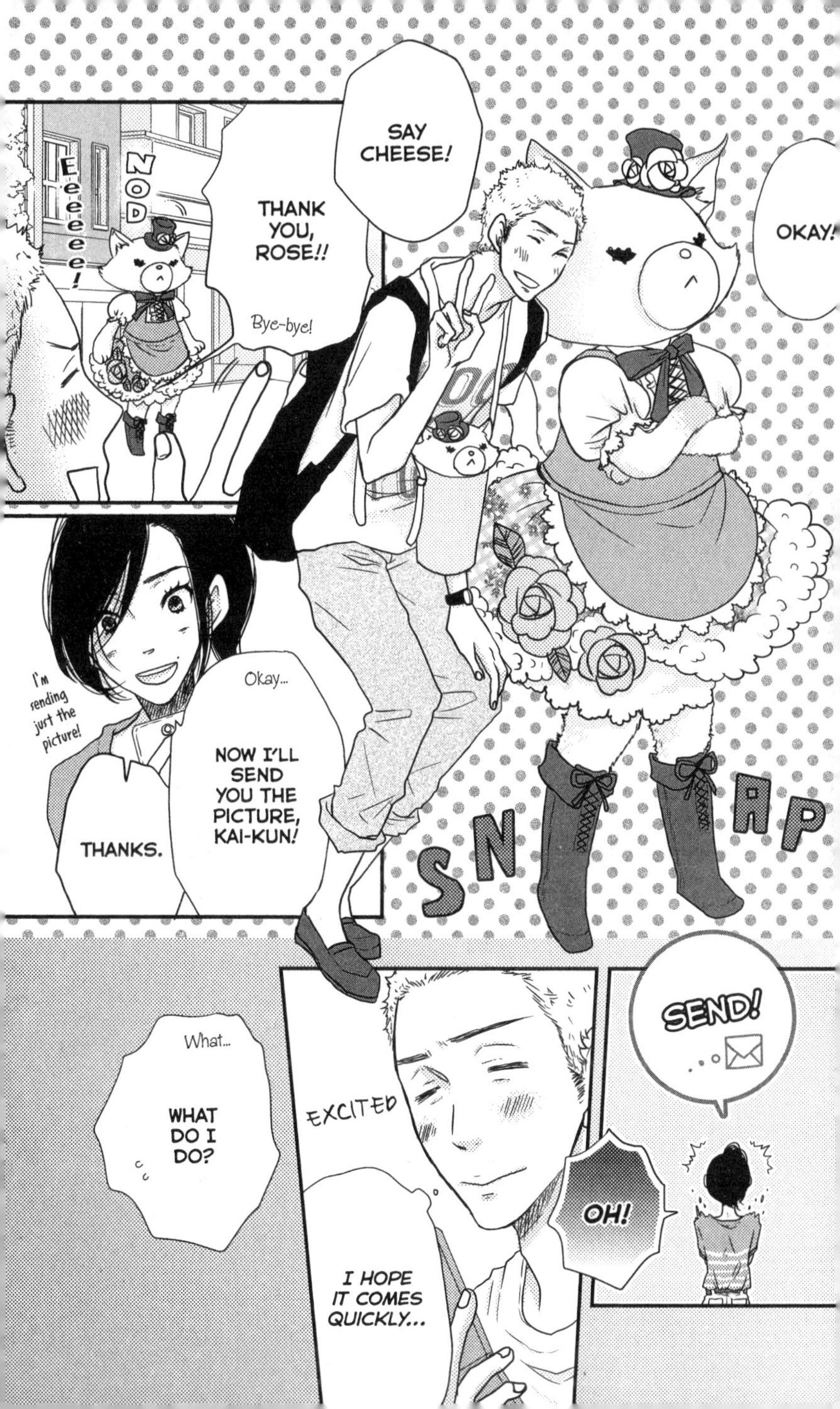
OKAY!
SAY CHEESE!
SNAP
THANK YOU, ROSE!!
NOD
Eeeeee!
Bye-bye!
Okay...
NOW I'LL SEND YOU THE PICTURE, KAI-KUN!
THANKS.
I'm sending just the picture!
SEND!
OH!
EXCITED
I HOPE IT COMES QUICKLY...
What...
WHAT DO I DO?

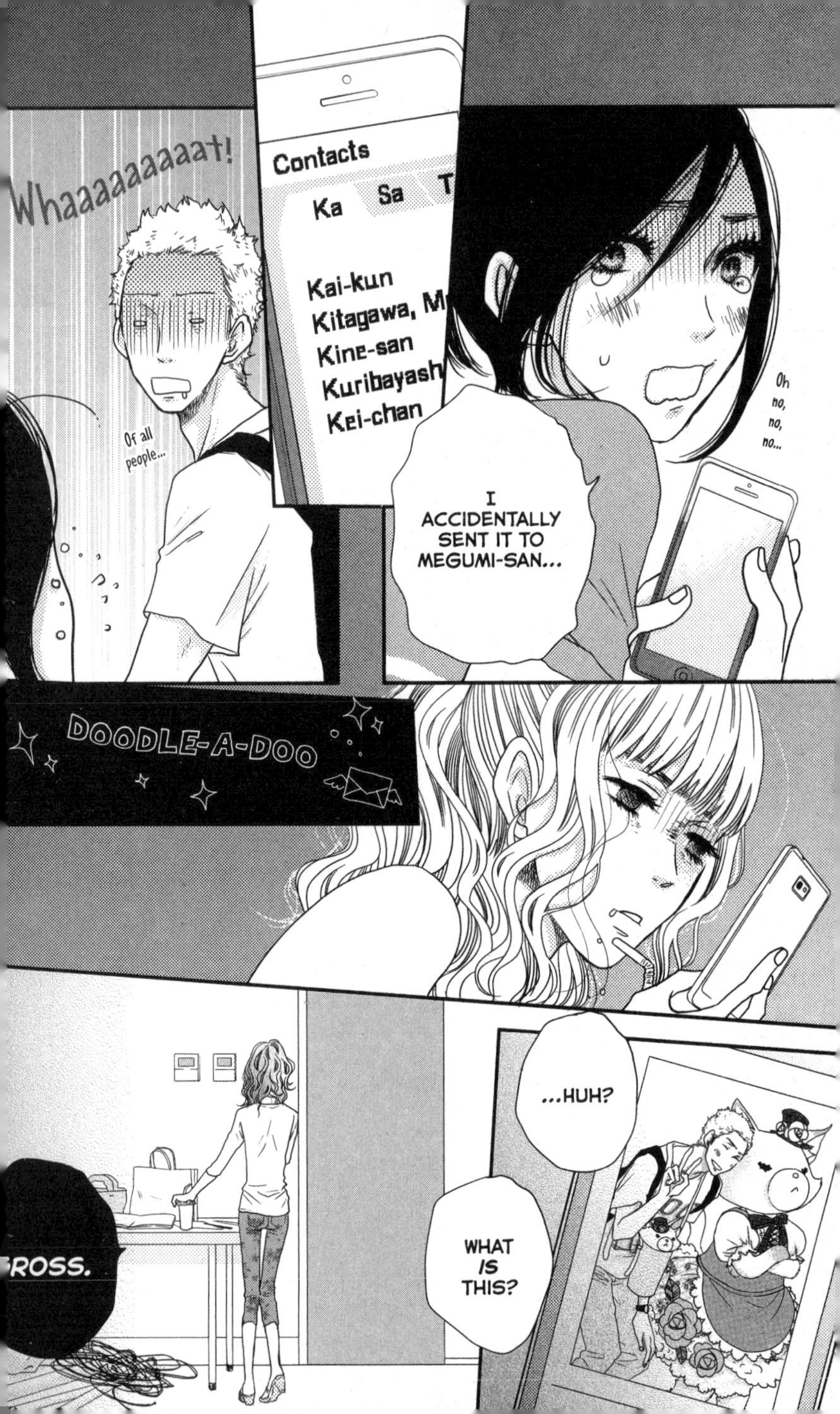

Oh no, no, no...
I ACCIDENTALLY SENT IT TO MEGUMI-SAN...
Contacts
Ka Sa T
Kai-kun
Kitagawa, M
Kine-san
Kuribayash
Kei-chan
Whaaaaaaaaat!
Of all people...
DOODLE-A-DOO
...HUH?
WHAT IS THIS?
ROSS.

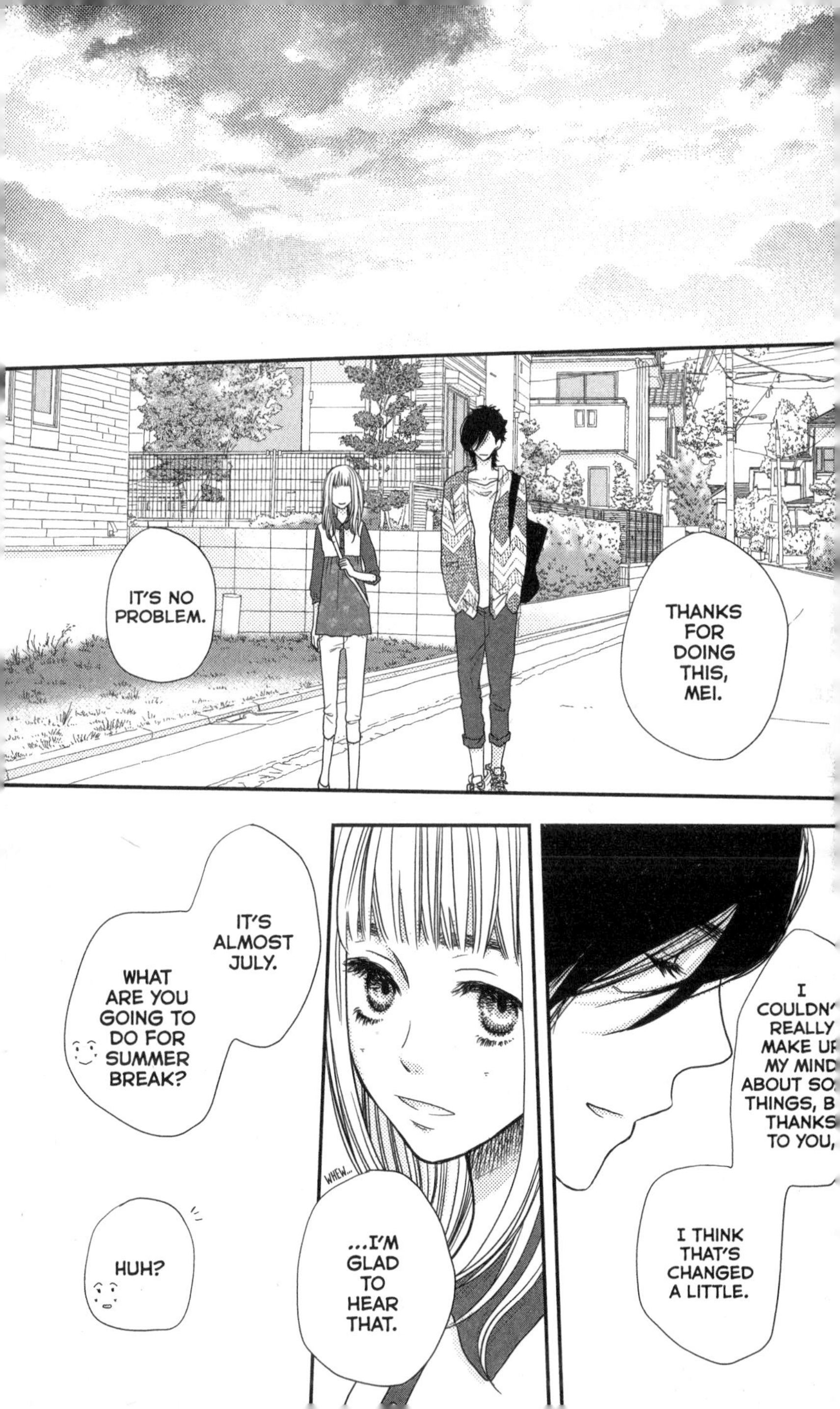
THANKS FOR DOING THIS, MEI.
IT'S NO PROBLEM.
I COULDN' REALLY MAKE UI MY MIND ABOUT SO THINGS, B THANKS TO YOU,
I THINK THAT'S CHANGED A LITTLE.
WHEW...
...I'M GLAD TO HEAR THAT.
IT'S ALMOST JULY.
WHAT ARE YOU GOING TO DO FOR SUMMER BREAK?
HUH?

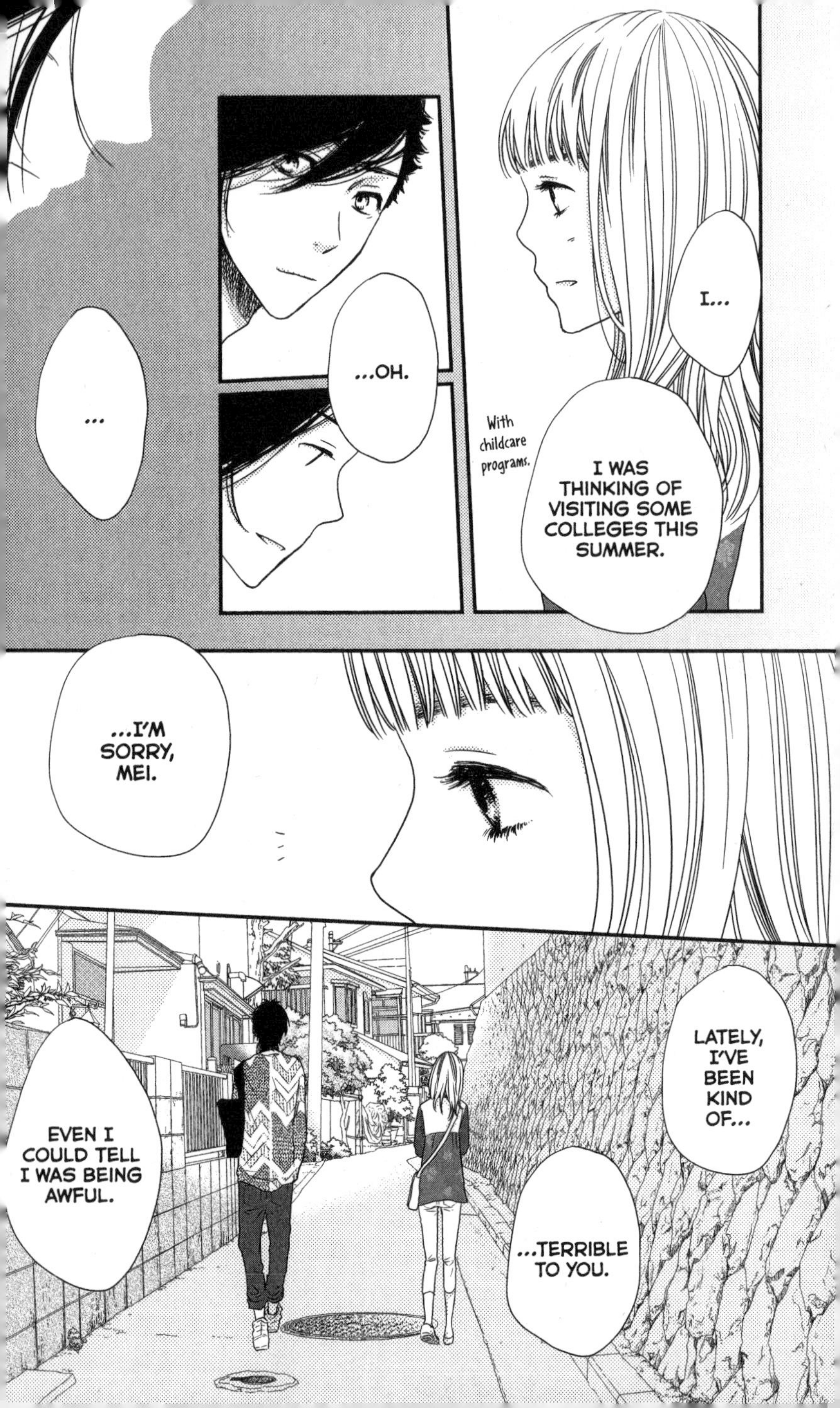
I...
I WAS THINKING OF VISITING SOME COLLEGES THIS SUMMER.
With childcare programs.
...OH.
...
...I'M SORRY, MEI.
LATELY, I'VE BEEN KIND OF...
...TERRIBLE TO YOU.
EVEN I COULD TELL I WAS BEING AWFUL.

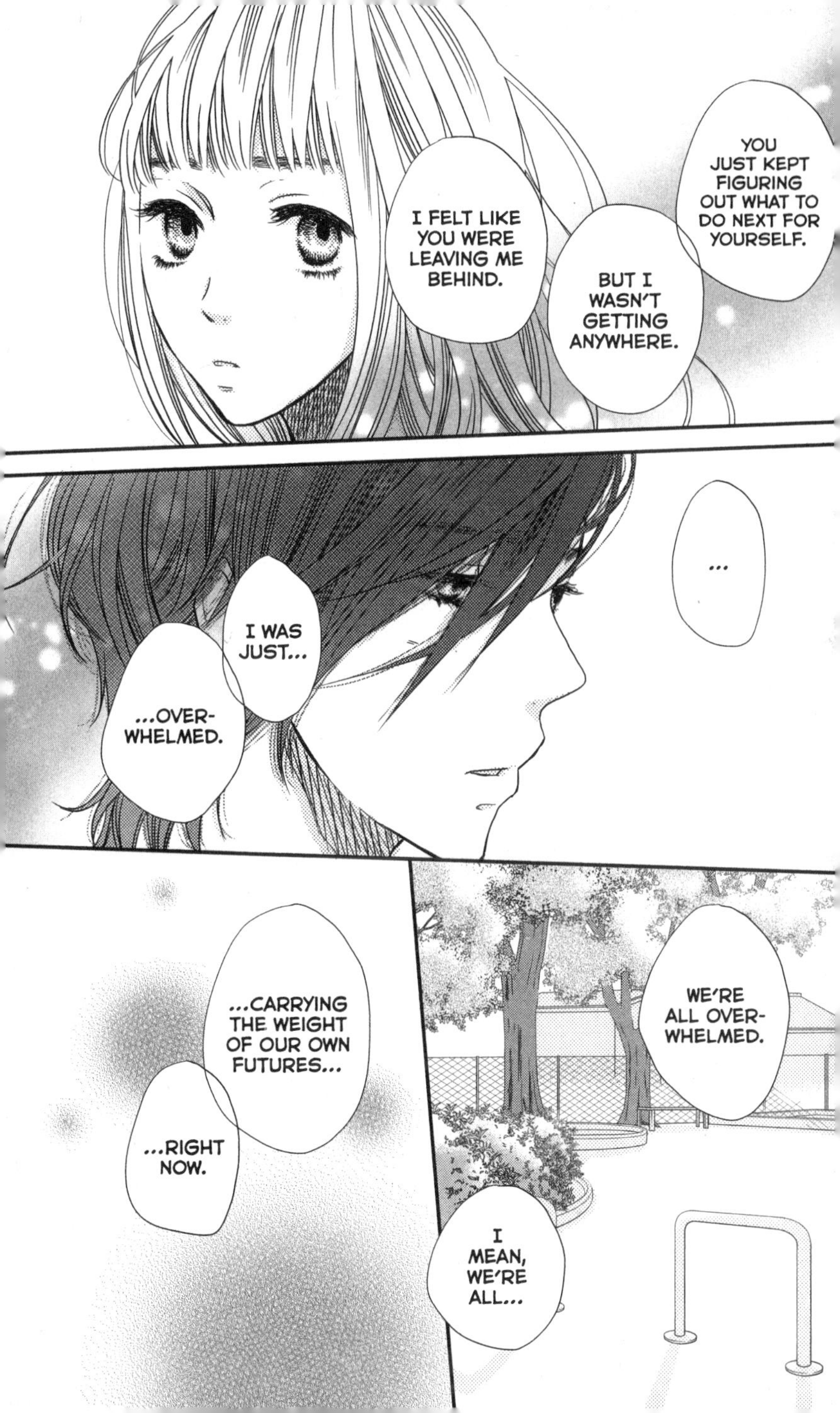
YOU JUST KEPT FIGURING OUT WHAT TO DO NEXT FOR YOURSELF.
BUT I WASN'T GETTING ANYWHERE.
I FELT LIKE YOU WERE LEAVING ME BEHIND.
...
I WAS JUST...
...OVER-WHELMED.
WE'RE ALL OVER-WHELMED.
I MEAN, WE'RE ALL...
...CARRYING THE WEIGHT OF OUR OWN FUTURES...
...RIGHT NOW.

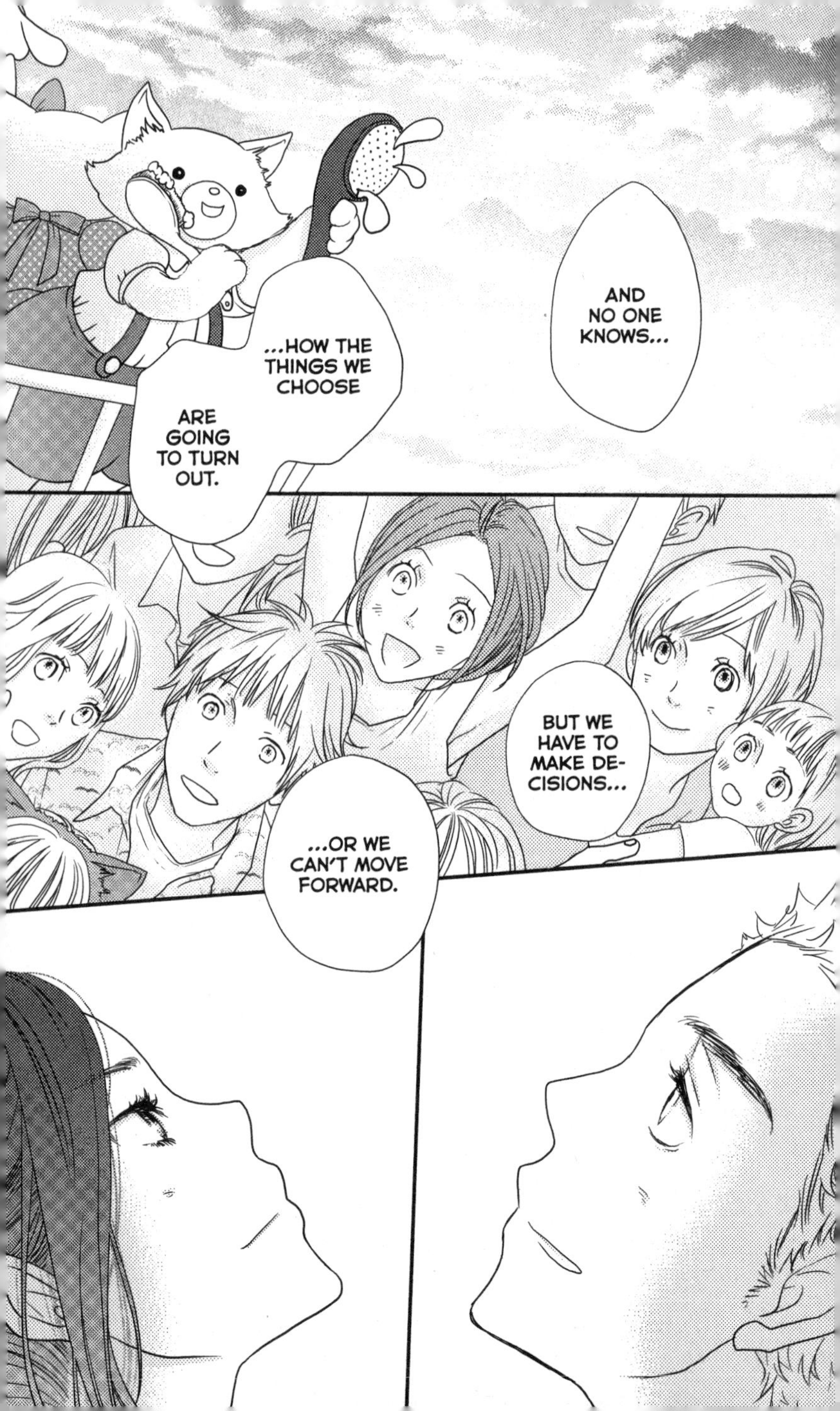
AND NO ONE KNOWS...
...HOW THE THINGS WE CHOOSE
ARE GOING TO TURN OUT.
BUT WE HAVE TO MAKE DE-CISIONS...
...OR WE CAN'T MOVE FORWARD.

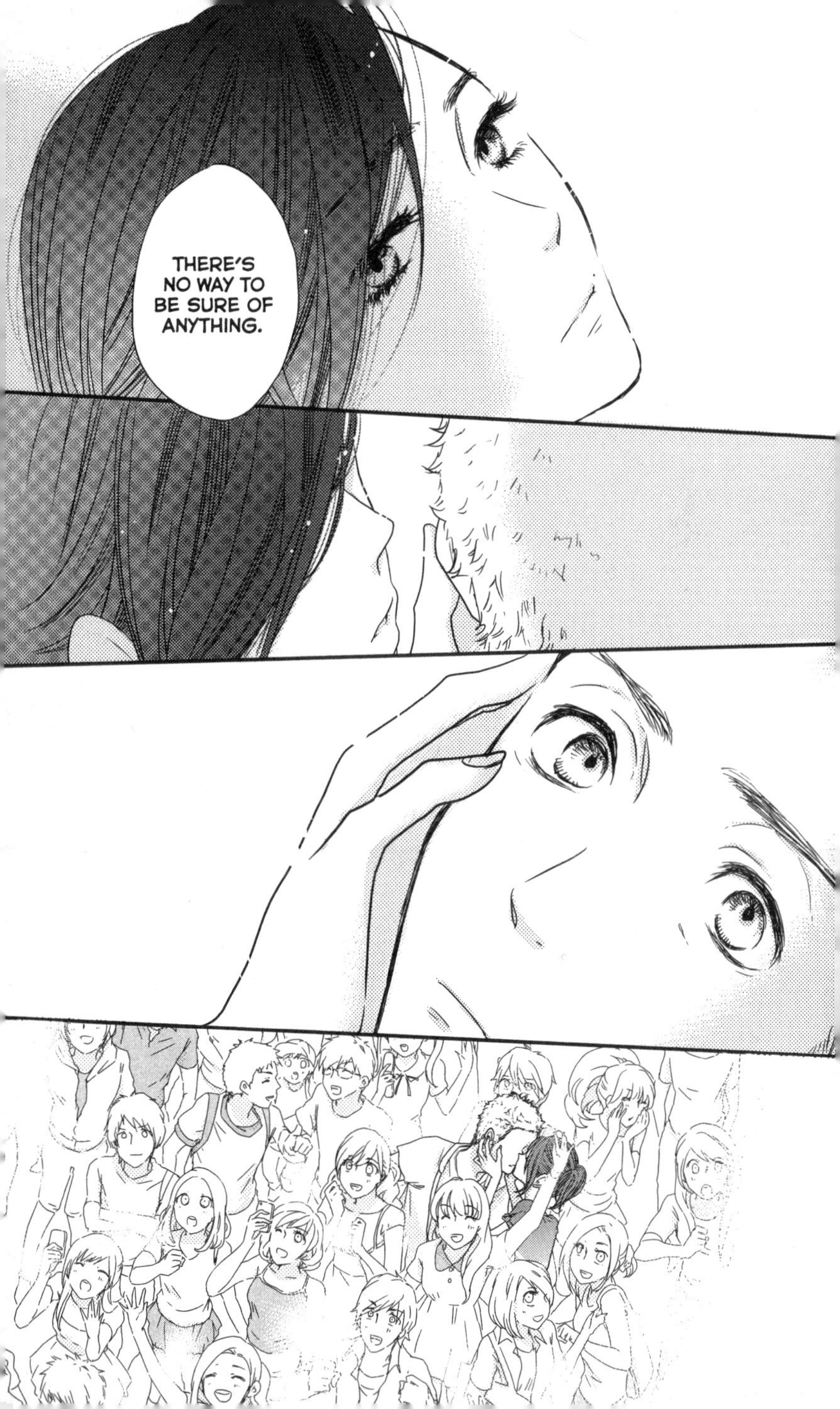
THERE'S NO WAY TO BE SURE OF ANYTHING.

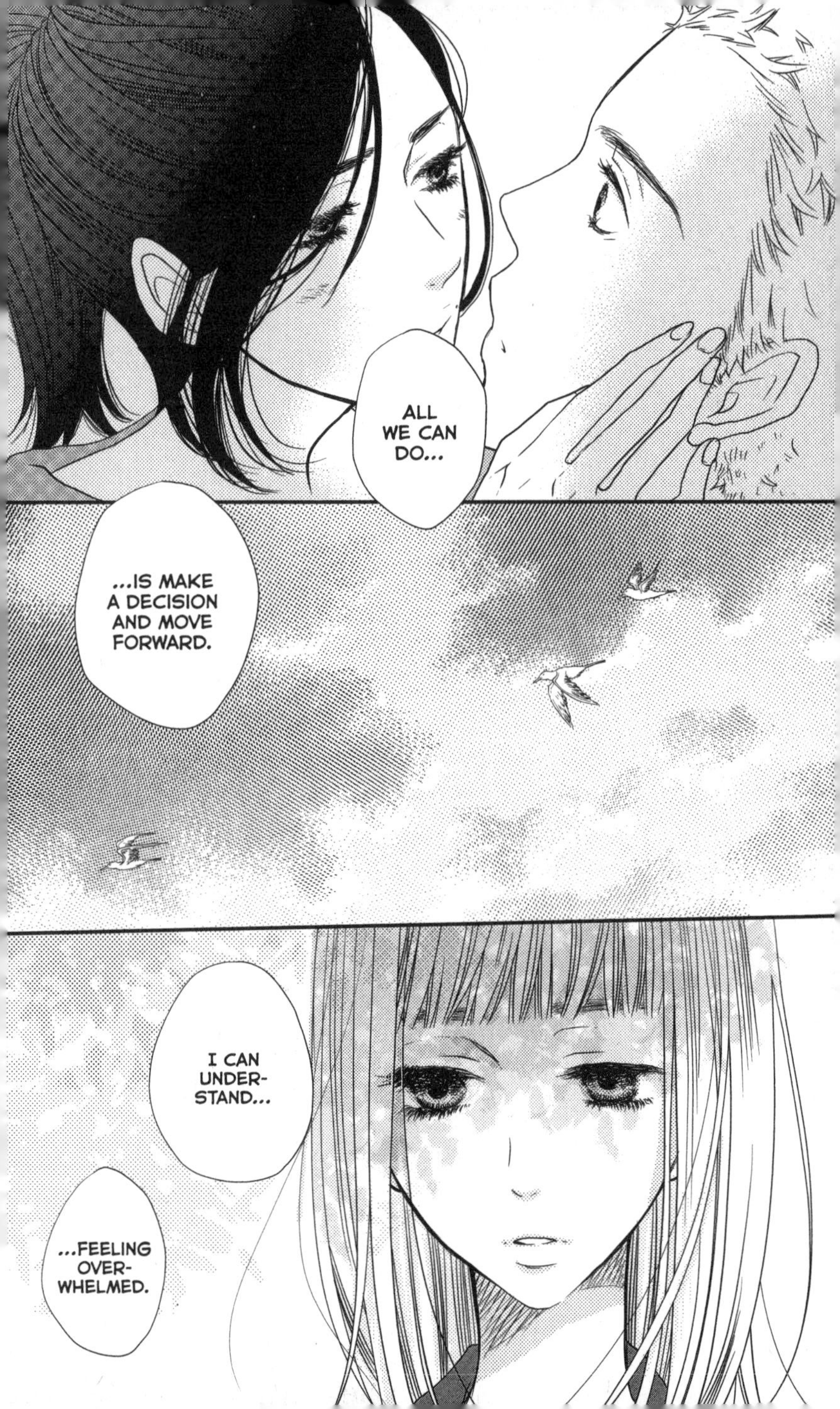
ALL WE CAN DO...
...IS MAKE A DECISION AND MOVE FORWARD.
I CAN UNDERSTAND...
...FEELING OVERWHELMED.

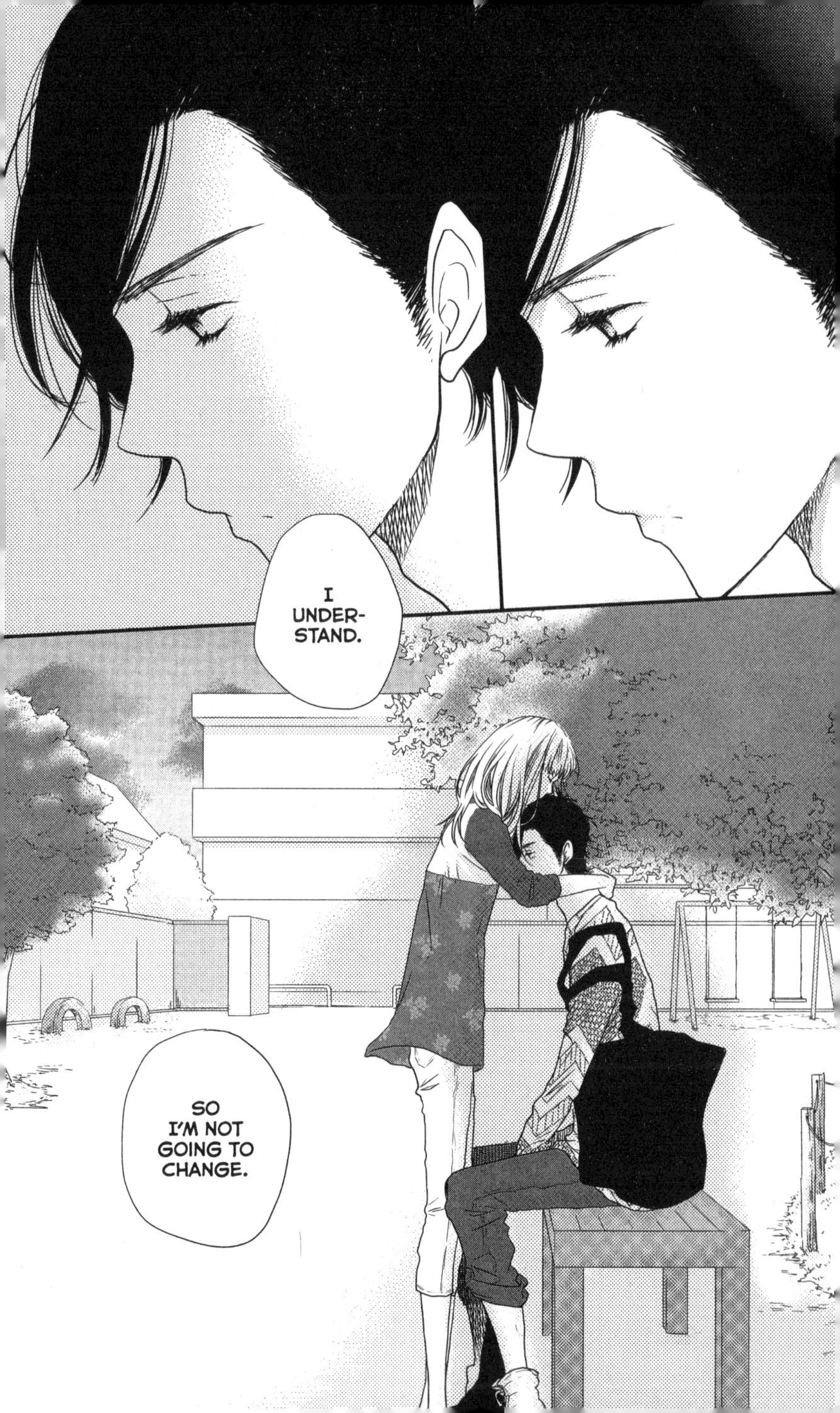
I UNDER-STAND.
SO I'M NOT GOING TO CHANGE.

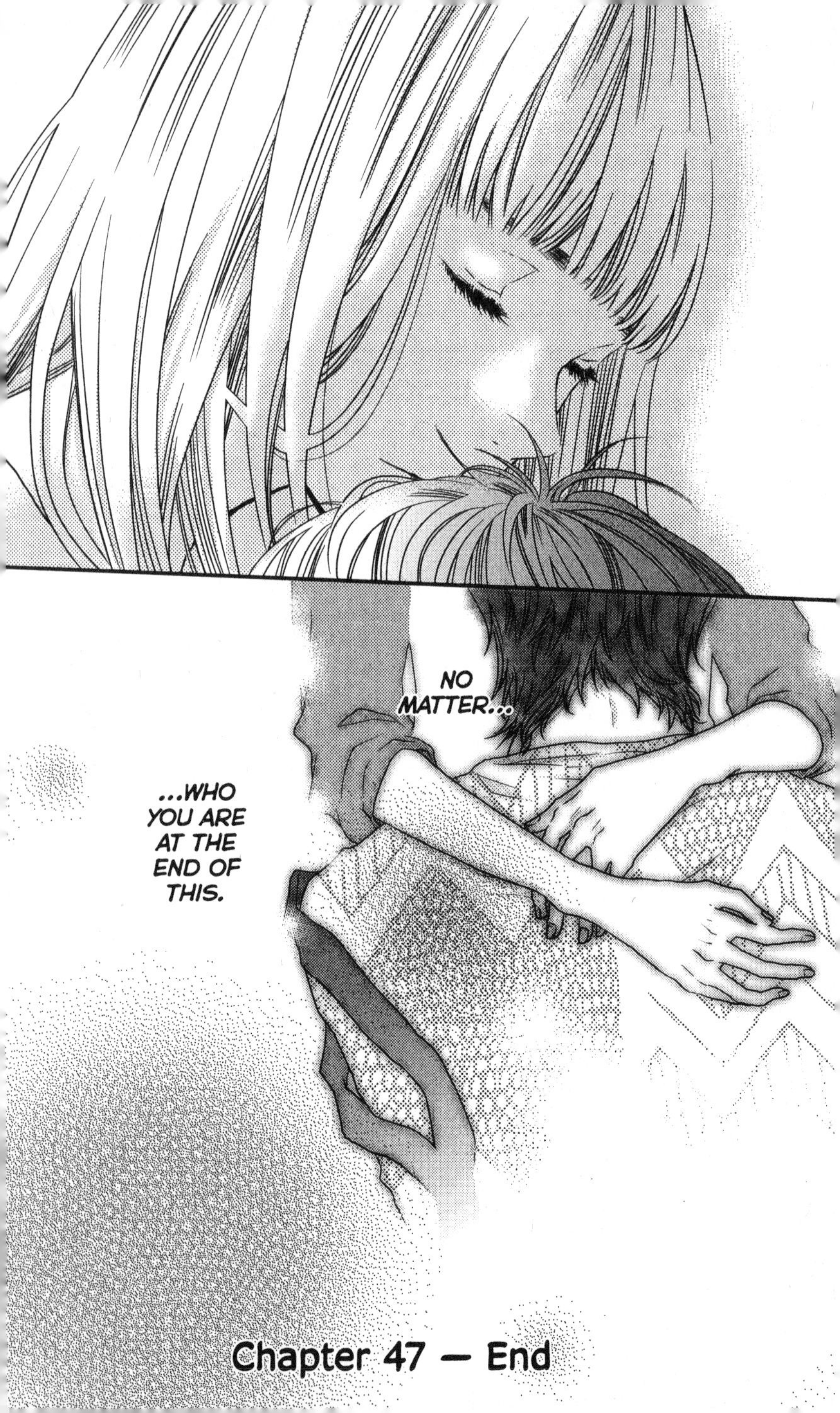
NO MATTER...
...WHO YOU ARE AT THE END OF THIS.

Chapter 47 — End

Say "I love you".

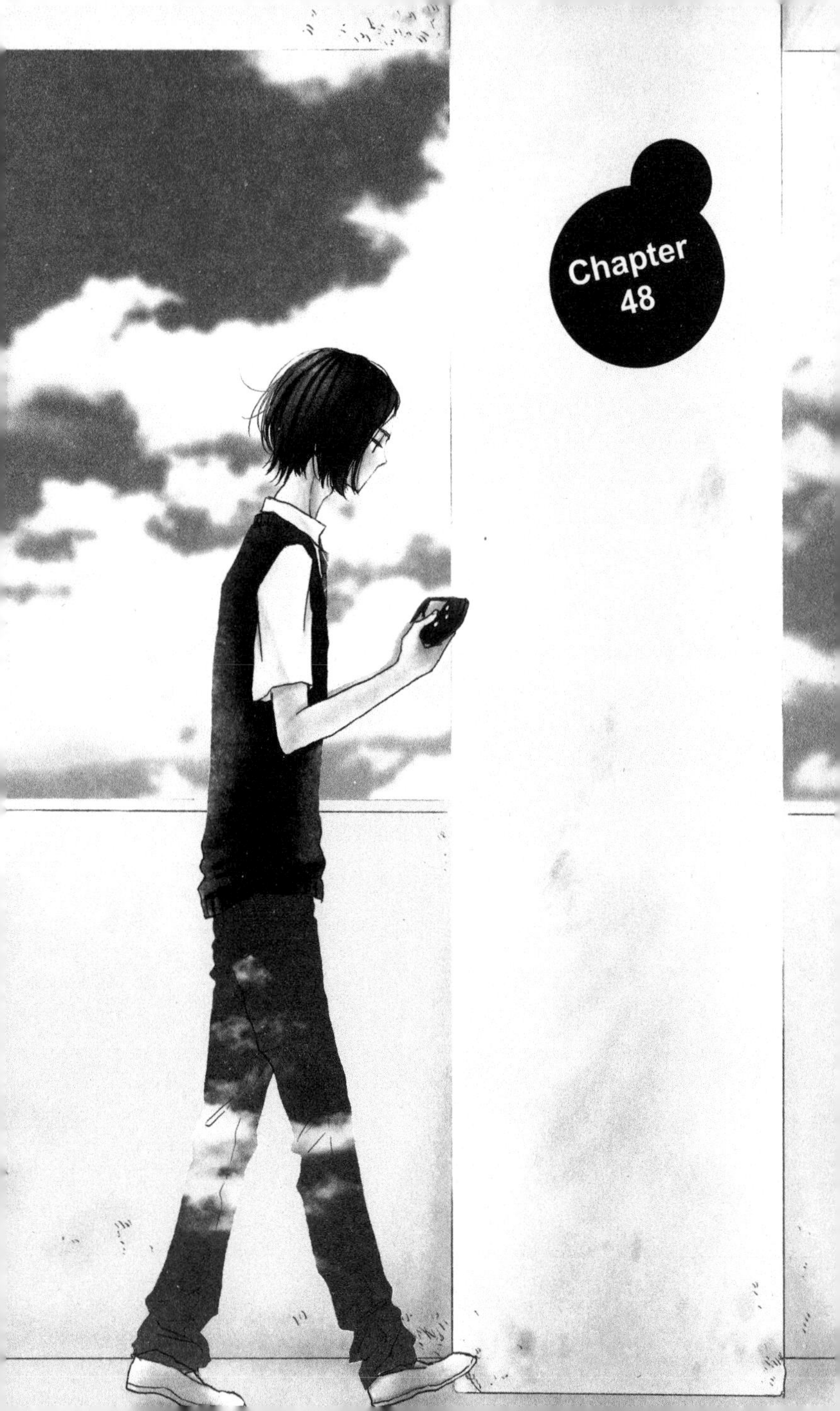
Chapter 48

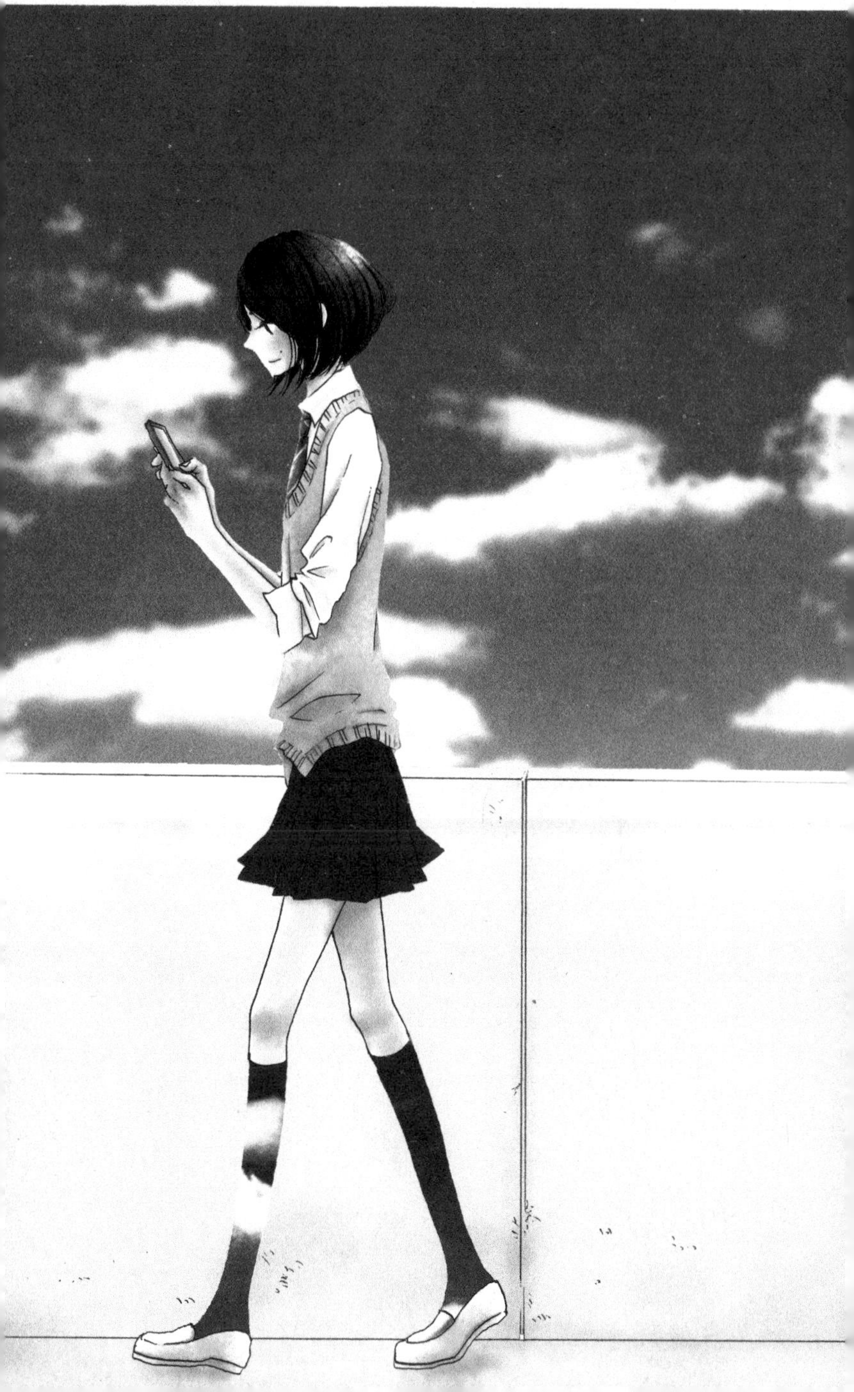

Say "I love you".

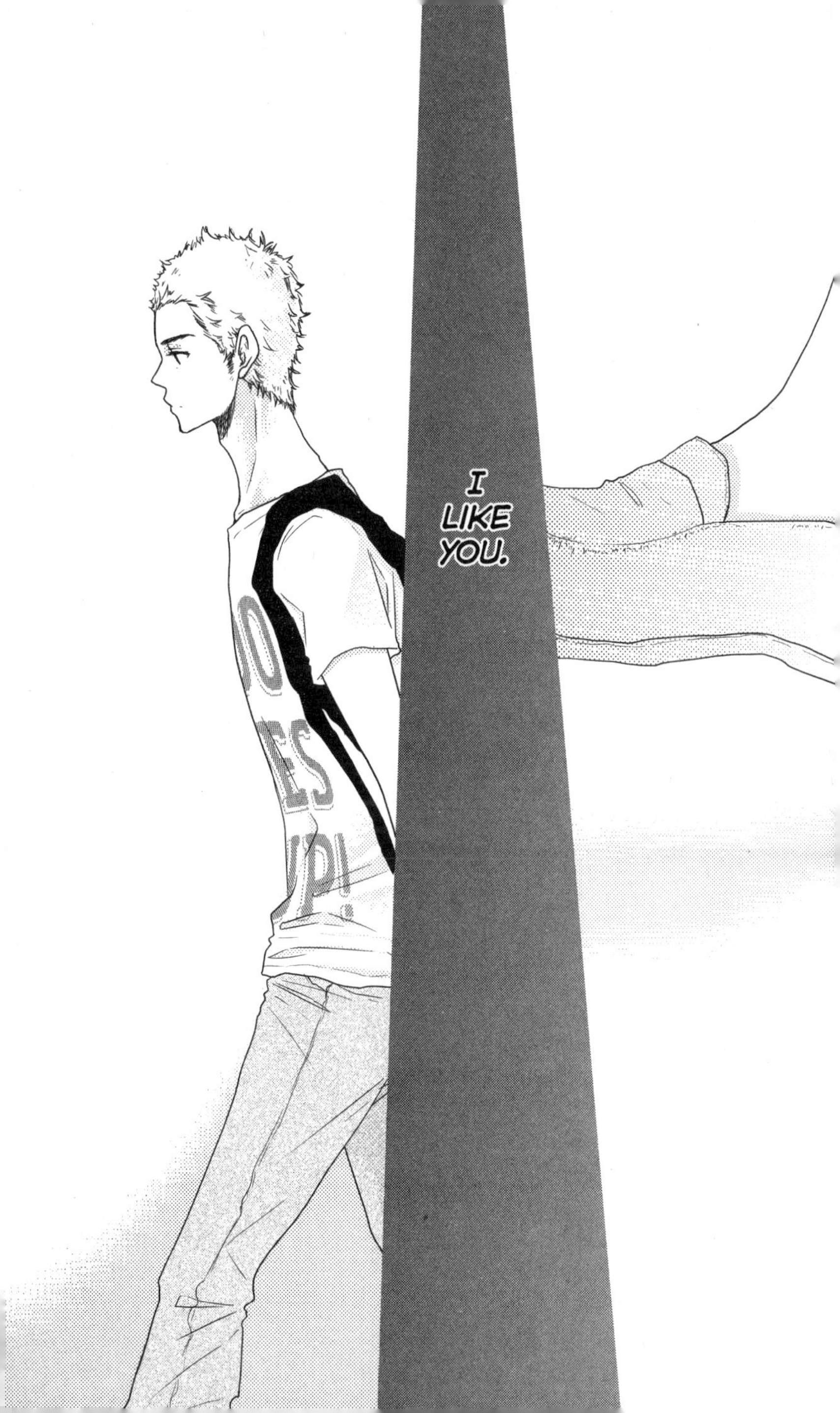
I LIKE YOU.

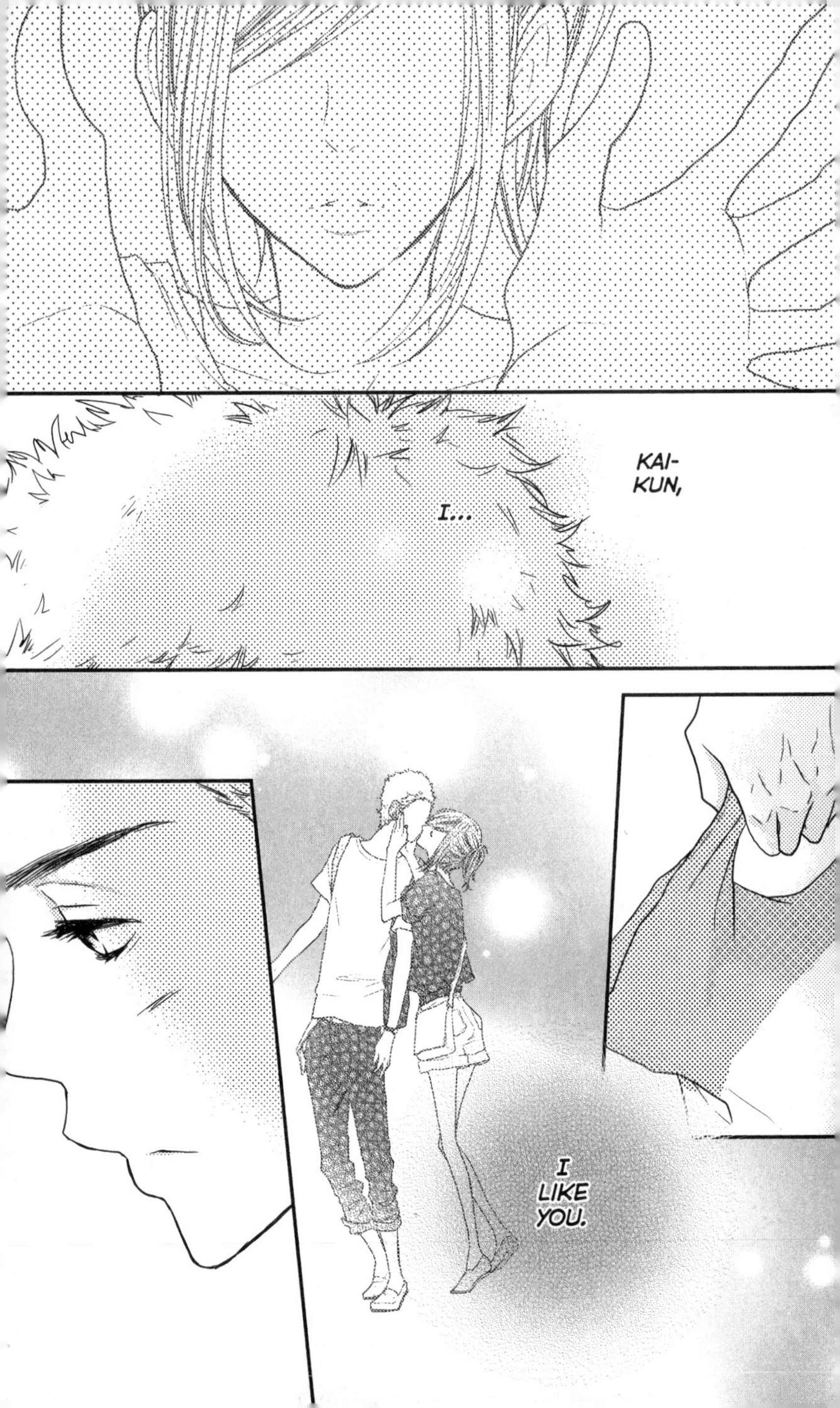
KAI-KUN,
I...
I LIKE YOU.

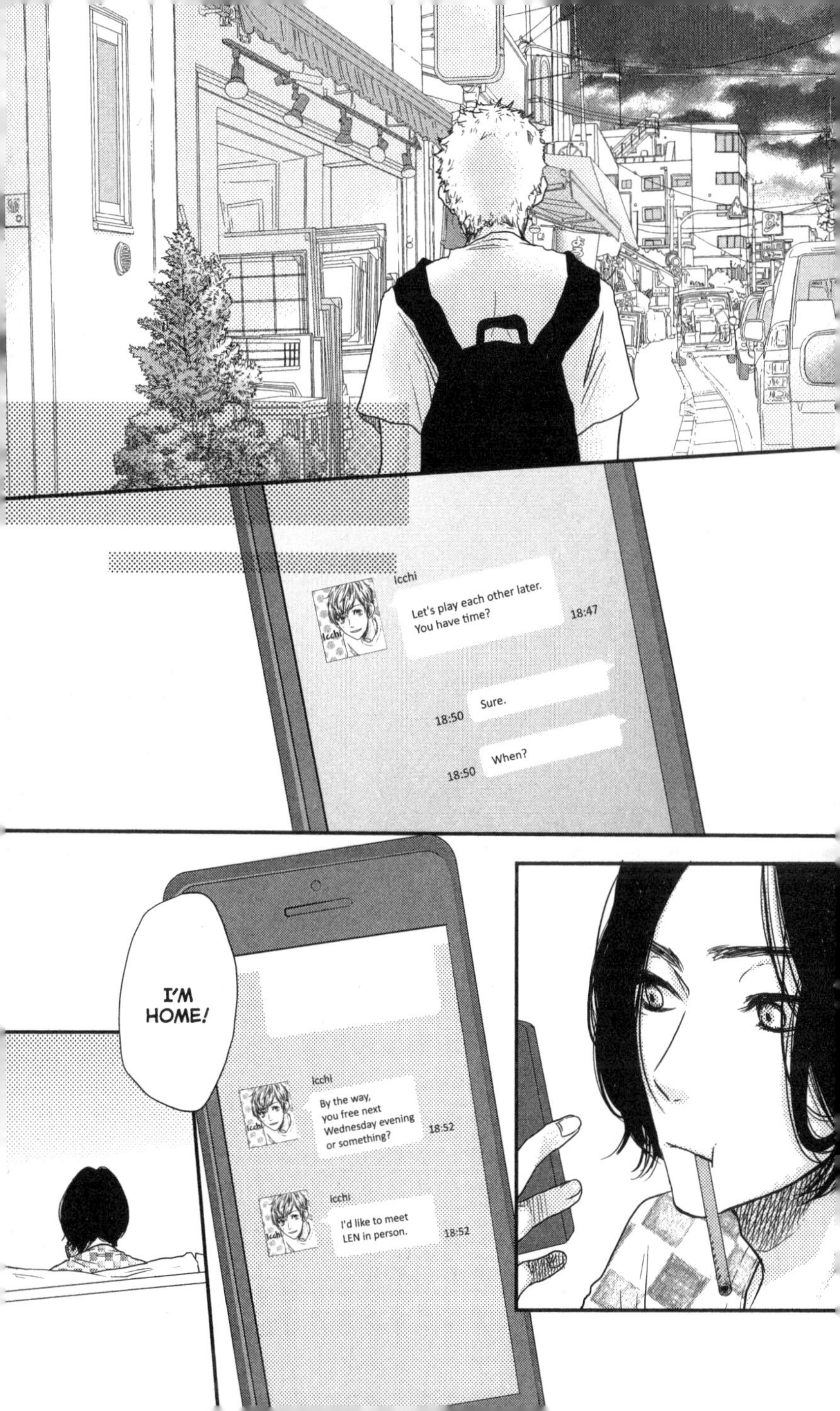
Icchi
Let's play each other later. You have time?
18:47
Sure.
18:50
When?
18:50
I'M HOME!
Icchi
By the way, you free next Wednesday evening or something?
18:52
Icchi
I'd like to meet LEN in person.
18:52

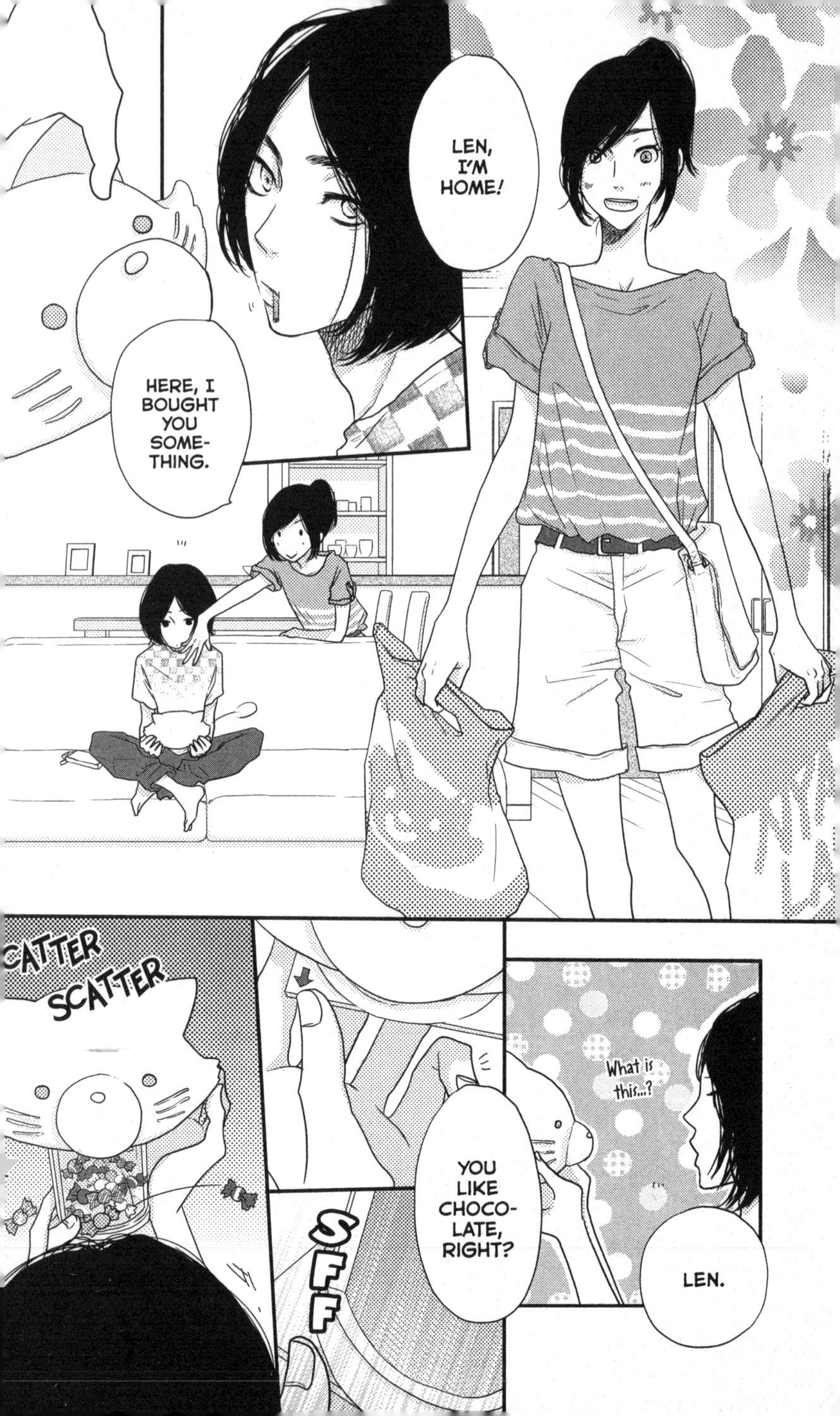
LEN, I'M HOME!
HERE, I BOUGHT YOU SOMETHING.
What is this...?
LEN.
YOU LIKE CHOCOLATE, RIGHT?
SFF
SCATTER SCATTER

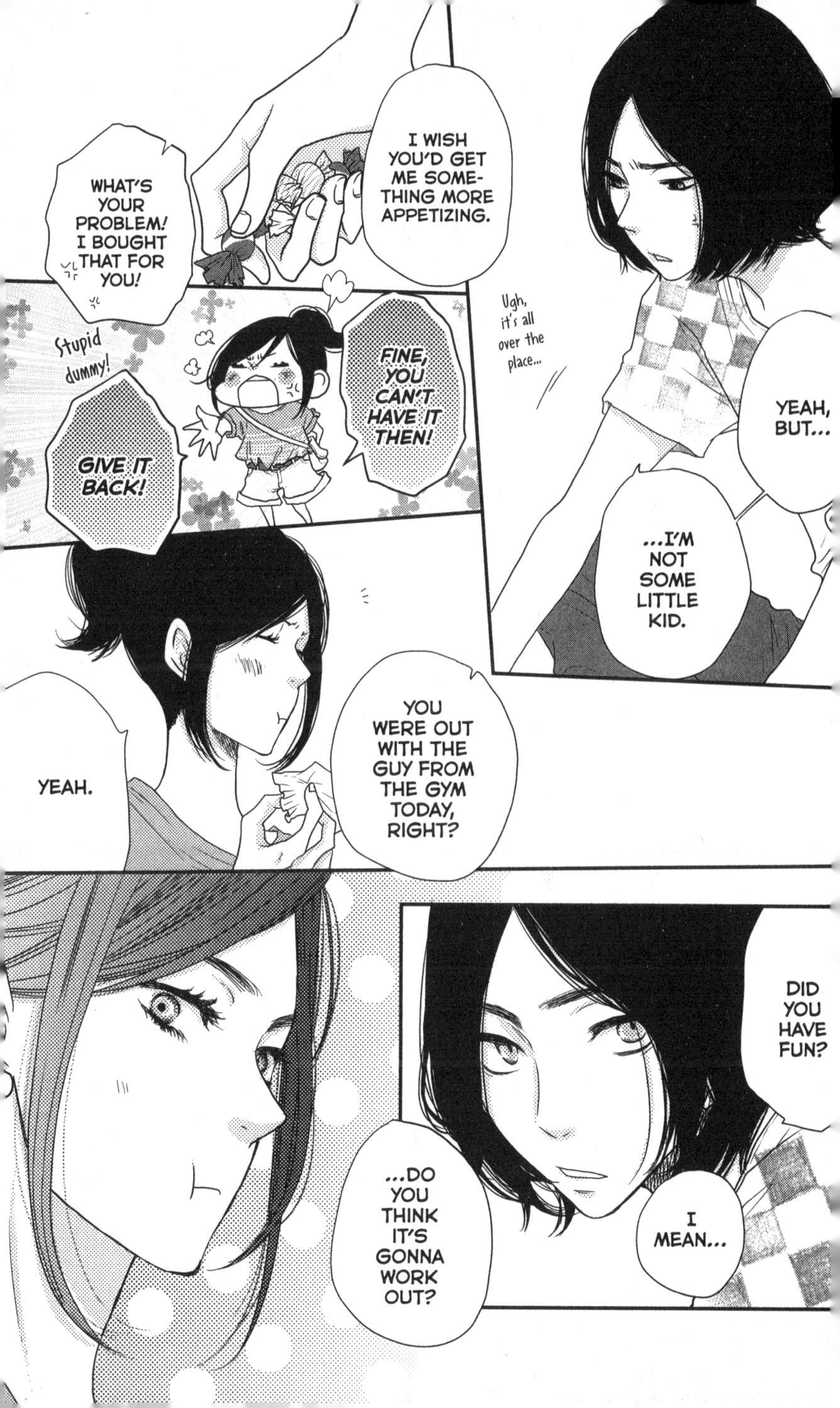
Ugh, it's all over the place...
YEAH, BUT...
...I'M NOT SOME LITTLE KID.
I WISH YOU'D GET ME SOME-THING MORE APPETIZING.
WHAT'S YOUR PROBLEM! I BOUGHT THAT FOR YOU!
FINE, YOU CAN'T HAVE IT THEN!
Stupid dummy!
GIVE IT BACK!
YOU WERE OUT WITH THE GUY FROM THE GYM TODAY, RIGHT?
YEAH.
DID YOU HAVE FUN?
I MEAN...
...DO YOU THINK IT'S GONNA WORK OUT?

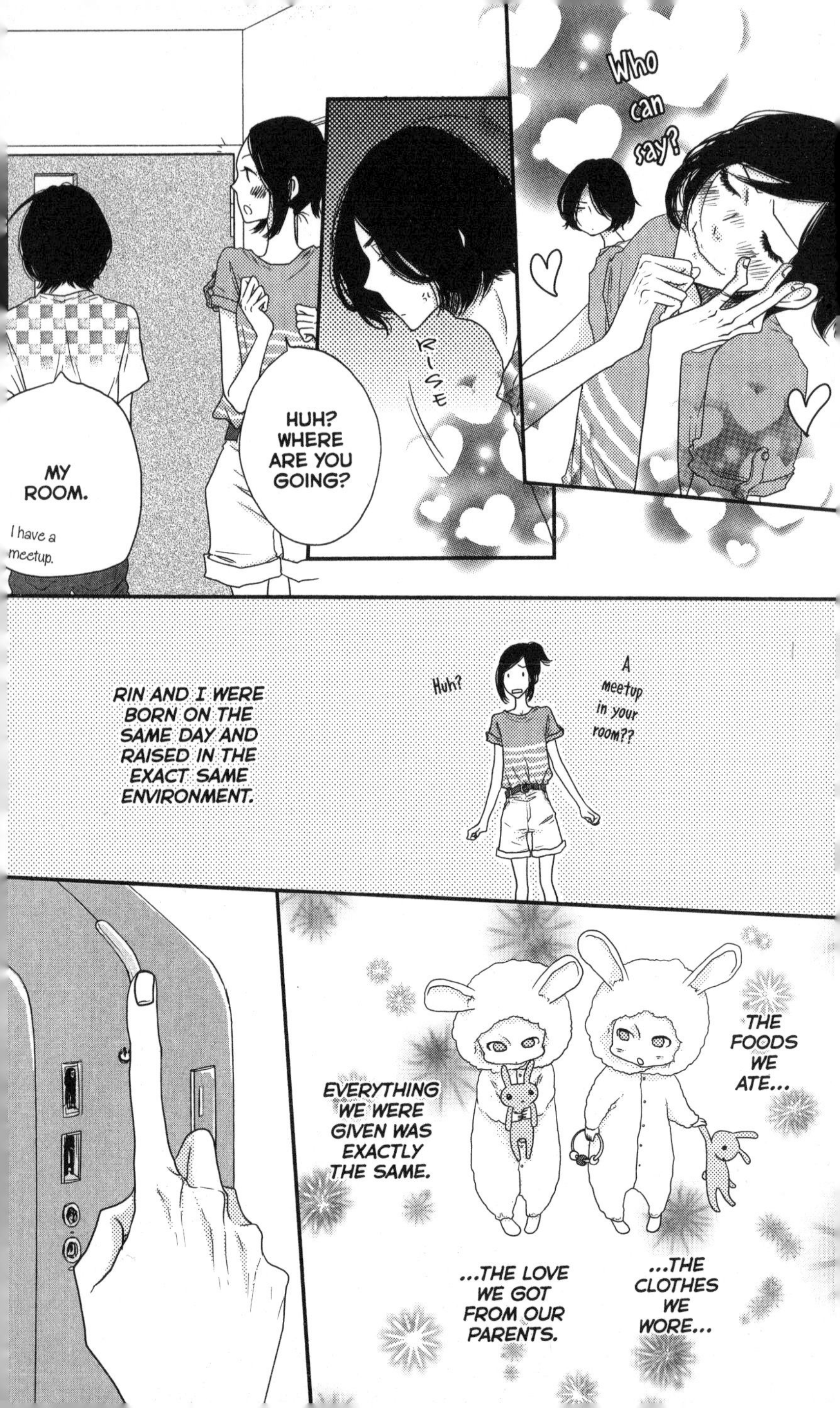
Who can say?
HUH? WHERE ARE YOU GOING?
MY ROOM.
I have a meetup.
A meetup in your room??
Huh?
RIN AND I WERE BORN ON THE SAME DAY AND RAISED IN THE EXACT SAME ENVIRONMENT.
THE FOODS WE ATE...
EVERYTHING WE WERE GIVEN WAS EXACTLY THE SAME.
...THE CLOTHES WE WORE...
...THE LOVE WE GOT FROM OUR PARENTS.

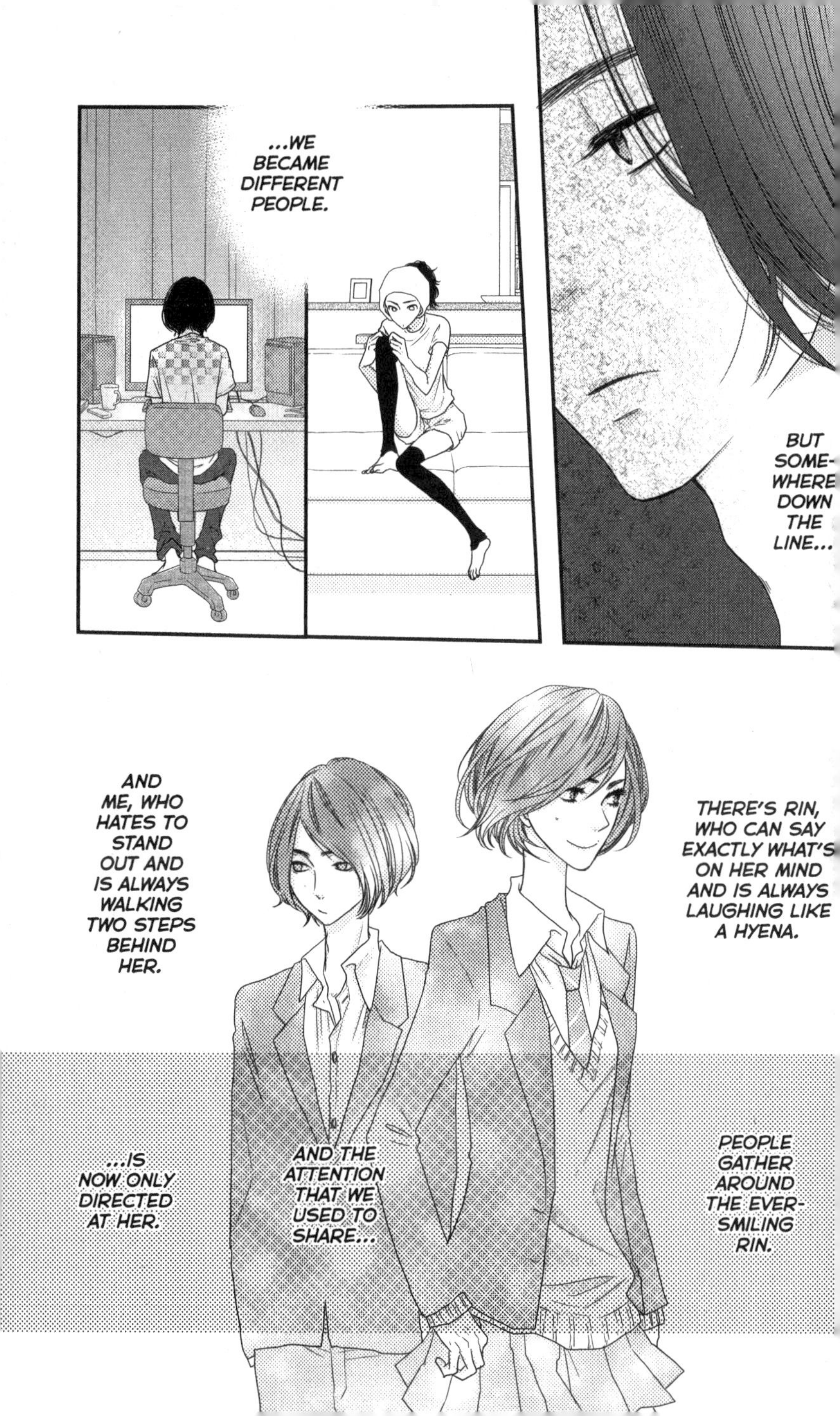
BUT SOME-WHERE DOWN THE LINE...
...WE BECAME DIFFERENT PEOPLE.
THERE'S RIN, WHO CAN SAY EXACTLY WHAT'S ON HER MIND AND IS ALWAYS LAUGHING LIKE A HYENA.
AND ME, WHO HATES TO STAND OUT AND IS ALWAYS WALKING TWO STEPS BEHIND HER.
PEOPLE GATHER AROUND THE EVER-SMILING RIN.
AND THE ATTENTION THAT WE USED TO SHARE...
...IS NOW ONLY DIRECTED AT HER.

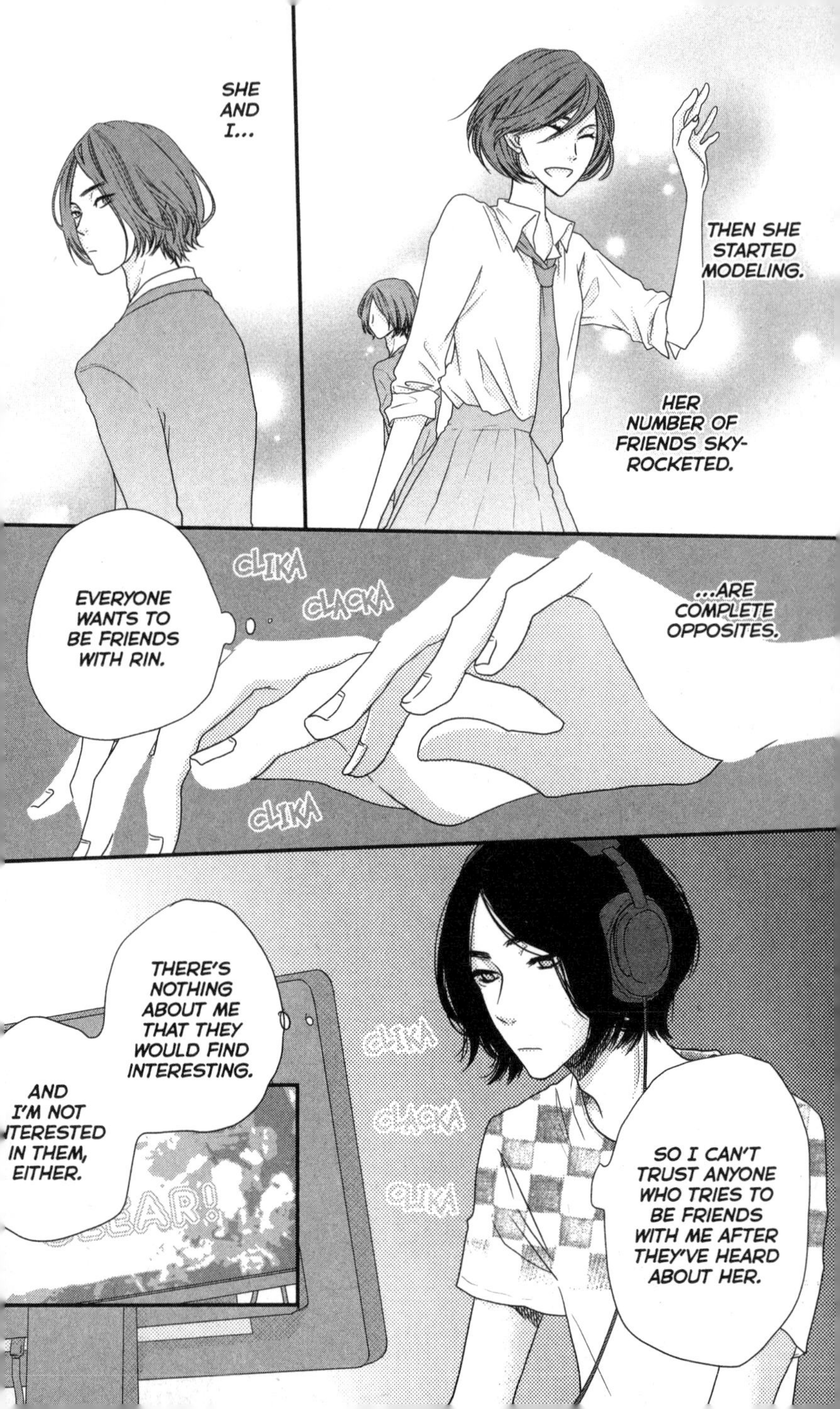
THEN SHE STARTED MODELING.
HER NUMBER OF FRIENDS SKY-ROCKETED.
SHE AND I...
...ARE COMPLETE OPPOSITES.
CLIKA
CLACKA
EVERYONE WANTS TO BE FRIENDS WITH RIN.
CLIKA
SO I CAN'T TRUST ANYONE WHO TRIES TO BE FRIENDS WITH ME AFTER THEY'VE HEARD ABOUT HER.
CLIKA
CLACKA
CLIKA
THERE'S NOTHING ABOUT ME THAT THEY WOULD FIND INTERESTING.
AND I'M NOT ITERESTED IN THEM, EITHER.

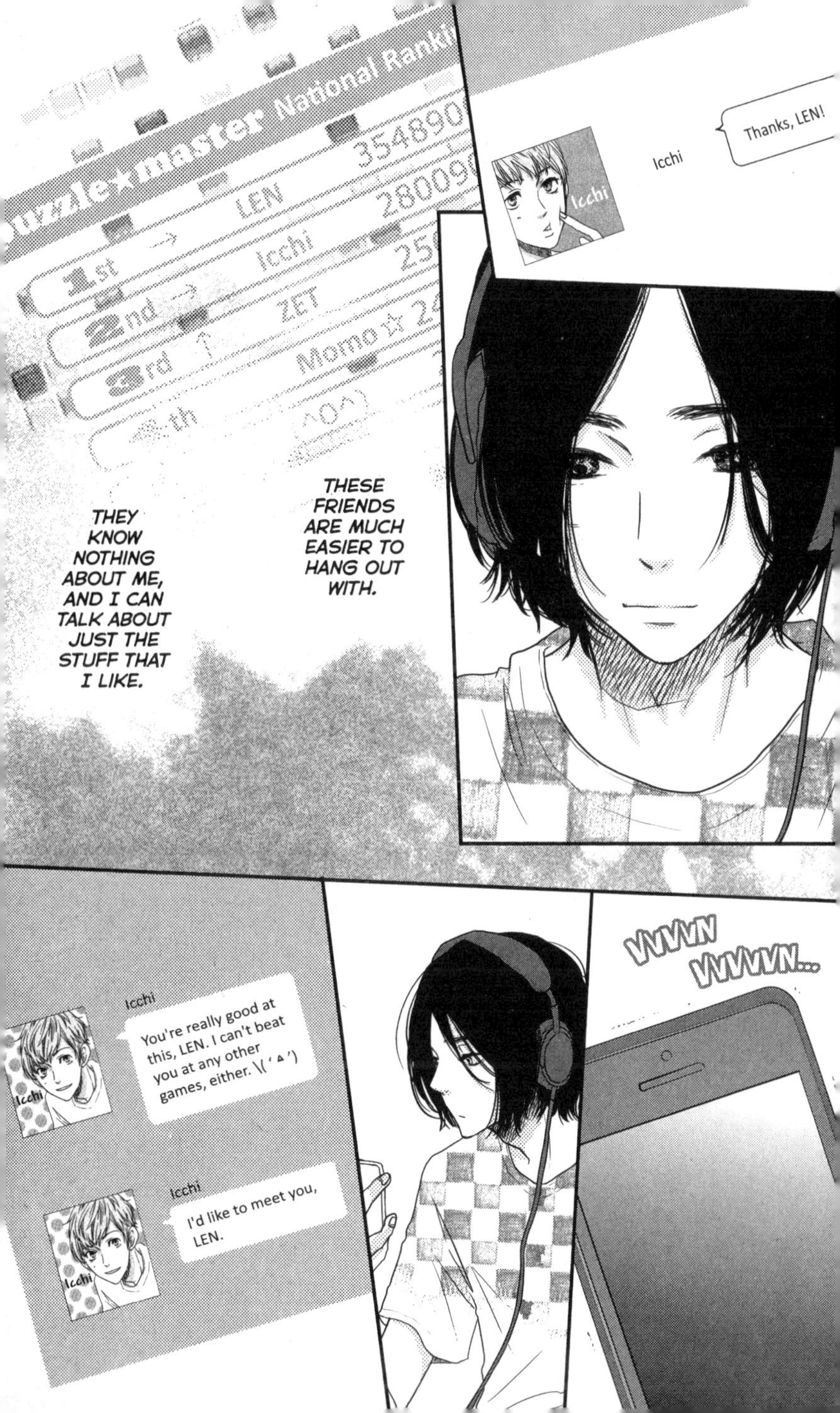
Icchi
Thanks, LEN!
uzzle★master National Ranki
1st → LEN 354890
2nd → Icchi 28009
3rd ↑ ZET 25
Momo☆ 2
th (^O^)
THESE FRIENDS ARE MUCH EASIER TO HANG OUT WITH.
THEY KNOW NOTHING ABOUT ME, AND I CAN TALK ABOUT JUST THE STUFF THAT I LIKE.
VVVVN VVVVVN...
Icchi
You're really good at this, LEN. I can't beat you at any other games, either. \(' ▵ ')
Icchi
I'd like to meet you, LEN.

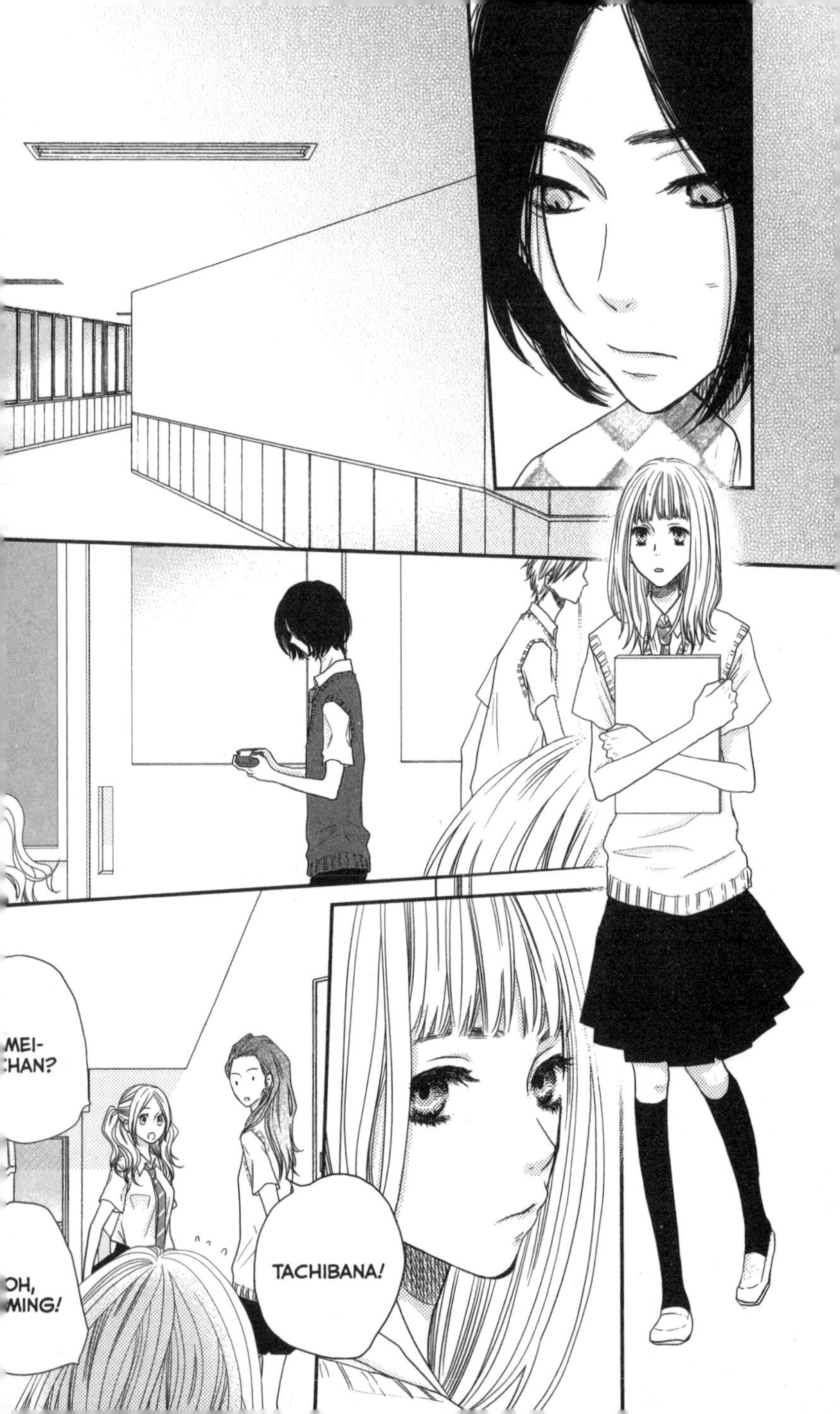
TACHIBANA!
MEI-
CHAN?
OH,
MING!

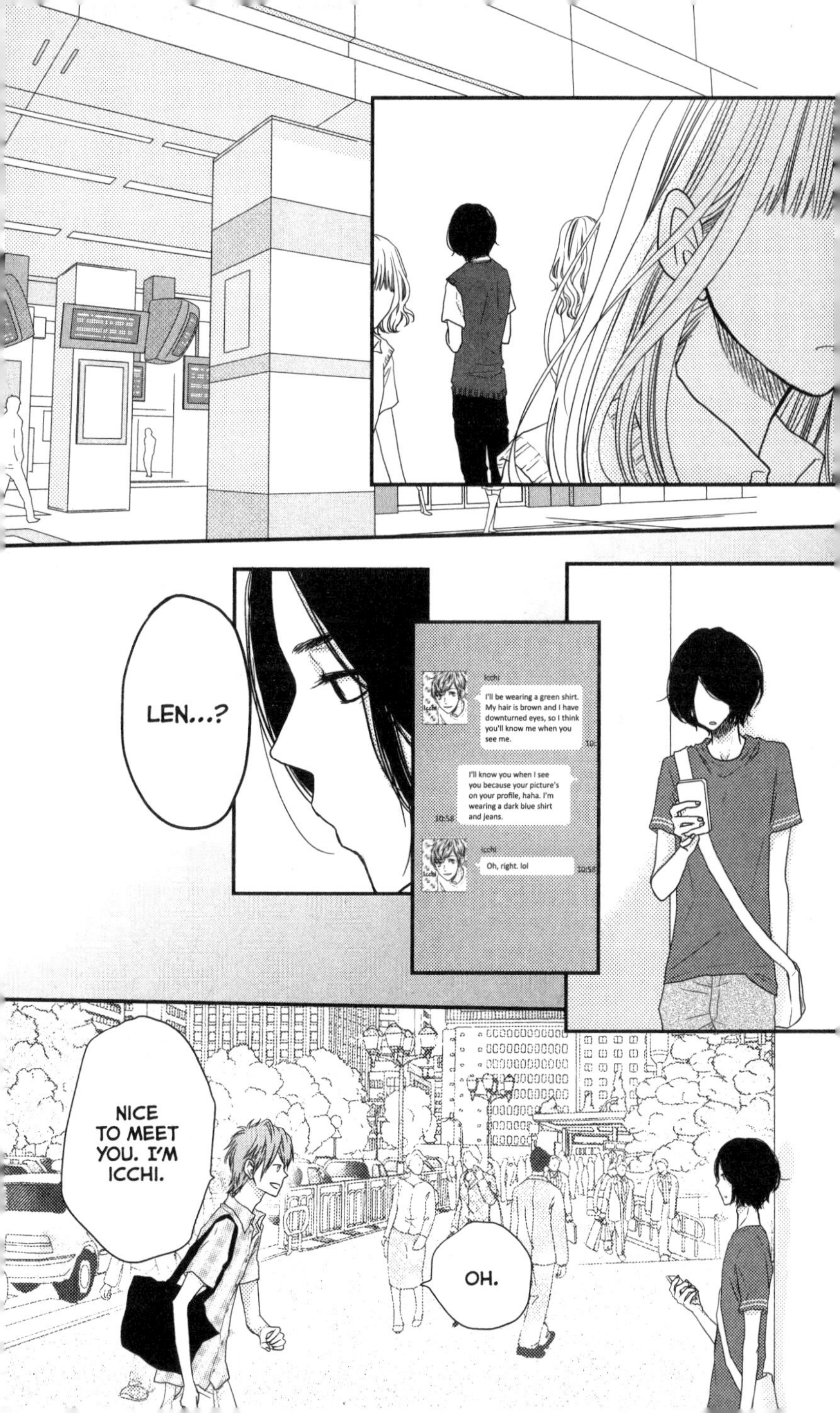
Icchi
I'll be wearing a green shirt. My hair is brown and I have downturned eyes, so I think you'll know me when you see me.
I'll know you when I see you because your picture's on your profile, haha. I'm wearing a dark blue shirt and jeans.
10:58
Icchi
Oh, right. lol
10:58
LEN...?
NICE TO MEET YOU. I'M ICCHI.
OH.

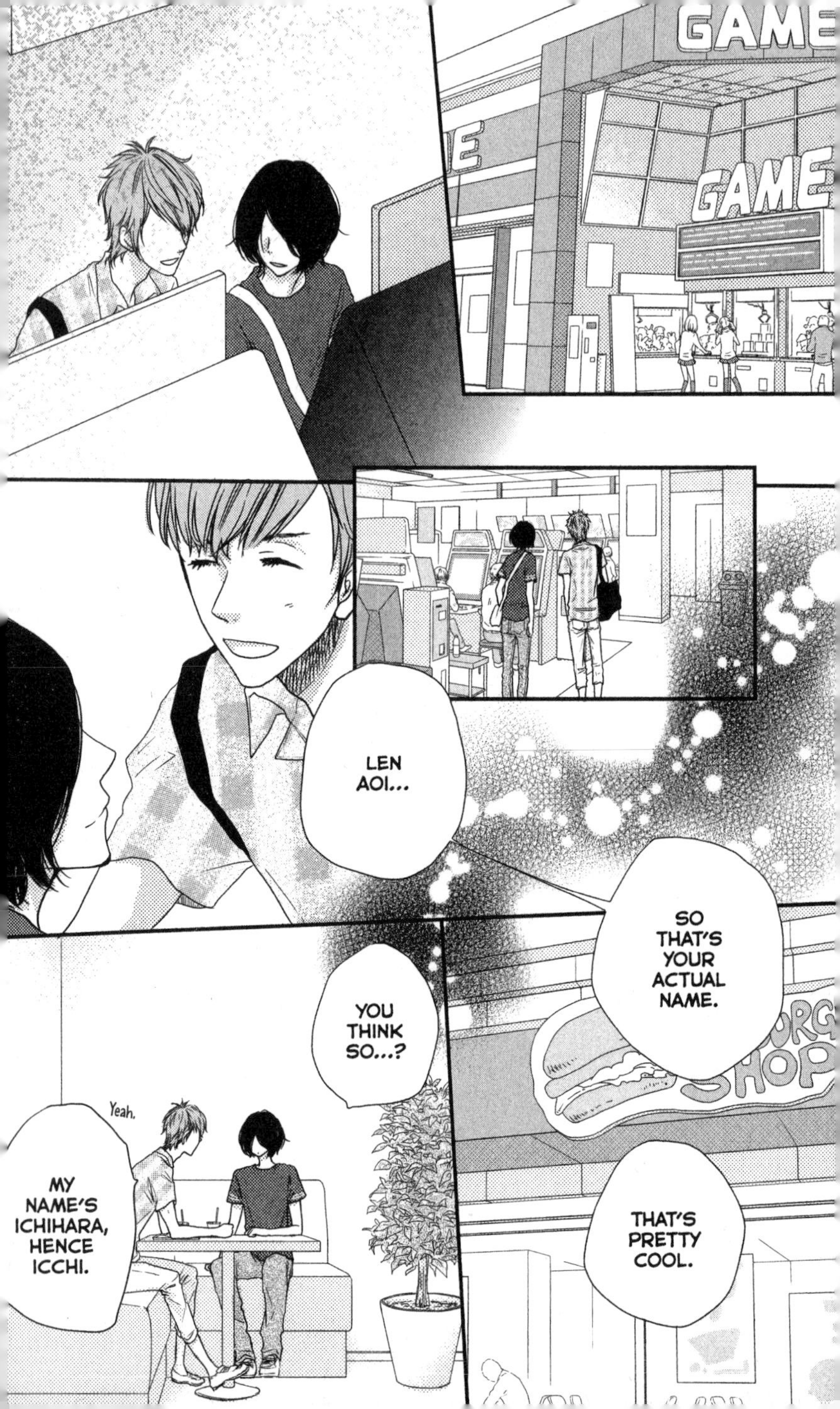
GAME
GAME
LEN AOI...
SO THAT'S YOUR ACTUAL NAME.
THAT'S PRETTY COOL.
YOU THINK SO...?
Yeah.
MY NAME'S ICHIHARA, HENCE ICCHI.

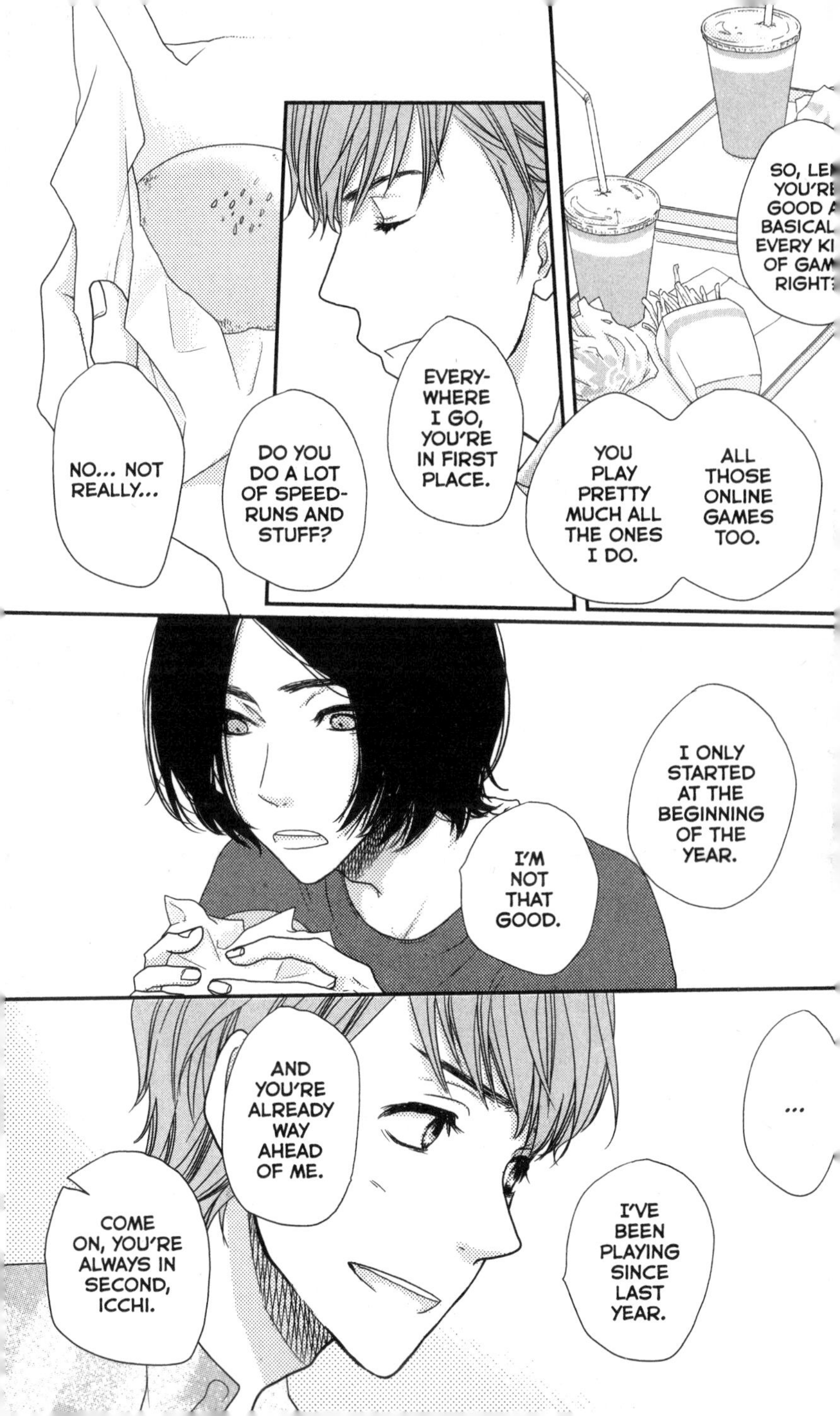
SO, LE YOU'RE GOOD A BASICAL EVERY KI OF GAM RIGHT?
ALL THOSE ONLINE GAMES TOO.
YOU PLAY PRETTY MUCH ALL THE ONES I DO.
EVERY-WHERE I GO, YOU'RE IN FIRST PLACE.
DO YOU DO A LOT OF SPEED-RUNS AND STUFF?
NO... NOT REALLY...
I ONLY STARTED AT THE BEGINNING OF THE YEAR.
I'M NOT THAT GOOD.
...
I'VE BEEN PLAYING SINCE LAST YEAR.
AND YOU'RE ALREADY WAY AHEAD OF ME.
COME ON, YOU'RE ALWAYS IN SECOND, ICCHI.

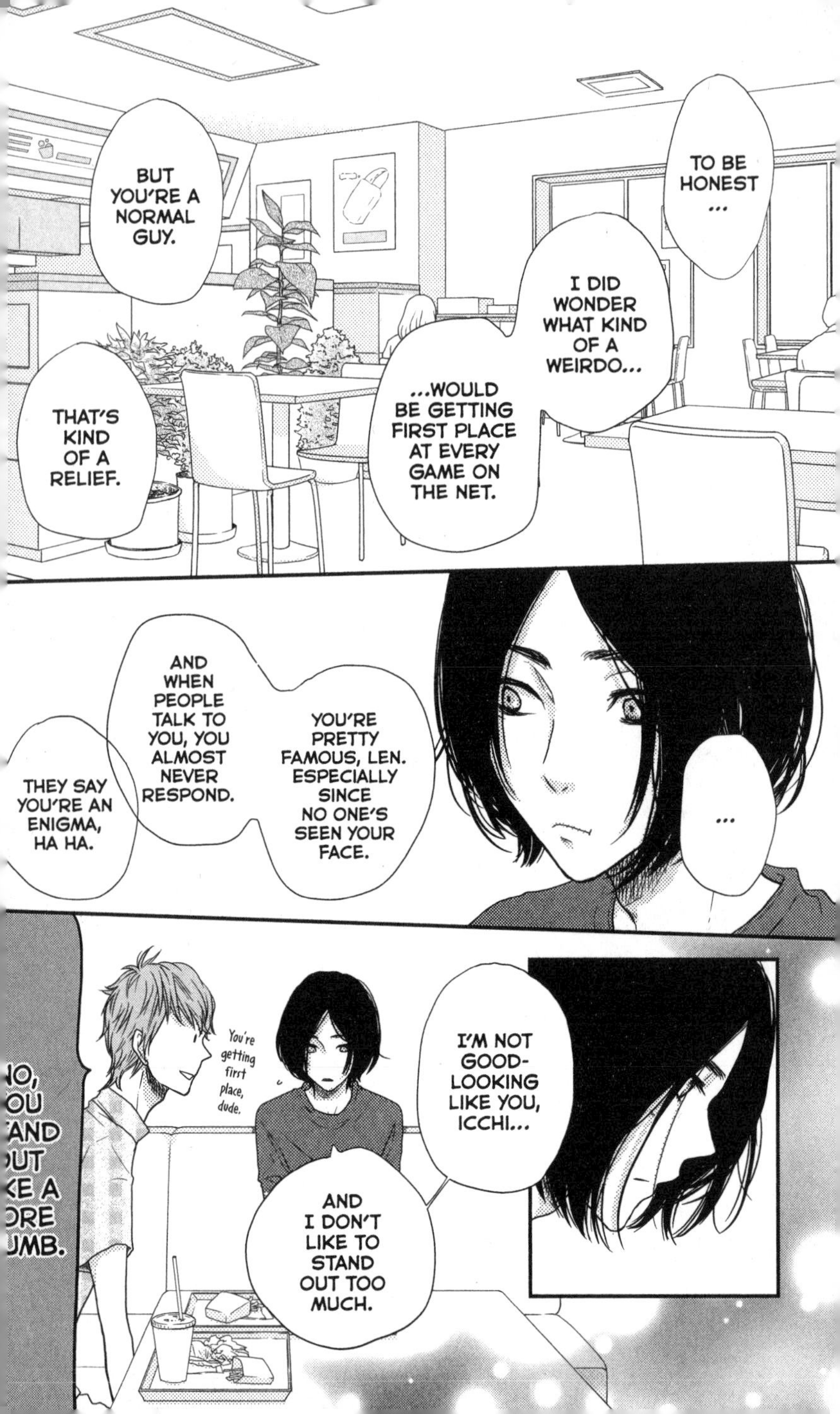
TO BE HONEST ...
I DID WONDER WHAT KIND OF A WEIRDO...
...WOULD BE GETTING FIRST PLACE AT EVERY GAME ON THE NET.
BUT YOU'RE A NORMAL GUY.
THAT'S KIND OF A RELIEF.
...
YOU'RE PRETTY FAMOUS, LEN. ESPECIALLY SINCE NO ONE'S SEEN YOUR FACE.
AND WHEN PEOPLE TALK TO YOU, YOU ALMOST NEVER RESPOND.
THEY SAY YOU'RE AN ENIGMA, HA HA.
I'M NOT GOOD-LOOKING LIKE YOU, ICCHI...
AND I DON'T LIKE TO STAND OUT TOO MUCH.
You're getting first place, dude.
O, OU AND UT E A ORE UMB.

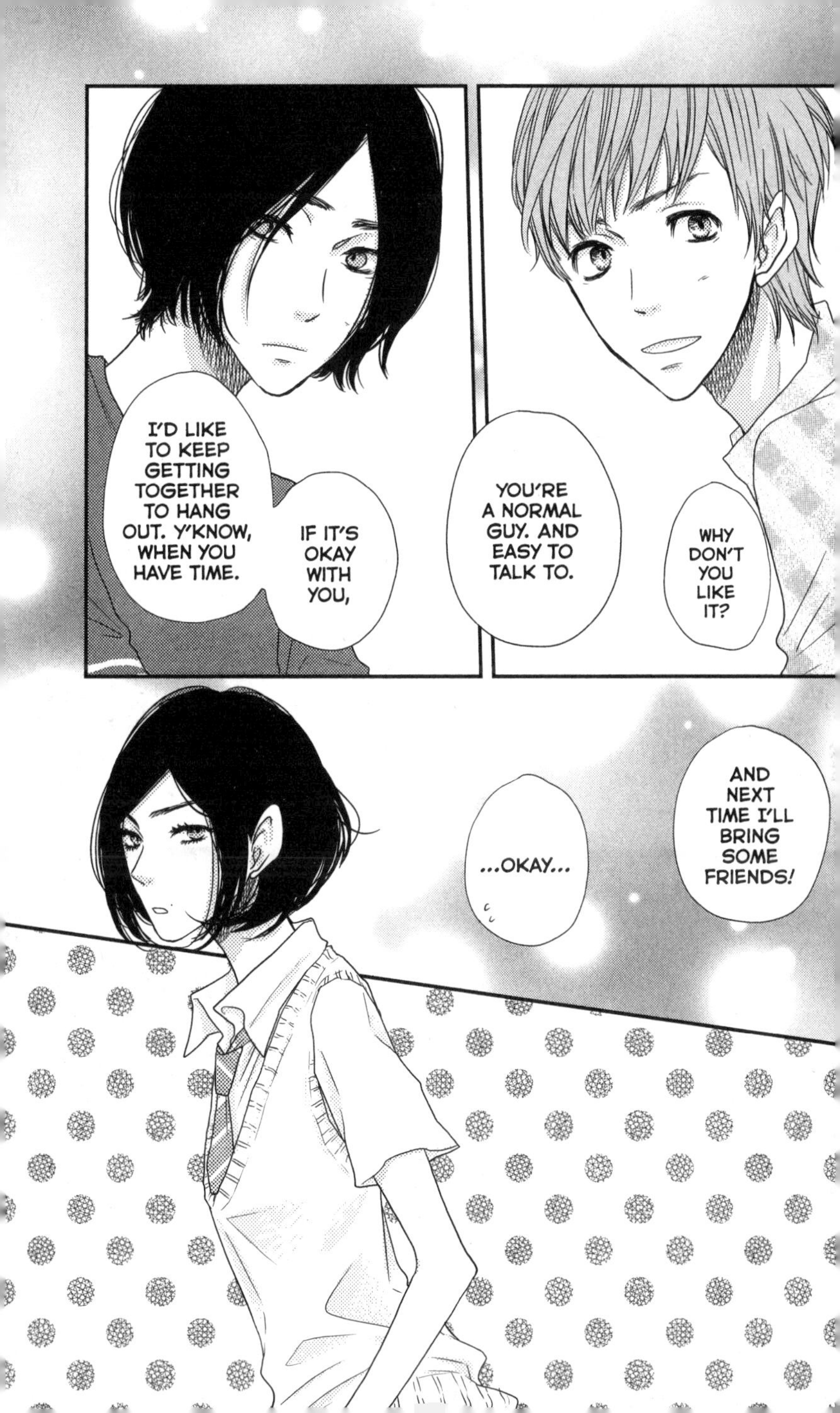
WHY DON'T YOU LIKE IT?
YOU'RE A NORMAL GUY. AND EASY TO TALK TO.
IF IT'S OKAY WITH YOU,
I'D LIKE TO KEEP GETTING TOGETHER TO HANG OUT. Y'KNOW, WHEN YOU HAVE TIME.
AND NEXT TIME I'LL BRING SOME FRIENDS!
...OKAY...

OOOH, WHAT'S THIS?

LEN-SAMA'S IN A GOOD MOOD TODAY! ♡

Uh.

OH YEAH, RIN.

But it's a good thing.

It really throws me off when he's not his emo self...

...

WHATEVER.

YOU CAN HANDLE IT ON YOUR OWN, RIGHT?

I CAN'T HELP AT THE GYM THIS SATURDAY. I HAVE PLANS.

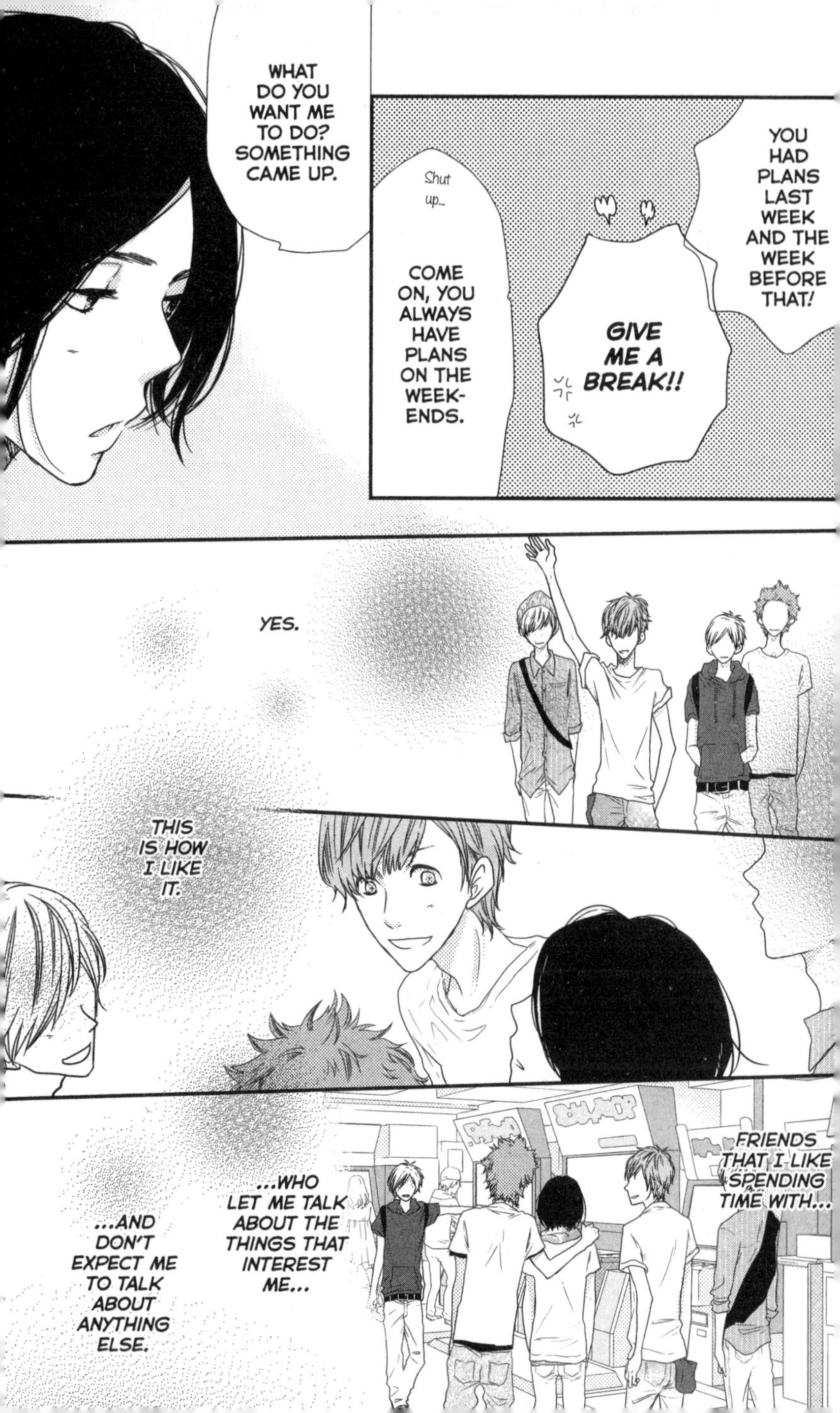
YOU HAD PLANS LAST WEEK AND THE WEEK BEFORE THAT!
GIVE ME A BREAK!!
COME ON, YOU ALWAYS HAVE PLANS ON THE WEEK-ENDS.
Shut up...
WHAT DO YOU WANT ME TO DO? SOMETHING CAME UP.
YES.
THIS IS HOW I LIKE IT.
FRIENDS THAT I LIKE SPENDING TIME WITH...
...WHO LET ME TALK ABOUT THE THINGS THAT INTEREST ME...
...AND DON'T EXPECT ME TO TALK ABOUT ANYTHING ELSE.

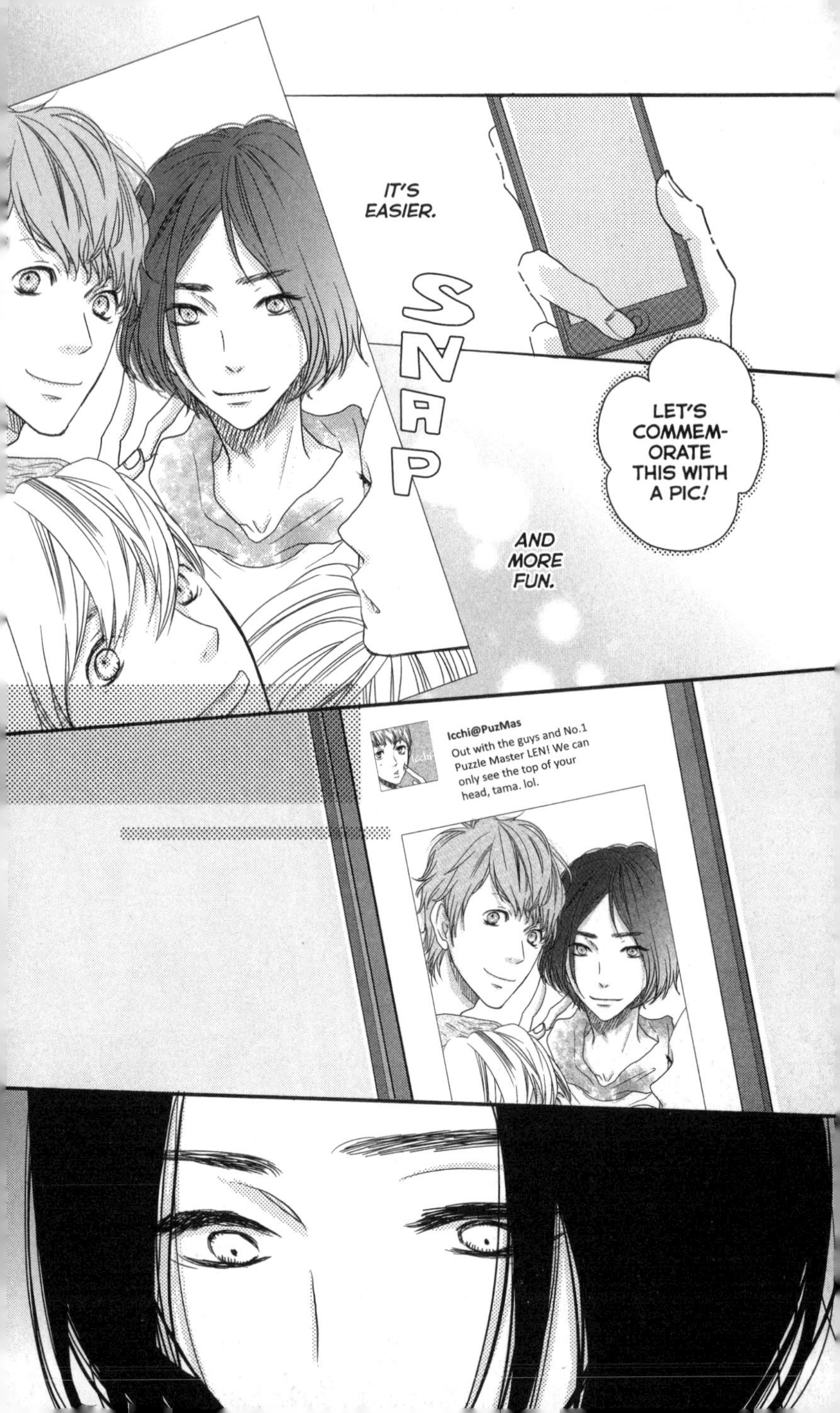
IT'S EASIER.
SNAP
LET'S COMMEMORATE THIS WITH A PIC!
AND MORE FUN.
Icchi@PuzMas
Out with the guys and No.1 Puzzle Master LEN! We can only see the top of your head, tama. lol.

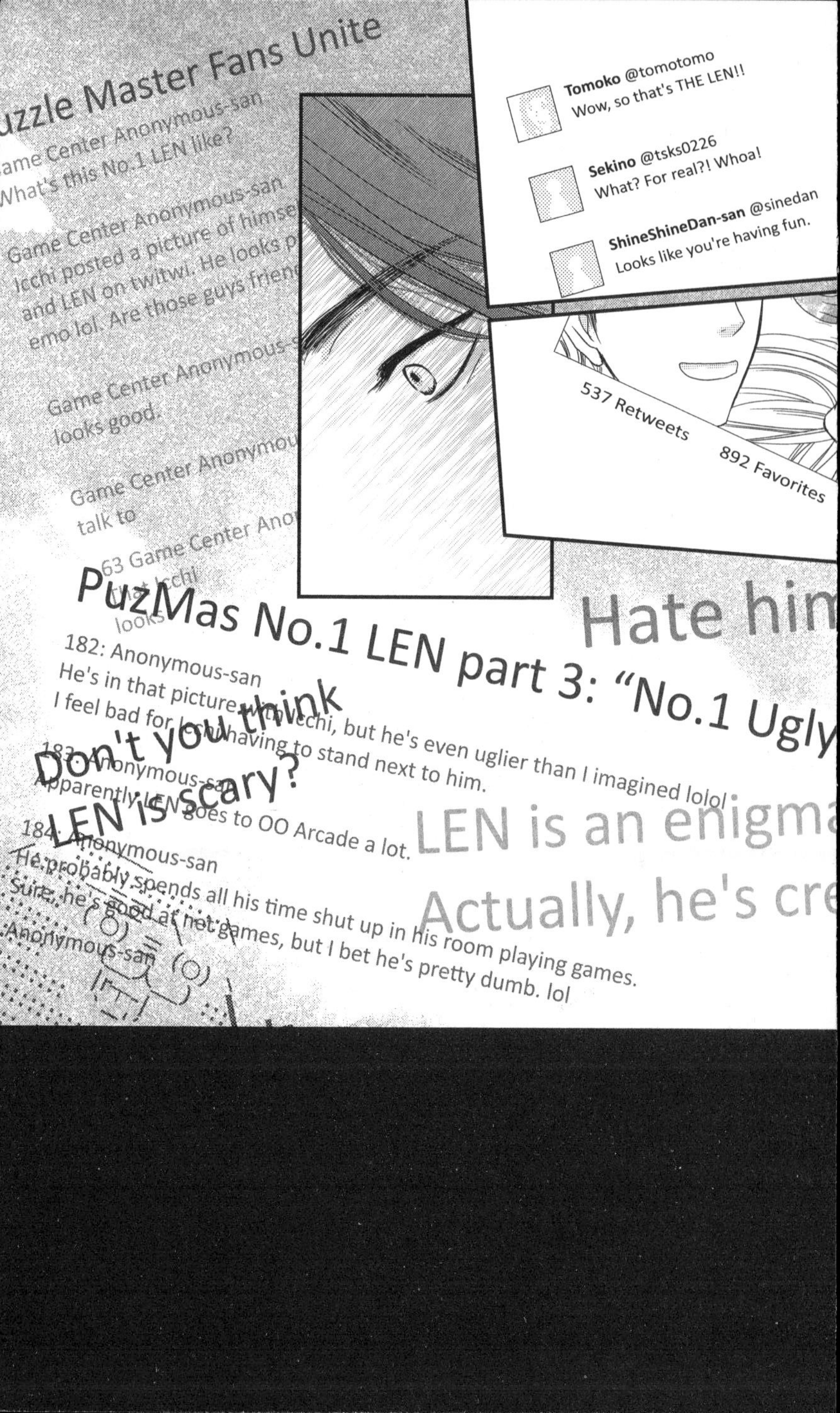
Tomoko @tomotomo
Wow, so that's THE LEN!!
Sekino @tsks0226
What? For real?! Whoa!
ShineShineDan-san @sinedan
Looks like you're having fun.
537 Retweets
892 Favorites
uzzle Master Fans Unite
ame Center Anonymous-san
What's this No.1 LEN like?
Game Center Anonymous-san
Icchi posted a picture of himse
and LEN on twitwi. He looks p
emo lol. Are those guys frien
Game Center Anonymous-s
looks good.
Game Center Anonymou
talk to
Game Center Anon
63 Game Center
Hate him
PuzMas No.1 LEN part 3: "No.1 Ugly
182: Anonymous-san
He's in that picture with Icchi, but he's even uglier than I imagined lolol
I feel bad for Icchi having to stand next to him.
Don't you think LEN is scary?
183: Anonymous-san
Apparently LEN goes to OO Arcade a lot.
LEN is an enigma
184: Anonymous-san
He probably spends all his time shut up in his room playing games.
Sure, he's good at net games, but I bet he's pretty dumb. lol
Actually, he's cre
Anonymous-san

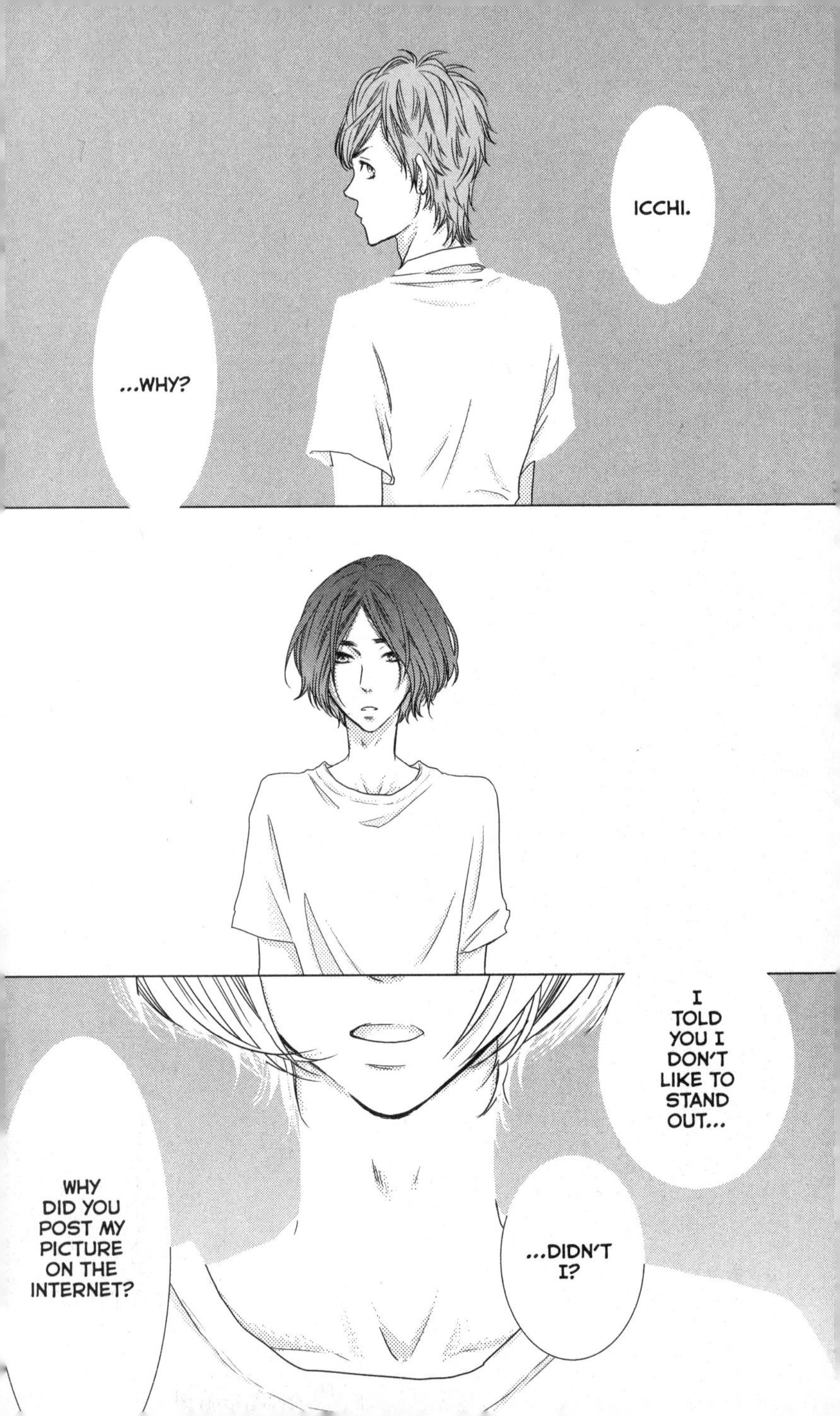
ICCHI.
...WHY?
I TOLD YOU I DON'T LIKE TO STAND OUT...
...DIDN'T I?
WHY DID YOU POST MY PICTURE ON THE INTERNET?

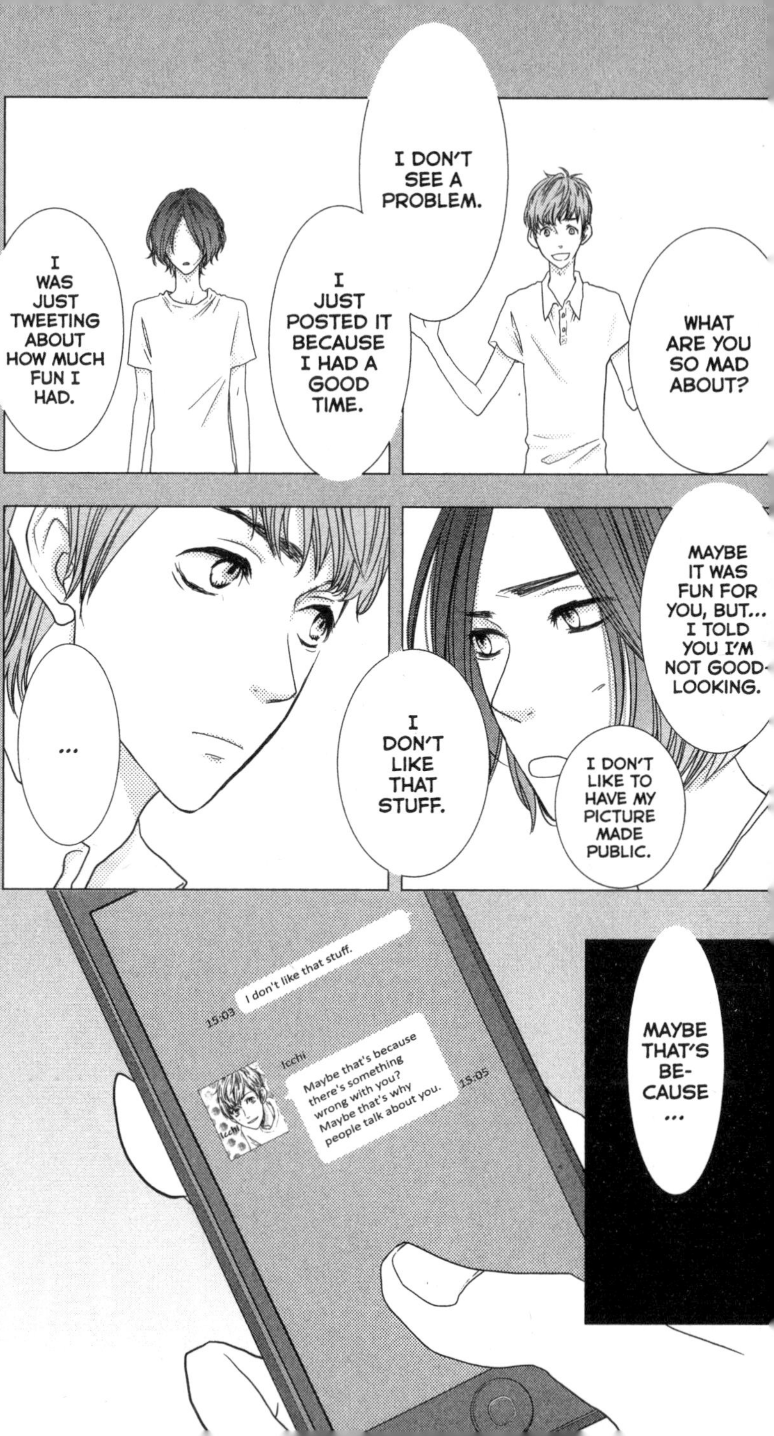
WHAT ARE YOU SO MAD ABOUT?
I DON'T SEE A PROBLEM.
I JUST POSTED IT BECAUSE I HAD A GOOD TIME.
I WAS JUST TWEETING ABOUT HOW MUCH FUN I HAD.
MAYBE IT WAS FUN FOR YOU, BUT... I TOLD YOU I'M NOT GOOD-LOOKING.
I DON'T LIKE TO HAVE MY PICTURE MADE PUBLIC.
I DON'T LIKE THAT STUFF.
...
MAYBE THAT'S BE-CAUSE ...
I don't like that stuff.
15:03
Icchi
Maybe that's because there's something wrong with you? Maybe that's why people talk about you.
15:05

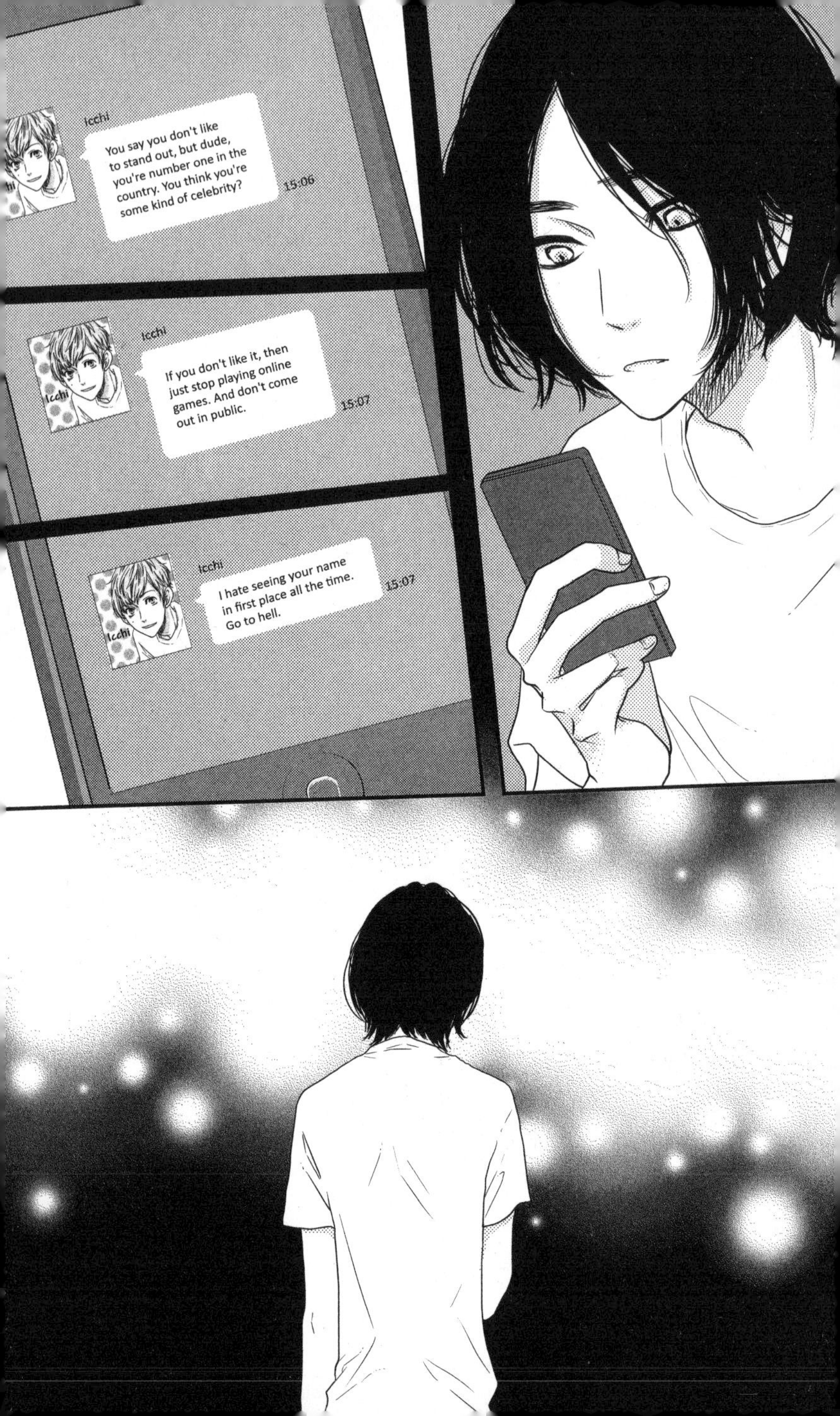
Icchi
You say you don't like to stand out, but dude, you're number one in the country. You think you're some kind of celebrity?
15:06
Icchi
If you don't like it, then just stop playing online games. And don't come out in public.
15:07
Icchi
I hate seeing your name in first place all the time. Go to hell.
15:07

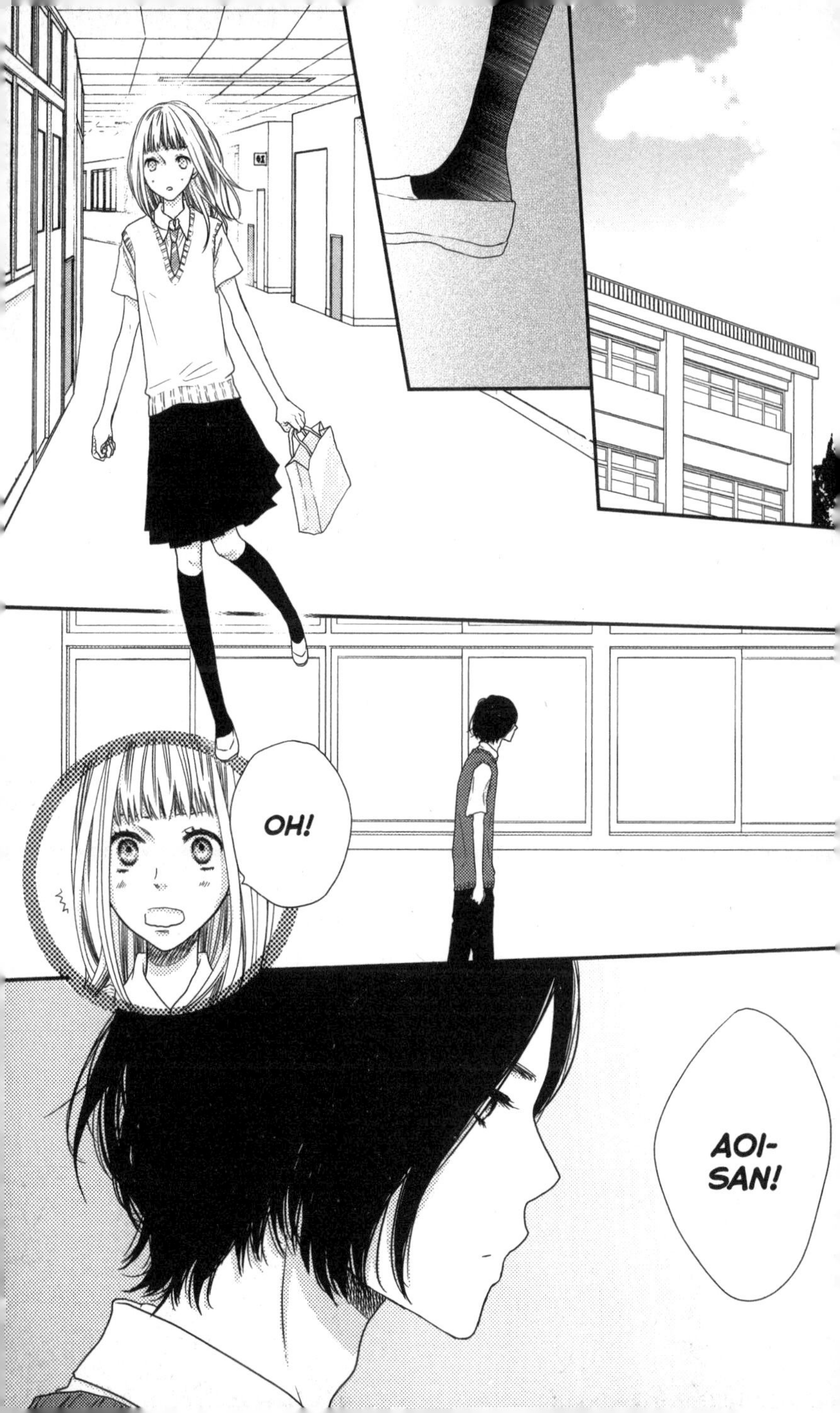
OH!
AOI-SAN!

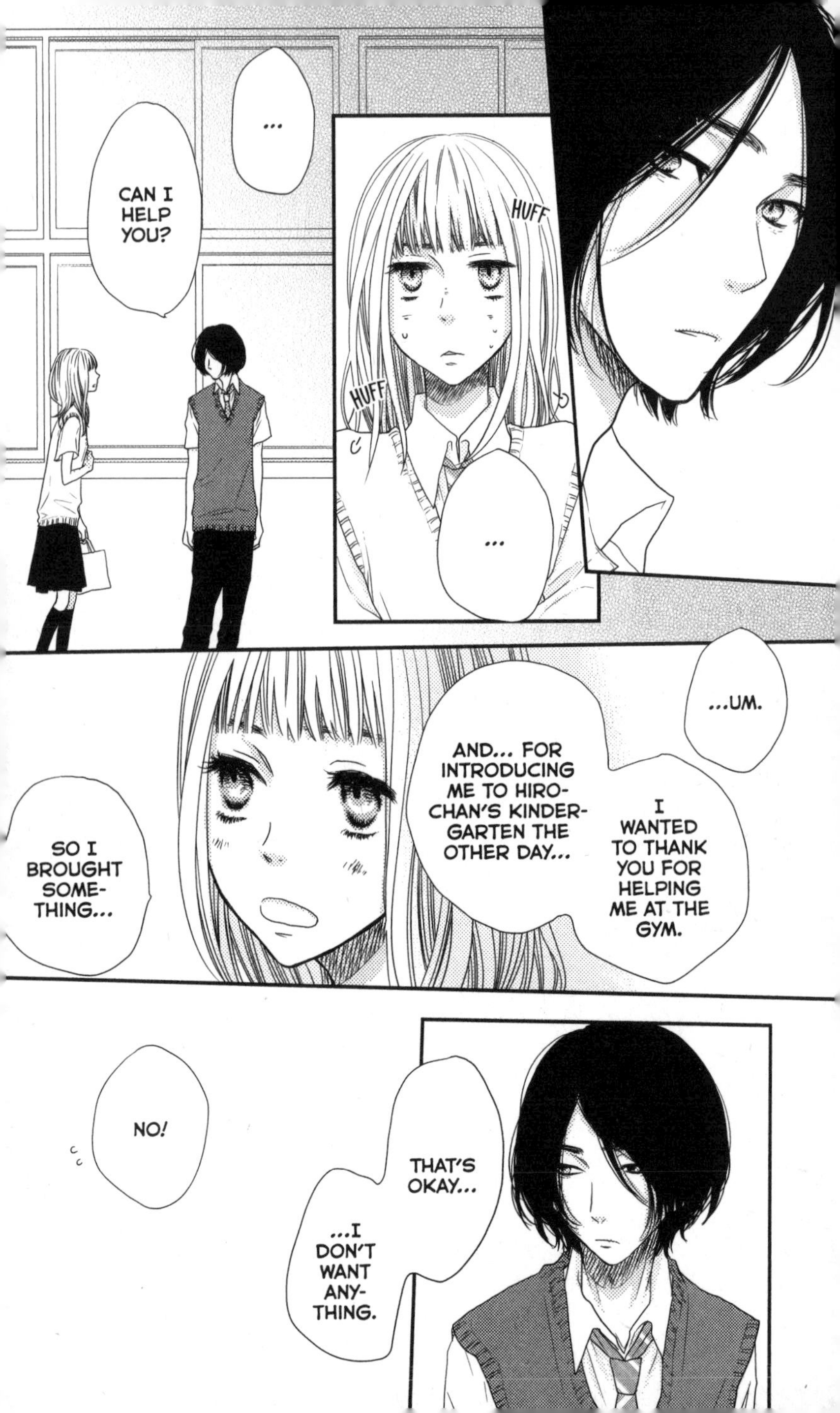
HUFF
HUFF
...
...
CAN I HELP YOU?
...UM.
I WANTED TO THANK YOU FOR HELPING ME AT THE GYM.
AND... FOR INTRODUCING ME TO HIRO-CHAN'S KINDER-GARTEN THE OTHER DAY...
SO I BROUGHT SOME-THING...
THAT'S OKAY...
...I DON'T WANT ANY-THING.
NO!

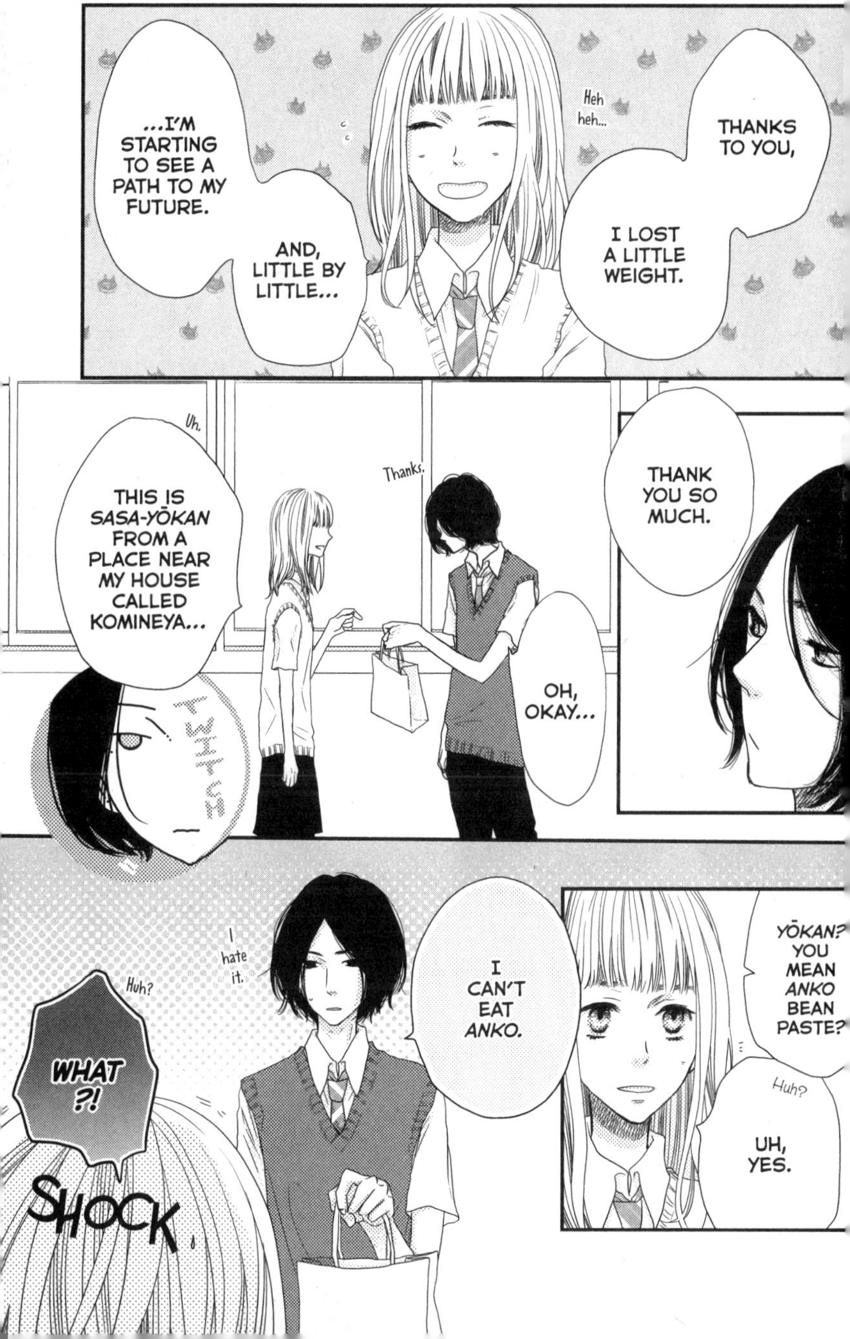

THANKS TO YOU,
Heh heh...
I LOST A LITTLE WEIGHT.
AND, LITTLE BY LITTLE...
...I'M STARTING TO SEE A PATH TO MY FUTURE.
THANK YOU SO MUCH.
Thanks.
OH, OKAY...
Uh.
THIS IS *SASA-YŌKAN* FROM A PLACE NEAR MY HOUSE CALLED KOMINEYA...
TWITCH
YŌKAN? YOU MEAN *ANKO* BEAN PASTE?
Huh?
UH, YES.
I CAN'T EAT *ANKO.*
I hate it.
Huh?
WHAT?!
SHOCK

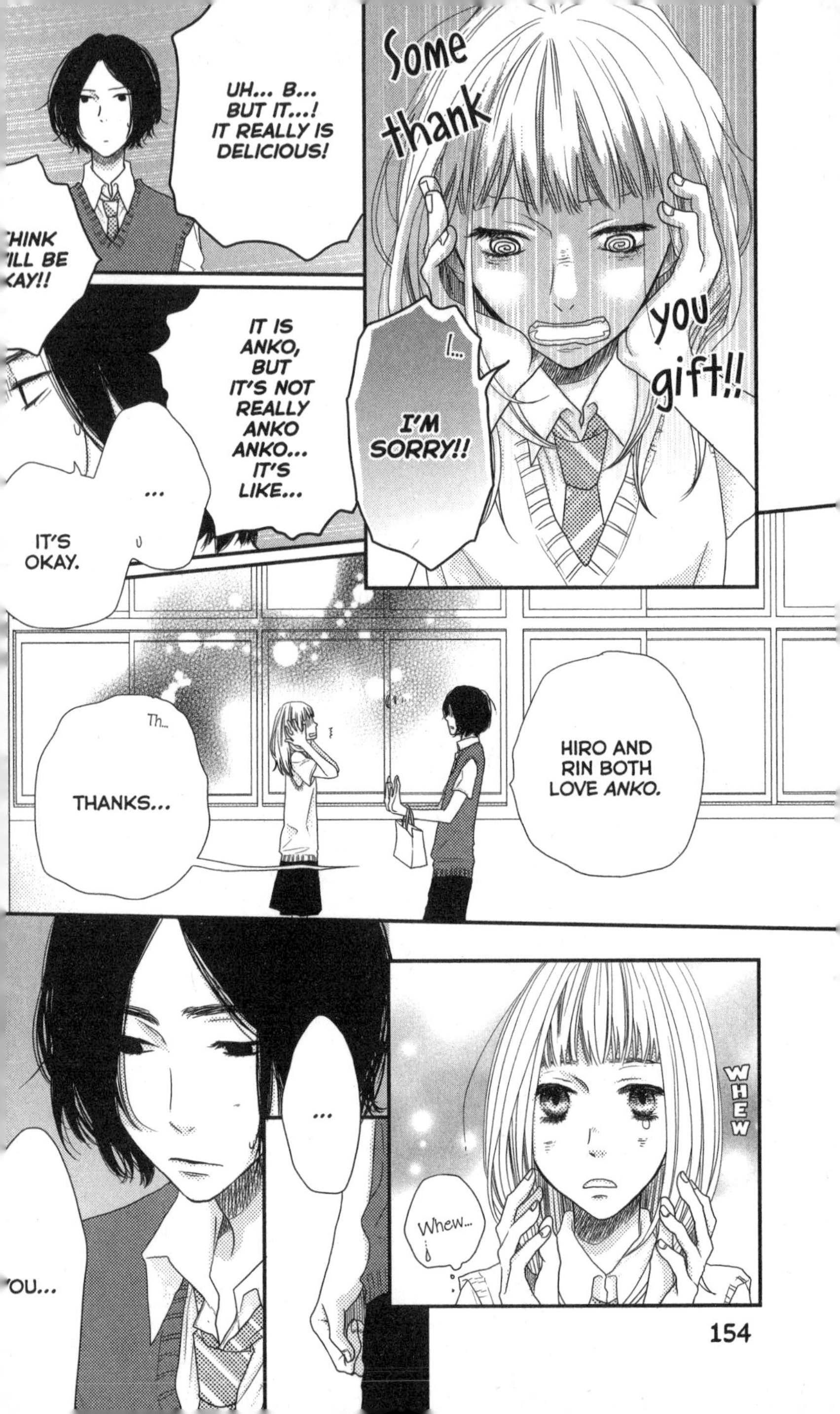
Some thank you gift!!
I...
I'M SORRY!!
UH... B... BUT IT...! IT REALLY IS DELICIOUS!
IT IS ANKO, BUT IT'S NOT REALLY ANKO ANKO... IT'S LIKE...
...
IT'S OKAY.
HIRO AND RIN BOTH LOVE ANKO.
Th...
THANKS...
WHEW
Whew...
...

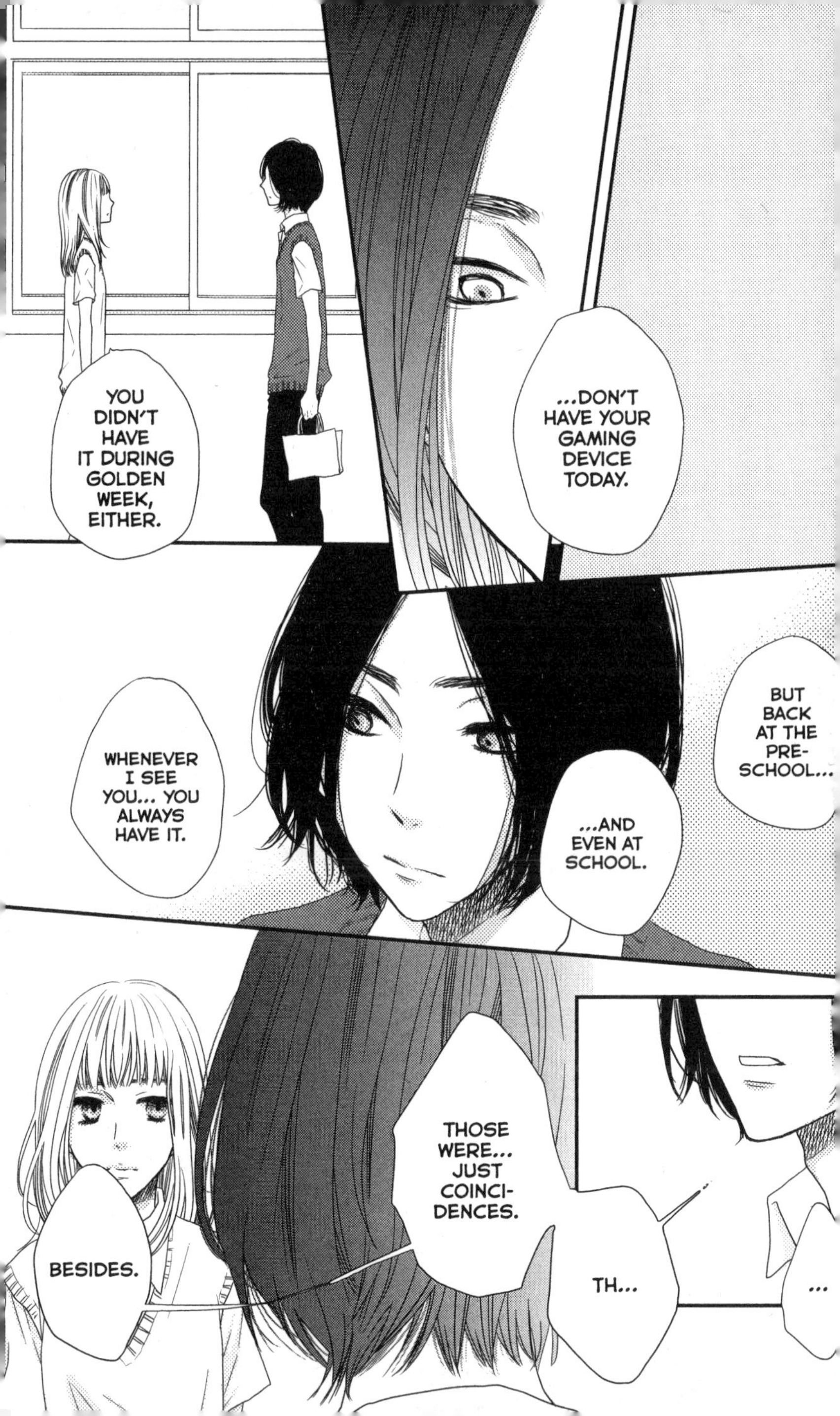
...DON'T HAVE YOUR GAMING DEVICE TODAY.
YOU DIDN'T HAVE IT DURING GOLDEN WEEK, EITHER.
BUT BACK AT THE PRE-SCHOOL...
...AND EVEN AT SCHOOL.
WHENEVER I SEE YOU... YOU ALWAYS HAVE IT.
...
TH...
THOSE WERE... JUST COINCI-DENCES.
BESIDES.

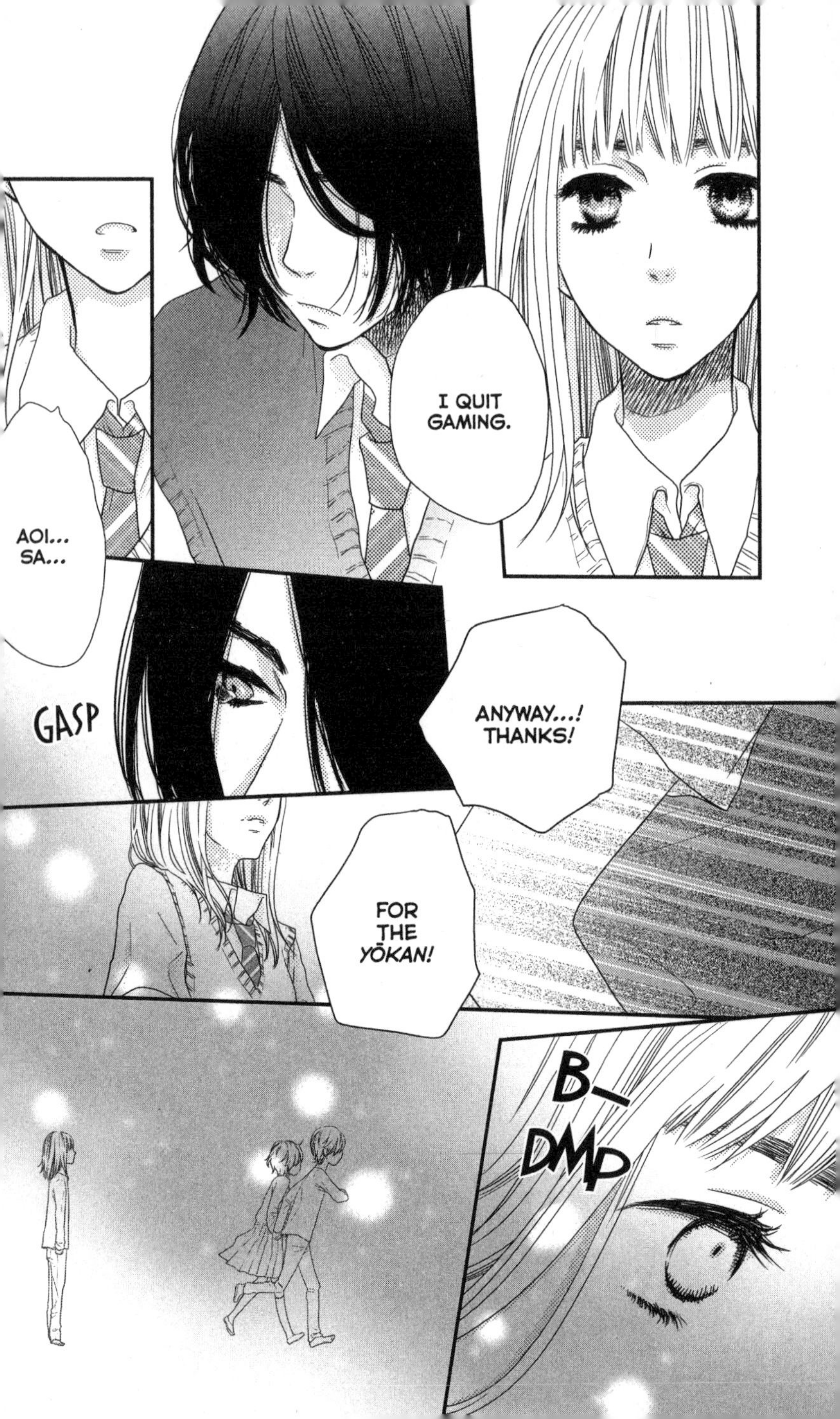
I QUIT GAMING.
AOI... SA...
ANYWAY...! THANKS!
GASP
FOR THE *YŌKAN*!
B—DMP

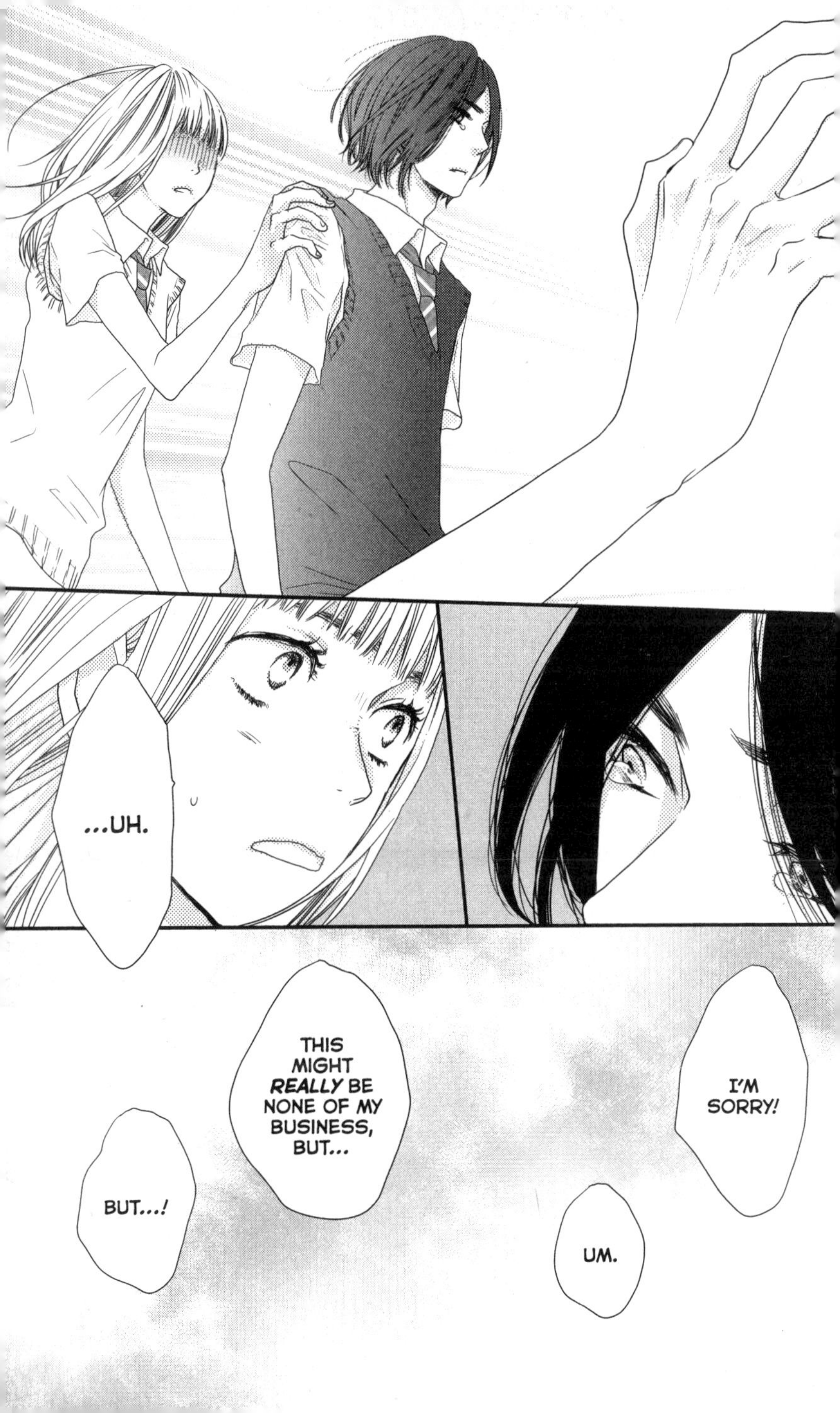
...UH.
I'M SORRY!
UM.
THIS MIGHT *REALLY* BE NONE OF MY BUSINESS, BUT...
BUT...!

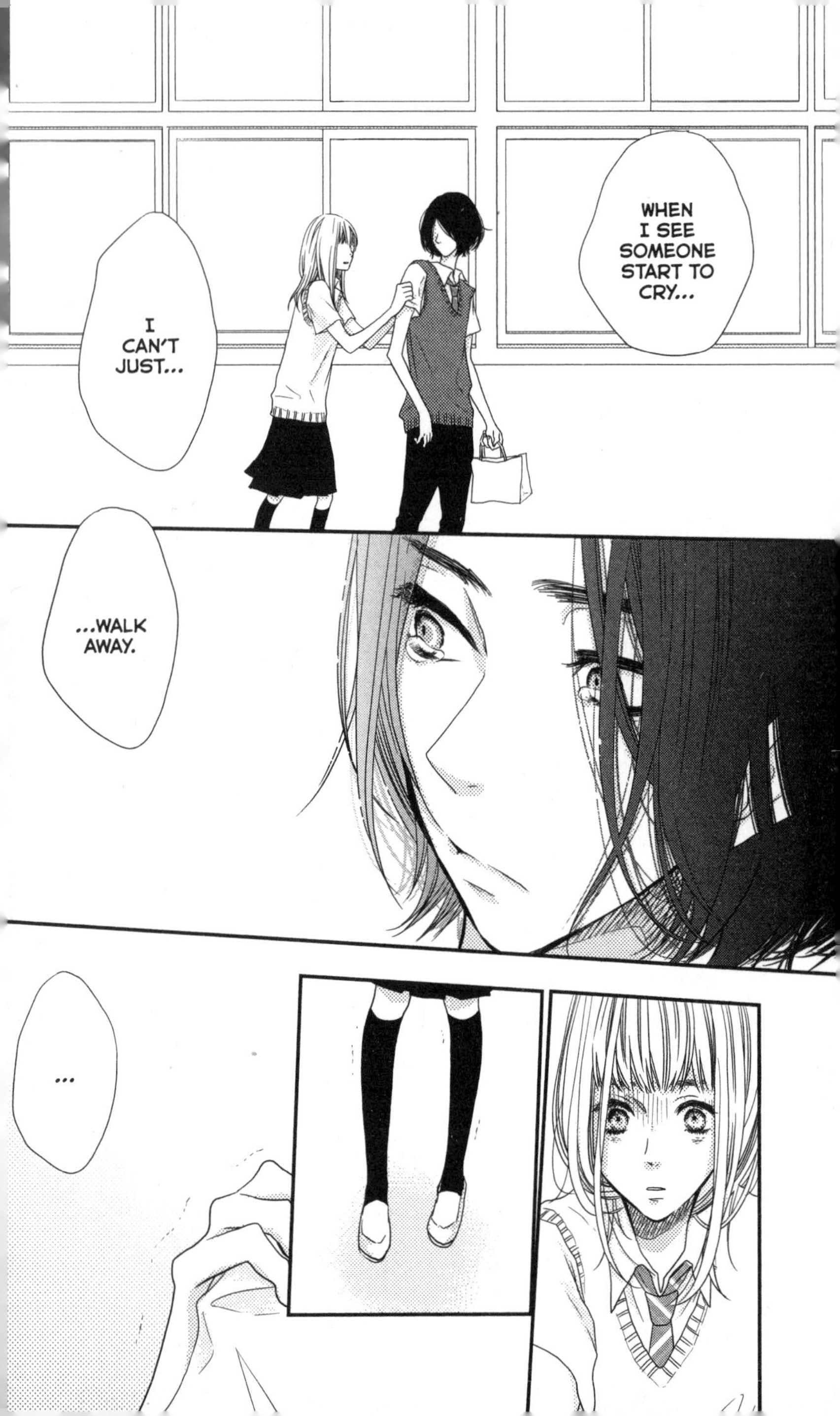
WHEN I SEE SOMEONE START TO CRY...
I CAN'T JUST...
...WALK AWAY.
...

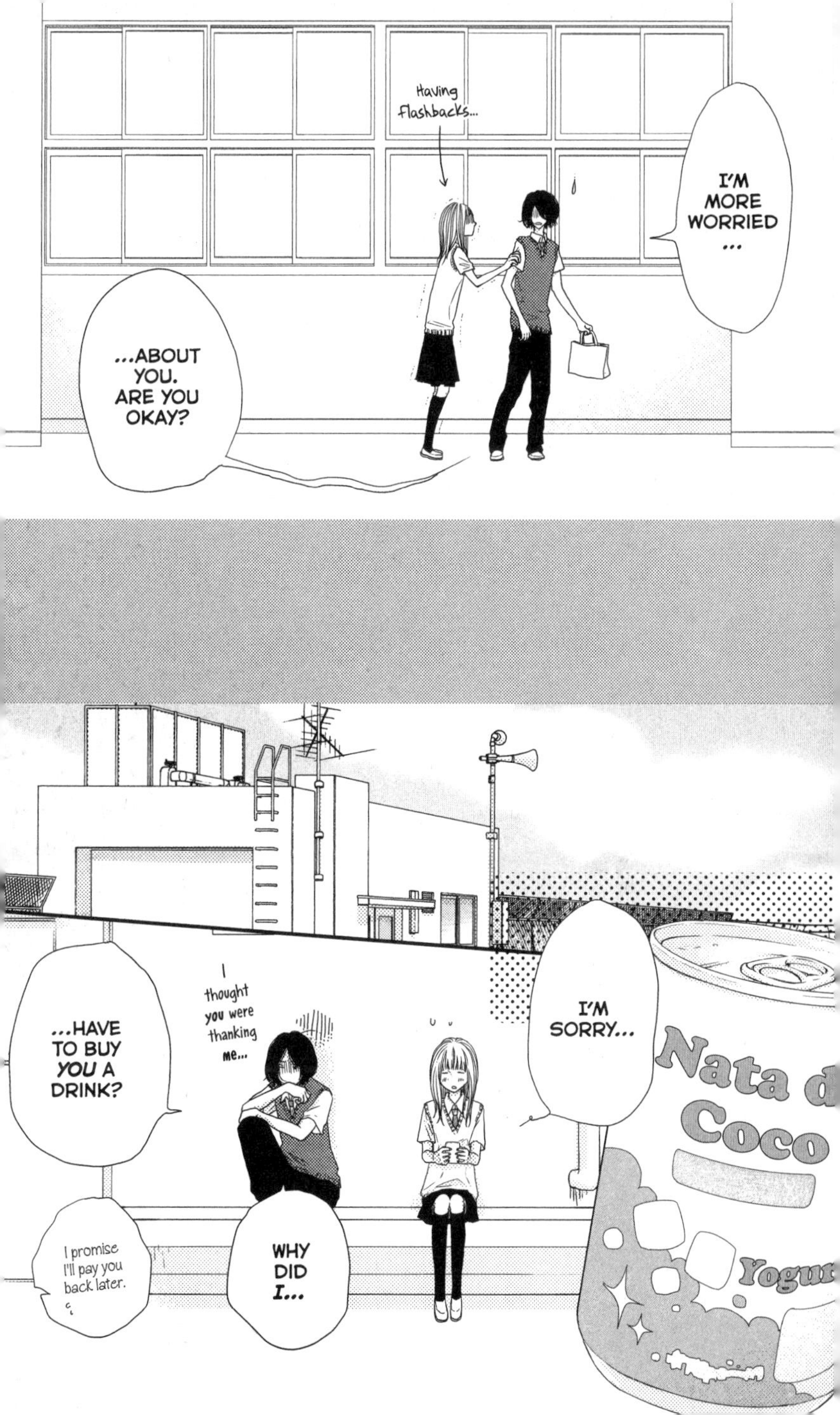
I'M MORE WORRIED ...
Having Flashbacks...
...ABOUT YOU. ARE YOU OKAY?
Nata d
Coco
I'M SORRY...
I thought you were thanking me...
WHY DID I...
...HAVE TO BUY YOU A DRINK?
I promise I'll pay you back later.

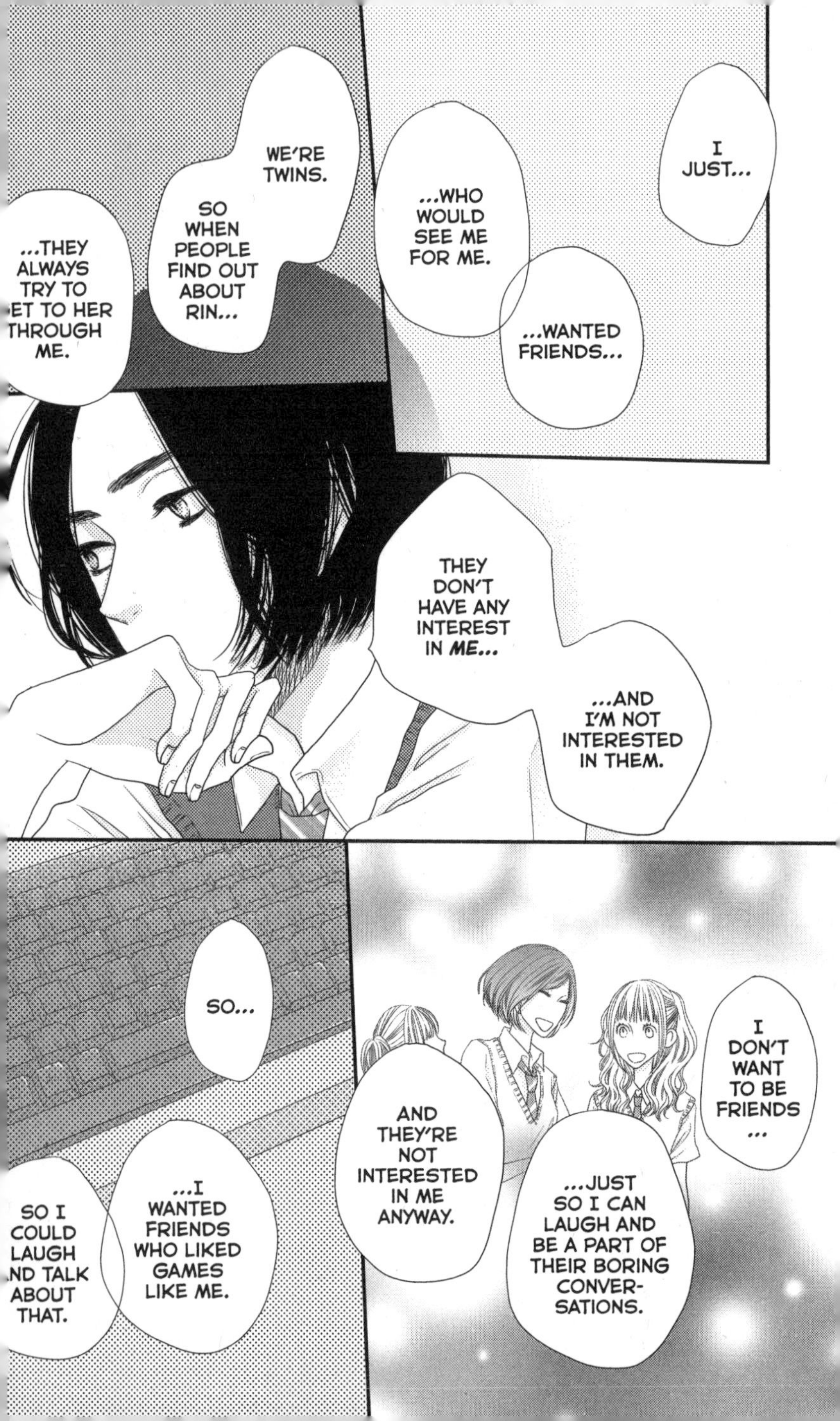
I JUST...
...WANTED FRIENDS...
...WHO WOULD SEE ME FOR ME.
WE'RE TWINS.
SO WHEN PEOPLE FIND OUT ABOUT RIN...
...THEY ALWAYS TRY TO ET TO HER THROUGH ME.
THEY DON'T HAVE ANY INTEREST IN *ME*...
...AND I'M NOT INTERESTED IN THEM.
I DON'T WANT TO BE FRIENDS...
...JUST SO I CAN LAUGH AND BE A PART OF THEIR BORING CONVER-SATIONS.
AND THEY'RE NOT INTERESTED IN ME ANYWAY.
SO...
...I WANTED FRIENDS WHO LIKED GAMES LIKE ME.
SO I COULD LAUGH ND TALK ABOUT THAT.

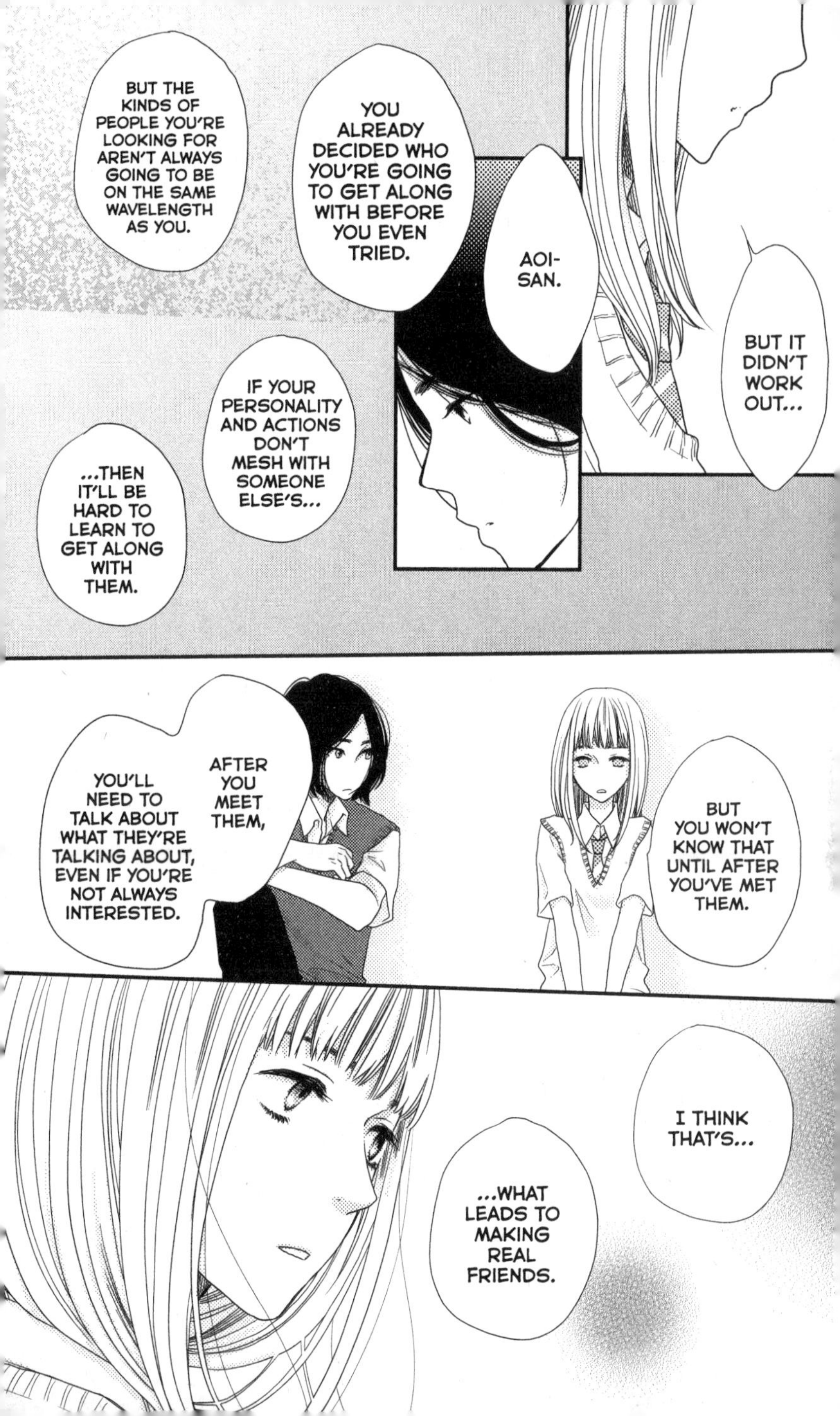
BUT IT DIDN'T WORK OUT...
AOI-SAN.
YOU ALREADY DECIDED WHO YOU'RE GOING TO GET ALONG WITH BEFORE YOU EVEN TRIED.
BUT THE KINDS OF PEOPLE YOU'RE LOOKING FOR AREN'T ALWAYS GOING TO BE ON THE SAME WAVELENGTH AS YOU.
IF YOUR PERSONALITY AND ACTIONS DON'T MESH WITH SOMEONE ELSE'S...
...THEN IT'LL BE HARD TO LEARN TO GET ALONG WITH THEM.
BUT YOU WON'T KNOW THAT UNTIL AFTER YOU'VE MET THEM.
AFTER YOU MEET THEM,
YOU'LL NEED TO TALK ABOUT WHAT THEY'RE TALKING ABOUT, EVEN IF YOU'RE NOT ALWAYS INTERESTED.
I THINK THAT'S...
...WHAT LEADS TO MAKING REAL FRIENDS.

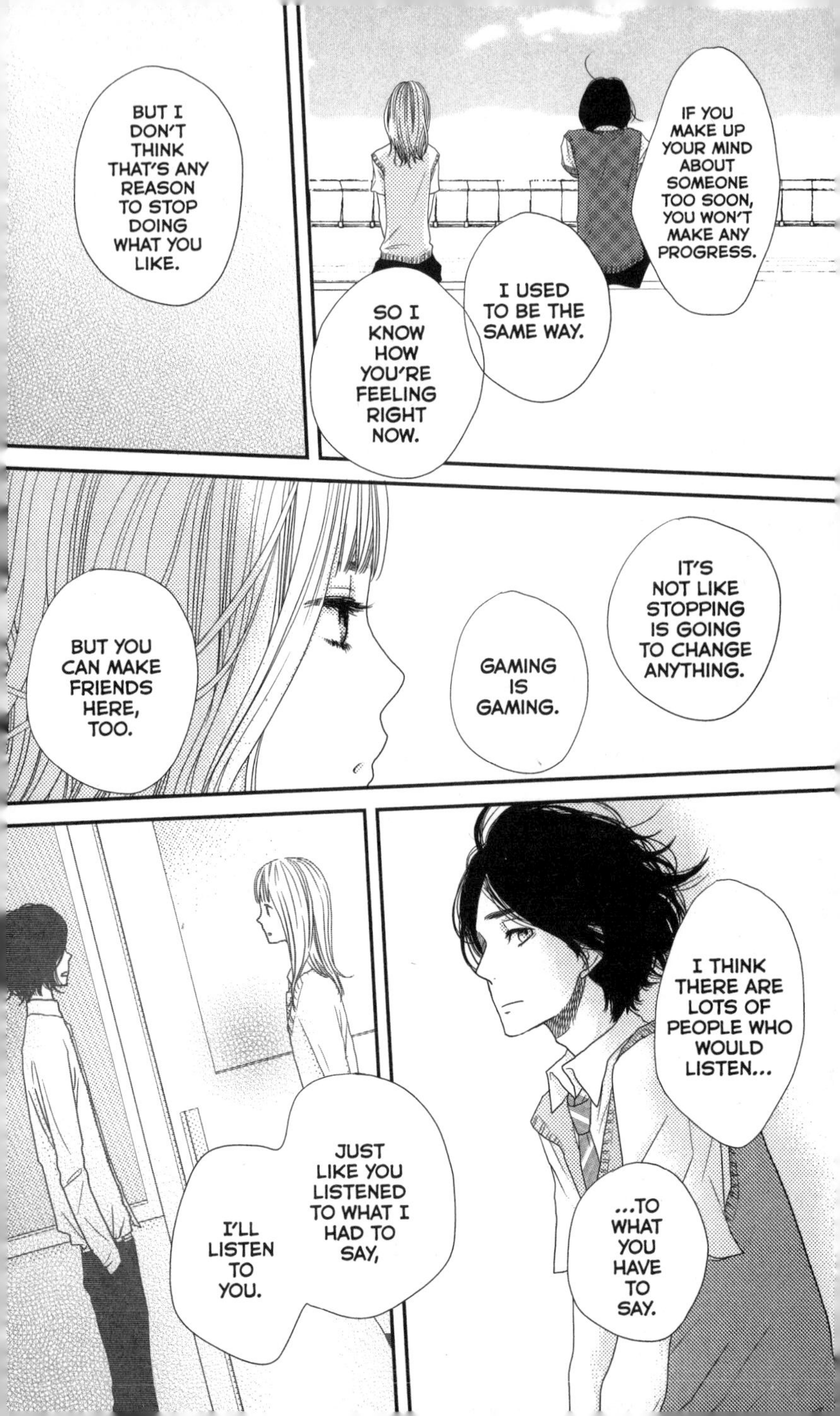
IF YOU MAKE UP YOUR MIND ABOUT SOMEONE TOO SOON, YOU WON'T MAKE ANY PROGRESS.
I USED TO BE THE SAME WAY.
SO I KNOW HOW YOU'RE FEELING RIGHT NOW.
BUT I DON'T THINK THAT'S ANY REASON TO STOP DOING WHAT YOU LIKE.
IT'S NOT LIKE STOPPING IS GOING TO CHANGE ANYTHING.
GAMING IS GAMING.
BUT YOU CAN MAKE FRIENDS HERE, TOO.
I THINK THERE ARE LOTS OF PEOPLE WHO WOULD LISTEN...
...TO WHAT YOU HAVE TO SAY.
JUST LIKE YOU LISTENED TO WHAT I HAD TO SAY,
I'LL LISTEN TO YOU.

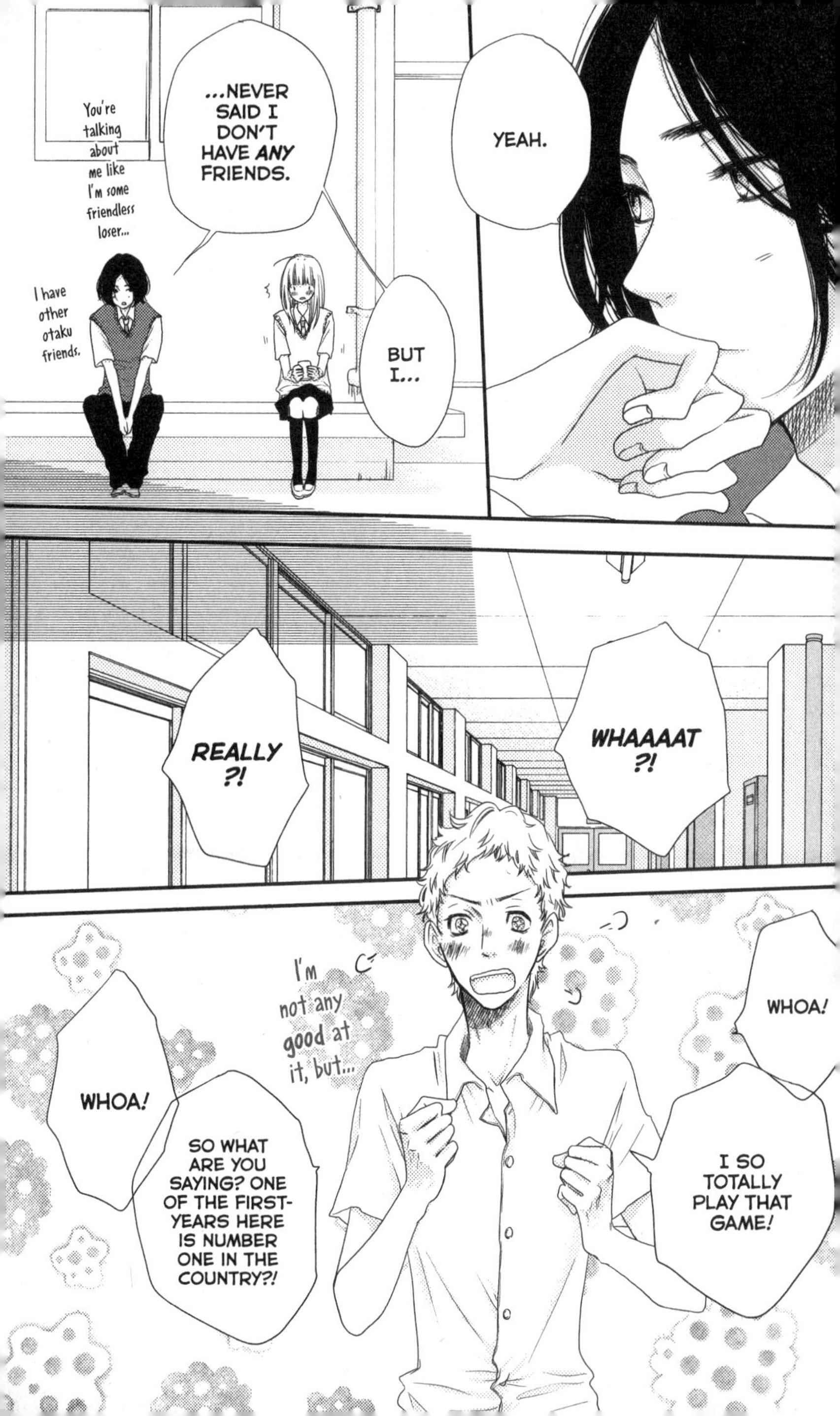
YEAH.
BUT I...
...NEVER SAID I DON'T HAVE ANY FRIENDS.
You're talking about me like I'm some friendless loser...
I have other otaku friends.
WHAAAAT?!
REALLY?!
WHOA!
I SO TOTALLY PLAY THAT GAME!
I'm not any good at it, but...
WHOA!
SO WHAT ARE YOU SAYING? ONE OF THE FIRST-YEARS HERE IS NUMBER ONE IN THE COUNTRY?!

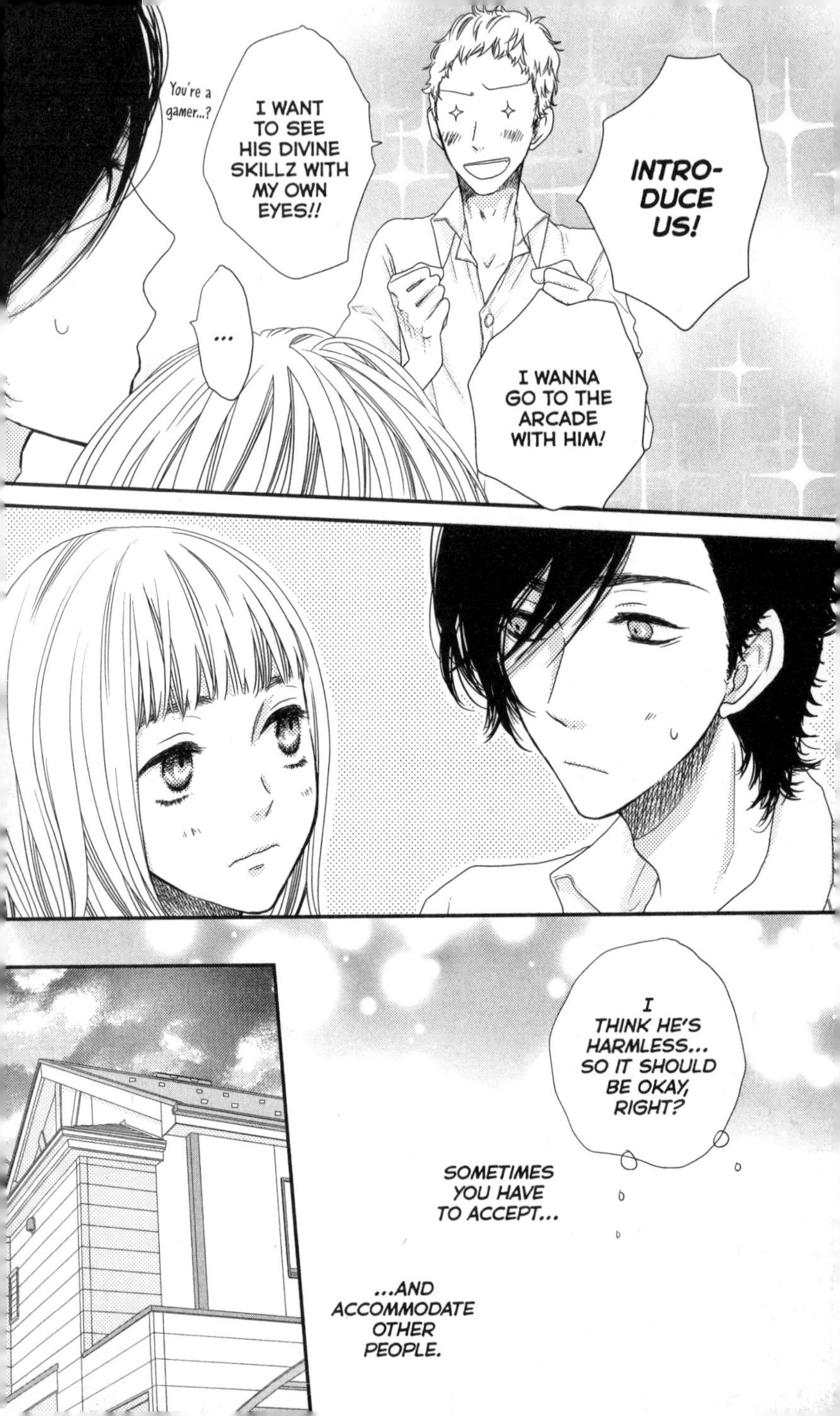
INTRO-DUCE US!
I WANT TO SEE HIS DIVINE SKILLZ WITH MY OWN EYES!!
You're a gamer...?
I WANNA GO TO THE ARCADE WITH HIM!
...
I THINK HE'S HARMLESS... SO IT SHOULD BE OKAY, RIGHT?
SOMETIMES YOU HAVE TO ACCEPT...
...AND ACCOMMODATE OTHER PEOPLE.

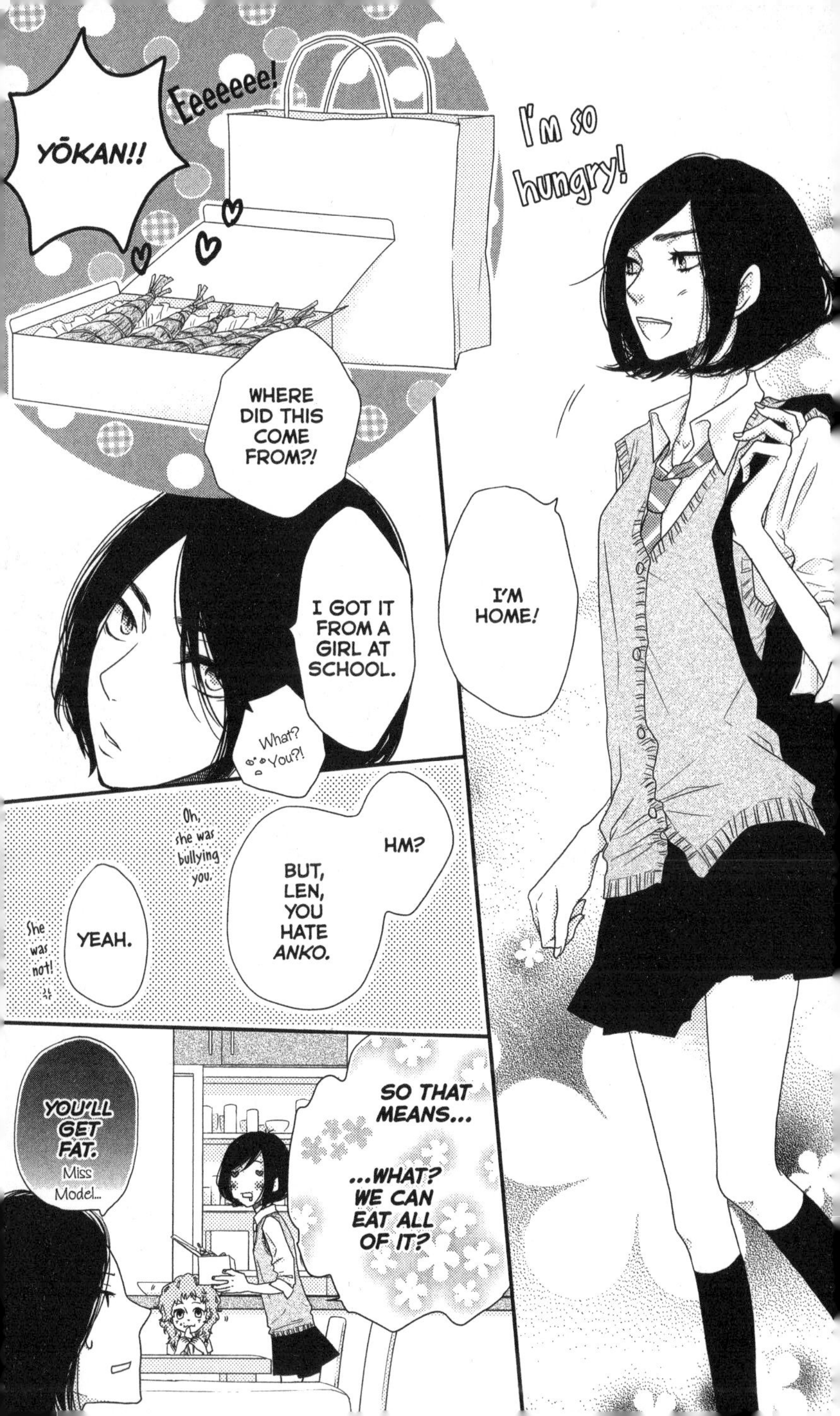
I'm so hungry!
I'M HOME!
Eeeeeee!
YŌKAN!!
WHERE DID THIS COME FROM?!
I GOT IT FROM A GIRL AT SCHOOL.
What? You?!
HM?
BUT, LEN, YOU HATE ANKO.
Oh, she was bullying you.
YEAH.
She was not!
SO THAT MEANS...
...WHAT? WE CAN EAT ALL OF IT?
YOU'LL GET FAT.
Miss Model...

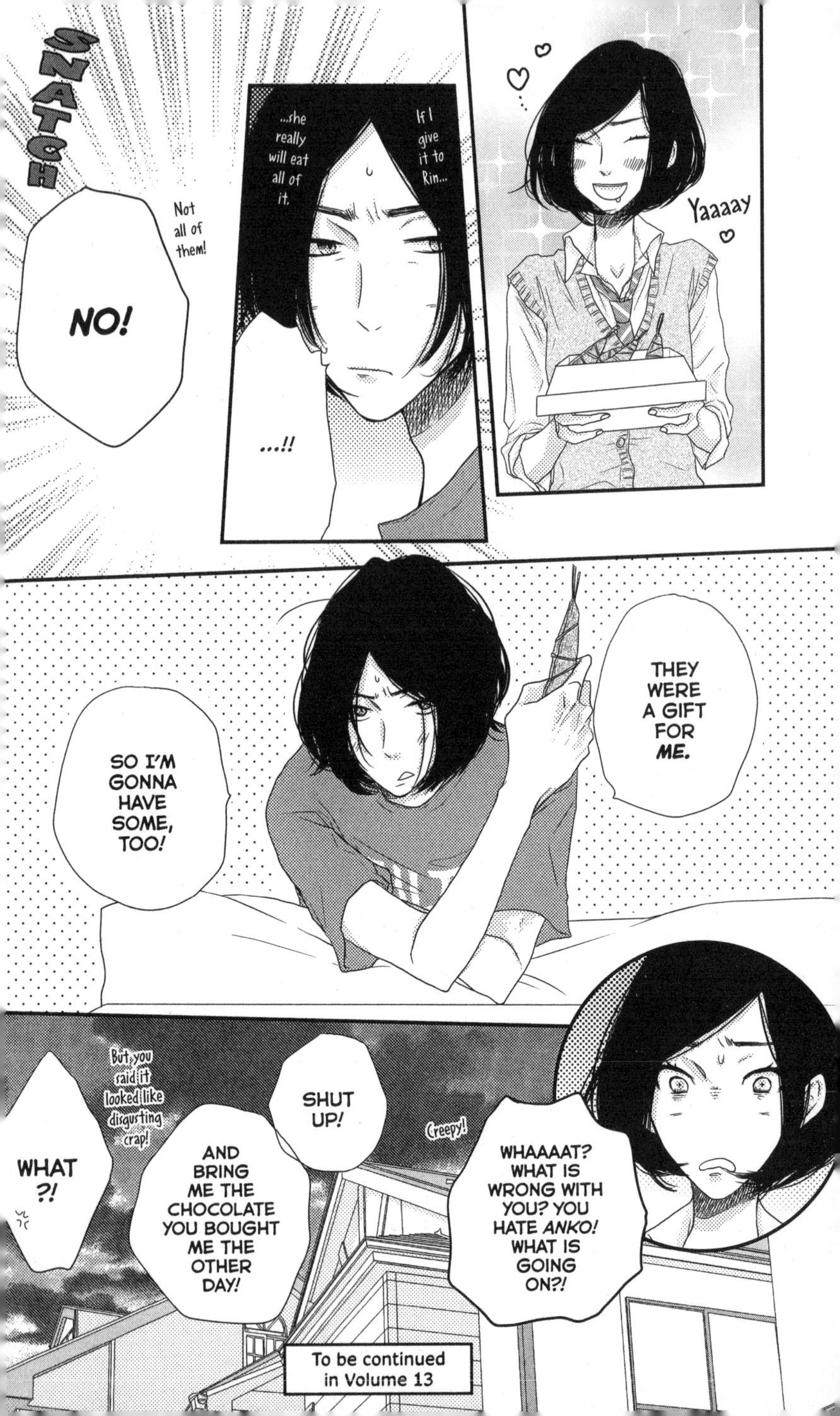
Yaaaay
If I give it to Rin...
...she really will eat all of it.
...!!
SNATCH
Not all of them!
NO!
THEY WERE A GIFT FOR ME.
SO I'M GONNA HAVE SOME, TOO!
WHAAAAT? WHAT IS WRONG WITH YOU? YOU HATE ANKO! WHAT IS GOING ON?!
Creepy!
SHUT UP!
AND BRING ME THE CHOCOLATE YOU BOUGHT ME THE OTHER DAY!
But you said it looked like disgusting crap!
WHAT?!
To be continued in Volume 13

Say "I love you".

AMATO ROSAW

lo, I'm Kanae Hazuki. This is volume 12.

're finally really getting into the career stuff. It brings :k memories... Speaking of the third year in high iool, I went job hunting then, too. My school wasn't nected to a college, so almost all the kids went job iting.

d, too, but it was like we were in the middle of an ice :... Everyone around me was taking employment tests l failing, taking tests and failing, over and over again. : more I watched, the more it seemed like too much a hassle, so then I tried to get into one company and ed their test, and I thought, "That's it! I'm just gonna w pictures! I'll draw and draw and draw and *someday* be able to make a living!" And with that idle thought in head, I graduated high school... I never did deal well h adversity... But that's enough about me...

s time, I've been thinking up career paths for Mei and nato and the other kids in the manga, and it's pretty 'd. Every day, I'm brought to tears by my own lack of owledge. I didn't go to college, and I've never really erienced "the real world." ...So I don't even know basics. Every day, I battle with anxiety... asking self, "Can someone like that really draw this manga?" l, my editor has been helping me out, and I've been e to get interviews and talk with people from various ds, and so I'm getting a lot of experience in things t you don't normally get to experience. At this late nt in my life, I feel like I've gone back to being a third-ır in high school trying to figure out my future, so to eak. I thought I hated studying, but now I am studying). Especially when it comes to Megumi—under normal :umstances, I would never know any of that stuff. : what I really want to draw is Megumi's growth. : the end product, so much as the growth.

: since I did get some interviews and talk to people, ope that I can bring at least a little of that into the nga, regardless of how good I am at it. The journey m childhood to adulthood—it may not be a really citing coming-of-age story, but I want to draw how :h of their hearts grows, and hopefully the readers l find some small thing to relate to.

loesn't matter how old you get; there's no end to ts. But having a first means growing. I'm going work so I can experience more firsts.

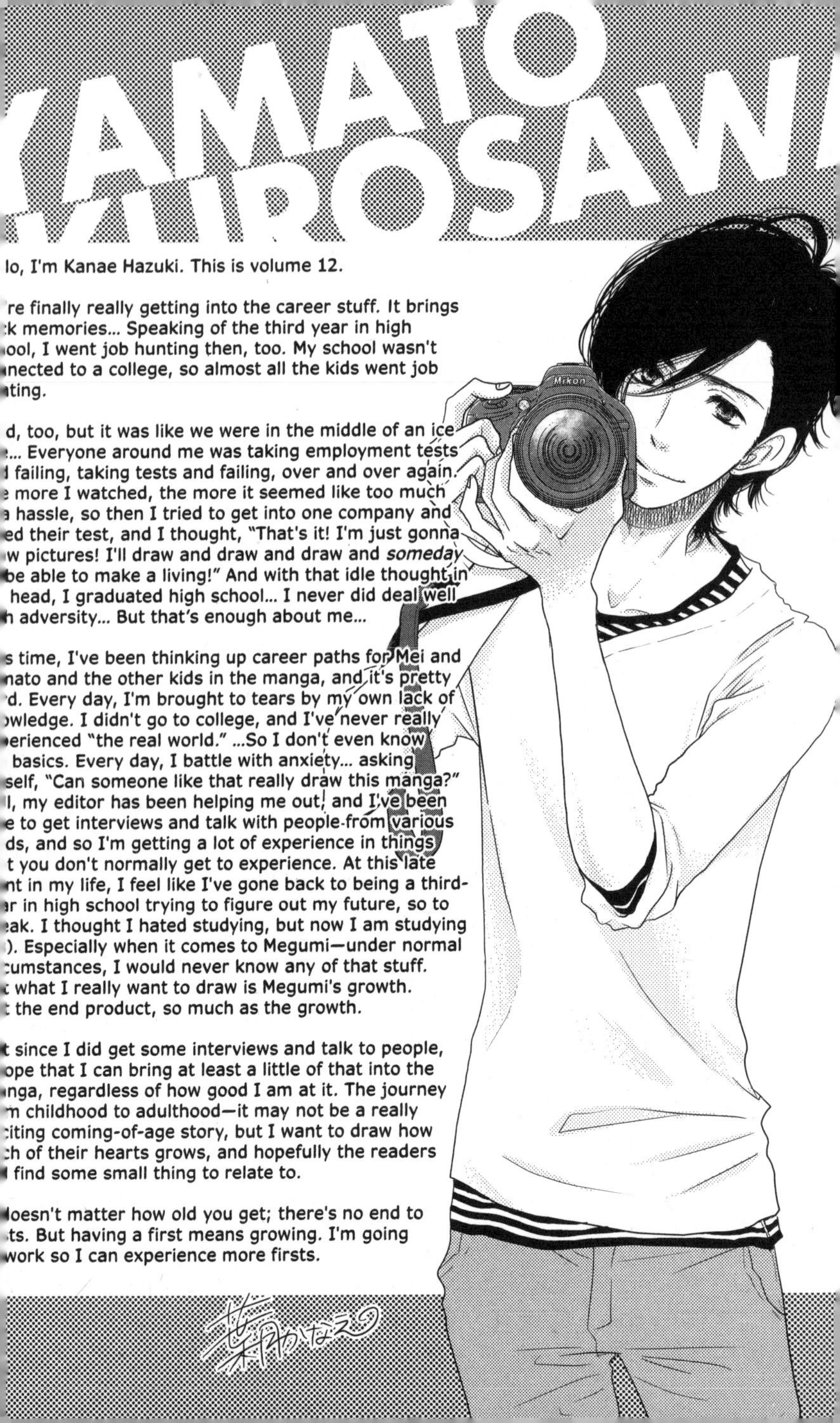
Nikon

葉月かなえ

TRANSLATION NOTES

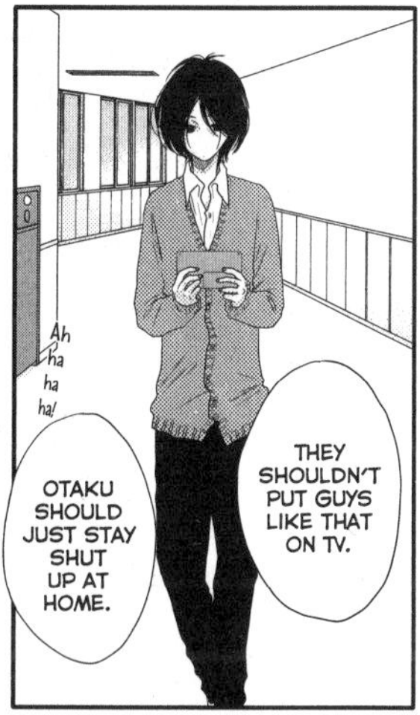
THEY SHOULDN'T PUT GUYS LIKE THAT ON TV.
Ah ha ha ha!
OTAKU SHOULD JUST STAY SHUT UP AT HOME.

Page 10: Otaku should just stay shut up at home
As many manga fans know, *otaku* is the Japanese word for geek, and is often used in a very derogatory manner. Here, the boy talking about them is making a play on words, because *otaku* also means "house," as in, *otaku* never set foot outside their homes.

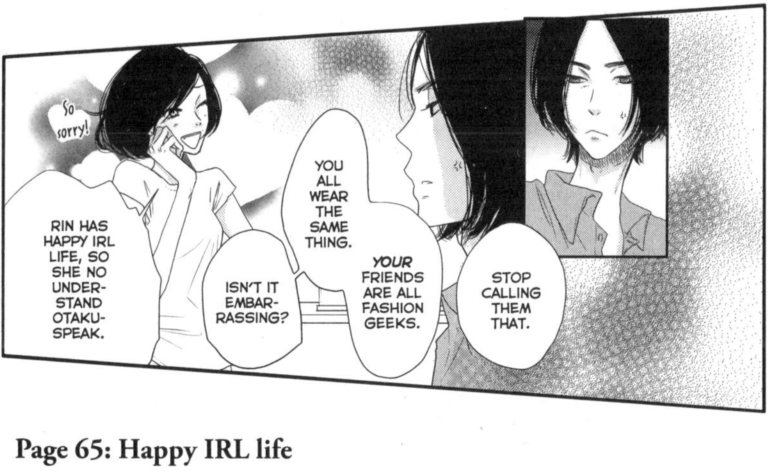
STOP CALLING THEM THAT.
YOUR FRIENDS ARE ALL FASHION GEEKS.
YOU ALL WEAR THE SAME THING.
ISN'T IT EMBARRASSING?
So sorry!
RIN HAS HAPPY IRL LIFE, SO SHE NO UNDER-STAND OTAKU-SPEAK.

Page 65: Happy IRL life
In Japanese internet slang, there's a word for someone who has it all together in the real world, and doesn't need to retreat to the internet to find a place to belong. That word is *riajū,* short for *riaru no seikatsu ga jūjitsu shiteru,* or "leading a fulfilled life in the real world [or IRL]." *Riajū* tend to be looked on by otaku with either longing or contempt.

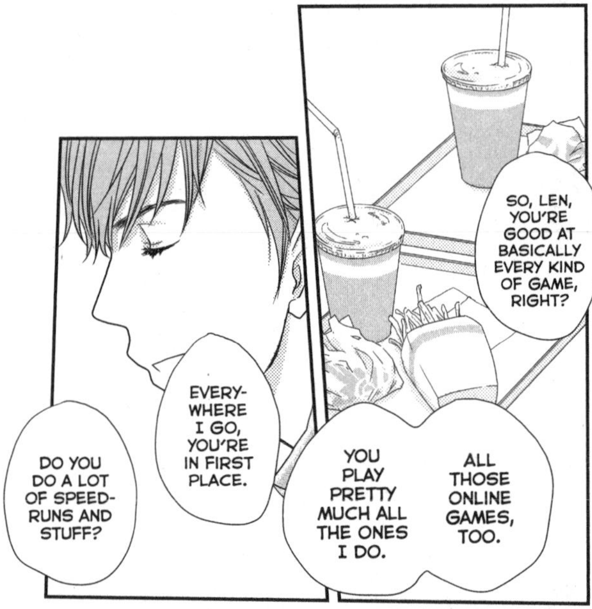
SO, LEN, YOU'RE GOOD AT BASICALLY EVERY KIND OF GAME, RIGHT?
ALL THOSE ONLINE GAMES, TOO.
YOU PLAY PRETTY MUCH ALL THE ONES I DO.
EVERY-WHERE I GO, YOU'RE IN FIRST PLACE.
DO YOU DO A LOT OF SPEED-RUNS AND STUFF?

Page 143: Speedruns

A speedrun is when a gamer plays through a game as quickly as possible, often for others to watch and be entertained. But Icchi really asked Len if he does a lot of *yarikomi,* which means roughly "to play a game as thoroughly as possible"—unlocking every possible achievement and earning every possible trophy. This can include speedruns, if a game requires the player to complete certain tasks within a specified time limit.

My Little Monster

OPPOSITES ATTRACT...MAYBE?

Haru Yoshida is feared as an unstable and violent "monster." Mizutani Shizuku is a grade-obsessed student with no friends. Fate brings these two together to form the most unlikely pair. Haru firmly believes he's in love with Mizutani and she firmly believes he's insane.

KC KODANSHA COMICS

NO.6

A PERFECT LIFE IN A PERFECT CITY

Shion, an elite student in the technologically sophisticated y No. 6, life is carefully choreographed. One fateful day, he es a misstep, sheltering a fugitive his age from a typhoon. ing this boy throws Shion's life down a path to discovering appalling secrets behind the "perfection" of No. 6.

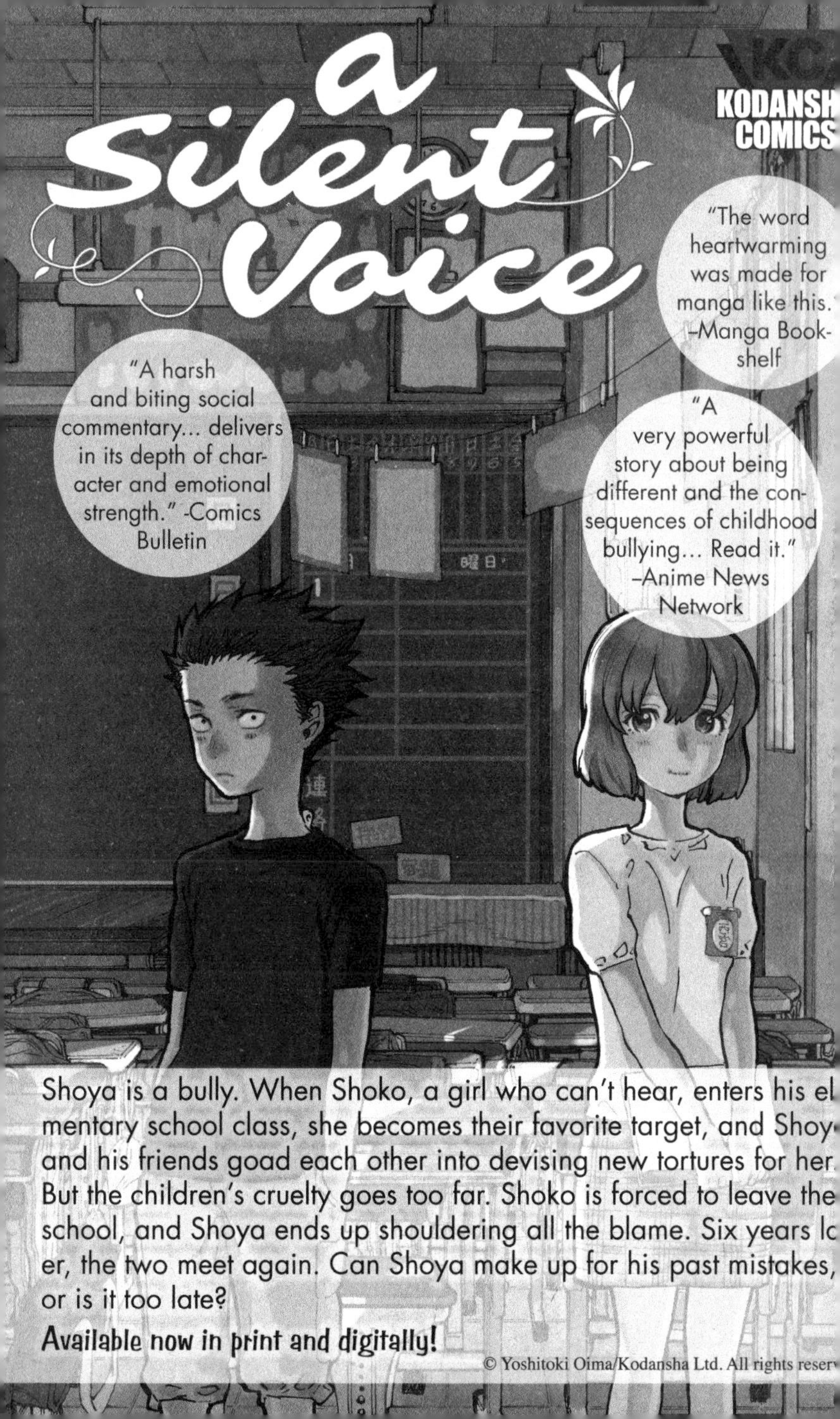
a Silent Voice
KODANSHA COMICS
"The word heartwarming was made for manga like this." –Manga Bookshelf
"A harsh and biting social commentary... delivers in its depth of character and emotional strength." -Comics Bulletin
"A very powerful story about being different and the consequences of childhood bullying... Read it." –Anime News Network
Shoya is a bully. When Shoko, a girl who can't hear, enters his el mentary school class, she becomes their favorite target, and Shoy and his friends goad each other into devising new tortures for her. But the children's cruelty goes too far. Shoko is forced to leave the school, and Shoya ends up shouldering all the blame. Six years l er, the two meet again. Can Shoya make up for his past mistakes, or is it too late?
Available now in print and digitally!
© Yoshitoki Oima/Kodansha Ltd. All rights reser

THE HEROIC LEGEND OF
ARSLAN

**READ THE NEW SERIES FROM THE CREATOR OF
FULLMETAL ALCHEMIST, HIROMU ARAKAWA!
NOW A HIT TV SERIES!**

"Arakawa proves to be
more than up to the task
of adapting Tanaka's
fantasy novels and fans of
historical or epic fantasy
will be quite pleased with
the resulting book."
-Anime News Network

ECBATANA IS BURNING!

Arslan is the young and curious prince of Pars who, despite his best efforts doesn't seem to have what it takes to be a proper king like his father. At the age of 14, Arslan goes to his first battle and loses everything as the blood-soaked mist of war gives way to scorching flames, bringing him to face the demise of his once glorious kingdom. However, it is Arslan's destiny to be a ruler, and despite the trials that face him, he must now embark on a journey

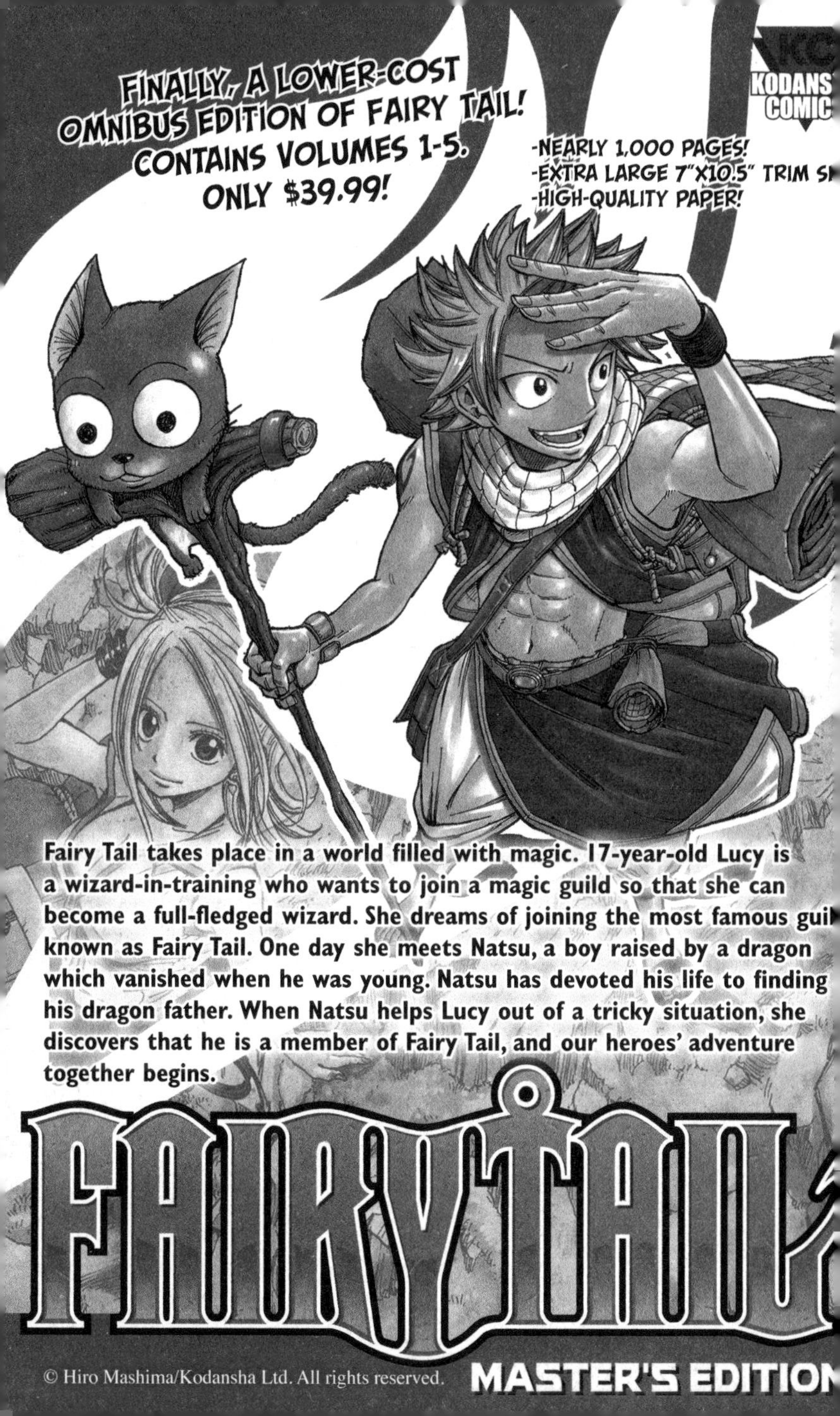
KC
KODANS
COMIC
FINALLY, A LOWER-COST OMNIBUS EDITION OF FAIRY TAIL!
CONTAINS VOLUMES 1-5.
ONLY $39.99!
-NEARLY 1,000 PAGES!
-EXTRA LARGE 7"X10.5" TRIM SI
-HIGH-QUALITY PAPER!
Fairy Tail takes place in a world filled with magic. 17-year-old Lucy is a wizard-in-training who wants to join a magic guild so that she can become a full-fledged wizard. She dreams of joining the most famous guil known as Fairy Tail. One day she meets Natsu, a boy raised by a dragon which vanished when he was young. Natsu has devoted his life to finding his dragon father. When Natsu helps Lucy out of a tricky situation, she discovers that he is a member of Fairy Tail, and our heroes' adventure together begins.
FAIRY TAIL
© Hiro Mashima/Kodansha Ltd. All rights reserved.
MASTER'S EDITIO

Say I Love You. volume 12 is a work of fiction. Names, characters, places, and incidents are the products of the author's imagination or are used fictitiously. Any resemblance to actual events, locales, or persons, living or dead, is entirely coincidental.

A Kodansha Comics Trade Paperback Original

Published in the United States by Kodansha Comics, an imprint of Kodansha USA Publishing, LLC, New York.

Publication rights for this English edition arranged through Kodansha Ltd, Tokyo.

First published in Japan in 2014 by Kodansha Ltd., Tokyo as *Sukitte iinayo.* volume 12.

ISBN 978-1-63236-042-7

Printed in the United States of America.

www.kodanshacomics.com

9 8 7 6 5 4 3 2 1
Translation: Alethea and Athena Nibley
Lettering: Jennifer Skarupa
Editing: Ajani Oloye
Kodansha Comics edition cover design by Phil Balsman